The World Debt Dilemma: Managing Country Risk

The World Debt Dilemma: Managing Country Risk

Irving S. Friedman

Council for International Banking Studies
Washington, D.C., and
Robert Morris Associates, Philadelphia, Pa.

Library of Congress Catalog Card Number: 83-13137
International Standard Book Number: 0-936742-12-7

Library of Congress Cataloging in Publication Data

Friedman, Irving Sigmund, 1915-
The world debt dilemma.
Includes index.
1. Loans, Foreign—Developing countries. 2. Debts, External—Developing countries. I. Title. II. Title: Country risk.
HG3891.5.F74 1983 336.3'435 83-13137
ISBN 0-936742-12-7 (R. Morris Associates)

Additional copies of this publication are available from the Order Department, Robert Morris Associates, 1616 Philadelphia National Bank Building, Philadelphia, PA 19107 (215) 665-2850.

To Henry Mueller who urged me to write a book on this subject and kept prodding, and

My daughter, Barbara, who throughout her prolonged illness urged me not to drop this effort.

Table of Contents

Preface

As this book goes to press (July 1983), the subject of external debt of developing countries continues to be regarded with great alarm everywhere. Descriptions like "debt bombs," "destroyed banking systems," "bail outs," "irresponsible lending," and "financial disasters" abound in authoritative, responsible, and expert circles, as well as in the popular and technical media. Although I regard the world debt situation as very serious, I find myself unable to agree with these widely held alarmist views. While I am deeply worried, I believe the world debt situation is still manageable.

The year 1982 was climatic for the evolution of international lending, the external debt problems of developing countries, the use of the rescheduling mechanism, and the employment of country risk evaluations and country risk management systems. Worldwide attention focused on these matters and on individual countries—particularly Argentina, Brazil, and Mexico. Statistical presentations, analyses, forecasts, and judgments were found throughout the media. Global and regional institutions dwelt at length on these subjects in their reports and their public addresses. Heads of state contributed their suggestions; conferences brought participants together to hear the views of those who had something to say. What had been technical subjects—largely within the province of economics, finance, and banking—now became popular subjects and grist in the political mills.

Preparation of this book began in 1978 when the need was perceived for more knowledge and understanding of country risk and debt renegotiations. Interest was already high in financial circles, but systematic analyses and exposition were rare. This book was designed primarily to help public officials, practitioners, teachers, and students in finance and economics understand better the role of commercial bank international lending, particularly to developing countries.

The needs of developing countries for external finance drove the process of increased borrowing and accumulation of external debt. The increasing reliance on commercial banks as sources of needed finance reflected the continued reluctance of creditors or donor countries to expand sufficiently their concessional assistance, either directly or through multilateral agencies like the World Bank or the regional development banks. Bond markets offering long-term, fixed-interest monies were largely closed to developing countries. These countries turned increasingly to floating rate credits based on U.S. prime rates or LIBOR or their equivalents in other money markets. Through the Eurocurrency markets, they could have access to the world savings streams. These borrowers tried to obtain the longest available maturities, cognizant that even longer maturities from banks would be relatively short for their project financing and other investment needs.

These developing countries also needed general balance-of-payments support to meet external deficits enlarged by such special factors as drought or overvalued exchange rates or by adverse international conditions like inflation or depression (or in our modern world, both). The International Monetary Fund was important as a certifier of a country's balance-of-payments management, but it was much too limited in financial resources to provide the funds needed to finance the balance-of-payments deficits of members when they occurred in a number of countries simultaneously.

The combination in the mid-1970s of large oil price increases, inflation, and food shortages hurt many countries. This situation was further compounded by the second round of oil price increases and the onset of world depression in the late 1970s. These countries turned to commercial banks to add to what they could obtain from the IMF and other official sources. The private banks responded to these demands from countries which met their individual criteria of country creditworthiness.

Banks were severely criticized by many for entering into these new areas of international lending. I believe the criticism was unjustified, and I had the opportunity to play a leading role in pioneering this new major source of development finance. I have never ceased advocating more official assistance for development and more financial resources for the IMF for balance-of-payments financing.

The expanded roles of private banking led to the use of new methods of assessing and managing country risks and to the invention of ways and means of dealing with country situations of arrears in debt servicing and major difficulties in servicing debt. Out of the increased lending to developing countries at floating interest rates came the so-called debt problem and the practice of restructuring, rescheduling, or refinancing debts to private or commercial lenders, not guaranteed by official creditor institutions. Debts to official creditors had long been the subject of renegotiation and restructuring. Fortunately for lender and borrower, we have not seen the recurrence of debt repudiation or debt defaults which characterized the 1930s, despite the serious and repeated balance-of-payments difficulties experienced by many countries.

In this book, I have dealt with the evolution of international lending, the resultant debt problem, and the rise in country risk analysis and management on the basis of over 30 years' experience in the IMF, the World Bank, Citibank, and most recently the First Boston Corporation. In these institutions, I was responsible for originating and managing their programs of evaluating countries and recommending appropriate policy actions.

At the IMF, my actions usually related to changes in exchange rate systems and restrictions on international payments and use of the Fund's financial resources. At the World Bank, the decisions related to lending by the World Bank and the International Development Association and recommendations on the development programs and policies of the developing countries. Much of what we did at the IMF in these matters was captioned by the word "conditionality." At the World Bank, we called it development policy.

At Citibank, these activities were summarized in the words "country risk." Country risk covered assessing countries for the risks involved in Citibank activities in the country not covered within the concept and practice of credit risk, that is, assessment of the individual borrowing entity within a country. Country risk also included definitions of lending exposure in foreign countries; establishing institutional ceilings and subceilings of such exposure for each country; allocating, reporting, and monitoring these exposures; and the management system which integrated the country risk system with the bank's line functions.

Other activities, such as exchanging views with authorities in the borrowing countries, participation in rescheduling of external debts, and heading a task force in these areas for the Association of Reserve City Bankers, were byproducts of these responsibilities. At First Boston, I continued those activities as advisor to private and official lenders and to borrowing countries.

This background gave me the opportunity to pioneer in these practices, but more important to learn and reach certain conclusions about these areas. This book offers me a vehicle to set down some of the lessons and to draw some conclusions. In so doing, we may find ways to harmonize the interests of lenders and borrowers, particularly in the developing countries.

The developing countries have now achieved the self-confidence to take advantage of the private international financial system to finance their needed inflows of resources. This self-confidence means they feel comfortable in negotiating loans effectively and advantageously. It also means they can manage their affairs to fulfill their contractual obligations to these lenders. The private lenders, on their part, need to feel comfortable that in lending to developing countries they are not accepting unacceptable risks. The private lenders do not, as yet, feel this comfort, and the whole process of their lending to developing countries remains vulnerable and fragile.

International lending will continue to play a critical role in the social and economic evolution of the poor, less modernized economies which encompass the large majority of mankind. Commercial bank lending is a highly sophisticated tool of modern economics and can play a major part in the evolution of most developing countries without resort to bail outs by creditor countries. It is hoped that in our eagerness to do something about present conditions, we will strengthen, rather than weaken, the present ability of private banks to play a constructive role.

The ultimate defense of international banking is the strength of the major banks in various countries. Part of their strength is capital—but only a minor part; much of their strength is the quality of assets. Of critical importance is the bank's ability to borrow. Transcending all in importance, however, are management skills and reputation. A well-managed major bank will enjoy a strong standing in financial circles even during periods of global disturbance. With such standings, it will have access to the liquidity it needs to meet contingencies as well as daily needs. Interbank relations are at the core of the international banking system.

My book tries to be a useful treatise on international lending, external debt, and country risk assessment and management in order to provide a better basis for evaluating current trends and the statements and opinions of others. Unfortunately, recent events have supercharged these subjects with emotion, short-circuiting thought, debate, and careful research. Perhaps this book will help focus on facts, analyses, and views to help foster the needed intellectual debate on the dilemma confronting developing countries. I hope this book will help to make us less prone to favor simplistic measures to deal with long-run fundamental, complex conditions. Too often, we confuse being practical with being simplistic. We must be practical, but our proposed remedies must face and deal with realities to be successful. The world debt problem is deeply rooted in the disparate needs of an exploding world population and its conflicting priorities, social dynamism, political immaturities, economic inefficiencies, and cultural transformations.

The dilemma is whether to defend and accelerate needed social and economic development by accumulating very large debts and debt-servicing burdens or slow down or end growth and run the risk of creating even more poverty, social disturbances, and political disruptions. For private lenders, the dilemma is to lend to the part of the world having most of the world's population and which may well prove over time to have the highest growth rates and market expansion, while knowing that such lending is replete with country risk. The alternative is to avoid the risks and leave these growing markets to more audacious and perhaps financially stronger competitors.

International lending to developing countries is still novel for most creditor countries and private lenders. It is likely to become even more important than it is now. My hope is that this book contributes to the knowledge and experience of lenders and borrowers and truly contributes to a constructive resolution of the serious financial difficulties now experienced throughout the world.

Irving S. Friedman
June 1983

Acknowledgments

Professor William Sihler of the Colgate Darden Graduate School of Business Administration, University of Virginia, merits special thanks. At First Boston, Dr. Elisabeth Rabitsch, my associate of many years, again demonstrated her personal loyalty and professional competence in her assistance, suggestions, and criticisms. John Mathis of Continental Illinois National Bank was very helpful in reviewing the manuscript and making editorial suggestions. Hank Mueller and Bob Parra at Citibank gave comments from the background of decades of experience in international banking. James Booth, at present at the University of California, helped in the research and thoughtful criticisms. My wife, Edna, as always made the book happen.

I.S.F.

1

Country Risk: An Overview

The central focus of this book is the subject of country risk. The large growth and diversification of international banking in the past decade have made country risk and its management a matter of critical concern for bankers and their regulators. It is even a concern for borrowers many of whom depend critically on continued access to international credit markets.

Private bank loans have to be regarded as among the most conservative and cautious sources of lending. Therefore, concern is legitimate as to whether the developing countries can meet their developmental needs with this source of financing. It is inevitable that as the amount of financing by private banks becomes larger and larger, the developing countries' own development strategies, policies, and implementation of policies on a year-by-year basis are going to be more heavily influenced by these conservative, cautious standards of private banks.

For example, private banks pay a great deal of attention to whether a country has a competitive exchange rate which promotes exports, to the strength and efficiency of the government and the private sector, to the honesty of government, to the existence of social order, personal safety, etc. Private banks also look at the depth of management of the public sector. Private business tends to deal with the middle management level of government. Those are the people with whom business people associate and whose performance is very important for them. The banker must know not merely how good the person at the top is but how good the subordinates are.

Correspondingly, private bankers look at the private sector to determine how vigorous and efficient it is, what kind of role is played by the multinational firms in the country, etc. The questions bankers ask include:

- Is domestic business efficient, enterprising, innovative, export-oriented, investment-minded?
- Are multinational firms efficient in the country?
- Is the country innovative?
- Is it productive?
- Is it growing?
- Is it investing?
- Is it diversifying exports?

These are the kind of questions private bankers want answered when they make any kind of credit decision. Basically, the private banker is considering the wisdom of granting credit and judging its acceptability. From the commercial banker's perspective, the first line of defense against country risk is good credit risk analysis.

Private Versus Official Lending

Advocacy of private bank lending to developing countries has been seen by some as arguing against government or official sources of financing. Such commentators seem to regard private bank lending as a substitute for official lending and that borrowers, by going to private banks, can avoid these other sources of finance. Creditor governments may, and at times will, argue that recipients of official assistance can instead rely on private sources of financing.

These commentators see certain constraints for the borrowing country in using official sources of funds: for example, International Monetary Fund (IMF) conditionality; limits on amounts available; delays in decision making; rules on competitive bidding in use of developmental loans, etc. These conditions of official lending at times serve as constraints. But official lending is cheaper, has longer maturities, is carefully supervised, and transfers technology. Private bank lending does not substitute for official lending. There is a need for the kind of help developing countries can get from the World Bank, the IMF, the regional development banks, and other similar institutions. Private banks cannot do what these multilateral institutions can do. On the other hand, official lenders cannot substitute for the private banks.

By considering what makes the viewpoints of private commercial banks unique in comparison with the viewpoints of the major multilateral financial institutions (IMF and the World Bank), it is easier to identify what steps enable private commercial banks to lend successfully overseas.

Risks in International Lending

Country risk covers contingencies which exist or may arise in a country outside the home country of a lending institution which can cause losses to income, reserves, or capital for reasons other than the credit risk. The exact content or scope of country risk is constantly redefined by experience, so definitions should not be solidified prematurely.

Definitions Unclear

Country creditworthiness is also a definition without clear or sharp boundaries. In the elementary sense, it is the consideration of those conditions which cause a lending institution to be willing to acquire assets in a particular country. This definition also is fluid. Here, too, experience is filling in the configurations and beginning to define boundaries. But the process of definition is only beginning. We are not even sure what constitutes a "foreign" loan, a "foreign" entity, a "foreign" borrower, or "foreign" funds. This book attempts to contribute to the process of achieving better, more precise, and more generally agreed on definitions.

The subject of country risk is paramount for banks with substantial international lending. The increasing functional need of such banks to establish ways and means to monitor country risk and manage their overseas loan portfolios has led to a new control function in a bank's organization. The methods that banks have used (or could use) to cope effectively with these new responsibilities are outlined in a number of subsequent chapters. Country risk analysis is a pursuit akin to the traditional credit check of potential borrowers but extended to a consideration of the macroeconomic creditworthiness of the nation in which the borrower is domiciled. It gathers relevant information for a bank to safeguard, plan, and manage its international portfolio.

Country risk evaluation has gained worldwide attention because of a seeming dilemma which confronts private banks engaged in lending overseas. On one hand, there is increased demand for bank credit from creditworthy borrowers in countries outside national borders. On the other hand, there is widespread concern in private and official quarters that such lending, if it continues to expand, will become insupportable by some borrowers and lead to major losses by the private banks. For many, the resolution of this dilemma is to curtail private lending abroad, particularly to developing countries, whether by the actions of the private banks or the regulatory authorities.

Private Bank Lending

Curtailing private lending would be a major contractionary force in the world economy. It would disrupt the adjustment process and the structural transformation now taking place in virtually all countries—developing and developed. Instead, international private bank lending should be allowed to expand so that it strengthens both borrowers and lending institutions. To do so, however, the keystone must be adequate knowledge of the world economy and its correspondent parts in the broadest senses of these words.

Risk in lending cannot be eliminated, but it can be managed to make expanded lending appropriate. If done, private bank lending can continue to facilitate the functioning of an increasingly interdependent global world economy. It cannot be done without following a process which combines knowledge of the complexities of the real world with the needs, perceptions, and experience of private bank lenders. This process will form an integrated business judgment.

Private banks have seen the expanding role of governments as borrowers or as guarantors of international borrowings by entities in their countries. To the extent that governments assume these roles, the banks face credit assessment needs which are no longer simply analyses of individual projects and their projected cash flow. The needs are rather synonymous with an assessment of the country itself.

Banks must judge the ease or difficulty in responding to perceived future difficulties in countries by reducing exposure or changing its composition to new levels and mixtures deemed more appropriate. This puts emphasis on what a lender can do, rather than what a borrower might do. Thus, in addition to judging the microeconomic creditworthiness of the individual private borrower, bankers have found it equally important to judge the macroeconomic creditworthiness of the country where a particular borrowing firm is domiciled.

Country Risk Management

To monitor and anticipate adverse internal or external macroeconomic events which could impair a nation's ability to service its debt, a new function is needed in most banks active in international lending. This new control function can create the ability to minimize losses arising from country risk contingencies. One purpose of adequate country risk management is to guide the international business decisions of a bank and its marketing department. Banks are still struggling to determine the kind of country risk management process needed, how to design and introduce it, and how to use it efficiently on a cost-effective basis.

This book explores different country risk management systems or processes in order to clarify some of the key characteristics of an efficient and trustworthy country risk management system. However, three management implications of the expanded role of private banks in international lending need to be remembered when reading subsequent chapters:

1. The need for definition and identification of country risks; how to assess, report, and anticipate risks to the lending banks.

2. The need to improve country knowledge and understand global trends and developments as these affect individual countries; the need to link macro- and microeconomics in arriving at better country judgments from the viewpoint of the lending bank.

3. The need to apply assessments to portfolio and other business decisions of the lending bank.

Objectives and Needs

Virtually no two banks involved in international lending have acted in the same way. Banks have responded in terms of what they thought their needs were and their capabilities to be. For example, some decided to go the route of participating in loan syndications, which limited their cross-border exposure and enabled them to rely on the country knowledge of other syndicate participants. Others decided to become capable of acting on their own. For the latter, the mode of response varied from having in-house capability to using outsiders and consultants. The reasons for different responses often have been sensible: size of portfolio and earnings and geographic location. Too often, however, banks neglected to build their own capability and were satisfied with prevailing views, with what was fashionable to think about a country, as expressed in the media or elsewhere.

Whatever the nature of the country risk assessment system used by private U.S. banks, the effectiveness and reliability of most systems do not measure up to need.

Banks need more time to evaluate the reliability of their country risk systems in light of experience, but we can say now that most banks need to improve their systems. Of primary importance are the business objectives of the particular lending institution. Insofar as the country risk assessment is generalized or abstracted from actual business situations and needs, it is meaningless. The basic objectives of a lending entity limit the potential universe of business involvement and hence differentiate the kinds of country assessment techniques required.

Business Strategy and Tactics

These objectives dynamically affect the next two management considerations: a general business strategy for the future and the tactical means envisioned to realize this goal. A bank's general strategy may include such long-term goals as the expansion of international business in preference to domestic or vice versa, or engaging in new kinds of international lending operations and new markets. The tactical dimension looks at the step-by-step logistics by which medium-term plans can be achieved. Examples of tactical decisions are what specific investment activities should a bank become involved in and how much liaison or collaboration is worthwhile with the staff of multilateral bodies like the IMF.

Out of the three deductive phases—objectives, general strategy, and tactics—comes a precise long-range business plan for the bank. In other words, a working statement can be written which enumerates for each country, in which the bank has an interest, the specific business opportunities that should be watched for by the marketing staff in different markets abroad. Only by defining and identifying the specific kinds of business activities the bank wants to engage in and in what countries, do we come to the first practical indication of what specific kinds of country risk the bank has to guard against. All this must be formulated before a bank even thinks about how to design a good country assessment and risk management process.

An illustrative example involves a decision to invest in a resort hotel in a foreign land. Did this decision take into account whether visiting foreigners could feel safe or welcomed in the country? If not, the bank may later be surprised and hurt by the occurrence of unforeseen adverse contingencies.

In short, the country risk assessment system must be predicated on the realities of a bank's business or it is liable to produce information and advice of little relevance to the bank's best business interests.

Three more steps can be added to molding a bank's country assessment and information system:

1. Identifying and defining a bank's specific exposure to country risk.

2. Combining that information with other ingredients of a bank's basic risk/reward equation.

3. Determining internal linkages—how country risk activities and information can be linked with the bank's regular international operations and needs in order to minimize the bank's vulnerability to country risk.

Rating or Ranking Systems

Contrary to the above deductive approach, in which the capabilities of the country risk assessment function are made to conform with a set of identified international banking needs, is the oft-used general country rating or ranking system, which is not related to a bank's business activities. The severest criticism of a country ranking approach is not that the information produced may be worthless, but that it is not germane to the specific business involvement of a particular bank. The idea that the multifarious nature of country risk might be reduced analytically to one or two summary country ratings is futile, except as a possible preliminary country screening device.

The *reductio ad absurdum* case of averaging the results of a number of different country rating systems is well described by Professor Roman Senkiew: "Of even more dubious value is the recent practice of conducting surveys of risk ratings that are produced by various diverse country risk analytical systems. It should be intuitively obvious that adding apples and oranges is more likely to lead to a loss, not a gain, of informative value."[1]

If bank management is overdependent on a general country analysis and rating scheme, it is possible that this bank's specific configuration of country risk contingencies remains poorly analyzed. Probably, the specific linkages of the country risk officers with the rest of a bank's international business were probably not specifically identified by bank management beforehand.

In past years, most internationally active commercial banks have focused on transfer risk. Country assessments are generally balance-of-payment analyses: Periodic reports are written by country officers who essentially analyze a country's balance-of-payments position. Some banks do use broader gauged analyses. However, knowledge of countries still lags behind awareness of the need for such knowledge.

Country Risk Function

Another major shortcoming of today's country risk management activities is insufficient linkage between the country assessment function and the day-to-day business operations of the bank. Country risk work as a staff function is typically conducted at corporate headquarters. This situation reinforces the country analysts isolation from the daily concerns of the line bankers. This need not be, however, the result of centralizing the final stage of country risk management at corporate headquarters.

Resolution of how the country risk officer* might best act to help determine what overseas lending is acceptable to the bank depends on achieving a close collaboration in the everyday functioning of the bank. Only if the country risk officer

[1]Roman Senkiew, "Utilizing Risk Assessments in Decision-Making." International Risk Management Symposium, New York, 1980.

*For a description of the functions of the country risk officer, see the Citibank country risk evaluation section in chapter 15.

is knowledgable about the entire gamut of the bank's affairs can this person be expected to act as a catalyst in making the right organizational connections to immunize the bank from these risks. By redesigning the bank's information system to anticipate and register new risks, country assessment can be linked functionally to the banking process.

Network Needed

The country risk officer should be less interested in writing a study than in establishing a working relationship between staff and line personnel. Perhaps the most important connection the country risk officer can make is with the credit policy committee or its equivalent. One form that might take is mandatory consultation with the country risk officer whenever individual foreign loans under review exceed a specific amount. Similarly, appropriate linkages will suggest themselves in many other tasks a country risk officer encounters, whether informing regulatory authorities, preparing a portion of the annual report, or cooperating with the bank's controller. Indeed, whenever a bank engages in a new type of business activity abroad, new circumstances of risk arise and corresponding linkages should be made within the bank to evaluate them.

Further, the country risk officer must grasp what various people in the field need in the way of information or other help. Field representatives need help. If the country risk officer can gain a reputation as an independent available source of ideas and information, his or her telephone may become the busiest in the bank. Auditors, for example, traveling to examine and certify the financial records of foreign branches might call up the country risk officers repeatedly to ask for interpretation about some recently unearthed peculiarity.

In summary, a bank's country risk management system cannot approach a mature stage until such a network effectively comes into operation. A formal country risk system would teach or induce the bank's other staff and line officers to become more actively on guard against country risk and more cognizant of its many forms. Given the notoriously poor quality of the economic and social data published by many countries, the first tip that something is awry is likely to come to bank employees in residence in that foreign country out of their myriad business and personal contacts. Thus, explicit elements of a bank's early-warning system may not be as important as the preparedness and alertness which such a system instills in the bank personnel. The formal country assessment system does not always provide the warning signal as readily as an alert country officer.

Integrated Skills

The aim in country risk work, when the process is matured, is to add country risk assessment capability to the ordinary regular minimal skills of a banker. In any bank of almost any size, these skills are not specialized skills of different people. A banker is supposed to be a manager of staff, handle people on the outside, understand credit risk, and handle funding. If an international banker, he or she has to understand foreign exchange. If the banker does not get the necessary training in these fields in school, or does not get sufficiently wide experience on the job, the major banks have training programs within their institutions, or use training programs organized outside the bank, often in academic institutions. The ability to do country risk assessment has to be part of the arsenal of a banker in a modern world.

Over time, I believe that there will be fewer people who are identified as only country risk analysts within a bank. The people who are part of the management structure will be bankers who are knowledgable about country risk in the same way that banks have controllers who are experienced in foreign exchange trading. These people are equally skilled because the basic management and intellectual qualities are common to the whole group. However, country risk work is not yet that matured. Banks still hire special people to do country risk assessments because line officers do not feel they have as yet acquired the general experience and intellectual preparation to do this work.

Country risk analysis and the management of this risk is thus a vital part of the process of international lending. The developing countries have been in the center stage of country risk analysis. This book deals with the evolution of this international lending, its outlook, its resulting external debt situations, experience with reschedulings or restructuring of external debt, and then returns to a more detailed examination of country risk assessment and country risk management systems.

2

Growth of International Lending

Country risk analysis and the introduction of country risk management systems by an increasing number of banks were not the result of abstract thinking about bank management or bank supervision. They resulted from a remarkable development in the 1970s—the tremendous expansion in international lending by major banks in the advanced industrial countries to borrowers around the globe. Lured by profits to expand financial services abroad, banks had to reconcile the eagerness to respond positively with the private character of the lender, whose ownership was shared by thousands. Managers of such lending entities, judged by their ability to create and sustain profits, were also judged by their ability to avoid losses and to maintain the financial viability of their institutions.

Ignorance is the mother of uncertainty and risk. Ignorance of conditions abroad was the great obstacle to earning profits from lending abroad. The markets for monies provided accurate signals on pricing and returns, but given the widespread ignorance and inability to fathom the future, the market signals could not be relied on to reflect country risk for a particular lender. Over time, market experience would validate or negate current lending decisions. But, in the meantime, ignorance could lead to major wrong decisions.

However, ignorance of country conditions, trends, and outlook could be overcome, and uncertainty and risks accordingly greatly reduced. Assessing countries became a new part of the science of banking; linking such evaluation to business decisions became part of the management of banks.

Emergence of Private Commercial Banks

We cannot hope to understand the role of foreign lending by private commercial banks except in historical perspective. The speed at which change was taking place in the 1970s warns us that those who plan the future as a continuation of the past and present are virtually certain to be wrong. On the other hand, historical perspective provides us with an understanding of the institutional framework within which change occurred.

Pre-World War I

In the nineteenth century, London was the financial center of the world, and it acted as an intermediary for foreign investment from various parts of the world, particularly continental Europe. Other important financial centers at the time were Amsterdam, Berlin, Paris, Milan, and New York.

International financial activities in this period took place within an international monetary system based on the gold standard. The United Kingdom played the dominant financial role while the U.S. and Germany grew to become industrial giants. In those years, the international financial markets were organized by a small number of highly influential investment houses in London, Paris, and New York. The international banker in the nineteenth century was English or French, not American.

Many years were to pass in this country before banking was divided between commercial and investment banking. America's banks grew in size as the American economy expanded. Banks sprang up across the nation as it moved westward. Although with few exceptions, the Eastern banks formed in the early days of the Republic remained the largest. The U.S. federal system of government inhibited the formation of national banks. At the same time, the pull of a continental economy meant much less attention was given to international opportunites than in other countries.

American banks went overseas on a highly selective basis, which explains many attitudes found today in U.S. banking circles. The rarity of foreign lending by U.S. banks in the nineteenth century helps account for the distrust Americans have for large magnitudes of foreign lending. At the same time, American banks were more global in viewpoint. The European banks came from colonial countries. Their overseas activities were relatively large in the colonies: the United Kingdom in Australia, India, Hong Kong, and Malaya; France in North and West Africa and the Near East; Belgium in the Congo; Portugal in Angola and Macao; the Netherlands in the Netherland East India (using the colonial names of now independent nations). American bankers also went to countries in which U.S. political influence was great or trade relations were important. But without a large empire, the U.S. view was broader and encompassed China, Japan, Argentina, and Mexico. These American relationships sharply differentiated the U.S. style of banking, as well as its geographical spread, from the European.

Post-World War I

During World War I, New York emerged as the world's leading financial center. The U.S. dollar began to replace the pound sterling and the French franc. The U.S. became the largest single exporter and importer in world trade. Enormous capital market facilities emerged in the U.S. The establishment of the Federal Reserve System just prior to World War I strengthened the position of the financial institutions in this country. World War I depleted the financial resources of the European countries and led to a depreciation of their currencies. It also brought the suspension of the gold standard.

The period between the two world wars, particularly the 1930s, witnessed a series of international financial crises. In the immediate period after World War I, attention and concerns were mostly concentrated on reparation payments and debts of the Allied governments to the U.S. It was soon evident that these government obligations were not regarded as strict obligations like private international debt. In essence, the problem was approached as a need for those countries that owed reparations or debts to create external financial surpluses with which to service the payment of these debts. Reparations and debts were to be repaid by net transfers of goods and services to victors and lenders. The conquered countries were to be "surplus" countries, while the victors were to be the "deficit" countries, welcoming imports from the reparation payers.

The debate about the ability of countries to meet reparation obligations or to repay war debts centered on the "transfer problem." This problem focused on the ability of debtor countries to earn the needed foreign exchange by running balance-of-payments surpluses and the willingness of creditor countries to experience external deficits financed by inflows from debtor nations. John Maynard Keynes gained international repute for his strong criticisms from the early 1920s that this transfer problem would prove most difficult for victors, as well as losers.

For the transfer approach to work, the principal creditor country, namely the U.S., would have to become a chronic deficit country in its international exchange of goods and services. In the major European countries, national priorities on economic growth, employment, improvement in living standards, investments, and savings would have to be subordinated to achieving external positions which would enable reparations to be paid by Germany and her wartime partners to the victorious Allies. This would enable the Allies to pay their debts to the U.S., debts incurred to fight the common war.

Reparation Defaults

The financial arrangements of reparations and war debts proved unreal and unworkable. The 1930s saw the end of the efforts to pay reparations and war debts. In some cases, the Allied war debts to the U.S. disappeared rather quietly; in other cases—Nazi Germany—nasty and loud. These failures left a residue of distrust and resentment which lasted for decades. Investors learned that even the loser and victor governments of Central (loser) and Western Europe (victor) could find themselves unable (and later) unwilling to honor these international obligations. Simultaneously, other international borrowers from private banks and other financial sources defaulted on their obligations.

The economic and financial crisis of the 1930s, miserably handled by the industrial countries, swamped the "newer" economies of Argentina, Brazil, Australia, and Mexico. Commodity prices, the main source of foreign exchange earnings for these countries, collapsed and stayed down for years. New monies from foreign sources became hard to obtain as financial crises arose in industrial countries. International efforts to avoid worldwide crises repeatedly failed. It took another world war to create the hindsight that its major cause was failure to end the worldwide Great Depression. Many international debts were not honored. Finland, with its staunch insistence on keeping its external financial record unblemished, became a household word for international honor.

The events of the 1930s led to widespread skepticism about international lending, particularly among Americans who were relative newcomers to big time international finance. Much of this skepticism remains today, and periodically reappears as it did when oil prices jumped in 1973 and developing countries became very large external borrowers. It appeared in 1981-82 when Mexico and Poland found difficulties in servicing their external debts.

There were cataclysmic events that occurred in the financial world during the 1930s. The failure of the Credit Anstalt bank in Austria, the abandonment of the gold standard, the introduction of floating exchange rates, and the severe restrictions on international trade and foreign exchange reflected a near collapse of the international payments system and financial markets. Instability in exchange rates encouraged speculative capital movements, and exchange rate adjustments were feared by international competitors which saw them as means of obtaining unfair competitive positions in shrinking world markets. Japan was often singled out for special criticism, because Japanese military and naval power accompanied its economic rise and expansion. Defaults by bond borrowers in foreign countries gave international lending a bad reputation among U.S. investors.

The memories of the 1930s were disturbing and still are, even now. Many a skeptic today, consciously or unconsciously, reflects the experience of the 1920s and 1930s. For many, the lessons drawn were that governments of developed and developing countries could not be relied on to give the highest priority to honoring their international financial obligations. Defending domestic conditions—whether the national economies or political systems, or principal sectors and subsectors, or individual firms—had higher priority. Protectionism could take many forms and would be adopted in practice, even though scholars and practitioners widely extolled the virtues of free international trade, competition, and the international division of labor. In the 1920s and 1930s, most countries favored orderly and stable international monetary relations but not at the expense of immediate national well-being or national entities.

World War II

From the experiences of the 1920s and 1930s, came the resolve not to recreate reparation and war debt problems after World War II. Instead, the U.S. provided huge quantities of goods and services to its allies on a lend-lease basis with the terms to be settled after the end of the war. There was a clear understanding on the part of the U.S. (the donor) and its allies (the recipients), that the financial obligations would be limited and sustainable, designed to avoid placing continuing burdens on the recipient nations. The quid pro quo for this generous finance was the commitment to fight in a common cause—to win the war.

The U.S. was the principal donor because it was by far the largest economy, had not been bombed, and was largely spared the horrors of the battlefield. The allies were all economically weaker, occupied, and bombed. The United Kingdom, France, European allies and China, thus, could not do militarily or economically what the U.S. could. The U.S. was not trying to profit from this good fortune. Even bitter complaints during the war that the allies were abusing the U.S. program to obtain goods for postwar use or strengthen their international commercial positions did not interrupt the steady stream of goods and services. China received very little, however, because Japan achieved a virtual military and naval blockade there.

The flows to the allies were offset, in part, by flows from the allies to the U.S., dubbed reverse lend-lease. In the same spirit, when Germany and Japan were vanquished, there were only limited reparations (Japan to the Philippines and Germany to individuals). No large-scale unmanageable financial obligations resulted from World War II, and the unpaid World War I war debts and reparations faded away.

What was seen as a major cause of international friction—huge reparations and external debts—was deliberately avoided. It did not happen accidentally; it happened because the U.S. and its allies had the vision to fight for victory in a manner which would not destroy the peace to follow. Nevertheless, these farsighted actions did not wipe out the memories of the 1920s and 1930s. Indeed, it may be said that the resentments of the 1920s and 1930s proved stronger and lasted much longer than the memories of financing World War II and lend-lease. It is the memories of the 1920s and 1930s which mingle with current events today and shape our judgments about the future.

Bretton Woods and the IMF

After World War II, the U.S. and the United Kingdom collaborated in restoring the international financial mechanism. It was a collaboration of the most powerful nation with the financially most experienced.

Most important was the Bretton Woods Agreement of 1944, which was achieved after three years of intense international discussions and negotiations. This agreement brought about the establishment of the IMF and the World Bank (the International Bank for Reconstruction and Development). Great emphasis was placed on creating an exchange rate system which was neither rigid like the gold standard nor flexible like the floating rates in the 1930s. In addition, the top priority was to restore the convertibility of the world's major currencies which had been destroyed by the widespread adoption of exchange controls and restrictions on international payments, during the 1930s and World War II. Convertibility and stability in exchange rates were necessary to support rapid nondiscriminatory growth in international trade and investment.

Exchange rate systems are not made stable or flexible by mechanisms; they are made stable or flexible by government policies and practices. The Bretton Woods system could have been flexible; the present floating exchange rate system can be stable. Even the degree of international monitoring depends primarily on national wishes—not on mechanisms. The major sterling devaluation of September 1949 was essentially a decision by the United Kingdom, which the other members of the IMF endorsed.

The present so-called floating rate system can readily be transformed into a system of internationally agreed changes in exchange rates without formally changing the IMF Articles of Agreément. On the other hand, the IMF Agreement, as it originally existed, did not prevent nations from taking unilateral action in the exchange rate field. No country could have prevented the U.S. from breaking the traditional tie between the dollar and gold in August 1971. Repeated assurances to the contrary did not prevent this national action of global importance. Similarly, virtually any country can act unilaterally. Its freedom or lack of it comes from its economic and political position not formal mechanisms.

Another major purpose of the Bretton Woods system was to achieve an international payments system free from governmental restrictions, or exchange controls, on international payments and transactions including purchase and sales of other national currencies such as the U.S. dollar. Currencies without such restrictions are commonly called convertible. Exchange rates and convertibility create the financial ballpark within which the game of international banking is played.

Dollar World

By the end of World War II, the only major currency which could be freely exchanged for other currencies was the U.S. dollar. Only a few other countries, economically small but closely tied to the U.S. economy (Cuba and Costa Rica), had convertible currencies. Foreign exchange markets had virtually ceased to exist in Europe and Japan. Payments among nations were made in accordance with regulations issued by central banks. Exchange quotas for specified international payments were set by these central banks. Countries aimed to conserve and allocate their foreign exchange.

Credits were largely intergovernmental, usually bilateral between two nations. An intricate web of so-called bilateral agreements channeled international trade and payments, according to government priorities, not market forces. Bretton Woods aimed to bring inconvertibility and bilateralism to an end among all member countries including nonindustrial countries after a few years. It proved to be a mammoth job, never fully finished, but largely accomplished by industrial nations 15 years after the end of World War II or approximately by the end of the 1950s.

The freedom gained for international payments around the end of the 1950s, through the efforts of the European Payments Union in the early 1950s and the IMF throughout this period, fostered the revival of private international capital movements, especially international banking. Without this freedom, the world economy and international trade could not have grown at unprecedented rates. International banking would have remained, at most, a mechanism for implementing government decisions, not an autonomous major factor in the growth of the world economy.

Marshall Plan

It was soon evident after World War II that the Bretton Woods institutions were too small to provide the external finance needed for the reconstruction of war-devastated Europe. The Marshall Plan was the answer for Europe. Lend-lease, which President Harry S. Truman quickly abolished in 1945, was a vivid memory in 1947 and had given a new definition of how to deal with an ally. The Marshall Plan was the peacetime lend-lease. Few events are of comparable international importance in explaining the economic and financial history of the world in the past three decades. Again, the roots of the Marshall Plan were deeply embedded in the experience with reparations and war debts after World War I.

The economic and financial reconstruction of Europe, largely accomplished by the early 1950s, made possible the revival and expansion of international private lending. The Marshall Plan, like lend-lease, had the built-in magic of being truly temporary. Both programs paved the way for other institutions and activities.

Thus, the late 1940s and the 1950s saw the reconstruction of Western Europe and Japan, within the framework of the international monetary system, agreed on at Bretton Woods. Growth in national economies and in international trade was sustained at levels higher than ever recorded. The poorer so-called developing countries were not excluded from this growth. The extension of convertibility of European currencies during the 1950s created the conditions for the establishment of true foreign exchange markets and enabled the private international credit mechanism to strengthen and expand. Nevertheless, funds lent and borrowed by governments, bilaterally and multilaterally, dominated the international financial scene, although the Eurocurrency markets came into existence in the mid-1950s.

Renaissance of International Banking

In the 1960s, internationally oriented private commercial banks became increasingly important in re-establishing modern and efficiently functioning international financial markets. Banks in such countries as Great Britain, France, Germany, The Netherlands, Belgium, Sweden, Japan, as well as the U.S., expanded their international activities, particularly their branches abroad. Several large private commercial banks in the U.S. were leaders in this effort. They began to expand their network of branch banks outside the U.S. By the early 1970s, this rapid expansion of branches was slowing down. As the international financial markets grew in size and depth during the 1960s, market instruments used, like syndicated loans, also increased in number and complexity.

In the late 1950s and early 1960s, however, the U.S. became concerned with its stubborn balance-of-payments deficits. These deficits had been welcomed after World War II. They helped create net financial transfers to industrial countries abroad to facilitate their rapid reconstruction and accumulation of more international monetary reserves, which were depleted by their war needs before lend-lease began. But by the end of 1945, the U.S. was eager to redistribute part of its gold reserves (concentrated there during the years before its entry into the war) particularly from the United Kingdom which had to pay for its war import needs.

Having started on the road of balance-of-payments deficits—financed partly by an outflow of gold and mostly by U.S. dollars—the U.S. found it difficult to reverse direction without governmental constraints.

The imposition of the interest equalization tax (IET) after 1963 on foreign securities purchased by U.S. residents was designed to reduce outflows of capital and improve the U.S. balance of payments. The tax strengthened the European financial centers. It accelerated the trend, begun in the 1950s, of re-establishing the former importance of European financial centers.

Dollar Lending

A rather novel aspect, reflecting the much-enhanced international role of the U.S. dollar, was dollar lending from these nondollar financial centers based on the acceptance of dollar deposits in London and other financial centers. In the 1960s, higher interest rates in Europe for dollar deposits attracted more U.S. dollar funds, and the Eurodollar market grew to a major source of funding. The worldwide activities of large transnational corporations required large amounts of capital abroad. The development of the Eurodollar market (bank credits and bonds), after 1963, was partly in response to the needs of such corporations as well as governments that needed U.S. dollar finance but wished to avoid the higher costs of borrowing in the U.S. For some U.S. dollarholders, deposits of dollars in London and elsewhere had (and still has) the attraction of being outside the sovereign U.S. boundaries.

During the 1960s, the private commercial banks created the international capability which was the foundation of their success in the early 1970s in coping with the severest economic and financial crises since the end of World War II. The main clouds on the international financial horizon before 1973-1974 were the continued U.S. balance-of-payments deficit combined with the uneven rates of inflation among countries. This characterized the persistent worldwide inflation. It repeatedly eroded existing exchange rate patterns and, more particularly, led to significant revaluations of nondollar currencies with respect to the U.S. dollar or, in other words, devaluations of the U.S. dollar. The expectation was that the U.S. dollar would be devalued repeatedly. The speculation was not whether but when, how much, and in what currencies. Recurring market pressures against the dollar resulted in repeated large-scale outflows of dollars from the U.S. to Europe, particularly Germany and Switzerland.

The European monetary authorities did not welcome the further increases in their international monetary reserves in the form of dollar holdings. In the first instance, an increase in such reserves was inflationary domestically because it involved a domestic monetary expansion. Second, it was in dollars, no longer a prized currency. The U.S. dollar was still the world's preeminent currency. But its convertibility into gold, at the fixed price of $35 per ounce, became impractical in the 1960s as dollar holdings abroad greatly exceeded U.S. holdings of gold. Yet foreign monetary authorities had the legal right to convert their dollar holdings at the fixed price of $35 per ounce.

This was not a serious problem, although a potential one, as long as holders of dollars held them more or less voluntarily. Gold was, after all, a nonincome-earning asset. Dollars could be held in interest-earning securities. When the confidence level, however, fell from willing holders to unwilling holders of dollars, the international monetary system went into a state of shock. President Richard M. Nixon, in 1971, ended the U.S. dollar's tie with gold, and the stable exchange rate system gave way, after an uncertain few years, to a floating rate system. Uncertainty and instability became the hallmarks of the international monetary system—and still are.

Unstable Currencies

Unfortunately, the basic causes of international currency instability, such as persistent inflation and the U.S. balance-of-payments deficits, were not tackled successfully. The world economy was already lurching when it was hit by the OPEC oil price increase in 1973-1974. The recession of 1974-1975 was the deepest of the post-war period. Inflation thwarted attempts to regain satisfactory levels of growth and employment, as governments fought excessively large balance-of-payments deficits and inflation essentially with strict monetary policy and rather weak budgetary restraints. National economic strategies diverged and business cycles did not synchronize while key commodity prices plunged. Nonoil-developing countries were the hardest hit as a group.

Aside from the increased value of oil, international trade expansion slowed down. Currency instability worsened, and speculative capital movements again dominated exchange markets and currency values. Simultaneous flights from and into the dollar, depending on guesses about the future, became frequent.

It is against this unfavorable background that private international bank lending has expanded since 1974.[2] Combined with the inherited concerns of the 1930s, it is not surprising that alarmist views about private international lending and borrowing have been prevalent. Nevertheless, private capital markets and the private banks demonstrated, for the remainder of the 1970s, that they could act under these conditions. In so doing, they did much to prevent a drastic deterioration in the world economy which would have meant even lower growth rates, more unemployment, more inflation, more distress in developing countries, reduced international trade, and strengthening of protectionism throughout the world. International flows of private bank capital played a key role in defending the world economy during the difficult years of 1974-1980. This success did not, however, come easily or automatically. It involved major redefinitions of a commercial bank's functions, capabilities, and management processes.

The trends and magnitude in international lending in the 1970s and early 1980s are especially significant because they probably represent a permanent feature of international lending. Ten years hence, it is likely that the present magnitude of

[2]F. John Mathis, ed., *Offshore Lending by U.S. Commercial Banks*, 2nd ed. (Philadelphia: Robert Morris Associates and Bankers' Association for Foreign Trade, 1981).

international lending will seem relatively small, just as the magnitude before 1974 now seems small. The secular trend of international lending is upward, despite the very large outstanding international loans, the very large demands on available foreign exchange to service these debts, and repeated needs to reschedule or restructure these debts. The process is not self-sustaining. It can be brought to an end by unwise policies of debtors, or creditors, or international agencies. If international private lending does not rise, it will lead to a major economic crisis unless the interruption is short-lived or public sources of finance substitute adequately for private sector lending.

Size and Character of Bank Lending

During the 1970s, the size of private commercial bank lending expanded rapidly. The Bank for International Settlements (BIS) estimated that total international lending by banks of the Group of Ten countries* (plus Switzerland, Austria, Denmark, Ireland, and offshore branches of U.S. banks), increased from about $125 billion at the end of 1970 to $893 billion at the end of 1978, and to $1,550 billion at the end of 1981 (see Table 2.1). This represents a more than 12-fold increase over the decade. These figures, however, include a substantial amount of redepositing of funds among the reporting banks themselves. Excluding this double-counting, the outstanding "net" international bank credit was estimated by BIS to amount to $945 billion at year-end 1981.

The growth in the dollar value of international bank lending in the 1970s was affected by the appreciation of the deutsche mark, the Swiss franc, the yen, and some other currencies used on a major scale in international lending. These appreciations raised substantially the dollar value of assets and liabilities in these nondollar currencies.

As far as the geographic distribution of lending is concerned, more than half of all international banking business is done among the Group of Ten (plus four) countries themselves. This, of course, reflects the extraordinary importance of these countries in international trade and investment. Other industrial countries at year-end 1981 accounted for only 6% of the total. The oil-exporting countries and Eastern Europe, taken as groups, account for 8.6%. Although much publicity has been given in recent years to private commercial bank lending to nonoil-developing countries, this market segment accounts for a comparatively small fraction of total international bank lending (see Table 2.2). The statistics provided in Table 2.2 tend to show higher numbers for developed countries, because these are the countries in which re-depositing takes place. Efforts are being made by the BIS, with the help of central banks around the world, to improve the external debt data. As of this moment, comparability among available statistics is quite unclear. More work has to be done before a satisfactory worldwide breakdown of international private bank debt is available.

*The Group of Ten countries includes Belgium, France, Federal Republic of Germany, Italy, the Netherlands, Sweden, the United Kingdom, Canada, Japan, and the U.S.

Table 2.1—External Claims as Reported by Banks in Major Financial Markets (billions of dollars at year-end)

Country or Region of Lending Bank	1978	1979	1980	1981*	June 1982
Banks in group of European countries reporting to the BIS**	$611.4	$776.0	$902.9	$998.4	$958.9
Domestic currency	109.4	136.3	151.7	151.8	145.0
Foreign currency (Eurocurrency market)	502.0	639.7	751.2	846.6	813.9
Banks in Canada	22.3	25.6	35.5	38.2	39.8
Banks in Japan	33.7	45.5	65.7	84.6	81.3
Banks in the U.S.	119.2	136.3	176.8	257.0	320.6
Branches of U.S. banks in the Caribbean and the Far East***	106.5	127.6	141.0	172.0	170.1
Grand Total	893.1	1,111.0	1,321.9	1,550.2	1,570.7
Less doublecounting due to redepositing among reporting banks	358.1	446.0	511.9	605.2	605.7
Net International Bank Credit†	535.0	665.0	810.0	945.0	965.0
Nonreporting banks in offshore centers††	—	135.0	175.0	239.0	248.0

* Beginning in 1981 including U.S. international banking facilities. Claims of banks in U.S. exclude all custody items except negotiable U.S. bank certificates of deposit held on behalf of nonresidents.

** The European reporting area covers Austria, Belgium-Luxembourg, Denmark, France, Federal Republic of Germany, Ireland, Italy, the Netherlands, Sweden, Switzerland, and the United Kingdom.

*** The Bahamas, Cayman Islands, Hong Kong, Panama, and Singapore.

† Grand total adjusted on a partly estimated basis to exclude doublecounting due to redepositing among the reporting banks. For Hong Kong, banks liabilities exclude those vis-à-vis the nonbank sector.

†† Estimates for nonreporting banks in offshore centers mentioned under *** and all banks located in Bahrain and the Netherlands Antilles.

Source: Bank for International Settlements, *Quarterly Reports on International Banking Developments* (Basel, Switzerland: BIS, various issues).

Sources of Funds: The Largest Banks

The figures presented give the broad magnitudes of international bank lending. Looking ahead, it is expected that the world's largest banks will also be the largest international lenders, although not necessarily in the relative order of their absolute sizes.

Which are the largest banks in the Western world and what is their geographical distribution? Ranked according to deposits at year-end 1981, the world's 25 largest commercial banks include only 3 U.S. banks, Japan had 7, the United Kingdom 5, France 4, and Germany 3. A decade before, the U.S. had 7 banks ranked among the

Table 2.2—External Claims as Reported by Banks in Major Financial Markets by Region of Borrower (billions of dollars at year-end)

Region of Borrower	1978	1979	1980	1981*	June 1982
Reporting countries**	$466.9	$588.3	$704.4	$820.6	$819.6
Offshore banking centers***	123.5	157.1	188.8	237.5	249.0
Other developed countries	63.9	72.4	85.7	99.0	104.3
Eastern Europe	47.5	55.9	59.8	60.7	54.1
Oil-exporting countries†	56.4	64.1	70.0	72.1	74.9
Nonoil-developing countries	120.8	155.6	193.3	229.9	241.7
Latin America	79.9	102.5	129.2	158.4	168.3
Middle East	6.5	7.8	9.7	11.5	12.6
Asia	23.1	31.0	38.5	43.0	43.7
Africa	11.3	14.3	15.9	17.0	17.1
Others	14.1	17.6	19.9	30.4	27.1
Total	893.1	1,111.0	1,321.9	1,550.2	1,570.7
Claims on nonbanks	N.A.	335.9	395.1	458.1	468.6

* Beginning in 1981 including U.S. international banking facilities. Claims of banks in the U.S. exclude all custody items except negotiable U.S. bank certificates of deposit held on behalf of nonresidents.

** The European reporting area covers Austria, Belgium-Luxembourg, Denmark, France, Federal Republic of Germany, Ireland, Italy, the Netherlands, Sweden, Switzerland, and the United Kingdom; Canada, Japan, and the U.S.

*** The Bahamas, Barbados, Bermuda, Cayman Islands, Hong Kong, Lebanon, Liberia, the Netherlands Antilles, Vanuatu, Panama, Singapore, and other British West Indies.

† Includes, in addition to OPEC, Bahrain, Brunei, Oman, Trinidad, and Tobago.

Source: Ibid.

25 largest, while Japan had 5, Canada, France, the United Kingdom each had 3, and Germany and Italy had 2 each. The change in country representation was, of course, partly caused by the appreciation of some major currencies in terms of the U.S. dollar, which increased the dollar value equivalent of their deposits. More important, the expansion of domestic, as well as international, business activities has brought more French and Japanese and German banks into the top ranks (see Table 2.3).

Some 20 different countries are represented (1981) among the world's 100 largest banks, compared with 15 countries a decade ago. Australia, Austria, Belgium, Brazil, Mexico, India, Iraq, Israel, and Spain have now banks ranking among the 100 largest. Besides a wider diversity of countries, international bank consortia combining banks from different countries have strongly gained in importance and in many instances have entered into lending activities in Third World countries.

A decade ago, U.S., banks, among the 25 largest, accounted for about 36% of the combined deposits. At the end of 1981, they accounted for only 14%. When looking at the 50 largest banks of the world, the U.S., a decade ago, accounted for 30% of the combined deposits but at year-end 1981 barely 12%.

Table 2.3—The 25 Largest Commercial Banks in the World (Ranked by Deposits Dec. 31, 1981, Compared with Dec. 31, 1970)

Rank	December 31, 1981	Country	Deposits (millions)	Rank	December 31, 1970	Country	Deposits (millions)
1	Bank of America NT & SA	U.S.	$95,985	1	Bank of America	U.S.	$25,643
2	Banque Nationale de Paris	France	93,864	2	Chase Manhattan Bank	U.S.	21,228
3	Credit Lyonnais	France	85,227	3	Citibank	U.S.	21,085
4	Barclays Bank	U.K.	82,070	4	Barclays Bank	U.K.	13,830
5	Credit Agricole Mutuel	France	81,533	5	National Westminster Bank	U.K.	11,726
6	Deutsche Bank	West Germany	79,179	6	Manufacturers Hanover Trust	U.S.	11,073
7	Societe Generale	France	78,872	7	Banca Nazionale del Lavoro	Italy	10,856
8	National Westminster Bank	U.K.	76,082	8	Royal Bank of Canada	Canada	10,668
9	Citibank	U.S.	72,471	9	Banque Nationale de Paris	France	10,452
10	Midland Bank	U.K.	72,325	10	Westdeutsche Landesbank	West Germany	10,097
11	Da-Ichi Kangyo Bank	Japan	67,514	11	Deutsche Bank	West Germany	9,793
12	Royal Bank of Canada	Canada	62,904	12	Canadian Imperial Bank	Canada	9,777
13	Fuji Bank	Japan	62,840	13	Morgan Guaranty	U.S.	9,589
14	Sumitomo Bank	Japan	62,133	14	Chemical Bank	U.S.	9,026
15	Mitsubishi Bank	Japan	59,129	15	Credit Lyonnais	France	9,010
16	Chase Manhattan Bank	U.S.	58,586	16	Bank of Montreal	Canada	8,438
17	Sanwa Bank	Japan	56,182	17	Societe Generale	France	8,436
18	Dresdner Bank	West Germany	55,000	18	Banca Commerciale Italiana	Italy	8,284
19	Westdeutsche Landesbank	West Germany	53,293	19	Sumitomo Bank	Japan	8,273
20	Industrial Bank of Japan	Japan	49,538	20	Fuji Bank	Japan	8,172
21	Lloyds Bank	U.K.	48,492	21	Bankers Trust	U.S.	8,086
22	Norinchukin Bank	Japan	47,967	22	Midland Bank	U.K.	8,036
23	Canadian Imperial Bank	Canada	47,592	23	Mitsubishi Bank	Japan	7,785
24	Hongkong and Shanghai	Hong Kong	47,563	24	Sanwa Bank	Japan	7,552
25	Barclays Bank International	U.K.	45,511	25	Industrial Bank of Japan	Japan	7,176

Source: *American Banker*, July 28, 1982, and July 30, 1971.

Table 2.4—Assets, Liabilities, and Equity Capital of the Ten Largest U.S. Banks (millions of dollars at year-end)

	Assets		Liabilities		Equity Capital	
	1981	1980	1981	1980	1981	1980
BankAmerica Corp.	$121,158	$111,617	$117,068	$107,709	$4,091	$3,908
Citicorp	119,232	114,920	114,951	111,029	4,281*	3,891*
Chase Manhattan	77,839	76,190	74,842	73,502	2,593	2,283
Manufacturers Hanover	59,108	55,522	57,208	53,814	1,900	1,709
Morgan (J.P.)	53,522	51,991	51,102	49,811	2,420	2,180
Chemical	44,917	41,066	43,365	39,709	1,502	1,307
Continental Illinois	46,972	42,089	45,261	40,564	1,711	1,525
Bankers Trust	34,213	34,202	32,882	33,042	1,331	1,159
First Chicago	33,562	28,699	32,291	27,498	1,272	1,202
Security Pacific	32,999	27,794	31,676	26,624	1,323	1,170

* Common stockholders' equity. Total capital funds (also including preferred stock, convertible notes, and long-term debt with original maturities of 15 years or more) totaled $7,157 million in 1981.

Source: Annual reports of the ten largest U.S. Banks

The ten largest banks in the U.S. range from about $32 billion to about $121 billion in total assets. BankAmerica and Citicorp are the largest. In this family of giants, Chase Manhattan, Morgan, Chemical, and Continental Illinois are mid-size giants. Bankers Trust, First National of Chicago, and Security Pacific are ordinary giants (see Table 2.4).

Among the ten largest U.S. banks, six have their headquarters in New York, two in California, and two in the Midwest. Their combined (consolidated) deposits, at year-end 1981, were valued at $432 billion, of which $227 billion, or 53%, were deposits at their foreign branches. At year-end 1981, total deposits on the books of BankAmerica Corporation stood at $94.4 billion, 42.3% of which were deposits at its foreign branches. Consolidated deposits at Citicorp amounted to $72.1 billion, of which $52.1 billion, or 72% were deposited at its foreign branches. Total deposits in Chase Manhattan amounted to $55.3 billion, and deposits at its foreign branches to $31.6 billion (see Table 2.5).

American banks have now accumulated very large assets overseas. Earnings from these assets constitute a substantial portion of total earnings. (More details will be found in a later chapter.) In 1981, the ten leading U.S. banks averaged 48% of total earnings from international earnings. Morgan Guaranty had the largest percentage with 63%, an increase from 58% in 1980. Bankers Trust also received over 60% of total earnings from overseas sources. Bank of America, Citicorp, and Chase derived more than 50% of their incomes from foreign sources. On the other hand, much lower percentages were experienced by Chemical Bank, Continental Illinois, Security Pacific, and First Chicago (see Table 2.6).

Table 2.5—Domestic and Foreign Source of Deposits and Income of the Ten Largest U.S. Banks, 1981 (millions of dollars)

	Holding Company Consolidated Deposits			Income*		
	Total	Foreign	Percent Foreign	Total	Foreign	Percent Foreign
BankAmerica Corp.	$94,369	$39,878	42.3%	$ 445	$245	55.0%
Citicorp	72,125	52,098	72.2	555	287	51.7
Chase Manhattan	55,300	31,581	57.1	444	247	55.6
Manufacturers Hanover	42,462	23,614	55.6	256	120	46.8
Morgan (J.P.)	36,024	21,278	59.1	375	235	62.7
Chemical	29,430	13,776	46.8	215	74	34.2
Continental Illinois	29,594	14,631	49.4	260	74	28.0
Bankers Trust	23,345	12,892	55.2	192	116	60.3
First Chicago	25,555	12,979	50.8	122	24	19.7
Security Pacific	23,446	4,704	20.1	207	51	24.8
Total	431,650	227,431	52.7	3,071	1,493	48.0

* After income taxes and before securities transactions

Consolidated Deposits (billions) of the Ten Largest U.S. Banks

1956	1960	1965	1970	1975	1978	1979	1980	1981
39.7	49.2	75.4	126.2	256.1	341.6	387.2	418.1	431.7

Source: *The American Banker* and the banks' annual reports.

As in all modern banking, earnings come essentially from interest differentials; the most common measure of interest differential is the spread over the London interbank offered rate (LIBOR). In recent years, the spread over LIBOR has tended to be narrow. And from time to time, banks have refused to participate in loan syndications because the spreads offered by the borrower were too low to be profitable to the lender. In lending to governments and government entities, the spreads have been narrow indeed, ranging from even less than 1/2% to somewhat over 2%. Spreads significantly over 1% were unusual between 1977-1980, but thereafter they began to reappear.

Spreads reflect, of course, the eagerness or reluctance of lenders. In a crude way, they also measure the market ratings on country risk. As country risk ratings, they are crude because many other factors affect spreads, including portfolio mix management. Unless conditions in financial markets change drastically, government borrowers are likely to pay narrower spreads than private borrowers. On the other hand, governments which lose their country creditworthiness cannot hope to bor-

Table 2.6—International Earnings as a Percent of Total Earnings*

	1975	1977	1979	1981
BankAmerica Corp.	54.7%	41.8%	37.5%	55.0%
Citicorp	70.6	82.2	64.5	51.7
Chase Manhattan	64.5	64.9	46.9	55.6
Manufacturers Hanover	49.1	60.2	48.8	46.8
Morgan (J.P.)	60.2	48.1	52.2	62.7
Chemical	41.6	38.8	31.7	34.2
Continental Illinois	13.4	16.6	16.5	28.0
Bankers Trust	58.6	82.8	51.7	60.3
First Chicago	34.0	21.0	3.6	19.7
Security Pacific	12.6	11.6	11.0	24.8
Composite	52.5	50.5	42.2	48.0

* Income before securities transactions
Source: Annual reports of the ten largest U.S. banks.

row by offering large spreads. In early 1982, it was safe to say that a country that offered to pay a spread of 3% over LIBOR would not be able to borrow at all. It would be regarded as too dangerous a country risk (see Table 2.7).

Uses of Funds: The Major Borrowers

The global spread of U.S. international banking is reflected by the geographical distribution of assets and liabilities of American banks' major foreign branches (see Table 2.8). It is noteworthy that in recent years European branches have declined in relative importance compared with branches in other parts of the world.

Thus, international banking has become of prime importance for American banks. Risks in international lending are ever-present and high. To wait for a low-risk global environment is simply to decide not to engage in international banking. Instead, the response of banks has been to create mechanisms to evaluate and judge these risks, to decide what are acceptable risks of doing business in foreign countries, and how to defend against adverse changes.

Table 2.7—Representative Terms on Syndicated Loans to Developing Countries

Country	Sovereign Borrower	Date	Amount (millions)	Tenor (years)	Spread (Percent over LIBOR)
Brazil	Eletrobras	3/82	70	8	2⅛
	Nuclebras	4/82	150	8	2⅛
	Itaipu Binacional	6/82	25	8	2⅛
	Eletrosul	8/82	135	8	2⅛
Mexico	Nafinsa	5/82	400	3	¾
	UMS	6/82	1,367	7	1½
	Pemex	6/82	60	4	⅞
	Pemex	8/82	300	9 mos.	½
Venezuela	BIV	4/82	170	3	⅝
	Inos	6/82	310	1	½
	Republic of	8/82	200	7	⅞
Panama	Republic of	5/82	225	8	1¼
Korea	Republic of	8/82	18	10	½
	EXIM/Korea	3/82	300	8	½
	KEB	5/82	300	2	⅜
				6	½
Philippines	United Coconut	5/82	42	10	⅞
	Ptet	5/82	110	7	1
				3	1⅛
	Cdcp	7/82	15	1	¾
	NPC	9/82	11	10	⅞
Indonesia	Republic of	4/82	300	10	⅜
	PT Perwick A.	8/82	28	3	1⅜
				5	1¼
Malaysia	Federation of	8/82	440	8	⅛
	Sabah Gas Ind.	8/82	25	10	⅜
Ivory Coast	Republic of	8/82	22	8	1½
	Republic of	8/82	11	8	1½
				4	1⅝
Morocco	BNDE	2/82	53	6	1⅛
	Samir	6/82	70	5	1
Nigeria	NNPC	4/82	80	4	¾
				4	⅞
				3½	1
	Bauchi state	7/82	32	8	⅞
Turkey	Central bank	1/82	70	8 mos.	1

Source: Euromoney Syndication Service, September 1982.

Table 2.8—Geographical Distribution of Assets and Liabilities of Major Foreign Branches of U.S. Banks*
(billions of dollars year-end)

	Assets					Liabilities				
	1976	1978	1980	1981	June 1982	1976	1978	1980	1981	June 1982
Europe	$86.3	$110.2	$140.8	$139.1	$132.1	$75.0	$95.8	$111.1	$105.3	$96.1
Canada	2.4	3.9	6.5	6.6	5.7	4.4	3.8	5.3	4.4	4.0
Latin America	40.0	50.0	72.7	72.7	57.5	23.7	28.1	41.7	42.0	30.2
Asia	28.1	39.2	51.5	63.0	63.8	30.0	38.9	52.5	59.4	54.5
Africa	5.9	7.9	8.7	10.2	9.8	2.5	2.9	5.7	4.7	4.0
Oceania	1.0	1.6	1.5	2.0	3.0	0.3	0.1	0.3	0.2	0.1
Puerto Rico & U.S. dependencies	N.A.	2.8	4.2	4.2	4.1	N.A.	2.0	3.6	5.1	4.4
Total	174.3	239.3	324.8	376.4	374.0	172.7	237.3	323.6	374.9	371.3

* Figures have been adjusted to exclude accounts between branches of the same bank.

Columns do not add to totals because totals *include* international organizations and the U.S., and prior to June 1978, Puerto Rico and U.S. dependencies.

Source: Federal Reserve, *Statistical Release E.11* (Washington, D.C.: Federal Reserve, various issues).

3

Sources of Funds to the Third World

Our attention will now focus on lending to developing countries. It is lending to these countries which has raised most questions about country risk. Lending to all foreign countries, however, results in some country risk, objectively or subjectively as perceived by the lender. Country risk evaluation and country risk management need to encompass countries of all kinds, as long as they are recipients of bank lending or other bank business. Nevertheless, it is useful to give special attention to developing countries.

We begin by looking at international bank lending to developing countries in historical perspective. There has been a transformation from dependence on official sources of funds, which was at its peak under the Marshall Plan, to greater reliance on private bank funds. This has raised problems for banks and the developing countries because an increasing share of funds are loans obtained on commercial terms, and therefore debt-servicing costs are higher per dollar borrowed. In general, banks can strengthen their loan portfolios by lending to developing countries, and these countries have a good ability to use these funds efficiently to generate growth to service their debts. The process of economic development implies that countries will have balance-of-payments deficits and be chronic debtors. But this must be balanced with extended foreign exchange generating capability. Less developed countries' persistent need for capital to support growth is the strongest reason why they will continue to service their foreign debt.

Historical Perspective

Private bank lending to Third World countries has fostered country risk analysis and its application. Ignorance about international banking combined with large and growing lending magnitudes and the memories of the 1930s were well-springs of concern. The process of overcoming these concerns has just begun and it may not be completed for years or decades. If these concerns halt international lending, it will diminish the profit-making opportunities of banks and reduce the ability of developing countries to evolve into modern more productive, more diversified economies.

New Funding Source

Commercial bank lending is proving crucial to the social and economic evolution of many developing countries. This source of financing enabled modernization and growth to maintain momentum in the 1970s despite the severe shocks of repeated multiplication of oil prices, large increases in balance-of-payments deficits, accelerating persistent inflation, restrained growth in developed countries, and increasingly severe global recessions. In the early 1980s, conditions became worse—global depression replaced recession, and many developing countries faced difficulties in servicing their external debts. If banks had to restrain lending to developing countries because of today's rescheduling problems, borrowing countries would lose a vital option in pursuing their national development objectives and avoiding substantial social suffering. Table 3.1 gives the magnitudes of net flows of financial resources, from all sources, to the developing countries.

The existence of private bank lending as a major source of funds for developing countries is still fragile and vulnerable, for it is still relatively novel for both borrowers and lenders. It involves decisions that are fraught with uncertainties. The purposes, magnitudes, and maturities of borrowing are continually evolving, and new countries have entered the universe of major borrowers.

New Borrowers

These new borrowers often do not have a long record of borrowing and servicing debt to private bank lenders since many are relatively new nations. Others have relied nearly exclusively on official sources of development finance. Some countries are and have experienced difficulties in servicing their external debt to official and private lenders. A further complication comes from the widespread misunderstanding of the lending policies and capabilities of commercial banks. Unfortunately, the degree of attention given these misunderstandings is not diminished by their inaccuracy.

Lenders are often portrayed as short-sighted, grasping, and driven by market forces to make loans which they themselves perceive as too risky, even to the point of imperiling their own institutions. Competition, it is argued, forces them to make poor decisions. From a very different viewpoint, it is often argued that if lending serves to make profits for the lender, it must be undesirable, unfortunate, or even harmful to the borrower! Thus, in the 1970s, international lending to developing countries was widely criticized as dangerous to lenders and undesirable for the borrowers.

In the 1950s and 1960s, prevailing attitudes were very different. Private bank lending to developing countries was steadily advocated and warmly endorsed by supporters of the developing countries and was not seen as unwise by observers of the lenders. Maximizing the availability of private sources of external finances, as long as the financial terms and usage were acceptable to the host country, was regarded as helpful to the developing countries. Now, however, attention focuses on the potential dangers and possible abuses of such borrowing to lender and bor-

Table 3.1—Total Net Resource Receipts of Developing Countries from All Sources (billions of dollars)

	1971	1972	1973	1974	1975	1976	1977	1978	1979	1980	Prel. 1981
Total receipts	**21.16**	**23.35**	**32.18**	**36.17**	**54.43**	**58.22**	**63.75**	**83.30**	**85.55**	**95.67**	**104.0**
Official Development Assistance	9.36	10.06	12.43	16.46	20.09	19.65	20.36	27.22	30.61	36.36	35.51
DAC bilateral	6.33	6.63	7.09	8.23	9.81	9.50	10.08	13.12	15.91	18.02	18.28
Multilateral agencies	1.33	1.39	1.96	2.82	3.84	3.87	4.83	6.00	6.20	7.74	8.00
of which: OPEC financed	—	—	—	0.12	0.16	0.42	1.23	0.96	0.26	0.29	0.41
OPEC bilateral	0.44	0.66	2.03	4.15	5.68	5.17	4.28	6.90	6.58	8.26	6.91
CMEA countries	1.26	1.38	1.35	1.26	0.73	1.05	1.09	1.20	1.80	2.14	2.12
Other countries, bilateral	—	—	—	—	0.03	0.06	0.08	0.10	0.12	0.20	0.20
Nonconcessional Flows	11.80	13.29	19.75	19.71	34.34	38.57	43.39	56.08	54.94	59.31	68.49
Multilateral of which:	0.90	1.01	1.28	1.83	2.58	2.68	2.94	3.09	4.16	4.85	5.00
OPEC financed	—	—	—	0.02	0.06	0.13	0.27	0.16	0.22	0.13	0.27
Direct investment	3.31	4.23	4.72	1.89	11.51	8.64	9.59	11.83	13.42	10.36	14.64
Bank sector*	3.30	4.80	9.70	10.00	12.00	15.00	15.50	22.87	19.67	19.00	25.00
Bond lending	0.30	0.52	0.58	0.28	0.42	1.22	3.20	2.67	1.14	3.10	2.50
Private export credits	2.71	1.44	1.15	2.40	4.42	7.22	9.11	10.22	9.49	12.20	10.59
Official export credits**	0.71	0.75	1.18	0.86	1.22	1.39	1.48	2.15	1.72	2.46	2.76
OPEC bilateral***	0.19	—	0.14	0.92	1.50	1.61	0.89	(1.01)	(1.00)	(2.00)	(3.00)
Other† of which:	0.38	0.54	1.00	1.53	0.69	0.81	0.68	2.24	4.34	5.34	5.00
CMEA countries	0.10	0.11	0.10	0.09	0.09	0.12	0.11	0.16	—	—	—
Memorandum Items:											
Private sector grants	0.91	1.04	1.37	1.22	1.34	1.35	1.49	1.65	1.95	2.31	2.02
Selected IMF Facilities, net††	0.05	0.30	0.36	1.74	3.24	2.98	−0.43	−0.85	0.52	2.61	6.18

* Excluding (i) bond lending and (ii) export credits extended by banks which are included under private export credits. Includes loans by branches of OECD banks located in offshore centers.

** Including supporting funds to private export credits.

*** Official flows only; no information is available on private flows.

† Apart from CMEA and "other donors" (Ireland, Luxembourg, Spain, Yugoslavia, India, Israel), includes DAC miscellaneous nonconcessional.

†† Oil facility, compensatory drawings and extended fund facility; loans by the IMF Trust Fund are included under ODA flows from multilateral agencies (1977=$180 million, 1978=$860 million, 1979=$680 million, 1980=$1,640 million, 1981=$430 million).

Note: Figures concerning non-DAC member countries are based as far as possible on information released by donor countries and international organizations completed by OECD secretariat estimates based on other published and unpublished sources. Therefore, it has not been possible fully to verify that they comply in all respects with the norms and criteria used by DAC members in their statistical reports made directly to the OECD secretariat.

Source: *Development Co-operation, 1982 Review* (Paris, France: OECD, November 1982).

rower. World growth, nevertheless, is increasingly dependent on private bank lending to secure satisfactory improvements in living standards.

Relationship Between Private and Public Lenders

A given magnitude of concessional assistance does finance a larger net inflow of resources than finance obtained on commercial terms. This obscures, however, the more fundamental point that these are not truly practical alternatives. Official assistance has been, and remains, inadequate for developing countries and, therefore, it must be strictly rationed. Developing countries do not borrow commercially because they masochistically enjoy paying higher interest rates or wish to borrow at shorter maturities. Nor do they borrow, for the most part, from private sources because they wish to misuse the funds by corruption and in wasteful consumption or to avoid needed adjustments in economic management, particularly changes in patterns of consumption, income, savings, and investment. They borrow to pay for imports of consumption goods, intermediate and capital goods and services and to pay for interest, dividends, and royalties.

No level of feasible borrowing from private commercial banks can make it possible for a country in balance-of-payments difficulties to avoid needed adjustments for more than a brief time. The lending criteria of private banks, moreover, tend to induce changes in the macroeconomic management of foreign governments, though such changes are not by custom explicitly stipulated in loan contracts. The lending policies of the banks give heavy weight to the quality of economic management. Private lenders that lend to mismanaged weak countries or for unproductive usage are likely not fulfilling the lending standards that must guide a private lender. Such loans are mistakes which are costly to lenders and borrowers. They are too costly to be countenanced for long and this is well known by the major international banks. Banks do not wish to have losses resulting from nonservicing debt. They appreciate that if they stop lending, conditions are created that make debt servicing more difficult. But they find it difficult to be guided by such considerations because they cannot know what other banks will do. The bank acts defensively, not only against the borrower but also against other lenders.

Official lenders, like the IMF and World Bank, can and do help induce needed changes in economic management by forcing such changes before agreeing to lend. Much of the ability of official lenders to insist on changes and achieve them depends, however, on their ability to point to the unwillingness of private lenders to continue lending while the country is mismanaged. They also point out that funds from private sources will be forthcoming if economic management is improved, as these official lenders recommend. Agreements with official lenders, particularly the IMF and the World Bank, are offered as strong evidence of intentions by foreign governments to manage their countries in a way likely to have the confidence and support of private lenders. Borrowers find that to raise substantial funds over significant periods of time, the criteria of private institutions come close to those of the international organizations and can be even more severe.

The notion that market competition creates widespread imprudent lending confuses the exceptional case with the general situation. Mistakes are made by private banks; more knowledge and experience are needed to minimize that likelihood but the unforeseen does happen. Portfolios of private banks must be managed to make the unexpected adverse shocks tolerable. Banks must also be managed to recognize favorable opportunities. Often the favorable opportunities exist because the conventional wisdom is dominated by irrational fears that cause competitor banks to shy away from otherwise acceptable, profitable opportunities.

Relationship Between Public and Private Funds

Can private bank lending to developing countries reduce the need for providing increased resources to official multilateral agencies? For project financing, private lenders are not likely to finance many needed and desirable activities, such as rural rehabilitation, building cities, education, and medical facilities, which have long gestation periods before they contribute to production capability. Productive use of a commercial bank loan is more definable in terms of increased productive capacity in the future by the borrowing entity. Otherwise, the loan is likely to be perceived as akin to general budgeting or balance-of-payments support.

Private banks usually prefer lending for directly productive purposes. Project finance from private sources is not likely to be available for countries which are deemed too risky to be creditworthy, yet they are properly eligible for loans from official entities. In addition, project identification and evaluation and the other technical assistance provided by an official institution can be critically important.

Combination of Funds

In some areas, like industry, mining, and energy development, official and private lending institutions acting together may well be involved. In our world, which is in urgent need of capital for productive output and infrastructure of all kinds, the problem is the global need for capital, management, and labor skills. In the developing countries, these elements are chronically in short supply. Many important projects in developing countries cannot be financed from beginning to end by official funds alone. Many projects will use private, as well as official, finance, if available, and in many cases, private sources have to provide the bulk of external finance, or the projects are not done.

If the borrowing entity and host country are acceptable credit and country risks, obtaining funds from commercial bank sources ordinarily will be attractive. The funds are primarily obtained in capital markets of industrial countries where interest rates are relatively low compared with interest rates and returns on capital in developing countries. Commercially borrowed funds from external sources are usually relatively cheap for a productive entity in a developing country. When they are not guaranteed by creditor governments, they are also untied to procurement and therefore can be used to buy goods and services on a worldwide competitive price basis, giving the most return for the monies spent. Such borrowed funds can also lead to more available external funds, if needed in the future.

As the project proceeds and the borrower services the loans fully and promptly, creditworthiness is strengthened for continuing the project and financing others. The simultaneous presence of multilateral official funds is helpful. Borrowing from private sources is compatible with and often helped by full utilization of official funds and technical assistance extended by bilateral and multilateral agencies.

The availability of private sources of funds may deprive a borrower sooner of official sources of aid. This can happen if official sources of funds are so limited that increasingly severe criteria for selection of countries becomes necessary. The existence of private sources of financing need not diminish significantly the overall magnitude of official assistance. It can, however, affect the allocation of official funds among developing countries.

Assuming a country is well managed and creditworthy, although it finances other investments from private sources, it may be unable to carry out certain investments, necessary for development, that require funds from official sources. The fault is found in the magnitude of available official finance. There is no reason, otherwise, why such countries should not receive loans from the World Bank or a regional development bank, for example, while making important use of private funds. If, however, the World Bank and other official sources continue to be severely restrained in their lending, developing countries that achieve strong standing with private lenders are likely to be pressured to reduce further their borrowing from such official sources.

Inefficient Use of Funds

On the other hand, the inability of developing countries to make efficient use of official funds has been one of the arguments against governmental assistance or lending. When and if developing countries are perceived to be efficient users of privately borrowed funds and establish a strong record of prompt servicing of such debt, there may be more willingness to provide official development assistance. Exaggerated concerns about the future of developing countries and emphasis on their inabilities, difficulties, and inefficiencies lead not to more official assistance but to less. In our eagerness to advocate more official development finance, we may neglect to note the strength, resiliency, and stubborn will of most developing countries to move forward. We may unwittingly encourage dissemination of the view that developing countries do not make effective use of external funds—at most, a partial truth.

It is interesting to note which countries have been the largest borrowers, and of these which have borrowed the most from private banks (see Table 3.2). Of the 20 countries that are the largest borrowers from *all* sources, only India and Pakistan have made relatively little use of private commercial banks. Also, bank assets in Iran have been reduced in recent years. Eighteen countries made substantial use of official and private sources of finance. Of these 18, leaving aside the special case of Iran, the 2 developing countries that had balance-of-payments difficulties and

Table 3.2—The 20 Largest Borrowers among Developing Countries, 1978-81
Ranked by Size of Disbursed External Term Debt, Outstanding at Year-End 1981 (billions of dollars)

Country	Total Disbursed External Term Debt Year-End 1978	1979	1980	Prel. 1981	Total Debt Service 1979	1980	1981	Est. 1982	External Positions of Private Com. Banks*** Year-End 1979	1980	Mid-1982	Reserves (ex. gold) Year-End 1980	1981	1982**
Brazil	44.4	50.8	57.0	65.6	11.4	13.7	17.3	18.5	27.3	29.5	36.6	5.8	6.6	4.2
Mexico	30.5	37.6	43.5	54.4	11.4	9.3	13.4	15.2	20.2	23.7	32.2	3.0	2.6	1.6
Spain	13.1	16.3	20.7	25.1	3.0	3.7	5.0	5.7	9.8	11.7	14.3	11.9	10.8	7.6
Korea	12.5	15.5	17.6	20.8	2.9	3.3	4.0	4.8	5.3	6.3	8.6	2.9	2.7	2.7
Argentina	7.9	12.6	15.6	20.0	2.1	2.8	3.7	4.9	6.5	9.5	12.2	6.7	3.3	13.1
India	15.9	16.5	18.0	19.4	1.1	1.4	1.4	1.7	0.6	0.5	0.9	6.9	4.7	4.5
Indonesia	14.5	15.1	16.6	18.2	2.2	2.0	2.7	3.4	3.5	3.7	5.0	5.4	5.0	3.1
Algeria	14.9	17.0	17.2	17.0	3.2	3.9	4.4	4.8	7.7	7.6	6.2	3.8	3.7	2.4
Yugoslavia	11.4	13.5	15.1	16.8	2.7	3.3	4.2	4.7	6.4	7.5	7.3	1.4	1.6	0.8
Turkey	6.8	11.6	14.5	15.5	0.9	1.1	1.6	1.9	2.5	3.1	2.8	1.3	1.3	0.9
Venezuela	9.7	12.3	14.7	14.9	2.8	4.7	6.0	7.8	8.1	10.0	11.0	6.6	8.2	6.6
Egypt	10.4	12.2	13.8	14.0	1.3	1.8	2.2	2.4	0.9	1.3	1.4	1.0	1.2	0.7
Chile	5.1	7.1	9.0	12.3	1.7	2.2	3.1	3.3	2.9	4.5	6.9	3.1	3.2	1.8
Philippines	6.2	7.4	8.5	9.5	1.3	1.1	1.6	2.1	3.5	3.9	4.5	2.8	2.2	1.7
Pakistan	7.6	8.4	9.2	9.5*	1.1	1.6	N.A.	N.A.	0.5	0.6	0.4	0.5	0.7	1.0
Iran	10.9	10.5	10.3*	8.5*	2.0	2.0	6.1	1.6	4.1	3.3	0.9	N.A.	N.A.	N.A.
Morocco	5.4	6.7	7.3	8.0	1.0	1.3	1.5	1.9	2.7	2.7	2.7	0.4	0.2	0.2
Greece	4.7	5.6	6.9	7.6	1.1	1.3	1.7	2.1	3.7	5.2	6.4	1.1	1.0	0.9
Peru	6.1	6.5	7.1	7.3	1.1	1.6	2.0	1.9	1.9	1.7	1.8	2.0	1.2	1.2
Nigeria	2.6	4.2	5.5	6.0	0.8	1.2	1.6	1.9	0.6	0.6	4.5	10.2	3.9	1.2

* Estimate.

** Year-end or latest available.

*** External positions of private commercial banks in G-10 countries, Switzerland, Austria, Denmark, and Ireland. Claims exceeding one year in maturity of private commercial banks only; does not include other commercial sources.

Source: OECD, Development Assistance Committee, November 1982; *Maturity Distribution of International Bank Lending* (Basel, Switzerland: BIS, December 1982); *International Financial Statistics* (Washington, D.C.: IMF, February 1983).

required renegotiation of their external debt as of the end of 1981 were Turkey and Peru. These countries accounted for about 3% of the medium- and long-term exposure of private banks in the 20 largest debtor countries combined. However, in 1982, several of the largest borrowers, including Mexico, Brazil, and Argentina, approached the banks for restructuring of their bank debts.

Private Bank Objectives

It is to be expected that private lenders will be more stringent than official lenders. Private banks are privately owned; losses on loans are major adversities; loan losses are carefully investigated by management, internal auditors, external regulators, shareholders, and security analysts. A bad lending record means the bank loses its own credit standing in private money markets—a modern bank must be a borrower in order to be a lender. A bank which has a poor record of loan losses will lose its needed financial standing as a borrower from the public or other banks. It can result in the demise of the bank. The private bank can make some mistakes, but that is all.

The record of loan losses in lending to developing countries has been remarkably good by any standard. A bank lending to entities in developing countries has a wide range of potential customers—multinational firms, locally owned enterprises, government enterprises, governments, foreign-owned and locally owned banks, central banks, etc. The lending bank can pick and choose. Credit mechanisms are available to assess the creditworthiness of the borrowing entity. Care can be taken to avoid the pitfalls of sloppy credit analysis. The resulting portfolio, leaving aside country and "translation" or exchange rate risks and focusing on credit risk, can be very attractive, particularly as loans in foreign currencies can earn attractive spreads over the cost of such funds.

Competition drives down spreads, at times to unattractive margins, although this is more likely with government borrowing than private firms. Banks can refuse to lend to governments, if the spreads are too narrow. The individual borrowers are creditworthy and very much need to remain creditworthy. As individual entities, they are in chronic need of more capital and not able to meet this need from earnings or equity investments. These borrowing entities can and do run into difficulties. They are not immune, but they can represent a high-quality group of borrowers. Their countries, moreover, can only temporarily afford to do without a net inflow of resources for development. Their need is not temporary, short-lived, or minor. A developing country without a net inflow of resources runs the risk of a rapid decline in growth combined with a rapid rise in inflation.

Developing countries do not ordinarily have the ability to reduce the level of total external debt. The composition of debt changes as past and existing lenders are repaid, while new borrowers incur new debts. As the composition of debt changes, there are consequent changes in the total cost of servicing lenders, usage of loans, impact on ability of economy to grow, export performance, etc. Meanwhile, the total level of debt usually rises because the developing country needs the net inflow of real resources from abroad.

Developing countries only have the capability to service debt if there is a continual net inflow of real resources. They can only reconcile their consumption, production, and development needs and service their external debt by remaining creditworthy. Financing balance-of-payments deficits by borrowing from private banks does not avoid the need to make domestic adjustments. These policy changes are needed to maintain external creditworthiness. Even drawings from the IMF are a form of increased borrowing needed to maintain or restore creditworthiness.

There are other reasons, besides lack of alternatives, why countries have preferred to borrow from private banks and not use available cheaper sources of foreign exchange. Borrowing from private sources can be arranged quickly and for large magnitudes. Borrowing from private sources avoids the appearance of domestic policies dictated by "foreigners." Borrowing from private banks is also not usually perceived as political.

Future Funding from Official Sources

The IMF and other multinational sources of funds may not be used because they may be regarded as continuously available or reserved for future contingencies. Official sources of funds are available like a country's international monetary reserves. Access to private bank sources may be perceived as less certain in the future. The theory is, therefore, borrow from private sources while it is possible. Many developing countries have even borrowed commercially for the purpose of increasing international monetary reserves. This is perceived both as a rather inexpensive form of image strengthening and insurance against future short-falls in availability of foreign exchange. Such reserves can be invested in interest-earning foreign currency assets.

The recent changes in IMF and World Bank lending policies may result in increased demands for loans or grants from member countries. Member countries may seek much larger assistance from the IMF for longer maturities, while members of the World Bank are given access to a new balance-of-payments facility which provides additional funds more quickly than the traditional project financing. The World Bank is also making efforts to help secure additional external financing for its projects by expanding its program of co-financing.

If country demands are substantial, the IMF and World Bank will need to supplement the resources available to them through an increase in IMF quotas or by borrowing from official and private sources. For the World Bank, this will probably require increases in capital which raises its ability to borrow on private capital markets. As an interim or partial measure, it may gain permission to increase the amount of loans it can make against existing capital—so-called gearing ratio—or not to count guarantee operations as equivalent to loans when looking at capital/asset ratios. The World Bank will continue to try to obtain more grant-like funds for its poorest members as International Development Association (IDA) contributions. Negotiations to increase the lending ability of these organizations were confronted by serious objections until the Mexican liquidity crises caused the U.S. to relax its fiscal conservatism somewhat.

New sources of funds would not, in the aggregate, substitute for previously used private sources. It would be additive, unless external actions, like governmental controls by industrial countries, restrict the movement of private capital to developing countries or donor countries restrict official aid or the activities of the multilateral agencies.

Limits on Private Bank Lending

The private banks of the world, considered together, are not close to the limits of their capacity to lend to developing countries, however capacity is judged. A common constraint concerns the capital of banks, and it is often a principal consideration in judging ability of banks to expand lending.

In some countries, capital availability is stressed more than in others. (For example, in the U.S., Switzerland, and the United Kingdom, more than in France, Italy, or Japan.) It is unusual that a modern bank must stop lending more to a particular borrower or into a particular country because of capital limitations. It may instead become more selective in making loans, choosing the best combination of less risk and more profitability, if it is achieving capital/asset ratios which the market or bank regulators perceive as high. Moreover, the existing level of loans outstanding leaves much room for changes in composition of advancing new funds as loans are repaid. The opportunities for contracting or expanding desired portions of a loan portfolio are large, even when capital adequacy is deemed by management to be an important constraint in total lending.

Even when legal ratios exist, defining the relationships between loans made and capital, there are market judgments about the bank which are usually more important than the bank's formal position with regulators. A bank which is regarded as weak in its capital base may find it more expensive to borrow in the money markets and may have to pay more than its competition to attract and keep deposits. "Weakness," however, is likely to be judged in light of the bank's portfolio composition and quality and reputation of management. If a bank is regarded as so weak in its capital base and otherwise as to damage seriously its financial credibility, it can lose its creditworthiness entirely. A bank which cannot borrow cannot lend. It ceases to be an intermediary between sources and users of savings; it ceases to be a bank.

Bank supervisors or regulators can bring pressure on a bank if they are concerned with inadequate capital. The bank may be urged to restrain lending until capital has increased, particularly if the bank cannot do so quickly.

The issue of capital adequacy has become of prime importance in international banking because the Federal Reserve System and other central banks have not been willing to be lenders of last resort—perhaps more clearly stated, a rescuer of last resort. Private banks can borrow from central banks but often at high penalty rates which cause important losses to the borrowing banks. The borrowing bank may, in effect, be borrowing from the central bank to support loans which it has made at interest rates lower than what it is paying to the central bank.

If, in case of difficulties with its own loans, a private bank could borrow at profitable or at least nonloss rates from the central bank, it could be much less concerned about the future and what it will bring for its own portfolio. Banks cannot, however, assume that central banks will rescue them. It is not ruled out, but it is not to be ruled in. Banks cannot expect to be rescued without risking changes in management and even ownership or tighter controls by the supervisory authorities. If the bank is seen as having enough capital to use for future difficulties, it will have less problems in maintaining its own creditworthiness. It could expect to have the option to borrow, if needed, instead of using capital.

U.S. banks usually operate within legal lending limits to any single borrower which is a small percentage of capital—say 10% or less. With respect to the 10% legal lending limit, U.S. banks operate under a regulation commonly referred to as the means and purpose test. Under this regulation, loans to foreign governments, their agencies, and instrumentalities will be combined if they fail to meet either of the following tests, which are applied at the time each loan is made.

- The borrower must have resources or revenue of its own, sufficient over time to service its debt obligations ("means" test).
- The loan must be obtained for a purpose consistent with the borrower's general business ("purpose" test). This does not preclude converting the loan proceeds into local currency prior to use by the borrowing entity.

The issue of capital adequacy arises only when a number of important borrowers are simultaneously in difficulties and cannot service their loans fully and promptly. This happens occasionally, particularly when downturns in business cycles are strengthened by monetary and credit policies designed to bring about "credit crunches" through relatively high interest rates. Collapses in real estate speculative booms furnish repeated examples of this phenomenon.

Capital Adequacy

International lending to developing countries brings concerns with capital adequacy into sharp focus. The concern is often with the totality of all credits extended to entities in the borrowing country—official and private, including the government itself. The fear is that the foreign exchange needed to service foreign loans, as well as meet other payments, will simply not be forthcoming because of foreign exchange shortages. The need will arise to ration foreign exchange among different needs, including servicing of external debt. The fear is that the debt to the private lender will not be serviced fully and promptly or may even be defaulted. If all the credits extended to entities in any one country are large, they could be a substantial portion of the total capital of a bank—even exceed the total capital. The income from such credits could be a significant portion of total income—perhaps the difference between a bank's ability to achieve a profit from all assets during a given time period.

This situation can be found in a number of banks in relation to their lending to developed countries, for example, to entities in the United Kingdom, Germany, and Japan. These are the major economic units of the world. They have many creditworthy entities in such countries which use foreign finance to carry on some of their activities. These countries are usually regarded as virtually as safe for a lending bank as the U.S. They are major lenders as well as major borrowers. They not only have strong international monetary reserves but more important they have good reputations in financial markets and can borrow readily what they need. In the U.S., domestic loan assets 20 times capital cause no heart palpitations. It is not surprising that loans in Germany or Japan equal to, say, two or three times capital do not disturb the lender's equanimity.

Lending to developing countries, however, is seen very differently. At best, these countries are rarely seen as "safe" from the viewpoint of country risk, despite their good record of avoiding defaults since the end of World War II. Therefore, a bank's total credits in any one developing country, however large or strong, equal to or somewhat more than its total capital, is likely to be regarded as excessive concentration from the viewpoint of country risk.

For many a creditworthy developing country, a bank would regard total exposure equal to capital as being excessive risk, irrespective of the importance the bank gives to capital/asset ratios in defending its liquidity and financial viability. This is the case because the likelihood of the country risk materializing is seen as much greater than in developed countries, with the attendant possibilities of large-scale defaults or servicing difficulties. Moreover, it is feared that difficult experiences in a developing country will happen simultaneously in other developing countries because of similarities of conditions and causes, for example, fall in prices of primary export commodities or rises in the prices of essential foodstuffs, capital goods, and oil.

The fear of inadequacy of capital because of difficulties in a developing country is compounded if there is fear of difficulties with credits extended domestically in the creditor country and to entities in other developed countries. This cannot be ruled out because difficulties experienced by developing countries often originate in the developed countries. Slow growth, strong inflation, and adverse business conditions which cause payments difficulties for domestic borrowers in the developed countries, as well as difficulties to borrowers in developing countries, are such problems.

Thus, there is an interaction between country risk and concern with capital adequacy in modern banking. The persistent inflationary environment encourages more borrowing at rates of increase more rapid than banks can build capital from earnings or new issues. Differences in perception of country risks among different countries result in tiering of countries when considering capital adequacy within a bank. Within the U.S., where country risk is usually regarded as zero, for example, a ratio of assets to capital of say 15 or 20 to 1 would be regarded as quite acceptable. In Germany or Japan, a ratio of 2 or 3 to 1 would be quite acceptable but not

20 or 30 to 1 as in the U.S. In the case of developing countries, ratios of 1 to 1 or less are more appropriate.

Large differences exist among countries. Few countries have the country credit-standing of Germany, Japan, and the United Kingdom, despite their large external indebtedness. For many developing countries, the magnitudes of exposure are so small as to be virtually immaterial from this viewpoint. Only the larger borrowing countries like Brazil, Mexico, Argentina, and Korea raise the capital adequacy issue in a significant way; yet these countries have been much more acceptable borrowers than other developing countries. It is when they are in balance-of-payments difficulties that their large external debts are seen as barriers to further large-scale borrowing.

Distribution of Lending

Perceptions of country risk can limit lending to developing countries at some level for any one lender. This limit is an individual bank limit or ceiling. It does not apply to the conglomerate of banks nationally or internationally. Only in the cases of Mexico and Brazil are the magnitudes for a few banks close to high in this sense. This analysis, however, does not mean that banks are not at their designated limits for certain countries. As discussed in a later chapter, country limits can be reached at a very small percentage of capital if the country risk is perceived to be significant. This percentage can rise or fall as country risk assessments change with changing country conditions. It is in the different perceptions of acceptable capital/asset ratios for any one foreign borrowing country that we find much more informative and meaningful reflections of perceived differences in country risks than in other measures like comparative interest rates (LIBOR plus spread).

Banks defend their financial viability essentially by asset/liability or portfolio management rather than capital. But in actual practice, capital also weighs significantly in the decision making of bank managers and in the shareholders' evaluation of a bank's financial strength and management. A bank's ability to lend increases over time as its scale expands in all dimensions—capital, deposits, assets, personnel, experience, etc. These expanding numbers may well reflect global and national inflations, rather than growth in real terms, but this expanding scale remains the measuring ruler for the banks.

The limits of any one bank lending to entities in any one country, as noted, will be influenced by its judgments on country creditworthiness and the quality of its portfolio. Individual banks may hold back on lending to some creditworthy countries for portfolio reasons, but other banks dealing with such countries will not. Similarly, capital adequacy can act as a general constraint on lending by a particular bank, but this applies to all asset acquisition—domestic and international. Lending to developing countries is a small portion of the portfolios of most, even large, banks. Huge increases in lending to developing countries can be accommodated within relatively small changes in the geographic composition of total assets. Portfolio quality and diversification are still much more important determinants of the magnitude of lending to developing countries than capital.

Net new private bank lending to developing countries is likely to continue to increase and encompass more and more developing countries. Competition will bring more banks around the world into this process. The ever-improving flow of instantaneous knowledge makes for highly efficient financial markets, which will keep down costs to borrowers, seen most clearly in the size of spreads over LIBOR, which vary, but remain relatively narrow. Interest rates and maturities will be commercial, reflecting cyclical variations, as well as the consequences of persistent inflation on money and capital markets of the world. Interest rates are likely to be high by historical standards of the developed countries but still acceptable when used productively in developing countries. Floating-interest rates heighten uncertainty domestically and internationally. They are seen as high when the borrowing country loses its creditworthiness but still has to service outstanding debt. The high rates are reasonable as long as the developing countries can continue to borrow.

The process of international lending can be beneficial to the developing countries and profitable for the banks. The principal dangers to lenders come from the crisis in the world economy into which we seem to be moving—continuing inflation, slow growth, high unemployment, inadequate investment, and reduced productivity with consequent increased exchange rate instability and pressures for protectionism in trade and payments. The developing countries cannot escape the consequences of continued serious adverse world economic events, but this is not an argument against lending to developing countries. Borrowers in such countries may prove to be more viable than in developed countries, and their countries will be keen to protect their country creditworthiness. However, frequent interruptions or delays in debt servicing and need for debt renegotiation will occur. Private lenders have a great stake in a viable world economy whether their borrowers are located at home or abroad.

Expanded IMF Role Needed

The deepening crisis of the world economy in the early 1980s is of critical importance in judging the future role of private bank lending to developing countries. Although relations with the IMF are explored more fully in a later chapter, it may be useful to comment here on the IMF because of its special role to prevent a financial breakdown of the world economy and in sustaining a viable system of international payments necessary for international banking expansion.

The IMF has to be much larger—by a factor of three or more—to play its proper role as the defender of the international monetary system in a world of structural as well as cyclical change. High levels of output and employment in a cyclical sense and satisfactory rates of growth in a structural sense are the content of world prosperity. The IMF must be able to provide temporary balance-of-payments assistance to deficit countries to avoid the need for policies inimical to domestic and international prosperity. Such undesirable measures include restrictions on payments, disorderly and unrealistic exchange rate systems, or highly restrictive fiscal and monetary policies leading to prolonged and deep depressions. Disruptions in the international payment and exchange systems protract and deepen recessions, strengthen and spread inflation, and impede needed structural changes to increase efficiency, productivity, and output. The achievement of a growing, noninflationary world economy is the test of the success of the international monetary system.

By 1970, an IMF of $100 billion was already necessary to cope better with the emerging problems of the 1970s. This was not done, and we were not able to cope successfully with the shocks and surprises of the 1970s. Instead we have had persistent global inflation, slow growth, and exchange rate instability. The need was not for more generalized international liquidity. The need was for an authoritative manager of an international monetary system capable of defending the system by the timely and strong support of its members. A comparable figure today to have an adequate IMF is more like $300 billion or more.

IMF Requires Substantial Increases

Why must the IMF be increased substantially? The Fund is a pool of currencies; it sells needed foreign exchange from this pool to countries which need the foreign currencies to meet international payments. In exchange, it gets the national currency of the country purchasing the foreign exchange. In the banking sense, the IMF does not have capital or assets and liabilities. It owns the contributed national currencies and gold. Its pool of currencies changes in composition but not in total nominal values, until countries agree to increase their contributions of national currencies. Thus, it is not a credit-creating mechanism like a commercial bank.

At any one time, only a portion of the IMF's currencies may be usable to make international payments—and countries need years to acquire the foreign exchange needed to repurchase their national currencies from the Fund with foreign currencies which other countries may need (hard currencies). The IMF management dare not run the risk of a "frozen" Fund, that is holding currencies which countries do not wish to buy because they are not used to making international payments. Nor can the IMF come even close to exhausting its supply of hard currencies without risking the paralysis of the system.

In order to judge the Fund's potential usage, any magnitude of resources seemingly available to it must be considerably deflated to determine the magnitude of internationally usable currencies which it needs to have. The Fund could use its gold, but it is likely to be reluctant in the future to use much of this bottom drawer of assets. It could expand by creating more Special Drawing Rights (SDR)*, increasing quotas, or borrowing from official and private sources. It has external borrowing arrangements with ten individual countries and Saudi Arabia. SDR creation is repeatedly resisted by some creditor countries which welcome the attractiveness of these assets but see their availability to debtors as too soft. Borrowing from private sources is likely to receive increasing attention as a major alternative to IMF reliance on official sources of borrowings like Saudi Arabia or

*The SDR is an unconditional reserve asset created by the IMF to supplement existing reserve assets and allocated to member countries in proportion to their Fund quotas.

increases in the Fund quotas. As of the end of 1982, the IMF was still reluctant to borrow from private sources.

The important thing is that the IMF be much bigger and give member countries a true option in how to handle their external financial needs when the world economy is experiencing simultaneously large balance-of-payments deficits, inflation, and recession. Some countries may still prefer to borrow from private banks or use their international monetary reserves for balance-of-payments purposes, but the choice will then be theirs.

A much larger IMF may not be used more proportionately to finance external deficits. The Fund's success is measured by achieving a healthy international monetary system, an expanding world economy, and controlling inflation, not by the magnitude of its foreign exchange sales. It must have the international stature that comes with the ability to finance, if needed. To achieve this, much of the Fund's resources must remain intact for contingencies. To do this, and still be a major source of financing, requires a much, much larger IMF.

Similarly, the multilateral and regional development banks can effectively intermediate a much greater international flow of savings than has been done. They could sponsor new mechanisms or institutions for such purposes. Financing by the expanded existing and new development institutions could be used for purposes for which private sources of funds are unavailable or inappropriate, rather than allocated by rather arbitrary country/sector/population criteria. In this way, these official institutions can contribute more to sustaining higher levels of output and growth on a sound basis in developing countries.

Even if these changes occur—at best years from now because such actions require the agreement of many countries—international lending by private banks will not only change in composition but also in total magnitude. The 1981 level of $36 billion in *net* lending by private banks to developing countries (including publicly guaranteed export credits) could well rise to about $75 billion per year *net* by the latter part of the 1980s. Expanded activities of the official multilateral institutions would mean that more potential borrowing entities can absorb more private capital efficiently, be regarded as creditworthy, and better able to service such debt. This debt will include borrowings by government entities as well as private corporations and individuals. Lenders will be able to respond to a broader spectrum of countries and borrowers in these countries. With more confidence in the quality of assets in their portfolios, private banks will be less concerned with capital adequacy. More banks in more countries will join the expanding group of international lenders, despite the need for restructuring and renegotiation of existing external debt.

Thus, a greatly expanded IMF and World Bank will not substitute for private banks. It is more likely to increase the total funds lent. The critical factors will be the judgments on country creditworthiness and the conditions of the world economy. A greatly expanded IMF, World Bank, and regional development banks would make the world economy stronger, and individual countries more creditworthy.

Private bank financing of development has matured to the point that it is a major, flexible, and efficient source of external funds, which can also be considered reliable as long as the country maintains its creditworthiness. This condition can be achieved for most of the developing countries, including China, India, and Pakistan. For the private banks, it means expanding their knowledge of countries and their ability to evaluate country risks and opportunities. From experience, they are gaining the skills and confidence to cope with inevitable uncertainties by diversification and spreading of risk on a global scale, including the developing countries. Lending to developing countries can strengthen the portfolios and thus the capital bases of the banks involved. For the borrowers, it means emphasis on productive usage of borrowed funds and good economic management. As the borrowers gain experience, they will appreciate, with increasing clarity and confidence, that maintaining their ability to tap directly into the world savings stream, through borrowing from private bank sources to support their development efforts, is to enhance greatly their chances of success. Countries that appreciate this first will make stronger borrowers.

New Forms of Lending Expected

Following are the kinds of lending to less developed countries expected in the 1980s:

• Floating-rate instruments rather than fixed rate instruments.

• Increased use of project financing compared with general purpose borrowing.

• Mechanisms whereby a development project can be broken down into different phases so that it might be more easily financed on shorter-term bases, say in five-year periods. A developing country must always recognize the risk of sunken capital, if new loans are not available as the old ones are repaid.

• Structuring projects so that they could be interrupted for a period of time and yet not lost. A developing country may want to structure suitable development projects with completion stretched out until the country qualifies as a longer-term borrower.

• Individual entities within developing countries will strive to become long-term borrowers, even if it is on a floating-rate basis and even if the country cannot hope to have access to long-term money in the foreseeable future. The novelty will be fixed-interest rates with longer-term maturities. The floating-rate mechanism may mean changing rates frequently, perhaps every six months or every year.

These suggestions exemplify the innovations and different forms of credits which may be created, just as market conditions created convertible debentures, certificates of deposit, and floating-rate notes. There may also be larger and more varied use of co-financing with the multilateral institutions. Perhaps multilateral institutions will be better able to give private lenders the benefit of their knowledge about borrowing countries and their knowledge about projects. The private banks will then have assurance that the borrowed funds are being used for productive purposes. The private banks would be used less for general balance-of-payments purposes and more for projects screened and endorsed by a responsible multilateral agency.

The multilateral agencies measure their success by the number of productive projects financed rather than their own financial contributions. Even if they make no financial contributions at all, their technical skill and reputation with private lenders would be major contributions. This is equivalent to what the IMF does when it gives its certificate of endorsement on stabilization programs and standby arrangements. The actual funds come mostly from other sources of finance.

The ability to lend and the desire to borrow exist. But the anxieties of the private banker cannot be ignored, and overcoming these anxieties must be part of the decision-making process. Therefore, the anxiety must be reduced to an acceptable level before lending can actually take place. Borrower and lender participate in the process of how to reduce this anxiety: The borrower tries to adapt his policies as much as he can to cause less anxiety, the private lender tries to improve his knowledge sufficiently to make sensible country judgments and integrate this knowledge into business decision making.

The private lender, all the time, wants to distinguish between anxiety that does not have an objective reality, that is not justified by facts, and anxiety that is justified by facts. That is credit and country risk assessment. Bankers are trained by books and experience to separate the important facts from really irrelevant considerations—to discard the irrelevant. This then provides a basis for a sound judgment and choice of terms and conditions of lending. The private banker will want to find ways and means for lending. Therefore, the 1980s are likely to be a very creative period for new instruments and new mechanisms because bankers have a strong incentive to lend and the environment will be difficult and risky.

In some form, the net inflow of capital into the developing countries will go on. Economic realities will dominate, and the large flow of funds of a debt character will cause continued concern. During the 1980s, borrowers, investors, and multilateral agencies will be thinking of ways and means to increase capital flows that are not of a debt character. People will be spurred on to the intellectual task of finding ways to maintain the needed net inflows of capital with lower projections of debt, although total debt keeps rising. The 1980s will be a period when innovation in debt and equity mechanisms will be sought and efforts will continue to increase international official development finance to those countries which cannot create the conditions for attracting the needed debt or equity capital.

External Debt Conditions

The current high levels of debt will not keep private banks from lending to those countries that want to borrow and are perceived by investors as being creditworthy. That group of countries will always be large enough—and likely to expand—so that the totality of foreign currency exposure of lending institutions will be rising. The present external debt situation—often referred to as the external debt problem—is likely to be greater than ever. Thus, we need to give special attention to the external debt conditions of developing countries. However, before doing so in subsequent chapters, it is necessary to address whether developing countries want foreign private banks to play a significant role in their development.

The answer is obviously critical for a judgment on the likely future of international lending to developing countries. Bank loans are made in response to demand, whatever the marketing efforts of the banks are to meet the competition for supplying these credits. Legitimate questions exist as to the wisdom of relying on private banks as providers of development finance. For country risk analysis, the question is crucial.

If borrowers in developing countries do not see the need for external finance from private lenders to be continuous and major, they are not likely to give the same top priority to servicing these debts and otherwise maintaining their creditworthiness with private lenders. Given the developing countries' chronic balance-of-payments needs, the "preferred creditors" will be those lenders seen as needed and available in the future. A past creditor without a future need to be used will always be at the bottom of borrowers' concerns. Country risk for such creditors will be much greater than country risk for creditors still needed and potentially available and so perceived by borrowers.

Developing Countries' Demand For Funds

Do developing countries want banks to play a significant role in development and be major sources of development finance? Commercial banks lend on commercial terms—the hardest available. Their borrowers do not expect concessional terms, such as lower-than-market interest rates or longer grace periods and maturities than prevail in private markets. Thus, commercial borrowings mean larger external debt accumulations and larger debt-servicing obligations than borrowings from concessional sources.

For countries with chronic need for net inflows of goods and services, loans from commercial banks finance smaller net inflows of such goods and services than the same magnitudes of monies obtained on concessional terms. The extreme examples are grants, which result in no debts and no servicing obligations; the maximum inflow of goods and services is financed. Certain credits like those obtained from the IDA come close to grants because their maturity periods are very long (50 years), grace periods very generous (20 years), and interest rates close to zero.

Loans extended by the World Bank and the regional development bank (Inter-American Development Bank and the Asian Development Bank) are much closer to financial market conditions. However, at fixed rates not far from rates at which the governments of the leading industrial countries borrow, and for extended maturity periods of 20 to 25 years, they are much more concessional than the terms developing countries can obtain from private banks. External debt and debt-servicing obligations are created by such concessional borrowing but less rapidly and in substantially smaller magnitudes. Grants and concessional loans and credits, thus, are preferred by developing countries. Yet borrowing from commercial banks has greatly expanded. Is this expanded role of private banks welcomed by developing countries? The answer is obviously yes, since borrowing has expanded but with what misgivings or qualifications.

Private Bank Involvement

An increasing number of developing countries want private banks to play a significant role in their development processes. There has evolved over some years—well before the OPEC crisis—a new awareness of what private banks are capable. That awareness goes far beyond the identification of a source of quick emergency help, as well as normal trade-related financing. Private banks are seen as part of an extensive, expanding, efficient nonpolitical international financial system providing a great variety of services and technical assistance. They are viewed as providing a major additional source of external finance to countries whose chronic problem is how to find adequate external finance.

Private banks help especially to finance the expansion of modernizing sectors, including agriculture as well as industry, mining, tourism, retailing, etc. All developing countries have modern sectors or firms—"islands of modernity"—which expand over time in relation to traditional sectors. Governmental and private entities are in these sectors. They need funds, and part can come from external sources. Although located in developing countries, they are thoroughly equipped to approach financial sources in foreign countries. When funds are obtained directly from overseas sources, the domestic entity becomes a borrower from a foreign lender.

More and more, this foreign lender is a commercial bank. Moreover, official and private entities in the developing countries keep large deposits with banks in industrial countries. In other cases, the domestic entity borrows from domestic sources, particularly domestic banks. These domestic sources, including domestic banks, in turn, obtain part of their funds from external sources through correspondent banking relations. Thus, directly and indirectly, foreign private banks are intimately part of the domestic development process. They add foreign exchange resources which add purchasing power to productive entities and in a form which is especially useful and scarce, namely foreign exchange.

Furthermore, private institutions are perceived as not political. They are able to coexist with a variety of socioeconomic systems and usually stay out of domestic politics. At the same time, they offer advantages to borrowers because of their diversities, competitiveness, international connections, lending capability (not limited by official budgetary restraints or need for intergovernmental agreements), flexibility, reasonable (market) terms, and speed of response. At times, the availability of finance on a nonpolitical basis has been seen as a way to reinforce the adoption or implementation of unpopular adjustment measures without the appearance of outside political interference or involvement.

Nations have developed increasing self-assurance and confidence, overcoming earlier anxieties that they did not know how to deal with foreign investment and that the presence of foreign banking entities brought the concomitant danger of foreign domination. Fears of "dollar diplomacy" were part of the heritage of many developing countries. This growth of self-confidence helps explain their increasing use of private borrowing, as well as their widening interest in having foreign-owned banks operate within their borders.

Oil Shock Effects

The private banks are also welcomed as a source of external finance because of the previously cited limitations on availability of official capital flows. Total official aid from all sources has risen over the years. For many years, however, there has been resistance among the industrial countries to increase their aid flows to levels that the developing countries felt could be used effectively. The surplus-oil-exporting countries have made substantial contributions, but thus far mostly to countries with which they felt special ties—Kuwait and Saudi Arabia to Egypt, Pakistan, and the Sudan; Venezuela to Jamaica and certain Central American countries; Nigeria to the African Development Fund. Channeling more of these oil funds through multilateral institutions, with relatively less emphasis on special ties, has run into the problem of declining oil prices and revenues. The ability of most oil-exporting nations to extend large-scale assistance to others has been reduced.

In theory, the huge increases in oil prices in the 1970s need not have resulted in larger balance-of-payments deficits for developing countries. One alternative might have been greatly reduced or even negative growth rates. The result might be loss of sunken capital in incompleted investment projects; even higher levels of unemployment; lower living standards; and greater social and political tensions. The borrowing developing countries turned to the official world to help avoid this kind of adjustment, and obtained considerable official aid from new as well as established donor or creditor governments and multinational institutions.

These sums were, however, much too small. Some developing countries tapped the world savings stream by borrowing large sums from private banks around the world, mostly U.S. banks because of the preeminence of the U.S. economy and efficiency of its banking system. Coincidentally, those countries mostly in need of private capital and with good creditworthiness were countries with strong financial ties to the U.S.; Latin America, Korea, Philippines, and Taiwan exemplify this situation.

International Intermediation

The types of international financial intermediation required for the developing countries to tap into the world savings stream could not be accomplished adequately by the domestic banks within the developing countries. Some developing countries like Brazil, Mexico, Korea, and India have entities that can and do part of the job of intermediating world savings on a competitive basis in world financial markets, like the U.S. and the Eurocurrency markets. Most domestic entities in developing countries need the international financial institutions to provide the links.

Many developing countries are interested in having foreign-owned banks in their countries. Such private banks, though foreign-owned, can play a useful role in encouraging and collecting domestic savings, as well as providing a distribution mechanism to channel domestic savings into various private and publicly owned industries and productive facilities, including the creation and improvement of long-term plant and equipment. Branches of foreign-owned private banks coexist with domestic government-owned and privately owned banks. There are many places where this is so: Brazil, Mexico, and India, as well as industrialized countries like France, Japan, and Germany. Thus, for developing countries that are creditworthy for private bank borrowing, the private banks help create a wider variety of options in selecting their development finance strategies, including financing in domestic national currencies.

Foreign-Owned Banks

The conviction is growing that the foreign-owned banks in developing countries offer an extra security for future problem periods. However, there is still widespread questioning whether the private banks will be foul-weather, as well as fair-weather, friends. On the other hand, in a few developing countries, domestic banks have reached sufficient strength to pressure their governments to limit the role of foreign banks in their domestic markets. They see themselves as able to perform efficiently and adequately the role of domestic and even foreign intermediation.

Thus, the resistance to foreign-owned banks found in some developing countries is a form of protectionism, rather than a fear of political domination or interference. Nevertheless, it exists, and it may become more important as these developing countries modernize their societies. Protectionism is an old phenomenon and still significantly influences the international exchange of goods and services, 200 years after Adam Smith!

This international exchange of goods and services continues to expand because of the common interest of countries in this expansion, and their interest in finding ways and means of overcoming particularly troublesome cases. It may be expected that international banking will have a similar experience in developing countries. The growth of foreign-owned private bank activity has not been confined to the wealthier or more advanced of the developing countries. The poorer countries in Asia and Africa also host many foreign-owned banks, while indigenous banks are creating their own international business.

Thus, in greatly varying proportions, private bank lending runs the entire spectrum among the developing countries, reflecting the great variety of activities and functions they perform. Even in countries not creditworthy for substantial amounts of foreign-currency term lending, the international private bank can safely finance foreign trade in self-liquidating transactions, as well as domestic- or local-currency banking. Banks in these countries can do a local-currency business without incurring foreign-currency risk. In these various ways, international private banks are active in some of the poorest developing countries, which are still largely dependent on official concessional aid for their external foreign-currency financing.

The diversification of the economies of the developing countries has been another factor in the growth of the role of private banks. Diversification means expanded modernization. This diversification and modernization have created more creditworthy borrowers who are eager to have more means of financing, particularly in foreign currencies at rates of interest prevailing in creditor, industrial countries.

Government Borrowing

Lending to governments and central banks has grown rapidly. Governments see themselves as strong borrowers, with preferred access to both local currency and foreign exchange. They are able to borrow on better terms than domestic private entities, even when the latter obtain government guarantees. Government borrowing can also be part of external debt management, trying to ensure usage of borrowed funds for high-priority activities as defined by the government—financing imports to dampen inflation or carrying on high-priority investment projects. It is often seen as a way of preventing excessive foreign-currency borrowing.

Governments may borrow to make their own payments. Frequently, however, the borrowed foreign-currency funds are added to other foreign exchange availabilities and allocated to public and private sector users through an official foreign exchange budget administered by the central bank. The increased lending by private foreign-owned banks to governments has set an example for increasing private lending to other entities in the economy. The acceptance by the government of the usefulness of private international banks becomes a model for other public and private borrowing entities.

It might be assumed that the banker's traditional preference to lend at short or medium term would have dampened the interest of developing countries in bank financing. It is evident that the cutting edge of economic and social development is long-term investment in plant, equipment, technology, and human capability. It has been increasingly realized, however, that with good project and country performance, the level of inflows of short- or medium-term funds can be maintained and increased. Maturities may well lengthen as confidence in a country is strengthened by experience. Also, while private banks do review creditworthiness with each decision to extend a new credit at maturity of the old, experience indicates that short- and medium-term funds can be used for longer term purposes if the borrower's, and the country's, economic performances are consistently and continuously perceived as strong.

Many developing countries are, nevertheless, eager to lengthen the maturities of their borrowings, well beyond the range of commercial bank practices. Mexican entities, for example, have gained access to the U.S. and Eurobond markets. But for other developing countries, this remains a target because it requires a strong and durable financial reputation with institutional investors. In the latter part of the 1980s, we may see other developing countries trying to achieve this capability, thus decreasing their relative dependence on other shorter-term sources of private external financing, including private banks. In the early 1980s, it does not seem feasible given the concerns with developing countries' financial situations.

The benefits of becoming—and remaining—creditworthy in the private bank markets are now seen to be of major proportions. Policies needed to maintain external creditworthiness with private banks are also needed to meet national development objectives. It is the maintenance of the country's economic and social development that is the prime purpose of policy measures. But if availability of private credits is also achieved, the process of development is greatly facilitated.

Recent history provides many examples of countries that made major changes in their economic programs and major improvements in balance-of-payments management to get their economies back to a satisfactory growth pattern. The purpose was also to strengthen their creditworthiness in private markets. Examples include Argentina, Indonesia, Brazil, Korea, Mexico, Peru, Jamaica, and Zaire. These cases exemplify the importance that developing countries attach to maintaining or regaining access to private credit and capital markets as a permanent feature of their external financial management.

There are, of course, many areas of uncertainty. There can be no certainty that because of the many benefits to developing countries of pursuing policies designed to keep them creditworthy, that such policies will be pursued or that time will not be needed for adjustment and that, in the meantime, debt servicing may be threatened or interrupted. These developments have already occurred repeatedly. No government, or other domestic or external entity, can guarantee the future behavior of governments and economies. This underlines the need for continuous assessments and monitoring of countries.

Brazil and Korea, whose private debts are already large and have maintained prompt servicing, pose urgent questions about their continuing to pursue the policies necessary to remain creditworthy. The answer seems to be in the affirmative. By their repeated willingness to adapt, many developing countries indicate the importance they attach to maintaining their external creditworthiness. When confronted by the ultimate need, many have reduced their rates of growth and employment.

The response of developing countries is predicated on the assumption that private banks will respond positively to demand for credit from creditworthy countries. The light at the end of the tunnel for a creditworthy developing country is achieving access to the external credit needed to maintain a growing economy. It is *not* the *end* of the need for a net inflow of capital, the old (and wrong) definition of the light at the end of the tunnel.

4

Emergence of the External Debt Problem

Before proceeding to discuss the experience of developing countries with debt renegotiation and implications for country risk analysis and debt management systems, it may be useful to summarize and review international lending to developing countries and the resulting external debt. In earlier chapters, the statistics on lending were given. Here we start with the end product—external debt. In economic jargon, the earlier data gave the flows, now we look at the stock.

Current Level and Growth in Indebtedness

At year-end 1982, total disbursed external term debt outstanding in about 150 developing countries (including the major oil-producing developing countries but excluding Eastern Europe) was estimated at about $626 billion (see Table 4.1). This total was up by 18% from $530 billion a year earlier and about seven times the amount in 1971.* Of the $626 billion outstanding at year-end 1982, about $139 billion, or about 22%, came from official creditors (from governments on a bilateral basis or from multilateral agencies); $413 billion, or about 66%, came from private creditors, mostly banks. The remaining $74 billion, or approximately 12%, represented credits extended to developing countries, primarily by OPEC members and centrally planned economies. Breaking down the $413 billion from private creditors, capital markets (bank loans other than export credits but including loans through off-shore centers, bonds, and other private loans) accounted for about $265 billion (or 42% of total funds) and export credits for $148 billion (or an additional 24% of outstanding term debt).

At year-end 1971, by comparison, official creditors held about $34 billion of the external term debt outstanding, accounting for 38% of the total, while private creditors held $47 billion, or more than 50% of the total. (In these statistics, export credits extended by private banks and guaranteed by governmental agencies, like

*The estimate was made by the Organization for Economic Co-operation and Development and published in November 1982. By comparison, the World Bank reported the external term debt of 98 developing countries (plus the East African community) and capital deficit-oil exporting less developed countries to have reached $462 billion at year-end 1982. Term debt, as defined here, is debt with original maturities exceeding one year. Short-term debt is not included here.

Table 4.1—Total Disbursed External Term Debt Outstanding in Developing Countries, 1971-1982* (billions of dollars at year-end)

	1971	1975	1976	1977	1978	1979	1980	Prel. 1981	Est. 1982
Total Disbursed External **Term Debt****	$90	$180	$220	$274	$345	$406	$465	$530	$626
DAC/ODA***	24	34	37	41	49	53	57	57	63
Multilateral agencies	10	22	26	33	40	47	56	65	76
Capital markets†	20	61	80	103	134	162	190	222	265
Bank loans	11	49	64	81	105	131	155	180	210
Export credits	27	42	51	65	85	100	114	128	148
Other††	9	21	26	32	37	44	48	58	74
Source of Lending as a Percent of Total Debt									
DAC/ODA	26.7%	18.9%	16.8%	15.0%	14.2%	13.0%	12.3%	10.8%	10.1%
Multilateral agencies	11.1	12.2	11.8	12.0	11.6	11.6	12.0	12.3	12.1
Capital markets	22.2	33.9	36.4	37.6	38.8	39.9	40.9	41.9	42.3
Bank loans	12.2	27.2	29.1	29.6	30.4	32.3	33.3	34.0	33.5
Export credits	30.0	23.3	23.2	23.7	24.6	24.6	24.5	24.1	23.6
Other	10.0	11.7	11.8	11.7	10.7	10.8	10.3	10.9	11.8
Annual Percent Nominal Increase	(16)	(24)	(22)	(25)	(26)	(18)	(15)	(14)	(18)

* Approximately 150 developing countries including OPEC countries.
** Includes external term debt whether public, publicly guaranteed, or nonguaranteed in the borrowing country.
*** Development Assistance Committee of the OECD/Official Development Assistance.
† Banks loans (other than export credits), including loans through offshore centers, bonds, and other private lending.
†† Includes lending by OPEC and centrally planned economies.
Source: *Development Co-operation, 1982 Review* (Paris, France: OECD, November 1982); *OECD Press Release*, June 23, 1982.

Hermes in Germany or the Export Credits Guarantee Department in the United Kingdom, are counted as assets held by private creditors.) The centrally planned economies accounted for almost $9 billion; credits from OPEC countries were at that time negligible.

After World War II and until the beginning of the 1970s, official creditors, both governments of developed countries and multilateral agencies, were the most important sources of debt capital to the developing world. The traditional official sources of external capital—both the donor countries'* Official Development Assistance (ODA) and the financial flows stemming from the multilateral financial institutions such as the World Bank and regional development banks—have long been inadequate to meet the developing countries' external capital requirements. Private sources of financing had filled these gaps to a certain extent for many years, with private commercial banks becoming an increasingly important constituent source.

A substantial and sudden increase in the flow of private debt capital occurred during 1974-1975 when the financing needs of the nonoil-developing countries multiplied as a consequence of the first oil shock and the severe worldwide recession then affecting the industrialized nations, persistent global inflation, and food shortages. In 1975, for the first time, the net flow of private financial resources from Development Assistance Committee (DAC) countries to developing countries exceeded official flows by a substantial margin (see Table 4.2). Since then, the financing needs of the developing countries have been increasingly met by the availability of funds from private sources.

In 1981, the net flow of financial resources from developed countries to developing countries amounted to about $88 billion, compared with about $17 billion in 1971. This is a fivefold increase over the decade. Over the same period, the net flow of funds from private sources increased from $7.5 billion to $54 billion, or about sevenfold. Even more significant was the increase in bank lending and private export credits (mostly private commercial bank credits and borrowing in the Eurocurrency market). These grew from $3.9 billion in 1971 to $39 billion in 1981, or tenfold over the decade.[3] In addition to the developed industrialized nations, some of the capital-surplus OPEC members have increasingly provided financial resources to some of the nonoil-developing countries, either through official development assistance, direct investments, or other types of loans.

The resulting rapid increase in external debt has resulted in large debt-service obligations for many developing nations (see Table 4.3). Total debt-service payments of developing countries to all lenders during 1981 were estimated at about $109 billion and are believed to have approached $130 billion in 1982. Interest payments accounted for $60 billion, or 46%, and amortization for about $71 billion, or

*The donor, or DAC, countries are Australia, Austria, Belgium, Canada, Denmark, Federal Republic of Germany, Finland, France, Italy, Japan, the Netherlands, New Zealand, Norway, Sweden, Switzerland, the United Kingdom, the U.S., and the Commission of the European Economic Community.

[3]Organization for Economic Co-operation and Development, *Development Co-operation, 1982 Review*, (Paris, France: OECD, November 1982).

Table 4.2—Net Flow of Financial Resources from DAC Countries to Developing Countries* and Multilateral Institutions, 1967-69 to 1981 (net disbursements in billions of dollars)

	Average 1967-69	Average 1969-71	1971	1974	1975	1976	1977	1978	1979	1980	1981
Total Net Flows	**12.7**	**15.7**	**17.4**	**22.5**	**44.8**	**46.0**	**51.5**	**70.6**	**75.4**	**75.4**	**88.0**
A. Official flows	7.0	8.1	9.0	13.8	17.7	18.1	19.1	25.3	25.7	32.6	32.2
ODA	6.4	7.1	7.6	11.6	13.8	14.0	15.7	20.0	22.8	27.3	25.6
Other	0.6	1.0	1.4	2.2	3.9	4.1	3.4	5.3	2.9	5.3	6.6
B. Private flows (market terms)	5.7	7.0	7.5	7.5	25.7	26.5	30.9	43.6	47.7	40.4	53.8
Direct investment	2.6	3.3	3.7	1.1	10.3	7.9	9.5	11.0	12.7	9.8	14.6
Portfolio investments	1.5	1.4	1.5	3.9	11.8	12.6	13.4	23.0	25.5	19.2	28.5
Export credits**	1.5	2.3	2.4	2.5	3.5	6.1	8.0	9.6	9.4	11.5	10.6
Capital markets & export credits***	3.0	3.7	3.9	6.4	15.3	18.7	21.4	32.6	34.9	30.7	39.1
As percent of the total net flow	23.6%	23.6%	22.4%	28.4%	34.1%	40.6%	41.5%	46.2%	46.3%	40.7%	44.4%
C. Grants by private voluntary agencies	—	0.6	0.9	1.2	1.3	1.4	1.5	1.7	2.0	2.4	2.0

* Approximately 150 developing countries.
** The bulk of which is officially guaranteed in creditor countries.
*** Mostly bank lending from banks residing in DAC countries but excluding lending by offshore subsidiaries of these banks.
Source: Ibid.

Table 4.3—Total Annual Debt Service of Developing Countries 1971-1982 by Source of Lending (billions of dollars)

Source of Lending	1971	1975	1976	1977	1978	1979	1980	Prel. 1981	Est. 1982
DAC countries and capital markets	9.2	22.0	27.1	36.3	51.7	66.5	75.8	95.9	115.2
1. DAC/ODA	1.4	1.8	1.9	2.0	2.3	2.6	2.8	2.9	3.4
2. Capital markets*	2.7	9.5	12.8	17.8	28.8	38.3	43.4	57.5	67.0
Private banks	N.A.	8.1	10.6	14.4	24.6	33.1	38.1	49.6	56.0
3. Total export credits	5.1	10.7	12.4	16.5	20.5	25.6	29.6	35.5	44.8
Multilateral agencies	0.9	1.7	2.0	2.6	3.3	3.8	4.8	5.6	6.7
Other	0.9	2.1	2.6	3.1	4.0	5.3	6.4	7.8	9.4
Centrally planned economies	0.6	0.8	0.9	1.1	1.4	1.7	1.8	2.1	2.5
OPEC countries	0.1	0.2	0.2	0.6	1.0	1.3	1.9	2.4	3.0
Other LDCs	0.1	0.4	0.5	0.5	0.6	0.8	1.0	1.3	1.9
Unspecified and adjustments	0.2	0.7	1.0	0.9	1.0	1.5	1.7	2.0	2.0
Total	11.0	25.8	31.9	42.1	59.0	75.6	86.9	109.3	131.3
Interest	3.3	9.3	10.5	12.9	17.6	26.0	37.2	48.5	60.1
Amortization	7.7	16.5	21.4	29.2	41.4	49.6	49.7	60.8	71.2
Annual Percent Nominal Increase	(15)	(19)	(24)	(32)	(40)	(28)	(15)	(26)	(20)

* Bank loans (other than export credits) including loans through offshore centers, bonds, and other private lending.
Source: Ibid and *External Debt of Developing Countries, 1982 Survey* (Paris, France: OECD, December 1982).

about 54% of the total. This compares with a total debt-service burden of about $11 billion and interest of about $3 billion, only one decade earlier.

Growth in Short-Term Debt

The rapid growth of the outstanding debt of Third World countries, the large debt-service obligation, and the growing share of debt to private lenders—debt which generally involves shorter maturities and harder terms than official credits—have caused widespread concerns. Are they warranted for lender or borrower? At least three major points need to be considered before answering this question.

1. Growth in the less developed countries' external debt which needs to be related to other national and world economic indicators.

2. Role of debt capital, particularly from private commercial sources at market terms, in economic development and the use made of debt capital in developing countries.

3. Differences and variations among individual borrowing countries and bor-

rowing entities within countries, which are substantial and need careful scrutiny by any prospective lender.

As for the growth in total debt, the borrowing requirements of the less developed countries are mirrored, to a certain extent, in the growth of world trade. Total world exports, measured at current prices, increased from $320 billion in 1971 to $1,840 billion in 1981. They are estimated to have declined to $1,695 billion in 1982. The 1981 total was almost six times the amount in 1971. Exports of the oil-exporting developing countries, measured at current prices, grew 12-fold over the same period, while exports of the nonoil-exporting developing countries were about 6.5 times larger than a decade ago.

The external debt of the developing countries has increased at an average of almost 20% a year from 1971 to 1981. If the nominal increase in external debt is deflated by the increase in export prices from industrial countries, in terms of U.S. dollars, then the real growth in external debt averaged about 7.5% a year. If the external debt is deflated by import prices of the nonoil-developing countries, then the real growth in external debt averaged about 5% a year (see Table 4.4).

It is noteworthy that over the same period, the real growth of the nonoil-developing economies taken as a group averaged about 5% a year. Thus, in real terms, external debt of the developing countries has increased roughly in line with the domestic growth of their economies. By comparison, from 1971 to 1981 the exports of the nonoil-developing countries, in real terms, grew at an average of over 8% per year.

Private Commercial Banks

During the 1970s, the private commercial banks emerged as the largest single source of external finance for the developing countries. In the past, I thought that the total external debt of developing countries might well rise from about $530 billion at the end of 1981 to about $1,500 billion at the end of this decade. This projection implied an annual average increase in total external debt of $100 billion (net of amortization payments). It implies gross borrowings of about twice that amount, namely $200 billion average per year for the decade. Of this total of $1,500 billion, as much as $1,000 billion was anticipated to come from private commercial banks. This was extrapolated from the experience in the 1970s when private commercial banks became the most important single source of private finance of the developing countries. It meant, if this analysis and outlook proved correct, that private bank exposure would quadruple in the 1980s, while exposure from other sources would about double.

Is this outlook still realistic in view of recent events in Poland, Mexico, Brazil, and Argentina? The financial needs of the developing countries have, if anything, become greater in today's world of global depression and the pressures to return to higher growth rates in the developing economies. The demand for capital will continue to increase. I still believe that the external debt of the developing countries will mount to the order of $1,500 billion by the end of this decade. It may well

Table 4.4—Growth in Exports and Disbursed External Term Debt (billions of dollars)

	Exports in Current Prices		External Debt Value	International Price Deflators		External Debt Volume		Annual Percent Change in Volume of Debt	
		Nonoil		1975=100		150 LDCs			
Year	World*	LDCs	150 LDCs	(1)	(2)	(1)	(2)	(1)	(2)
1971	319.7	48.8	90	54	48	167	187	+16.0	+14.7
1972	378.8	58.2	99	60	51	165	194	−1.2	+3.7
1973	527.4	84.7	119	72	63	165	189	0.0	−2.6
1974	779.4	121.3	145	90	91	161	159	−2.5	−15.9
1975	803.1	117.0	180	100	100	180	180	+11.8	+13.2
1976	915.0	137.7	220	101	100	218	220	+21.1	+22.2
1977	1041.6	164.7	274	109	106	251	258	+15.1	+17.3
1978	1200.0	188.0	345	123	116	280	297	+11.6	+15.1
1979	1523.8	244.9	406	142	138	286	294	+2.1	−1.0
1980	1868.6	312.5	465	160	178	291	261	+1.7	−11.2
1981	1840.4	321.2	530	154	177	344	299	+18.2	+14.6
1982**	1750.0	300.0	626	151	N/A	415	N/A	+20.6	N/A

* Excluding centrally planned economies.

** Estimated

The international price deflators: (1) Export unit values (prices) of industrial countries, in terms of U.S. dollars. (2) Import unit values (prices) of nonoil-developing countries, in terms of U.S. dollars.

Source: International Monetary Fund, *International Financial Statistics* (Washington, D.C.: IMF, February 1983); Organization for Economic Co-operation and Development, *Development Co-operation, 1982 Review* (Paris, France: OECD, November 1982).

be higher. The question, however, remains whether the private commercial banks will contribute as much as earlier anticipated. At the moment, there is no clear answer to this crucial question. Intuition tells me that private banks will be back lending to developing countries, after they have crossed the current rough patch. Private banks will be willing to lend because international lending to developing countries can be done at acceptable risk and is profitable to the banks.

Is Borrowing Excessive?

A judgment on whether developing countries have borrowed excessively in the past depends on the use to which their external debt has been put. Developing countries, because of their relatively low output and income and low rates of economic growth over time, have for many years required the net inflow of financial resources from abroad to supplement domestic savings and to add to the foreign exchange available from export and other hard currency earnings. Many of these countries also have had to supplement their domestic savings and foreign exchange to be able to adjust to external pressures created in the world economic environment, such as the oil shocks of the 1970s, the severe recession of 1974-75, repeated crop failures and food shortages, and global persistent inflation.

The immediate adjustment needs and the longer-run development needs often merge. This has been a prime factor in the expansion of external borrowing. Nevertheless, it does not answer the question whether the borrowing has been excessive. The growth in external indebtedness of a borrowing country is not excessive if the borrowed funds are used to defend or implement sound development strategies, with consequent lasting improvements in the levels and composition of private and public savings, output (agricultural and industrial), investment, and consumption pattern.

The question whether Third World countries have borrowed excessively cannot be answered generally. Each borrowing country's performance must be examined carefully and by separately assessing each of the borrowing entities within a country. On a global scale and in proportion to the total savings stream of the industrialized creditor nations, lending from the developed to the developing world does not appear to be excessive.* Most probably without the substantial increase in the availability of financial resources to nonoil-developing countries in the past five or six years, their foreign trade would have declined, the short-term adjustment process of many countries seriously impaired, and economic stagnation or even severe recession in the borrowing countries would have been widespread and inflation even worse.

Given the growth rates which the developing countries have maintained in recent years despite the adverse international environment, it seems reasonable to conclude that most of the borrowing has been productively used but much has not. Fortunately, the returns on productive use of capital are so high in developing countries, although often delayed in fruition for many years, that much of borrowed funds can be wasted and still the total is not excessive. For a developing country, the wastage, however, has a very high opportunity cost and over time will create very serious management problems. Much of the positive improvements from borrowing have long time lags before the desired and needed benefits are achieved, even when the borrowing is well used.

Variable Performance

There have been, as expected, wide differences in the performance of borrowing countries. Those developing countries which have established a strong creditworthiness with the private financial community are among the largest borrowers. These countries have large amounts of external debt outstanding and large debt-service obligations. They tend to be more modernized countries in many aspects of their economic and social life. These countries have achieved a relatively high growth performance through adopting coherent development strategies, diversifying their economies, creating a broader modern economic base, and sustaining

*The world's savings stream (excluding the centrally planned economies) totals at the present time about $2,000 billion or more per year. The largest portion by far are domestic savings channeled into domestic investments. The proportion of the world's savings that moves across national frontiers and the proportion of world investment that is financed from external sources have increased substantially during the past decade.

high economic growth rates—total and per capita. These countries are carrying heavy debt-service obligations and their debt-service ratios—interest and amortization payments in relation to the total export earnings—are very high. Their debt-service requirements have, however, usually been more than matched by the inflow of new debt capital. In fact, their high debt-service ratios have reflected their strong external credit standing.

The economic management and performance of these countries have been perceived by the international financial community as making them creditworthy and warranting confidence in their ability to service the outstanding debt in the future. Among the countries that maintained a sound economic management over a sustained period have been Brazil, Mexico, Argentina, Korea, and Taiwan. In noting the countries that have borrowed significantly from private banks, these countries will be among the most significant. Generally speaking, these countries did not borrow excessively, even though their external debts and debt servicing were large. As the experience of Mexico, Brazil, and Argentina in 1982 indicated, these countries could lose their creditworthiness with external private lenders. In this respect, they experienced sharp declines in borrowings from private sources, which aggravated existing external deficits. Their problem arose, however, not from the size of existing debts but from loss of confidence in economic management of their difficult conditions.

Mismanaged Countries

Those countries that have suffered from prolonged mismanagement not offset by exceptionally favorable international environments are at the other end of the spectrum. Despite a substantial inflow of external resources in the past, they have not been able to maintain a satisfactory growth rate; in such cases the countries have had a period of declining total and per capita output, rising inflation, overvalued exchange rates, loss of international reserves, and loss of a satisfactory credit standing with lenders. Because these countries were usually not able to pursue domestic policies that would regain previous creditworthiness, they had no practical alternative but to ask their creditors, whether official or private, for debt renegotiations or rescheduling. Examples have been Zaire, Peru, Turkey, and others which have gone through debt renegotiations in past years. (Debt renegotiations are examined in some detail in chapters 7-10.)

These countries had borrowed excessively, not because of the magnitudes of debt servicing, but because economic management did not succeed in increasing total savings and total productive investment, with accompanying benefits in output, employment, income, and consumption. When these countries lost their ability to borrow from private external sources, they had no choice except to slow down growth often to zero, despite great resulting hardships. Improved economic management was unavoidable. With better management, borrowing was resumed, and the new level of debt was higher.

These experiences illustrate the difficulty in judging whether borrowing is excessive. Poor economic management can transform a country which has made, on balance, good use of borrowed funds and has not had servicing difficulties into a country which has borrowed excessively. All countries have to be monitored carefully and continuously, even though they have enjoyed long periods of strong creditworthiness.

Limited Borrowing

There is another group of countries whose economic management has accepted a low economic growth rate with limited external borrowing. Among this group are Thailand and Burma. Some countries, particularly India, are among the Third World's largest borrowers, but mostly from official sources and on concessional terms, reducing the magnitude of annual debt-servicing charges on their balance of payments. Private-source debt is small in relation to their total external obligations. Yet creditworthiness with private investors is highly prized and defended because it is needed for day-to-day financing of international trade and is a potential cushion in case of adversity. These countries may be presumed not to have borrowed excessively, but yet some like India have repeatedly experienced debt-servicing difficulties.

Neither relatively low debt levels nor low debt-servicing obligations eliminate the chronic vulnerability of developing countries to external payments difficulties. The key element in deciding whether a developing country has been borrowing excessively in recent years is the separate assessment of that country—the country's economic performance and its future prospects. Economic management, however, does not take place in a vacuum but in a worldwide framework of events and developments. Governments of poor countries are frequently limited by the inherent characteristics of their countries—poor natural resources, inadequate capital, unfavorable geographic locations, an untrained labor force, and hostile climatic conditions. They can be victims of their own pasts—disturbed political and social conditions encouraging capital flight, inadequate income distribution, etc. In addition, they are also subject to pressures from the external worldwide environment.

A common international environment does not mean, however, a uniform impact of this environment on national conditions. These uneven impacts must be part of the country analyses, which attempt to inquire as deeply and continuously as possible into the factors which determine the ability and willingness of a country to provide the foreign exchange needed to meet its international obligations. As in other matters, a frequent trap is reliance on superficial analyses which, in turn, rely on simplistic ratios, in this case, usually debt-service ratios. As in corporate finance, there are no simplistic ratios that give reliable answers on financial viability, strength, and attractiveness to investors and lenders. Their use can be a snare and a delusion. Excessive debt is debt that is used unproductively or cannot be serviced, irrespective of size. Even low levels of debt are not sufficient protection by themselves against excessive debt.

Key Points on External Debt

In evaluating external debt, certain key points should be taken into consideration.

- Always keep the distinction clear between servicing of individual loans and credits and servicing external debt of a country as a whole. This is particularly important in considering the likelihood of repayment or servicing difficulties. An individual borrower may be able to service its own loans from earnings and income and yet not be allowed to service such loans because of the general shortage of foreign exchange or vice versa.

- These two aspects come together in concerns with the balance of payments and its management. Will countries have difficulties in providing foreign exchange to borrowers to meet their individual debt-servicing obligations? If faced with such difficulties, will they result in delays or even defaults in servicing the individual credits? This is particularly poignant for countries likely to be in balance-of-payments difficulties and for private lenders to such countries. Balance-of-payments conditions and outlook are of central importance, but special attention needs to be given to why and how current account deficits are generated. The size of servicing requirements and management of the external debt are usually important elements in this general assessment of balance-of-payments outlook and responses. But they emerge as difficulties only after the country is losing its external creditworthiness. Nevertheless, sizable external debt can be a good starting point for alerting credit and loan officers to the need for careful investigation of the country environment and how it may impinge on individual debt servicing.

- Attention centers on these balance-of-payments conditions and outlooks, even if individual borrowers have the national currency needed to buy such foreign exchange from national authorities or in foreign exchange markets.

- On individual loans or credits, it is essential to ensure that credit evaluations are done in the broad framework of country and global conditions.

- Neither individual lender nor individual borrower normally expects outstanding loans to be rescheduled or refinanced. The need may arise despite efforts to avoid reschedulings or refinancings through careful credit assessments. But such occasions must be the exception, or the lending bank as well as the borrowers, eventually may be in serious trouble.

- The first line of defense against country risk is a good credit risk system. It integrates knowledge of countries with individual credit judgments. Country analyses may cause the individual credit to be questioned, either on the ability of a country to provide needed foreign exchange or because more net earnings are needed to pay a higher price (via devalued currency) for the foreign exchange needed to service the foreign currency debt. The focal point of credit analysis remains the individual credit—the individual borrower.

• Banks must expect debt to be fully and promptly serviced and repaid. Despite careful professional country work, a loan can be jeopardized because a country gets into difficulties which result in individual borrowers being unable to obtain needed foreign exchange, or foreign exchange made more costly in local currency than expected at the time of the borrowing. We cannot expect to foresee all adverse events. Poor knowledge and judgment based on poor knowledge about country conditions are, however, not acceptable excuses for misjudging the significance of a country's external debt and debt-servicing obligations. Ignorance can be overcome. Lending standards based on inadequate knowledge are poor lending standards.

• External lending may continue to be strong, and external debts of countries rise further. Banks need to know how to assess the implications of existing external debt if they are to engage substantially in international lending.

5

Commercial Banks and International Multilateral Agencies

Before discussing the historical experience with debt renegotiations, it is useful to give special attention to the relations of banks with the IMF because the Fund has been of major importance in international lending and in coping with external debt problems when they have arisen. The IMF affects country risk for developing countries as well as other countries in a number of ways. For some countries, it is a source of international liquidity through the use of the Fund's resources or creation of SDRs. The IMF also can be part of the international monetary reserves of a country if the so-called gold tranche has not been fully used.* It can be a source of the equivalent of borrowed foreign currency on terms more favorable than commercial banks offer. For example, a member country sells its currency to the Fund for needed internationally usable currencies with the obligation to "repurchase" such currencies at some future date with internationally convertible currencies. These drawing rights are equivalent to medium-term credits. The amounts, however, are limited by the IMF's quotas and policies on use of its resources.

Purpose of IMF

The IMF was originally conceived as a source of assistance for countries with temporary balance-of-payments difficulties. Balance-of-payments deficits were seen to be reversible through changes in external conditions, the adoption of domestic policies of an essentially nondeflationary character, or exchange rate changes. Reversing a country's balance-of-payments deficit might well imply a change in the exchange rate or changes in domestic monetary or fiscal policies. Payments adjustment was not to involve intensification of restrictions on current payments or moving from convertibility to inconvertibility of the currency of the country in balance-of-payments difficulties.

*The gold tranche is that portion of the country quota contributed to the fund assets which does *not* consist of the national currency of the contributing member. It is a small portion of the total quota. It is commonly regarded as equivalent to the creditor position of a country in the fund. The use of the gold tranche eliminates this creditor position. The use of the gold tranche is automatic—not subject to conditionality.

The founders of the IMF did not feel, however, that a member's use of its resources was necessarily to be regarded as indicating a need by the member for major policy changes. It was narrowly and precisely perceived as a need for temporary balance-of-payments financing. Soon after the IMF began its operations, however, the use of its resources was frequently related to adoption of major policy changes, referred to briefly as conditionality, by the borrowing country.

Access to IMF resources by member countries is governed by a wide range of policies. These policies create differing degrees and composition of conditionality depending on causes of difficulties, previous use of Fund resources, and members' ability to adjust in ways compatible with IMF purposes. Certain amounts of access are not subject to policy conditions, or the policy conditions are very easy to fulfill. These are unconditional drawing rights. They are governed by financial provisions such as the need to repurchase (repay) and "charges" (interest rates) but do not require policy changes by member countries wishing to use IMF resources. Members that have made large use of the Fund's resources relative to their quotas are regarded as in the "higher" credit tranches. Their further use of the Fund is subject to increasingly stringent conditions, although the specific content varies with the individual cases.

Countries that come to the IMF for drawings (or the right to draw in the future) in the higher credit tranches are often in financial trouble. The IMF often deals with workout or near-workout cases. In such cases, emphasis is placed on policies to ameliorate or eliminate the immediate difficulty. Such countries may well need the Fund's presence to reinforce those within the government and central bank who wish to adjust exchange rates or institute major changes in domestic monetary and fiscal policies. They may also need the IMF's technical assistance in central banking, fiscal affairs, and exchange controls. Such countries are often desperately short of foreign exchange.

Financial Resources

Access to the IMF's financial resources can be critically important, particularly since the private banks may be reluctant to lend new monies during these difficult times. In practice, borrowing again from private sources probably will be possible sooner if the country pursues stabilization policies endorsed by the IMF. Under these conditions, relations between the commercial banks, the country in difficulty, and the IMF become urgent and complicated.

The countries with the most severe difficulties are likely to need the largest access to the Fund relative to their quotas. Such countries will face strict conditions for using the Fund and can expect imposition of a wide range of economic policies including fiscal, monetary, incomes, exchange rates, and exchange restrictions. Conditions set forth by the IMF may cover such other areas as external debt management and treatment of foreign investment. These conditions are often outlined in standby arrangements, which assure a country access to an agreed amount of resources during a specified period, usually one year, provided conditions are met by the country. More recently, these arrangements are for three or four years and are called extended arrangements.

It is often expected that the Fund resources will not actually be used. Rather, the principal benefit to the country results from the certification of economic management. The certification not only indicates the intention of the government but also lays the basis for the Fund's monitoring the country's performance with respect to the agreed conditions. Thus, in relation to the financial ability to service debt and increasing confidence in the economic management of the country—two vital factors in judging country risk—the IMF can and does play an important role.

For a country with balance-of-payments difficulties, the use of various unconditional IMF drawing rights may well be attractive because it does not imply the country is mismanaged. This implication is hard to avoid when domestic so-called stabilization programs result from conditional drawings on Fund resources in the higher credit tranches.

Similarly, borrowings from banks by countries in balance-of-payments need but not yet requiring stabilization programs usually do not damage and may even strengthen a country's international financial standing. The implication is, at least, that the country is receiving passing grades from the international banking community for its domestic economic and balance-of-payments management despite the expanded payments deficit. This is particularly true for developing countries that chronically need a net inflow of external resources, even when well managed.

Most countries perceive themselves to be reasonably well managed, even though outside technical advisors or assigned IMF personnel may be part of the country's management team. Many such countries borrow internationally from private banks, even though they could exercise their access to Fund resources. Indeed they have strong incentives to use the Fund because drawings on it are less costly than other sources of external finance. Moreover, the IMF repayment schedules are less rigid than repayment schedules of banks. However, a country may wish to preserve its capability to draw on the Fund should trouble arise in the future. The difference in cost between borrowing from commercial banks and drawing on the Fund is significant, but frequently cost is not important for governments.

IMF and Country Risk for Private Banks

The relationships between the private banks and the IMF have become a major aspect of international lending, especially to developing countries. They are critical for understanding the private banks' attitudes on country risk or lending in a risk-laden world.

Relationships between the private commercial banks and the IMF are ad hoc, informal, and varied. Each bank, indeed each banker, would describe the relationships somewhat differently. Aside from the publications of the IMF and its press releases, there are usually no formal arrangements for either transmitting information or exchanging views with private banks. Generally this applies both to relationships with countries of ordinary conditions and countries with extraordinary conditions requiring stabilization efforts and use of the Fund's resources.

The IMF usually does not publicize the content of its arrangement with countries and whether or not the agreed policy changes are being implemented. Months may pass after a country has ceased to implement such agreements, and the private banks would not know this. Unless the IMF makes available its country evaluations to private outside entities in a manner which can be used daily by banks, commercial banks have only limited benefit in their daily lending decisions. Even so, continuous help may be obtained from IMF publications, particularly its statistical monthly, *International Financial Statistics.*

Despite these limitations, the relationships between the banks and the IMF are often important and mutually beneficial. Attempts at formal arrangements run into difficulties because of the IMF's governmental character and the private character of commercial banks. The staff also must avoid injuring its members by giving opinions that may cause banks to reduce credits to a member. The IMF cannot even seem to be entering into relationships that affect the ability of member countries to obtain credits from banks—a matter of crucial importance to its members—without the knowledge and approval of its members.

The staff works for the member countries. In many respects, those who work for the IMF are employees of member governments. An important part of their work is helping members find and adopt good economic policies or stabilization program. The work is sensitive, delicate, and difficult. It requires the full confidence of member governments. The staff does not owe any allegiance or have any obligation to private commercial banks or any other entity. Such a relationship would destroy the staff's effectiveness with member countries.

IMF Conditions

The Fund, moreover, may not be able to include in its conditions for use of its resources, requirements that affect a country's creditworthiness for private bank lending. These conditions include the treatment of foreign investment or even a needed exchange rate change. Also, the IMF cannot alter a country's past record in servicing its obligations to foreign lenders. Thus, the Fund can be helpful, but it cannot substitute for a bank's responsibility to make its own evaluations and judgments on country risk.

In their loan contracts, private banks do not establish economic conditions for countries before lending to them. However, they must examine whether actual and likely economic policies, conditions, and outlook meet their criteria of country creditworthiness for lending. Thus, private banks, particularly in cases where unfavorable events have damaged a country's creditworthiness, may well wait to see whether an IMF-agreed program is initiated or what conditions are being met before making their own decisions on lending commitments. In addition, private banks must apply a similar set of criteria to the many countries for which the Fund may not have established specific conditions in standby arrangements. So far, only relatively few IMF members have had standby arrangements at any given time. The value of the Fund to private banks would be greatly enhanced if it informed the private banks of its current judgment on countries with which it does not have standby arrangements. However, this raises obvious sensitive issues for an international agency.

Differing Views on Creditworthiness

Banks differ greatly in their views on a country's creditworthiness. Any given bank or group of banks cannot commit another bank or group of banks. Often, they cannot commit themselves until the time for decisive action arrives. Bank officers may or may not represent the views of others in the same bank or group of banks. A bank's views of a country's conditions and policies often depend on the particular banker with whom one happens to speak. Thus, the views of individual bankers may not necessarily be those of their institutions.

Commercial banks, for their part, are guided by their private needs and obligations. They cannot divulge to IMF staff members confidential information detrimental to the banks' borrowers, depositors, or shareholders. Moreover, individual banks are separate entities with greatly differing interests and objectives in any particular country and with separate decision-making mechanisms and responsibilities. In this institutional sense, there is no international banking system with a centralized management. The private banks have no equivalent of the IMF or even the BIS for central banks, which provides a mechanism for international collaboration and cooperation on monetary matters.

Commercial banks are likely to lend to countries not perceived to be in difficulties requiring major changes in economic policy or management. Thus, the typical relationship of a private bank with the IMF is that of a private bank lending to a Fund member country *not* seen to be in serious balance-of-payments difficulties or needing new stabilization policies. Certain problems or adversities might be foreseen, such as a decline in commodity prices, a rise in the cost of imports, or the introduction of external protectionist measures affecting export earnings. These, however, are warning signals. They do not indicate by themselves that the country will experience difficulties or conditions warranting a cessation of lending by commercial banks or a reduction in foreign currency exposures therein.

Information Source

Adverse economic developments imply the need for a country to adjust its policies. There is always the need to judge whether and how a country will adjust and to conclude whether such actions would be unfavorable to private banks that have been lending to entities in that country. In making these judgments, the IMF is a useful source of information, but private banks must, in most cases, rely nearly entirely on their own capabilities in reaching their business decisions.

Banks do not rely on the Fund for judgments on countries not in trouble. The IMF is in contact with all the member countries by its work at headquarters or by field missions to the country. It may well be giving technical advice and obtaining much information and valuable insights into the country. This work, however, does not usually result in publications or reports for use by outside private entities. Fund staff can be visited by private bankers. The staff is helpful, but its job is to help member countries, not private banks. Fund publications are the principal way of sharing its knowledge with the world, not giving the world the benefits of its confidential activities. This unpublicized work involves nearly all the countries to which private banks are lending. The workout country cases are exceptional. Nevertheless, it is the Fund's role in such cases that has made it important because what the Fund does is visible and the outcome can be of guidance to the private banks. Although usually limited to a few countries at any time, this workout role of the IMF is very important for private lenders. It adds to the comfort level to expect that if the borrowing country gets into difficulty, the Fund will assist it to recreate acceptable economic management and to have financial help. The former is more important to the private bank lender, unless the latter is exceptionally large.

Are the IMF and Private Banks in Conflict?

The question arises whether countries that need major adjustments in policies and would otherwise adopt stabilization programs, presumably with the assistance and endorsement of the IMF, can avoid this action by borrowing from private commercial banks. This is more likely to be the case where other sources of financing are truly unconditional, that is, the country—even though perceived to be in difficulties—has the right and ability to obtain resources without substantive changes in policy or management despite the need to do so. This situation may well exist when using the limited unconditional access a member has in the IMF or analogously when using its own monetary reserves.

This is not true of borrowings from private banks. Banks do not lend significant sums without serious consideration of the country risk. In certain circumstances, banks may be willing to have exposures within a country with little or no attention to country risk. For instance, loans guaranteed by government institutions in creditor countries may be undertaken with little attention to country risk in the borrowing country. However, these are exceptional situations. The majority of international lending does not involve creditor government guarantees. Moreover, international lending is to countries in which the lending institutions already have significant exposure. Marketing considerations, particularly profitability, may well create incentives or internal pressures within a bank to lower standards of country evaluation. Similar pressures operate to lower standards of individual credit evaluations. Less obvious but ever present, however, are internal control mechanisms to prevent dangerous lowering of credit or country evaluation standards. High-risk interest-rate premiums, for example, are not acceptable reasons for lending to countries with a too high-risk environment.

Private Bank Influence

Banks will voice their concern to borrowers about the country's past performance and its outlook for the future, irrespective of its known relations with the Fund. The expressed concerns of private banks do not go unheeded. The governments of borrowing countries are well aware that if existing difficulties are allowed to proceed to crisis, they will lose their access to external sources of finance. This conditionality is informal but constant and weighty. Lending by private banks thus encourages domestic policies that avoid situations, particularly balance-of-payments difficulties, which would simultaneously require drastic policy changes and cause a cessation of commercial bank lending to the country.

For countries that have not yet created a stabilization program but are seen as close to external debt or balance-of-payments crises, informal exchanges between major private lenders and the Fund staff and the government are likely. These exchanges cannot be regarded as part of a mechanism whereby the IMFs views become part of the decision-making process for private commercial banks. Indeed, because the Fund is intergovernmental, it may be reluctant to talk to banks during such sensitive periods. The IMF may refuse to have relationships with private outsiders, even very informal ones, if the situation in a country becomes delicate.

During such periods, the Fund and private banks may simultaneously, but separately, be in very close contact with the borrowing country. But the banks have to be guided by their own knowledge and by any overt actions of the IMF rather than information received from the Fund. At such times, knowledge of Fund procedures is very important or the private bank can easily misinterpret IMF actions. Sometimes, the sending of an IMF staff mission to a country is viewed by a private banker that a country is in special difficulties, especially if the banker is worried about exposure in that country. The private banker does not know whether the field visit is a routine one scheduled long ago or indeed is a response to new conditions and is a sign of possible difficulties. Do not expect the IMF to tell which it is.

What Banks Want

Stabilization programs under standby or extended arrangements which involve renegotiation of debt with commercial banks create special conditions and relationships. (They as yet represent only a small fraction of total stabilization cases as discussed in later chapters.) Each case is different and commercial banks at such times feel great risk and see their actions as part of the stabilization program being evolved by the country with the help of the IMF. Usually banks are involved in the following actions:

1. Banks assess a country's situation and review their exposure to position themselves to defend against losses.

2. If the risks in maintaining or increasing exposure are regarded as great, banks take steps to maintain or reduce existing exposure or otherwise make exposure less vulnerable. As repayments under amortization schedules permit, they replace old

borrowers with new borrowers deemed stronger. Or they advance shorter term loans to old borrowers and reduce average maturities of their portfolios.

3. A country may ask banks to maintain their levels of exposure or reduce their exposure in a particular way, by maintaining their short-term exposure and reducing their term exposure as maturities fall due and are paid. Demonstrated willingness to have a stabilization program endorsed by the IMF weighs heavily in obtaining a favorable response from the banks.

4. A country can ask creditor banks to consider restructuring outstanding debt or additional lending as part of a stabilization program. A country can explore the timing of renegotiation or even new credits if it adopts and implements a stabilization program endorsed by the Fund. Banks make clear their institutional standards of country creditworthiness and lending criteria.

5. If approached by a country for rescheduling or new money, banks probably request IMF assurance that the country has indicated its willingness to prepare a stabilization program for which it will seek Fund endorsement. At the same time, some banks, usually those with the largest portfolios in the country, express their own views to the country and probably to the IMF on what needs to be done to restore the creditworthiness of the country with the private banks.

6. Any commitments obtained from banks on rescheduling, restructuring, or new money probably are subject to adoption or implementation of stabilization measures and usually are tied to performance under programs endorsed by the IMF, that is, with performance criteria agreed with the Fund.

7. Banks principally involved may arrange for some coordinating mechanism to work with other banks concerned, at least during the formation and implementation of the stabilization program or until more normal conditions and relationships with the borrowing country are restored. Lead banks may coordinate their activities by forming an informal coordinating committee. They may help arrange for visits to creditor countries by country officials who explain their problems and programs to other bankers. IMF representatives and others from multilateral institutions might also be present. These are *not* the multilateral debt renegotiation meetings dealt with in subsequent chapters in this book.

8. The IMF can try to provide the "masse de manoeuvre" (large foreign exchange fund) needed for stabilization. This is, perhaps, accomplished by giving appropriate waivers on limits of drawings by a member country on Fund resources or by permitting front-end access to resources plus support from other multilateral institutions. This could be particularly appropriate when the commercial banks feel that a considerable period of time for implementing a program and seeing its beneficial effects is needed before they can provide additional credits. Private banks are not expected to perform this support or aid function prematurely. In exceptional cases, a relatively quick contribution from banks to a program agreed on with the IMF can restructure country debt profiles. Such cases are covered in subsequent chapters.

9. If external funds are needed to assure the feasibility of implementing the

stabilization program, and such funds cannot come from existing multilateral institutions or other official funds, the commercial banks may well be a major, or even the most important, single source of external finance. Considerable time may, however, lapse before banks have confidence in the new situation and outlook. In making their decisions, banks have the benefit of discussions with officials of the country, the IMF, and other multilateral institutions involved. If implementation of the program progresses satisfactorily, banks can begin increasing their exposure to a country by extending new loans in totals larger than repayments under old loans. Since banks are likely to be very cautious and worried lenders at this stage, this new lending may be phased—usage or draw-down according to agreed schedules. Based on performance criteria, such as linking to drawings from the Fund, the banks can phase their new credits in a schedule parallel to the IMF's. The pattern of phasing might well be inverse: The Fund starts high and comes down; the banks start low and come up.

10. Commercial banks probably try to avoid restructuring outstanding debt unless it means risk of default or is seen as an alternative to the borrower's pressure to receive new credits in relatively substantial amounts. The banks try to get the country to keep servicing its debt as originally contracted. For countries with stabilization programs, restructuring of past debt may be difficult to avoid. The terms and conditions of restructuring debt will probably be greatly influenced by the country's willingness to negotiate an arrangement with the IMF in the upper credit tranches. The banks will probably relate debt restructuring to the agreement with the Fund on a stabilization program. However, in contrast with new or additional credits, the agreed restructuring could come into effect at the beginning of the stabilization program, rather than delayed to assure that the program is reasonably well implemented.

11. If the IMF will not certify the effectiveness of the good efforts of a country in difficulties, private banks can be expected to take whatever defensive measures they deem advisable and feasible. Countries in difficulties are quickly aware when this happens.

Banks influence the stabilization programs primarily because debt renegotiation or new lending will not occur in substantial amounts until the country's economic management performance meets the country creditworthiness criteria of the lending banks. Borrowing countries and the IMF are well aware of these criteria from bank actions in other cases and through informal exchanges of views with bankers at all stages. This early contact with banks can happen because the need for a stabilization program preferably endorsed by the IMF is not appreciated until after the country is convinced it has lost the confidence of external private bank lenders and will not recover it without a stabilization program to help restore its credit standing.

12. Re-establishing creditworthiness with private banks or restructuring past debt to private lenders are of crucial importance to the success of the country's stabilization program and are so perceived by the country and the IMF. Bankers

may invite country officials and officials from the IMF, World Bank, and other multilateral institutions to participate informally in their deliberations. This process is facilitated when concerned private banks form a coordinating group which meets with representatives of the government, the IMF, the World Bank, and other institutions. However, this group does not preclude any individual bank from conducting its own informal bilateral discussions with the country's officials, the IMF, or any other institution. Such groups facilitate communication on country conditions and strengthen the process of negotiating and implementing stabilization programs. In such cases, the banks do not take any responsibility for the stabilization policy packaging, although their informally expressed views will have an important effect on the measures actually adopted. The formal conditions for private bank loans are set forth in loan contracts, not in government stabilization programs or arrangements endorsed by the IMF.

Good Relations

In summary, in most countries, 20 or 30 banks account for the bulk of international lending. But many, many banks around the world have a stake in any stabilization program in a particular country. This was dramatically illustrated in Zaire, Peru, Turkey, and Mexico. Questions arose on their external indebtedness and the responses of private banks to requests for debt relief and more credit to help in the implementation of stabilization programs and achievement of more normal conditions. In many if not most countries, there is no precise or complete knowledge of outstanding external debt to commercial banks. Nor is any system, however designed and administered, likely to obtain the full accounts.

Within these constraints, the private banks and the IMF maintain important working relationships. The staffs share information and judgments, and the member countries often give their blessing and encouragement to such informal relations. The officials of the countries usually welcome the informal contacts and exchanges in hopes they will facilitate obtaining the needed external financing.

Banks repeatedly have urged countries, informally, to turn to the IMF when their external financial standings come into question, are seriously impaired, or in danger of becoming so. In some cases, countries have been reluctant to have standby arrangements in the higher credit tranches and resisted the urgings of the private banks to do so. In other cases, countries did not wish to do anything which was not routine in their relations with the IMF. In all cases, to the best of my knowledge, no decision to avoid a fund standby was taken because the countries were advised that they could borrow from the bank without need to change their economic policies as might be required by the IMF itself. In a few cases, bank lending went to countries that the IMF staff would rather have seen turn first to the Fund. This is not likely to happen when banks know that this is the case, and it is clear that the IMF regards further debt accumulation by the borrowing country as unwise and dangerous for private lenders.

World Bank and Regional Development Agencies

The World Bank and regional development agencies, such as the Inter-American Development Bank and the Asian Development Bank, can play a parallel role to that of the IMF. They are important sources of external financing for specific projects. In addition, more finance can be made available to help countries with balance-of-payments difficulties cope with structural adjustments. Such finance can be particularly helpful during extraordinary crises like severe drought or the recent very large oil price increases. In these situations, these agencies provide additional external finance available to the developing country more quickly than usual.

As with the IMF, the financial activities of these multinational institutions are not related to servicing external private debt. However, since most financial resources are fungible, anything that increases net availability of foreign exchange will facilitate the servicing of debt. In this sense, borrowing from a private bank strengthens the ability of the borrowing country to meet its obligations to the IMF, the World Bank, and other similar institutions. But it also works in reverse.

The World Bank and the regional development banks also help improve the economic management of a country. This is done by assisting countries in their efforts to formulate development programs and policies and carefully identifying, evaluating, and supervising investment projects to which these international institutions have contributed some portion of the financing. In many cases, these institutions attach conditions to their lending, such as fiscal, monetary, industrial, and export policies or realistic pricing policies on services produced by the project. Often the technical assistance provided by the development finance institution may be more important than the finance. In any case, the perception that a developing country is well regarded by such an institution has a strong positive effect on the bank lenders.

The World Bank and the regional development agencies collaborate with private bank lending through various schemes. These agencies have sold participations in their loans to interested investors and provided financing with private banks for an agreed project. Another important technique is described as co-financing, an abbreviation for complimentary financing. Co-financing activities still represent a small portion of total official lending, but they are growing in importance. It is too early to assess how important they will be, but they can diminish country risk for a private bank if structured carefully.

Co-Financing

In co-financing agreements, these official multinational institutions assume that developing countries are not going to default on their loans. These institutions see themselves continuing to enjoy their preferred creditor position and do not expect to experience any difficulties in repayment. Private banks hope this also will apply to them in case of difficulties. In these co-financing operations, the multinational institutions and the commercial banks enter into separate loan agreements with the borrower. The commercial loans are on market terms and are often related to official loans through an optional cross-default provision. Because of such cross-default clauses, covering both the private banks and the official lenders, private bank loans are regarded as less likely to be subject to default or delay in servicing. However, default is not likely in any case, and the technical and financial participation by these agencies in a co-financing is probably more important than the cross-default provisions. As a result of multinational agency participation, the project is likely to be well examined, evaluated, and monitored.

These development institutions can also be important sources of country information. Much of the information they generate is confidential and limited to internal use, but plans are under way to make useful information available to private banks that participate in co-financing agreements.

6

The Road to Debt Renegotiations

We have reviewed how international lending inevitably gave rise to the problem of servicing the consequent debt. We now turn to the experience with external debt renegotiation. The assessment of this experience is greatly influenced by an understanding of the debt-servicing problem.

Debt servicing, as we have seen, involves the outflow of resources from the borrowing country with which to obtain the foreign exchange needed to service debt. Given the assumption that developing countries suffer from a chronic shortage of goods and services, it is not surprising that the external debt problem which requires an outflow of goods and services has been part of the literature and analysis of economic and social development for many decades. It is part of the considerations which led to the formation of the World Bank and the bilateral and multilateral efforts to assist the less industrialized countries after World War II into the 1950s, 1960s, and thereafter. From the very beginning of these discussions, a few concepts have dominated thinking, analysis, and policy making in international development finance and external debt renegotiations.

Indicators of Debt Problems

First and foremost is the so-called transfer problem, namely the ability to export the goods and services from borrowing countries to creditor countries either directly or indirectly, to obtain the "surpluses" in foreign exchange needed to pay amortization and interest. In turn, this analysis assumed that debts to foreign countries would be repaid, not only in the technical and practical sense that a particular loan was repaid but also in the broad sense on the macroeconomic level, that the total level of external debt of the borrowing country would be reduced by a net outflow of its resources to the creditor countries.

From this logical premise, it was almost inevitable to go to the next step: To recognize that the ability to provide such net outflow would prove very difficult for a poor country. From this point of view, it was aptly described as a "burden," the need to service debt described as a "problem," and measures to reduce the amount which had to be serviced described as debt relief. Thus, from the early days, advocates of assistance to developing countries were advocates either of grant assistance or loans on very generous terms, much below commercial lending terms. These loans were soon labeled "concessional," particularly with respect to maturities, amortization schedules, and interest rates.

Foreign Exchange

The next step was also logical. The best indicator of likely difficulties was the proportion of foreign exchange available to the country, especially that earned by the country, which had to be earmarked for servicing external debt. Varying degrees of sophistication were applied to this concept; foreign exchange earnings could include not only earnings from commodity exports but also services like tourism. Expected or reliable inflows of capital could be added to earnings. Detailed and sophisticated analysis of economies could provide projections of foreign exchange inflows from exports of goods and services, capital requirements, and even projections of possible capital inflows.

Sophisticated analysis could provide deeper understanding of the total external payments requirements of the countries. Debt-service requirements could now be seen as a part of total payments requirements, including payments for the inflow of goods and services required by the importing developing country. Further elaboration led to measuring debt-service burdens in relation to available international monetary reserves of a country. Such international monetary reserves could be used to supplement foreign exchange earnings and other inflows of foreign exchange to finance international payments or, looked at more narrowly, to service external debt.

Measures of adequacy of international monetary reserves were used widely. These included relation of the magnitude of available reserves to import requirements. Again, these measurements were elaborated. For example, drawing rights under the IMF could be regarded as equivalent to monetary reserves to the extent that they were readily available to a member country to make international payments.

External Debt

These lines of reasoning led to the conviction that the external debt problem was essentially a problem of countries that had high levels of debt for the size of their economies, their rates of growth, or the rates of growth in export earnings. Countries with low levels of debt did not, it seemed obvious, have external debt problems.

This approach was flawed and proved inadequate. It resulted in poor guidance to those concerned with economic and social development or with the evaluation of the significance of external debt in international lending and borrowing by developing countries. It relatively neglected a much more fundamental point about developing countries. As noted earlier, a developing country requires a net inflow of resources over a significant period of time. It requires this net inflow even to maintain existing standards of living given the burgeoning population and urbanization of all developing countries. It is only in the mythical kingdom of zero population growth and no modernization that we can think of a developing country not needing an inflow of resources over a long period of years, even decades.

This net inflow can be obtained in many different ways, including cartels for export prices and other similar ways, like commodity agreements. These give windfall gains in foreign exchange that can be used to pay for imports of goods and services, if the price-fixing proves successful. The net inflow can be financed by grants, loans, direct investments, and charity. What is critically important from the viewpoint of external debt analysis is that no level of external debt—even a very low level—can be serviced without difficulty by a developing country. It cannot be expected to have an external surplus unless borrowed funds are included in making up the surplus. It starts with a deficit, yet it must have the means in foreign exchange of financing a net inflow of resources. Despite the outflows needed to meet debt-service payments, it must also pay for essential imports for consumption, production, and investment.

The level of debt or debt servicing are not the prime determinants of difficulties. Developing countries can virtually find it impossible to finance what is a low level of debt and debt servicing, if they cannot find the ways and means of maintaining a net inflow of capital. In terms of debt, it means being able to borrow more than is being paid back, unless it is obtaining adequate grant funds. The critical element is the effective functioning of the mechanism to obtain this net inflow of capital from abroad. Short periods of time without such net inflows can be tolerated by curtailing imports, use of domestic stocks, or by the drawdown of international monetary reserves. At best, these are temporary bridging devices from one period of net inflow of resources to another.

Persistent Need for External Funds

At all times, it is important to know the size of external debt, debt-servicing requirements, profiles, composition of creditors, and so forth. They are major components of country analyses and evaluations of external debt. To assess their significance accurately, however, means finally and decisively to move away from reliance on debt-service ratios, however sophisticated. More profoundly, it means to move finally and decisively to recognize that developing countries are inherently or structurally deficit countries at all stages of output—total or per capita. It means to recognize that as long as lending is the principal form of transfer of capital to finance goods and services, the external debt of developing countries will rise. The alternatives are to substitute official grant money for loans, whether official or private, or to cope with the problems created by economic stagnation in a world which is expanding its population by a billion people per decade, mostly in the developing countries. The possibility of equity capital becoming a major substitute is logically present, but it cannot be regarded as a likely or probable alternative in anything like the magnitudes required for the foreseeable future.

Stressing debt-service ratios tends to focus attention on countries with large debts and on rescheduling terms of outstanding debts to reduce the amounts which must be paid each year to service this debt. This approach obviously has some validity. It focuses attention on the new terms of rescheduled debt. However, it detracts from the fact that even with rescheduled debt, the country remains in balance-of-payments deficit requiring new net inflows of capital. Therefore, the need remains acute for the country to find these additional external funds. Unless official sources of such funds are available, the country will need to re-establish its creditworthiness with private lenders quickly or again it will be in serious balance-of-payments difficulties. In the following pages, attention is focused on ways and means to achieve this creditworthiness. Among other things, we examine suggested rescheduling terms in light of their likely impact on future creditworthiness, particularly the speed of achieving the needed financial standing with external sources of funds.*

Early Debt Problems

In its earlier years, the IMF found that a number of its member countries needed to reschedule their debt. These countries were almost entirely in Latin America. The debt reschedulings were seen as part of their balance-of-payments difficulties and the outcome of their inability to follow domestic policies which could avoid such difficulties. These countries were usually experiencing rapid inflation, overvalued exchange rates, internal and external governmental controls over economic behavior, weak monetary policies, and large unbalanced budgets. It was not assumed that the external debt of these countries was the primary source of their difficulties. Their debt reschedulings, which are discussed below, did facilitate their balance-of-payments management but were not usually a major element in the policy changes needed. Moreover, the external debt that was renegotiated was debt to official creditors or guaranteed by official creditors. Generally speaking, the creditor world was highly skeptical of the policies of these countries. But by and large, it did not see these debt renegotiations as having general major significance.

In the 1960s, the issue of external debt was largely the result of concern that the debt-service burden reduced the funds available for financing an inflow of needed goods and services rather than actual need for debt rescheduling. Indonesia and Ghana did require major debt reschedulings, but these were exceptions and these cases involved debt to official creditors, not to private banks. Perhaps more important, the need to reschedule was seen as the consequence of extraordinary domestic upheavals.

In Indonesia, it was a bloody civil war. Ghana was a less dramatic case of mismanagement by its charismatic first president, Kwame Nkrumah. Again, as in

*The importance of a new intellectual perception of the external debt problem was driven home to me by my experiences in the IMF in the 1950s, the World Bank from 1964 to 1974, and at Citibank from 1974 to 1981.

the Latin American cases, they were not seen as indicators of a widespread need to renegotiate debt. Nevertheless, anxiety about the external debt problem grew in the 1960s. This anxiety frequently resulted in more concessional aid to developing countries. Support was also increasing to channel such aid through multilateral institutions, like the World Bank and the Inter-American Development Bank.

At the World Bank, the external debt problem was followed on a country-by-country basis and was the subject of an extensive staff study at the beginning of 1970. Great care was taken in the World Bank's country reviews to scrutinize the common member countries of the IMF and World Bank individually to determine which might be regarded as prospective debt difficulty countries. The staff study looked ahead to try to judge the 1970s and its conclusions may be summarized as follows:

Out of developing countries under investigation, 28 were recognized as prospective debt difficulty countries and 52 were not. Out of the 28 prospective cases, 9 countries actually did conduct debt renegotiations in the 1970s and in the first two years of the 1980s, but 19 countries did not. Indonesia had a debt renegotiation in 1970, but none during the following decade. Out of the total of 52 countries which were not considered prospective debt difficulty cases, 10 actually had debt renegotiations during the 1970s. Kampuchea and Zaire which had debt renegotiations in the 1970s were not part of the study.

Countries Identified in 1970 as Prospective Debt Difficulty Cases

Bolivia	Algeria	Iran
Brazil	Greece	Pakistan
Chile	Morocco	Indonesia
Colombia	Tunisia	Korea
Ecuador	Turkey	Philippines
Mexico	U.A.R.	Ghana
Nicaragua	Yugoslavia	Guinea
Paraguay	Afghanistan	Sudan
Peru	Ceylon (Sri Lanka)	
Uruguay	India	

Countries Perceived as Prospective Cases in the 1970s and Actually Had Debt Renegotiations

Bolivia	Chile	Nicaragua
Peru	Turkey	India
Pakistan	Ghana	Sudan

Countries Perceived as Prospective Cases in the 1970s but Actually Did *Not* Have Debt Renegotiations

Brazil†	Algeria	Afghanistan
Colombia	Greece	Sri Lanka
Ecuador	Morocco	Iran
Mexico†	Tunisia	Indonesia
Paraguay	U.A.R.	Korea
Uruguay	Yugoslavia	Philippines
		Guinea

Countries *Not* Perceived as Prospective Cases but Did Have Debt Renegotiations

Sierra Leone	Gabon	Togo
Liberia	Jamaica	Madagascar
Central African Republic	Senegal	Uganda
Costa Rica	Kampuchea*	Zaire*

Those identified as prospective debt difficulty countries were mostly countries in Latin America and Asia, and a few in Africa. Many of the African countries were either newly independent or had not yet come into existence as independent nations. The World Bank study led to the conclusion, which also seemed borne out by individual country work, that all countries with large debts could be regarded as prospective debt difficulty countries.

Lessons Learned

No strong correlation was found with such economic variables as per capita income, growth, or even export performance. There also seemed to be no reasonable correlation between good and poor economic management and being a prospective debt difficulty country. Of critical importance, it was believed, was the magnitude of the external debt and the terms on which this debt had been incurred.**

The experience of the 1970s and the first two years of the 1980s demonstrated that a number of countries identified as prospective debt difficulty countries, in fact, had debt renegotiations in the decade after 1970. These nine countries were Bolivia, Chile, Nicaragua, Peru, Turkey, India, Pakistan, Ghana, and Sudan. Indonesia was also spotted as a likely debt difficulty country, but actually it did not re-

†Had debt renegotiations in 1982.

*Not included in the study.

**As the leader of the study, I recall how disappointing it was, after a number of months of work by a group of excellent people, that we found it hard to reach beyond the conclusion that the level of debt was the factor to watch and that having or tending toward a high level of debt was the real danger signal.

schedule after the 1970 rescheduling. However, the study did not identify about the same number that did experience debt renegotiations in the 1970s.

Had the increases in oil prices and food shortages been anticipated or had there been more general acceptance of my own conviction of the persistence of global inflation into the 1970s, the study undoubtedly would have produced a much longer list of prospective debt difficulty countries. Virtually all developing countries might have fallen into that category. It might have been seen that the economic management criteria could not be judged by past performance like per capita growth rates or export growth rates. It would have been perceived more clearly that good economic management for a developing country means creating not only economic but the political and social conditions for repeated crisis management. The study group would have probably delved more deeply into the alternatives for developing countries in coping with crises and concluded that quantitative indicators have limited value. Knowledge and judgment of a country, how it can and might react to crises, its perception of the need for creditworthiness, the prevailing lending criteria of public and private lending institutions, the general world economic climate, and so forth, all proved to be much more important in assessing the significance of external debt and external debt obligations than the quantitative indicators then used and which are still widely used today.

It is these experiences which indicated the need for new approaches to the external debt problem. The external debt renegotiations which have taken place in the past decade or so continued to be greatly influenced by the debt-service ratios approach. However, there is an alternative approach for handling debt management problems. Economic management should be made the focal point of attention. Changes in terms and conditions of the outstanding debt are still important but become more and more subordinated to achieving changes in economic policies. These policies aim to help the country again become creditworthy. Thus far, a major specific result of this alternative approach has been that the rescheduling country is urged to go to the IMF and obtain its endorsement for a new set of economic policies.

Recent Experience

The experience in recent decades with external debt renegotiations was helpful in providing the experience needed for coping with the problem of assessing country risk by private bank lenders in the latter years of the past decade. This experience demonstrated that any lender to a developing country is at significant potential risk at any level of external debt. At the same time, lenders can achieve an understanding of the borrowing country which enable them to assess and manage this risk to be compatible with the need for prudence by a private bank.

The 1970s' experience with debt renegotiations was not seen as isolated exceptional events when they happened. Instead, there were widespread expectations that a number of developing countries would soon need to reschedule their external debts and that these exercises would probably involve private, as well as official, creditors. Each experience was seen as precedent setting. Questions of comparability between countries and between private and public creditors gained importance. In the existing environment, each experience was also interpreted as indicative of general vulnerability of the international banking system, arising from the lending of major banks to developing countries. The following chapters indicate what did happen.

Amount at Risk and Countries of Concern

Before analyzing the experience of the developing countries involved in debt renegotiation during the past three decades, it may be helpful to summarize the global amounts in international lending to all developing countries and consequent external debt as reported by the World Bank. More details on individual countries and comments on the significance of external debt are also presented.

External debt of developing countries is reported in two broad categories: debt owed to official lending entities and debt owed to private lending entities without creditor government guarantees. Simultaneously, this debt is subdivided into two other categories: debt owed by public entities or guaranteed by public entities in the borrowing country. Another division is between short term (maturity of one year or less) and term (maturity over one year).

The external debt of developing countries has rapidly increased over the past two decades. The external public or publicly guaranteed disbursed term debt, over one year, of developing countries amounted to about $16 billion at year-end 1960, rose to about $60 billion at year-end 1971, and jumped to $370 billion at year-end 1981.[4] Debt-service payments on this public term debt by less developed countries rose from less than $2.5 billion in 1960 to almost $6 billion in 1970 and are estimated to have reached $60 billion in 1981. Interest payments alone on public debt in 1981 came to about $29 billion.*

In addition, the private nonguaranteed term debt increased substantially over the same period. Information on private nonguaranteed debt before the 1970s is incomplete. However, it is estimated that this type of debt rose from about $10 billion in 1970 to about $94 billion in 1981, and thus added significantly to the debt-servicing obligations of the developing countries.

Thus, public and nonguaranteed private term debt of developing countries combined reached by year-end 1981 something like $465 billion, depending on the

[4]Debtor Reporting System, *World Debt Tables* (Washington, D.C.: The World Bank 1982/83 selected volumes). This includes medium- and long-term debt, with an original or extended maturity of more than one year, which is a direct obligation of or has repayment guaranteed by a public body in the borrowing country. Short-term and private nonguaranteed debt are not included in these figures. Capital-deficit oil-exporting countries are included. These statistics do not have the same coverage as OECD statistics which are used in chapter 4. The World Bank statistics are given here to facilitate comparison with economic performance indicators.

*In these World Bank statistics "guaranteed" debt is debt guaranteed by the borrowing country. In other statistics, guarantees refer to creditor government guaranteeing lenders.

number of countries covered by these statistics.[5] These figures represent a sixfold increase over the past decade, or an average annual growth of more than 19% in the external indebtedness of developing countries.

As for the sources of borrowed funds, developing countries have increasingly turned to private creditors in the capital-exporting nations. The trend to private sources of finance already began in the late 1950s and early 1960s. Official creditors (creditor governments on a bilateral basis and through multilateral agencies) have correspondingly declined in relative importance over the past decade.

Within the category of private sources, most significant by far was the growth in funds supplied by private finance markets. Private financial markets at year-end 1971 accounted for only 18% of the less developed countries public term debt outstanding at that time, while by year-end 1981 their share in the total had grown to about 49%.

By 1981, official creditors accounted for about 45% and private creditors for about 55% of the developing countries total public term debt. Nevertheless, while private lending to developing countries was increasing during the 1950s, 1960s, and early 1970s, it was still less important than official lending. Therefore, when countries renegotiated their external debt in those years, the negotiations were conducted exclusively between individual less developed countries governments and their official creditors. Only since the latter part of the 1970s have private commercial bank creditors also entered into multilateral debt renegotiations with developing countries. No repudiation of all outstanding financial obligations by a government has occurred over the past three decades.*

From the mid-1950s to the end of 1981, 26 developing countries were involved in a total of 56 multilateral debt renegotiations with official creditors, either under the auspices of creditor clubs, or similar creditor consultative groups and consortia, covering loans from official sources—loans either provided or guaranteed by creditor country governments or official agencies. The number of countries involved in external debt renegotiations with official creditors remained small until recent years.

In the 1950s, only two countries were involved in debt renegotiations within a multilateral framework: Argentina in 1956 and Turkey in 1959. The Hague Club was established in 1955 in order to move toward a multilateral settlement between Brazil and its European creditors. The actual reschedulings, however, were carried out in 1961 and 1964. In the 1960s, there were 14 renegotiations involving 6 addi-

[5]The World Bank statistics are based on 98 developing countries, the OECD statistics on over 150 countries (including capital-surplus oil-exporting countries.) Furthermore, there are conceptual differences in these statistics which are discussed in greater detail elsewhere in this volume. *Development Co-operation, 1982 Review*, (Paris, France: OECD November 1982).

*A *repudiation* of a loan is the explicit declaration by the debtor government to stop forever interest or principal payments as originally agreed on. A *default* is a formal declaration of inability to service debt which entitles creditors to invoke the protective clauses in loan contracts relevant to this situation, like seizure of assets or recourse to agreed collateral.

tional countries, besides Argentina and Turkey. From 1970 to the end of 1980, the number of multilateral renegotiations increased to 31 and involved another 8 countries in addition to those 6 which had also participated in renegotiations during the 1960s. In 1981 alone, 8 more countries sought or conducted renegotiations, 4 for the first time. In 1982, 5 countries conducted renegotiations with official creditors, 1 for the first time. The countries are listed in Table 6.1, page 92.

Thus, in the 1950s and 1960s and, indeed into the 1970s, debt renegotiations were experienced by a small number of countries. Some countries, however, experienced repeated problems either because the difficulties reappeared (Argentina, Turkey, and Chile) or the original rescheduling was on a "short-leash" basis covering payments for a limited period ahead (Brazil and Indonesia). In the late 1970s and early 1980s, the number of countries involved in debt renegotiations markedly increased. Perhaps more important is that many of these contries have used this device repeatedly.

In judging country creditworthiness, lender's to developing countries must be influenced by whether the country has resorted to debt renegotiation to meet external payments difficulties and if so, when and how often, as well as why the difficulties recurred. With the growing importance of private capital markets in lending to developing countries after the mid-1970s, private commercial banks increasingly entered into and participated in multilateral debt renegotiations with developing countries including Peru, Zaire, Jamaica, Turkey, Nicaragua, and Sudan. This was followed in 1982 by renegotiations with several major debtor countries including Mexico, Brazil, and Argentina.

Accumulation and Ability to Service External Debt

In developing countries, the net flows of external capital are as a rule inward, and not outward, even in countries with large external debts and therefore relatively large capital outflows in the form of amortization payments. This has been the case in virtually all developing countries for the past 30 years.

As noted earlier, developing countries need to borrow to offset deficits in their balance of international payments. It is not a sign of economic weakness for a country to be in external deficit, to finance development from capital inflows as well as domestic savings, or even to finance its investments with funds borrowed on commercial terms. If the country is well managed and remains creditworthy, it can continue to borrow and thus ease the burden of repayment. It needs to be emphasized, however, that this does not mean that the country can assume past debts will automatically be renewed and only incremental borrowing needs negotiating. Borrowers borrow gross; statisticians record *net* flows.

Domestic or External Public Debt

A central distinction exists between domestic public debt and external public debt. The former can readily be repaid through a government's access to tax revenues and central bank financing, while the servicing of external debt depends on a country's foreign exchange earnings, other inflows of foreign exchange like equity investments and borrowed funds, and on international reserves available in adequate amounts.* Balance-of-payments difficulties or liquidity crises result from a shortfall in foreign currencies needed to meet a country's external payments needs including servicing its external debt.

Even if the inflow of capital continues over many years and the country's external indebtedness increases, amortization payments will not create a debt-servicing problem as long as the payments are offset by the additional inflow of funds. Conversely, interruptions in these inflows of additional funds can quickly cause serious payments difficulties, even at relatively low levels of external debt. It is necessary to differentiate clearly between the statistical phenomenon that inflows of capital are equal to or exceed outflows for amortization and interest and the economic phenomenon reflected in the balance of payments. They are related phenomena because the government's need to borrow externally is partly due to its need to provide foreign exchange to debtors in the country to service their external debts.

Servicing external debt, however, is only a fraction of total foreign exchange requirements of a country to make international payments. Payments for imports and services and investments abroad are usually much larger than payments for servicing accumulated debts. External borrowing, like other inflows of foreign exchange, becomes part of the pool of foreign exchange available to a country to meet all its international payments. These funds are allocated by the central bank, if exchange controls exist, as they usually do in developing countries.

Borrowed funds are *not* obtained for servicing of foreign debt. Analysts often act as though they are, but this is a statistical illusion. Countries need to finance all their international payments. Their ability to borrow (country creditworthiness) is a function of how they meet all their international payments, not only debt servicing. A country which is falling behind in meeting payments to foreign suppliers can lose its creditworthiness with bank lenders even when it is fully and promptly servicing its debts to such lenders. Similarly, it cannot use inadequate inflow of borrowed capital as an excuse for not servicing bank lenders. Only when its total inflows are inadequate for total payments, is the stage set for external debt renegotiation—it is simply impractical to "renegotiate" all payment obligations. It does happen that payment obligations due to foreign suppliers rather than lenders are "renegotiated"—a new payments schedule is agreed on—but when this happens the negotiations are usually conducted separately from the banks.

Domestic Difficulties

When debt-servicing difficulties arise, they usually do not originate in changes in external financial markets, but rather unfavorable domestic or balance-of-payments conditions. Internal inflation, overvalued exchange rates, large fiscal

*It may be added that in the case of private sector borrowings, the net return on investment must cover the cost of borrowing whether the loans were obtained from domestic or foreign sources of financing.

deficits, or overexpansionary monetary policies are likely to be the causes of debt-servicing difficulties. These domestic adversities may be caused or enhanced by unfavorable external conditions like global inflation, recession, and high interest rates in money and capital markets of industrial countries. But the countries can remain creditworthy and thus avoid the need to reschedule debt if they can adjust and manage the domestic resistance to the adjustment policies. The ability to avoid renegotiations of external debt often depends on the severity of needed domestic adjustment measures.

Over the past decade, exceptional events have added to the marked strengthening of the underlying trend of international indebtedness. Structural changes in the international economy, including the repeated increases in the price of oil, persistent global inflation, and prolonged periods of slow growth in the developed countries which has an adverse impact on both volume and price of commodity exports from the Third World, have been creating acute problems for many developing countries. The management of their economies has become increasingly complex. Under severe resource constraints, governments have had to adjust their development patterns and economic structures to the substantially changed international economic environment. Favorable developments in some countries, as well as unfavorable, can cause difficulties for other nations. Countries everywhere have had to undertake programs of adjustment to meet existing or avoid impending balance-of-payments crises.

The question arises whether countries can continue to service rising levels of external debt or whether they should reduce their levels of external debt. In many countries, foreign debt has not just been rising in absolute terms but also in relation to national income. The nominal value of outstanding debt, of course, has been eroded by persistent global inflation. Nevertheless, severe economic dislocations on a worldwide scale could result from any attempt to reduce and keep reduced the volume of currently outstanding external debt. In fact, developing countries will require substantial net additions of international capital, whether as grants, direct investment, concessional loans, or commercial credits, to continue their economic and social development and avoid virtually intolerable domestic conditions.

Use of Borrowed Funds

The implications of holding down external debt can be seen by a closer look at the usage of borrowed funds. External financing can be sought by the public sector or by the private sector, with or without official guarantees. The main objective of public sector borrowing in a developing country is primarily to build infrastructure, which usually has a high import content and takes years or decades to produce the fruits of the investments. The main objective of the private sector borrowing is usually investment to produce more products more efficiently so that they may be sold more profitably. It is more likely that foreign funds invested by the private sector will be used for productive purposes yielding relatively quick return than funds invested by the public sector.

All borrowings by the public sector in international capital markets provide budget and balance-of-payments support for the developing country. Foreign borrowings to replenish the country's international reserves perform the same function, but delayed or indirectly by making possible other external borrowings.

However, there is always the inherent possibility that the externally borrowed funds are financing consumption rather than strengthening the productive capacity of the borrowing country. Net inflows of external capital are used by governments to increase consumption directly, but this is often done for worthwhile reasons, that is, to overcome famine. More important is what happens to domestic consumption. Foreign borrowing can be used to subsidize consumption at the expense of investment. In the short or medium term, increased consumption can reduce domestic savings, decrease exports or increase imports, reduce investment in domestic production, and widen the balance-of-payments deficit. Anything which increases consumption ultimately increases the demand for imports. There is no product or output that is purely domestic. The import demand comes both from the import content of some of the factors of the production or distribution process and from the generation of higher incomes resulting from increased production. The "importer" may be far removed from the original producer, but he is there. Holding down external borrowing does not necessarily cause savings to rise by reducing consumption. It may simply mean less investment as foreign savings are not available as a substitute for domestic savings. The needed increased savings, if any, come from other policies, not holding down borrowing.

Net capital inflows may also finance such social investments as education and health, where the balance-of-payments gains are only realized after many years or decades. Social expenditures, however, are indispensable in a developing country. They will increase the need for external financing. Holding down foreign borrowing may well cause a postponement of such investments, but their need remains. The balance-of-payments impact is, at most, only delayed.

The margin of increased imports financed by external capital is often of major importance in determining a country's modernization progress, even though, in general, net inflows of foreign funds account for the financing of only a small portion of import payments. Export receipts of developing countries may ordinarily be expected to cover 80% to 90% of imports and other foreign exchange expenditures. The export-to-import ratio may be even higher in some cases. The net inflow of capital, though seemingly small in proportion to total economic output, can be continually important in relation to the often scarce domestic resources available for investment. In practice, capital inflow is essential for financing imports of goods and services needed for the country's economic development. When the balance of payments is in difficulties, imports for productive purposes are likely to be among the sacrificed imports. Other needs are seen as more urgent or sensitive. Reducing foreign borrowings directly impairs the investment/development program. The notion that developing countries can reduce the total level of external debt is unrealistic, unless the idea is supposed to be only for very short periods of time.

Good Management Essential

Mismanagement of the domestic economy of a developing country must lead to debt-servicing problems. Mismanagement leads to balance-of-payments difficulties and loss of country creditworthiness. Economic management does not take place in a vacuum, and there are important limits to any government's actions. Governments are not only limited by the inherent characteristics of their countries but are often victims of their own or previous governments' past actions.

Typical examples of disruptive past actions include excessive nationalism discouraging foreign equity inflows; technology and technicians; disturbed political and social conditions encouraging capital flight; emigration of skilled people; inheritance of weak or inadequate entrepreneurial skills; and discouraging environment for productive activities resulting from failure to realize earlier promises. Deflating excessive expectations of improved living standards to more realistic levels becomes increasingly more difficult for most developing countries. Yet failure to do so is a major handicap in creating the preconditions for modernization by investment.

There are no uniform rules by which countries live. Acceptable food consumption levels in one developing country may be much too low for others. Educational facilities acceptable in some are not acceptable in others. A governmental role in activities such as manufacturing is anathema in some countries but is taken for granted in others. These kinds of constraints must be taken into account in judging what countries can do in managing their balance of payments. Experience has shown the importance of domestic economic policy measures, like encouraging domestic savings or encouraging internationally competitive manufacturing. These are basic determinants of a country's ability to service external debt rather than the level of debt.

Likelihood and Anticipation of External Debt Problems

The nominal value of outstanding debt, by itself or related to other economic variables, is not sufficient to indicate actual or potential debt servicing problems of a developing country. Nevertheless, understanding the basic characteristics of the external debt of developing countries is essential for understanding not only debt problems but also the nature of the debt renegotiation process.

The nominal value of debt outstanding is made up of different types of debt, which provide the "debt profile" of the country. Total debt must also be adjusted for the effects of inflation. Debt can be incurred with official creditors and private creditors. Official loans can contain grant elements, ranging from zero to around 90%. To make different types of debt comparable, debt must be discounted to its present value. The discounted present value of the debt is the amount required for a country to pay off its entire debt obligations. The creditor would be as well off as had he received the service payments on schedule, because the creditor could invest the money at the same interest rate which was used in discounting the nominal debt to its present value. For example, Eurocurrency debt (with virtually no grant element) has the same nominal and discounted value; the present value of IDA debt (86% grant element) is 14% of its nominal value; the present value of DAC/ODA debt (around 60% grant element) is 40% of its nominal value, etc. Very soft debt—with a high grant element—is essentially the same as grant assistance.

Debt-service obligations of a country are a more relevant measure for its debt management. The debt service is determined by the structure and terms of outstanding debt. An important distinction, however, has to be made regarding the amortization—or repayment of principal—of the debt and the current cost which relates to the interest payments on the loan.

Amortization is repayment of capital. Capital has presumably been used to increase productive capacity in the short or long run. This increased productive capacity is presumably greater than the initial investment. Amortization payments repay the initial capital. The borrowing country has or keeps the increased physical capacity, which directly or indirectly translates over time into increased domestic output and an improved balance of payments. Thus, well-used debt in one sense raises little concern about amortization payments. Nevertheless, the time schedule for amortization is often very different from the timing of the realized benefits of the investment like borrowing medium-term money (five years) to finance a long-term project like new cities or dams. In such cases, new inflows of capital are needed to offset amortization payments made when the increased output has not yet been realized.

As for interest payments, they are always costly. When used to increase output, interest is financed by the earnings of the increased output. Care must be taken to avoid the use of borrowed funds in such a manner that the total stream of benefits over time does not cover at least the stream of interest payments. This need is complicated by the use of floating-interest rates, which not only are volatile and unpredictable but often behave very differently from the prices for the increased outputs resulting from investments.

These debt-servicing problems arise from differences in the time profiles of borrowings and usage which are dependent on the structural character of the borrowing nation. This is not the same as the distinction between debt-servicing problems of a longer run nature and temporary debt-servicing problems. Longer-run problems can arise from persistently inadequate domestic policies; for example, when a developing country allocates continuously a substantial portion of its net external capital inflow to consumption, unprofitable investment, or too much to investments which require a much longer period for realization of benefits than the scheduled servicing of the external debt incurred to make the investment. Temporary debt-servicing problems can occur when other factors, more transitory, make the borrower unable to offset servicing payments through new borrowing. For example, due to a change in the creditors' perception of the country's creditworthiness, because of maintaining an overvalued exchange rate, private commercial banks' current exposure limits, crowding out by other borrowers, or if debt-service payments are "bunched" in certain years, etc. Because of the structural character of the balance-of-payments deficits, a developing country can expect it will need to increase its external indebtedness in the longer run. In practice, increases in external debt may be relatively much larger than other economic indicators, even in real terms. Borrowers must expect difficulties in meeting debt servicing from time to time. They are well advised to have policies on how they would meet such difficulties ready for implementation.

The borrowing countries' responses to debt-servicing difficulties differ substantially and countries are faced with different alternatives. Countries can, at least theoretically, decide to reduce their total international payments by adjusting downward their development programs or domestic consumption of imported goods, rather than seek debt renegotiations. Countries can take administrative measures aimed at increasing supply and curbing demand for foreign exchange by imposing import and payments restrictions, while requiring surrender of foreign exchange income. Or they can seek to increase even further the volume of external borrowing. When available, they can use their international monetary reserves, including their drawing rights in the IMF. When corrective measures are not taken or are inadequate, countries may well experience exhaustion of their international reserves or the accumulation of payments arrears. These countries may need to approach their creditors to obtain a rearrangement of the stream of debt repayments.

Early-Warning System

In this context, the question arises whether it is possible to devise single or composite statistical indicators which would signal imminent or approaching external debt difficulties. Everyone involved would like to have a simple, reliable system of early warning of difficulties, even though this is still short of warning of the need or desire to renegotiate debt. Some relevant statistics are available such as the current account position in the balance of payments, debt-service ratios, exchange rates, inflation rates, exports and imports, as well as the level and change in international reserves. But much of the relevant data, like government expenditures, investment, and savings, are usually not available on a timely and complete basis for an economic forecast. It is even more questionable to combine them in a framework with valuable predictive capability.

Instead of simple reliable quantitative indicators, early-warning systems are more complex. They need, for example, to include qualitative factors which cannot be statistically measured and yet are often of decisive importance in seeing difficulties and in assessing a debtor country's future international creditworthiness. These factors also include the availability of additional financial resources to finance the country's external debt servicing. In addition, conditions in the lending countries are also of decisive importance. Lending and borrowing are two-sided transactions. The need for a borrower to renegotiate debt may well be deeply rooted in the conditions in lending countries, such as depressed conditions leading to low prices for imports of primary products. Simplistic early-warning systems, among other faults, focus on conditions in borrowing countries.

Measures of Economic Performance

Tables 6.1 to 6.16 summarize some of the principal measures of economic performance of 12 countries which had debt renegotiations with their creditors in the second half of the 1970s. This list of 12 consists of countries with widely differing characteristics, ranging in population from less than 1 million (Gabon) to 45 million (Turkey), in per capita output from $220 per year (Zaire) to $2,160 (Chile) and $3,680 (Gabon). Average per capita output rates during the period from 1970 to 1979 also vary substantially. Real output per capita of Jamaica, Nicaragua, Sierra Leone, and Zaire declined during that period, while Turkey and Bolivia until 1978 and 1980, respectively, maintained positive growth rates (see Tables 6.1 and 6.2).

There are some common features. Expansionary monetry and fiscal policies had an adverse effect on the balance of payments. Government expenditures rose rapidly, either as a result of overambitious development plans or in response to social needs and political pressures. Public sector deficits were usually financed through credit creation to avoid drastic cuts in expenditures and increasing unemployment. The rapid increase in the domestic banking system's net claims on the government (see Table 6.3) and, connected with it, a considerable growth in domestic money supply financed domestic price inflation (see Tables 6.4 and 6.5). Government fiscal deficits continued to grow relative to the countries' output of goods and services (see Table 6.6). Some maintained high levels of investment relative to total output, long-term development plans of the public sector mostly concentrated on infrastructure projects with little immediate payoff and only a delayed impact on productivity, output and export earnings. Overvalued exchange rates were frequent (see Table 6.7).

Primary product exports were the major source of foreign earnings for most of the 12 countries. The high concentration in a few export commodities and falls in primary commodity prices in the 1970s (copper, iron ore, coffee, cocoa, sugar, sisal, jute, for instance) adversely affected export earnings for almost all of the countries (see Table 6.8). The situation was aggravated by a shortfall from expectations in export earnings at a time when rising oil prices made imports much more costly while capital goods continued to rise, although much more gradually (see Table 6.9). This adverse movement in the terms of trade was often compensated for by incurring additional official short-term debt as compensatory financing from multilateral agencies such as the IMF. However, official funds were usually not available in adequate amounts.*

Current account deficits in relation to gross domestic product (GDP) rose sharp-

*Although the compensatory financing facility of the IMF, originally established in 1963, has steadily expanded over the years, drawings are still not adequate to cover fully the shortfall in export earnings. In the late 1960s, the World Bank staff prepared a proposal in response to a request from UNCTAD to deal with unexpected declines in export earnings to prevent disruption in development. This proposal gained widespread international support, but was a casualty of general lukewarm attitude to foreign aid of the U.S. government in the late 1960s and fears within the World Bank that this additional facility would detract from the funds available to the World Bank and IDA for other more traditional purposes.

Table 6.1—Population, Per Capita Product, and Average Annual Growth Rates, 1970-1979 (Twelve countries which entered multilateral debt renegotiations between 1970 and 1981)

Country	Population (millions)		GNP at Market Prices ($ millions)		GNP Per Capita ($millions)		Growth Rate (%)	
	Mid-1979	Mid-1980*	1979	1980*	1979	1980*	Population 1970-79	GNP Per Capita (real) 1970-79
Turkey	44.2	45.4	61,020	66,080	1,380	1,460	2.5	3.5
Bolivia	5.4	5.6	2,960	3,190	550	570	2.6	2.3
Chile	10.9	11.1	20,660	23,980	1,890	2,160	1.7	0.8
Jamaica	2.1	2.2	2,400	2,250	1,100	1,030	1.6	−3.7
Nicaragua	2.6	2.7	1,570	1,930	610	720	3.3	−1.6
Peru	17.1	17.6	14,520	16,470	850	930	2.7	0.2
Gabon	.6	.7	2,210	2,420	3,420	3,680	1.1	5.2
Liberia	1.8	1.9	940	980	520	520	3.4	0.5
Sierra Leone	3.4	3.5	860	950	250	270	2.6	−1.2
Sudan	17.9	18.4	8,060	8,640	450	470	2.7	1.5
Togo	2.4	2.5	970	1,020	400	410	2.4	1.2
Zaire	27.5	28.2	5,750	6,340	210	220	2.7	−2.6

*Preliminary. Source: *1981 World Bank Atlas* (Washington, D.C.: The World Bank, February 1982).

Table 6.2—Change in Real Gross Domestic Product (annual percent change)

Country	1971	1972	1973	1974	1975	1976	1977	1978	1979	1980	1981
Turkey	10.2%	7.4%	5.4%	7.4%	8.0%	7.9%	3.9%	2.9%	−0.4%	−1.1%	4.4%
Bolivia	4.9	5.8	6.7	5.2	6.6	6.1	4.2	3.3	1.8	0.6	*
Chile	9.0	−1.2	−5.6	1.0	−12.9	3.5	9.9	8.2	8.3	6.5	6.3
Jamaica	3.1	9.2	1.4	−4.1	−0.6	−6.1	−1.6	−0.3	−1.5	−5.4	2.0
Nicaragua	4.9	2.6	5.0	12.3	3.0	5.8	7.6	−7.9	*	*	*
Peru	5.1	5.8	6.2	6.9	3.3	3.1	−1.2	−1.8	3.8	3.0	3.9
Gabon	*	*	*	*	*	*	*	*	*	*	*
Liberia	5.0	3.8	−2.5	7.4	−15.1	4.0	−0.8	3.9	4.4	−4.7	−5.0
Sierra Leone	1.7	−1.1	3.1	4.0	3.0	−3.0	1.4	0.3	7.4	3.0	6.2
Sudan	*	*	*	*	*	*	*	*	*	*	*
Togo	*	*	*	*	*	*	*	*	*	*	*
Zaire	6.0	0.1	8.1	3.1	−5.0	−5.2	0.8	−4.7	−3.3	2.5	*

*Not available. Source: International Monetary Fund, *International Financial Statistics* (Washington, D.C.: IMF, Yearbook 1982 and February 1983).

Table 6.3—Change in the Domestic Banking System's Net Claims on the Government (annual percent change)

Country	1971	1972	1973	1974	1975	1976	1977	1978	1979	1980	1981
Turkey	29.9%	−0.8%	−21.6%	38.9%	143.1%	37.2%	86.9%	62.6%	78.4%	128.4%	28.1%
Bolivia	18.4	21.2	4.1	−76.0	185.6	59.8	11.6	65.7	100.7	66.9	27.0
Chile	170.0	188.9	716.7	437.7	410.7	122.1	80.6	9.0	4.7	−44.1	−71.0
Jamaica	53.6	−75.3	10.1	−9.4	152.5	101.0	38.2	33.4	68.8	4.1	39.0
Nicaragua	43.7	−4.1	−49.1	−347.9	−173.3	41.3	59.6	239.0	*	*	39.6
Peru	42.5	34.0	30.1	−9.4	54.7	114.4	47.5	55.2	−7.2	68.6	58.7
Gabon	*	*	*	*	*	*	98.1	−69.5	149.3	−3.0	*
Liberia	*	*	*	*	−34.3	37.8	−1.2	377.2	50.4	67.9	27.2
Sierra Leone	225.2	17.0	61.0	52.6	146.4	89.3	11.6	52.3	38.4	32.1	39.1
Sudan	16.7	16.6	14.9	17.0	51.9	46.9	66.1	21.5	16.0	13.0	32.8
Togo	−23.0	−37.8	−18.5	−34.0	−156.4	−17.1	59.5	234.0	−35.9	14.4	216.3
Zaire	33.0	20.4	16.1	74.1	37.0	82.0	43.5	46.2	28.7	21.2	53.0

*Not available. Source: Ibid.

Table 6.4—Change in Money Supply (annual percent change)

Country	1971	1972	1973	1974	1975	1976	1977	1978	1979	1980	1981
Turkey	23.6%	22.4%	32.5%	27.8%	31.3%	28.0%	39.0%	37.4%	58.2%	57.8%	34.7%
Bolivia	15.3	25.4	34.3	43.4	11.6	36.1	20.6	12.1	16.6	42.6	19.6
Chile	*	*	*	*	*	*	107.8	66.5	64.0	56.6	−6.1
Jamaica	23.8	9.6	19.9	27.2	20.6	3.0	38.3	16.4	8.9	40.6	−10.2
Nicaragua	5.7	23.8	53.6	10.7	−4.3	24.4	5.9	−7.4	*	*	38.6
Peru	10.0	28.6	24.8	41.1	16.8	25.9	20.8	45.4	70.3	57.9	46.6
Gabon	12.5	26.9	24.1	66.8	54.7	76.4	−8.0	−6.2	−4.9	9.9	21.9
Liberia	*	*	*	*	*	*	*	*	*	*	*
Sierra Leone	11.8	19.1	23.7	13.4	9.8	19.8	17.1	27.1	18.7	19.6	−0.4
Sudan	7.7	16.9	21.5	34.9	18.6	24.7	42.4	28.0	32.8	31.5	39.6
Togo	16.4	−1.2	−3.1	115.0	−14.7	52.0	10.4	32.2	10.5	5.6	44.8
Zaire	1.8	23.8	24.3	32.7	16.2	46.2	56.0	56.9	0.9	75.3	52.8

*Not available. Source: Ibid.

Table 6.5—Change in Consumer Price Index (annual percent change)

Country	1971	1972	1973	1974	1975	1976	1977	1978	1979	1980	1981
Turkey	15.7%	11.9%	15.3%	15.9%	19.2%	17.3%	27.1%	45.3%	58.6%	110.2%	36.6%
Bolivia	3.6	6.5	31.6	62.8	8.0	4.5	8.1	10.4	19.7	47.2	32.1
Chile	19.4	79.1	351.9	505.5	374.6	211.8	91.9	40.1	33.4	35.1	19.7
Jamaica	5.3	5.4	17.7	27.2	17.4	9.8	11.2	34.9	29.1	27.1	12.8
Nicaragua	*	*	*	*	*	2.8	11.4	4.6	48.1	35.3	*
Peru	6.9	7.1	9.5	16.9	23.6	33.5	38.0	57.8	66.7	59.2	75.4
Gabon	3.9	3.5	6.3	11.9	28.4	20.2	13.9	10.7	7.9	12.3	*
Liberia	−0.8	3.9	19.6	19.0	14.0	5.6	6.2	7.3	11.6	13.8	8.2
Sierra Leone	−1.6	5.5	5.6	14.4	19.9	17.2	11.6	7.6	21.2	11.1	23.3
Sudan	1.5	13.5	15.3	26.1	23.9	1.7	16.7	19.9	30.8	25.4	19.8
Togo	6.7	7.7	3.6	12.8	18.1	11.6	22.5	0.4	7.5	12.4	19.6
Zaire	5.8	15.9	15.6	27.5	29.0	80.7	69.0	48.5	108.6	42.1	34.9

*Not available. Source: Ibid.

Table 6.6—Government Budget Surplus (Deficit) in Relation to Gross Domestic Product (percent)

Country	1971	1972	1973	1974	1975	1976	1977	1978	1979	1980	1981
Turkey	−3.4%	−2.2%	−1.9%	−1.8%	−1.3%	−2.0%	−6.1%	−4.3%	−6.3%	−5.7%	*
Bolivia	−3.8	−3.4	−3.3	*	*	*	−5.1	−3.9	−7.2	−7.2	*
Chile	*	−12.5	−6.9	−5.1	0.1	1.2	−1.0	−1.0	4.9	5.5	*
Jamaica	−3.7	−4.1	−5.2	−7.7	−7.9	−15.4	−14.3	−16.6	−15.2	*	*
Nicaragua	−2.5	−3.6	−3.3	−5.5	−5.8	−4.0	*	−7.7	−7.1	*	*
Peru	−3.1	−3.7	−3.9	−3.1	−5.5	−6.3	−7.5	−5.1	−0.6	−2.8	−4.9
Gabon	*	*	−10.9	−4.2	−8.0	−22.0	*	*	*	*	*
Liberia	2.8	3.2	2.5	1.3	0.6	−2.5	−3.4	−7.3	−16.0	−9.6	−13.0
Sierra Leone	−1.1	−2.3	−3.1	−4.4	−10.5	−8.8	−7.0	−6.7	−7.1	−11.8	−9.3
Sudan	0.3	−0.8	−1.8	−0.8	−4.9	−3.2	−7.2	−5.3	*	*	*
Togo	*	*	*	*	*	*	*	*	*	*	*
Zaire	−7.3	−7.0	−9.6	−18.0	−11.2	−21.9	−11.4	−10.9	−4.9	*	*

*Not available. Source: Ibid.

Table 6.7—Fixed Capital Formation in Relation to Gross Domestic Product (percent)

Country	1971	1972	1973	1974	1975	1976	1977	1978	1979	1980	1981
Turkey	17.0%	17.4%	17.9%	18.6%	19.6%	23.2%	22.5%	20.3%	18.4%	16.2%	16.3%
Bolivia	14.4	15.2	17.3	15.1	18.4	18.9	19.0	20.1	16.6	12.1	*
Chile	15.4	12.5	13.1	12.4	10.1	8.7	9.0	14.7	15.3	17.1	18.6
Jamaica	27.8	25.5	25.8	22.0	23.3	16.6	11.7	13.3	17.4	14.5	18.2
Nicaragua	15.5	15.1	19.3	23.5	22.6	20.2	22.8	14.2	8.3	*	*
Peru	12.6	12.8	12.6	15.2	17.4	16.6	14.6	14.0	14.4	17.0	19.4
Gabon	*	48.1	37.5	51.8	62.6	73.5	58.1	35.0	30.3	*	*
Liberia	19.7	21.8	20.6	23.0	26.4	32.7	33.2	33.6	31.5	21.4	19.1
Sierra Leone	13.6	12.0	11.2	11.8	13.3	11.6	10.8	11.7	12.4	14.8	18.3
Sudan	9.6	8.7	10.6	11.2	14.2	19.6	13.4	11.2	*	*	*
Togo	16.2	18.5	19.0	15.3	22.8	24.7	34.8	45.7	46.9	*	*
Zaire	28.5	32.1	25.2	30.6	28.5	22.9	34.7	17.3	12.8	15.8	*

*Not available. Source: Ibid.

Table 6.8—Percentage Change in Export Earnings (three-year moving average)

Country	1971	1972	1973	1974	1975	1976	1977	1978	1979	1980	1981
Turkey	11.5%	22.7%	44.6%	43.7%	93.8%	93.2%	85.3%	16.9%	5.1%	15.0%	28.6%
Bolivia	6.3	4.9	13.3	48.5	39.3	38.2	7.2	13.2	10.8	15.2	14.0
Chile	4.3	−10.1	8.3	31.8	29.2	23.4	6.0	17.9	27.0	35.0	29.6
Jamaica	14.4	12.0	6.6	26.2	24.0	17.7	−1.0	2.3	9.1	12.3	8.8
Nicaragua	5.6	15.6	14.5	26.4	17.3	26.2	18.7	17.9	3.2	*	*
Peru	3.5	4.8	4.1	20.7	15.5	10.3	5.2	12.2	35.6	33.8	25.2
Gabon	11.3	16.8	29.0	64.3	64.5	53.4	14.1	6.0	15.4	18.9	*
Liberia**	9.6	7.7	15.5	22.0	18.2	12.9	4.2	8.9	5.5	9.6	2.2
Sierra Leone	3.3	1.7	7.2	14.4	5.4	−2.6	−0.3	12.4	21.3	18.4	1.8
Sudan	8.4	8.3	14.7	9.4	12.1	14.4	21.0	14.7	1.5	11.6	21.2
Togo	7.7	0.6	4.7	57.8	50.0	50.0	1.9	20.7	22.5	*	*
Zaire	7.7	2.3	13.1	32.9	19.7	8.3	−5.2	*	*	*	*

*Not available. **Merchandise exports. Source: Ibid.

ly in most countries, particularly Turkey, Bolivia, Chile, Sierra Leone, Sudan, and Togo. Current account deficits were persistent for nearly all the countries throughout the second half of the 1970s except Gabon and Peru in 1979 and 1980 (see Tables 6.10 and 6.11). But this condition is common for nearly all developing countries.

Debt-service payments on public and publicly guaranteed external debt took larger and larger shares of available export earnings, although the percentages differed markedly from country to country. One reason for these differences is that in some countries, such as Turkey, the debt-servicing obligations of private debtors were relatively large compared with other countries with predominantly public debt (see Tables 6.12 and 6.13).

All 12 countries lost international reserves following the impact of the first oil-price shock. Reserves were replenished by some countries in the late 1970s but not sufficiently in proportion to rising import costs. In 1981, for example, imports were 19 times larger than international reserves (available at year-end 1980) in Jamaica, and 46 times larger in the Sudan. Special cases were Gabon (where imports in 1977 soared to more than 100 times the amount of available reserves at the end of the preceding year) and Liberia (where import costs in 1981 amounted to more than 150 times the amount of available reserves at the end of the preceding year). See Tables 6.14, 6.15, 6.16. Several countries again suffered considerable reserve losses in 1981 or 1982.

The net inflow of external capital from all sources into the 12 countries in 1975 to 1981 is shown in Table 6.17. The proportion of official development assistance in the total inflow of external capital varied widely from country to country. In 1979, official development assistance accounted for almost all the external capital available to Jamaica and Sierra Leone, for over 50% of the external capital flowing into Zaire, but only for 33% flowing into Turkey and Bolivia, and about 20% flowing into Peru during that year.

Profiles Vary

Since the mix of various kinds of borrowing differs among developing countries, debt-servicing profiles vary by terms and conditions of past borrowings. The causes for this variation in mix are many: the level of a country's modernization, export capacity, and diversification of its economy; its government attitudes toward foreign borrowings; political relations with aid-extending governments; and shares of the lending programs of the regional development banks. A number of developing countries have regarded term borrowing from commercial sources on commercial terms as undesirable, at least in principle, particularly for investment. Some governments have seen this source of funds as threatening domestic policies thought to be disapproved of by foreign private lenders, for example, large-scale government ownership of productive facilities or extensive use of price, wage, production, and foreign payments controls. Others fear excessive influence of foreign interests or competition with domestic entities. Still other governments fear it weakens their case for concessional funds.

Table 6.9—Export Coverage of Imports (percent)

Country	1971	1972	1973	1974	1975	1976	1977	1978	1979	1980	1981
Turkey	76.8%	97.9%	121.1%	96.3%	38.1%	48.2%	37.2%	56.7%	49.6%	40.4%	55.7%
Bolivia	95.5	92.9	99.1	126.0	77.5	90.4	84.1	66.3	67.7	85.9	76.0
Chile	84.8	67.3	83.3	88.5	78.6	104.3	80.2	71.6	78.6	75.1	55.4
Jamaica	74.2	73.6	70.2	90.0	78.3	75.3	94.2	93.9	84.8	84.7	76.5
Nicaragua	81.9	105.3	72.3	62.1	69.4	92.8	79.1	95.5	114.9	*	*
Peru	93.8	94.3	81.8	70.9	52.0	58.4	68.6	90.7	118.9	98.5	71.5
Gabon	107.8	94.4	90.5	120.0	99.2	96.9	102.2	108.5	122.0	126.5	*
Liberia	*	*	*	*	80.6	87.3	76.8	76.3	80.4	84.9	84.4
Sierra Leone	81.6	91.4	80.6	67.3	66.1	65.5	70.0	59.6	52.3	53.4	52.7
Sudan	89.9	86.3	105.1	60.4	51.6	78.1	84.2	79.7	66.4	65.4	56.3
Togo	80.1	67.6	70.4	165.9	60.0	75.5	64.4	53.3	55.1	*	*
Zaire	75.5	67.1	78.7	78.1	61.4	56.3	45.8	*	*	*	*

*Not available. Source: Ibid.

Table 6.10—Current Account Balance (millions of dollars)

Country	1971	1972	1973	1974	1975	1976	1977	1978	1979	1980	1981
Turkey	$507	$789	$1,354	$1,474	$−1,848	$−1,964	$−3,229	$−1,216	$−1,479	$−3,538	$−2,376
Bolivia	−2	−4	13	137	−130	−53	−118	−331	−358	−118	−287
Chile	−198	−472	−279	−291	−490	148	−551	−1,088	−1,189	−1,971	−4,814
Jamaica	−172	−197	−248	−92	−283	−303	−42	−50	−139	−166	−337
Nicaragua	−44	22	66	−257	−185	−39	−182	−25	180	*	*
Peru	−33	−31	−263	−725	−1,540	−1,193	−922	−192	784	62	−1,513
Gabon	18	−4	−43	165	−9	−49	6	74	248	387	*
Liberia	*	*	*	*	−91	−58	−137	−158	−135	−105	−65
Sierra Leone	−20	−9	−29	−61	−67	−60	−50	−120	−188	−183	−143
Sudan	−42	−49	28	−271	−428	−138	−90	−109	−248	−320	−639
Togo	−3	−13	−6	132	−76	−27	−87	−217	−201	*	*
Zaire	−125	−365	−279	−472	−593	−830	−1,451	*	*	*	*

*Not available. Source: Ibid.

Table 6.11—Current Account Balance in Relation to Gross Domestic Product (percent)

Country	1971	1972	1973	1974	1975	1976	1977	1978	1979	1980	1981
Turkey	4.0%	4.8%	6.5%	5.0%	−5.1%	−4.8%	−6.8%	−2.3%	−2.1%	−6.2%	−4.5%
Bolivia	−0.2	−0.3	1.0	6.3	−5.3	−1.9	−3.6	−8.7	−7.9	−2.1	*
Chile	−1.9	−3.8	−2.5	−2.5	−5.7	1.3	−3.7	−7.1	−5.8	−7.0	−14.6
Jamaica	−11.0	−10.9	−13.0	−3.8	−9.8	−10.1	−1.3	−1.9	−5.7	−6.2	−11.5
Nicaragua	−5.4	2.5	−6.0	−17.0	−11.7	−2.1	−8.1	−1.2	12.4	*	*
Peru	−0.5	−0.4	−2.8	−6.3	−11.3	−8.9	−7.3	−1.8	5.7	0.4	−7.5
Gabon	*	−0.9	−5.9	10.7	−0.4	−1.6	0.2	3.1	8.5	*	*
Liberia	*	*	*	*	−14.9	−9.2	−19.4	−20.4	−15.3	−11.5	−7.7
Sierra Leone	−4.7	−2.1	−6.0	−10.9	−10.5	−10.8	−7.6	−14.9	−19.3	−16.6	−12.8
Sudan	−1.9	−2.0	1.1	−7.6	−9.9	−2.6	−1.3	−1.4	*	*	*
Togo	−1.2	−3.7	−1.5	24.3	−12.6	−4.8	−12.7	−25.3	−19.7	*	*
Zaire	−5.9	−15.8	−9.5	−13.1	−15.4	−23.4	−31.4	*	*	*	*

*Not available. Source: Ibid.

Table 6.12—Debt Service on Public or Publicly Guaranteed External Term Debt (millions of dollars)

Country	1972	1974	1976	1977	1978	1979	1980	1981
Turkey	$224.2	$240.9	$310.9	$362.5	$428.5	$627.0	$1,001.0	$1,168.3
Bolivia	40.1	68.1	103.4	152.8	350.5	258.7	274.1	278.6
Chile	97.6	278.6	755.2	885.8	1,214.8	1,258.0	1,374.5	1,663.2
Jamaica	28.9	64.0	111.3	152.0	194.4	199.7	202.3	352.0
Nicaragua	32.3	50.4	76.2	101.9	99.2	55.6	76.5	184.2
Peru	183.1	432.8	455.0	653.3	752.7	923.2	1,504.4	1,895.0
Gabon	22.3	41.1	82.8	136.8	308.7	357.2	389.8	299.8
Liberia	16.6	19.5	21.4	26.5	26.4	72.5	37.6	34.4
Sierra Leone	10.7	14.5	22.0	17.1	39.3	45.6	41.9	50.5
Sudan	50.8	61.8	96.9	75.7	89.6	68.8	92.9	110.7
Togo	5.3	8.5	23.1	56.8	47.8	37.0	60.1	40.4
Zaire	60.9	187.0	88.0	114.4	139.4	169.7	317.5	212.0

Source: *World Debt Tables, 1982/83 Edition* (Washington, D.C.: The World Bank, February 1983).

Table 6.13—Debt Service Payments on External Public or Publicly Guaranteed Debt in Relation to Total Export Earnings (percent)

Country	1972	1974	1976	1977	1978	1979	1980	1981
Turkey	17.7%	11.2%	10.9%	14.1%	14.0%	19.3%	25.7%	18.7%
Bolivia	18.0	11.2	16.2	21.8	49.6	30.2	25.9	24.7
Chile	9.9	12.0	31.1	33.8	40.7	26.5	21.9	27.2
Jamaica	4.6	6.1	11.8	15.1	16.6	16.4	14.2	23.5
Nicaragua	10.0	10.9	12.1	13.9	13.6	8.1	*	*
Peru	15.7	23.0	25.9	30.5	31.1	22.2	31.0	44.9
Gabon	7.2	4.1	6.1	9.2	20.8	17.6	16.0	*
Liberia	6.8	4.9	4.6	5.9	5.2	13.5	6.4	6.5
Sierra Leone	8.0	8.4	16.4	10.5	19.0	19.1	15.5	24.4
Sudan	13.7	13.8	13.9	9.6	12.1	9.5	9.0	8.7
Togo	6.5	3.6	12.2	24.3	15.7	10.7	*	*
Zaire	8.0	11.1	7.5	8.9	*	*	*	*

*Not available. Source: Ibid; *International Financial Statistics* (Washington, D.C.: IMF, Yearbook 1982 and February 1983).

Table 6.14—International Reserves, Minus Gold at Year-End (millions of dollars)

Country	1971	1972	1973	1974	1975	1976	1977	1978	1979	1980	1981
Turkey	$631	$1,265	$1,969	$1,708	$918	$978	$620	$833	$767	$1,274	$1,285
Bolivia	40	44	55	176	139	151	211	170	178	106	100
Chile	170	97	122	41	56	405	426	1,090	1,938	3,123	3,213
Jamaica	179	160	127	190	126	32	48	59	64	105	85
Nicaragua	58	80	116	104	122	146	148	51	*	*	*
Peru	381	442	526	925	425	289	357	390	1,521	1,979	1,209
Gabon	25	23	48	103	146	116	10	23	20	107	199
Liberia	*	*	*	14	14	17	27	18	55	4	7
Sierra Leone	38	46	52	55	28	25	33	35	47	31	16
Sudan	28	36	61	124	36	24	23	28	67	49	17
Togo	40	36	38	54	41	67	46	70	65	78	151
Zaire	91	123	173	119	48	50	134	126	207	204	152

*Not available. Source: Ibid (IMF).

Table 6.15—Percentage Change in International Reserves (annual percent change)

Country	1971	1972	1973	1974	1975	1976	1977	1978	1979	1980	1981
Turkey	107.6%	100.5%	55.6%	−13.3%	−46.2%	6.5%	−36.6%	−34.3%	−7.9%	66.1%	0.9%
Bolivia	20.7	11.9	23.9	221.0	−20.8	8.3	39.7	−19.6	4.9	−40.5	−5.9
Chile	−50.2	−43.1	25.6	−66.2	36.0	624.7	5.3	155.6	77.8	61.1	2.9
Jamaica	28.7	−10.8	−20.2	49.5	−34.0	−74.2	47.5	23.0	8.5	64.6	−18.9
Nicaragua	19.6	37.9	45.1	−10.1	16.4	20.1	1.6	−65.8	*	*	*
Peru	28.6	16.2	18.9	75.9	−54.0	−32.0	23.3	9.2	290.2	30.1	−38.9
Gabon	72.2	−8.5	106.0	115.8	41.4	−20.5	−91.5	127.7	−10.8	434.0	85.0
Liberia	*	*	*	*	0.0	23.7	58.7	−34.1	205.6	−92.5	78.0
Sierra Leone	−2.5	21.1	11.4	5.4	−48.0	−11.3	32.5	4.2	34.2	−34.5	−47.7
Sudan	28.6	27.6	72.2	102.8	−70.7	−35.2	−2.1	22.9	137.3	−27.7	−65.1
Togo	14.4	−9.9	3.8	43.8	−24.4	61.6	−30.8	51.8	−6.4	18.5	95.2
Zaire	−33.2	35.6	40.3	−31.2	−59.7	4.9	166.2	−6.1	64.4	−1.2	−25.7

*Not available. Source: Ibid.

Table 6.16—Ratio of Imports to International Reserves†

Country	1971	1972	1973	1974	1975	1976	1977	1978	1979	1980	1981
Turkey	0.9	0.6	0.4	0.3	3.1	6.4	7.1	8.7	7.9	12.5	8.8
Bolivia	6.5	6.1	6.7	8.6	3.6	5.0	5.5	5.0	7.5	6.9	12.8
Chile	3.9	8.6	18.2	21.8	57.0	41.6	8.1	9.8	5.5	4.3	3.5
Jamaica	5.4	4.8	5.8	9.2	7.5	10.0	33.0	26.1	24.5	26.3	18.7
Nicaragua	5.6	4.7	5.6	6.2	6.3	5.6	6.3	5.2	11.7	*	*
Peru	3.9	3.2	3.8	5.0	3.6	7.1	10.8	7.5	9.0	3.2	3.0
Gabon	13.0	21.0	17.5	12.2	9.6	12.5	137.9	73.8	95.7	*	*
Liberia	*	*	*	*	36.7	38.4	34.8	24.0	38.2	13.1	155.6
Sierra Leone	3.5	3.7	3.9	4.9	4.2	7.2	9.2	10.4	13.1	10.8	12.9
Sudan	18.1	15.4	12.9	12.1	7.9	24.5	39.4	40.2	38.2	23.4	46.3
Togo	2.9	3.0	3.4	3.7	5.4	6.1	5.4	12.4	9.0	*	*
Zaire	7.4	12.4	11.7	12.5	14.0	43.7	55.7	*	*	*	*

†Current year's imports divided by international reserves at end of preceding year. *Not available. Source: Ibid.

Table 6.17—Net Flows of Resources to Individual Countries from all Sources* (millions of dollars)

Country	1975		1976		1977		1978		1979		1980		1981	
	Total	ODA**	Total	ODA**	Total	ODA**	Total	ODA**	Total	ODA**	Total	ODA**	Total	ODA**
Turkey	$419.6	$83.1	$653.4	$137.5	$907.4	$93.4	$1,356.1	$178.0	$1,850.9	$584.8	$1,877.6	$1,002.4	$1,979.3	$735.4
Bolivia	101.9	56.6	124.7	71.2	170.0	93.5	231.9	145.9	430.5	156.5	157.0	170.0	229.0	169.6
Chile	−227.2	128.3	−60.9	8.2	−125.0	11.2	129.0	7.6	288.6	−27.1	409.0	−9.7	1,435.0	−7.0
Jamaica	94.6	25.3	−12.1	25.5	74.0	33.2	110.6	122.0	90.4	97.5	186.4	116.0	231.2	154.7
Nicaragua	92.3	41.4	81.3	39.2	67.9	36.5	48.5	41.6	119.7	115.1	240.1	220.6	232.8	170.2
Peru	590.8	74.4	368.8	74.1	428.8	96.6	380.4	142.7	868.3	199.5	625.1	203.1	810.3	233.3
Gabon	149.0	63.4	118.3	34.0	284.5	27.5	88.0	43.8	−43.7	36.7	−27.2	55.8	96.0	43.5
Liberia	652.5	21.1	308.2	26.9	711.2	33.6	713.0	48.0	356.7	80.7	416.9	97.9	656.3	108.5
Sierra Leone	24.8	18.1	25.8	15.1	34.5	26.2	46.1	40.2	60.5	53.2	94.2	90.9	65.9	61.2
Sudan	662.3	298.5	636.6	368.8	417.5	231.0	518.9	337.6	633.3	560.5	715.8	630.1	690.9	680.4
Togo	55.7	41.8	72.0	43.0	120.6	64.1	267.0	102.4	210.8	109.6	180.9	91.0	50.6	62.9
Zaire	643.4	204.5	489.2	193.6	510.5	260.5	703.2	316.8	732.5	416.4	756.3	427.5	628.2	393.6

* Excludes grants by private voluntary agencies and flows from Council For Mutual Economic Assistance (CMEA) countries. Bank lending included only insofar as reported by Development Assistance Committee countries.

** Official development assistance (ODA) from all sources but excluding CMEA countries.

Source: *Development Co-operation, 1981 Review,* (Paris, France: OECD, November 1981 and earlier issues); *Geographical Distribution of Financial Flows to Developing Countries* (Paris, France: OECD, 1982).

As might be expected, the largest external borrowers are those with absorptive capacity for productive use of such borrowed funds and therefore with higher proportions of modernized economies. Nevertheless, the ability of a developing country to obtain private sources of credit is also related to its domestic social and political attitudes and policies which reflect its willingness or eagerness to approach such private sources. These attitudes are not a function of stage of economic development or per capita income. Countries like India and Pakistan, for example, have borrowed mostly from official sources of financing but could join Mexico, Brazil, Korea, Taiwan, and Indonesia in borrowing from private creditors, particularly from private commercial banks, if they so decided.

Common Characteristics

As seen from the various tables in this chapter, underlying economic and balance-of-payments conditions differ considerably from country to country. Nevertheless, it is possible to identify common factors and deficiencies in economic policies that ultimately lead to a debt renegotiation. In this sense, it is possible to devise an early-warning system, but such a system will *not* consist of a few quantitative indicators which can be readily computerized and give neat and clear signals.

A rather common feature is relatively rapid accumulation of debt and increasing balance-of-payments deficits, frequently occurring in a five-year period immediately preceding the debt renegotiation. All these countries suffer from the basic and prolonged imbalance in the demand for and the availability of resources, that is, a resource gap as noted earlier. In an attempt to fill this resource gap, countries tried to increase rapidly their external borrowing, largely on commercial terms and often short term. If their borrowings had closed or hedged the resource gaps, the problem might be considered solved. In these cases, such successes, at most, were brief. If domestic fiscal and expansionary monetary policies failed to close these gaps, the gaps continued and were "closed" by inflation. Governments were not able to control demand and to increase domestic supplies, given the supply constraints inherent in the developing economies. The results were rapid inflation, often accompanied by overvalued exchange rates, disrupted investment, poor export performance, and severe pressures on the balance of payments. These developments often led to a decline in confidence at home and abroad in the management of the economy and the outlook for the country. Capital flight often heightened the difficulties. Under these pressures, the countries sought relief from their debt-servicing obligations, mostly after they reduced other external payments below levels compatible with a continuing viable economy.

The reasons for inflationary financing were manifold.[6] In many cases, when social and economic development plans were accelerated beyond the availability of long-term development capital, governments not only resorted to borrowing from the domestic banking system but they also resorted to short-term and

[6]Irving S. Friedman, *Inflation: A World-Wide Disaster* (Boston: Houghton Mifflin, 1980).

medium-term external borrowing from private creditors, particularly suppliers and contractors. Mismatches between loan usage for relatively long-term investments and loan maturities were increasingly frequent under such conditions. Thus, external borrowing was a form of inflationary financing although it resulted in an increased flow of goods. This financing, however, helped to perpetuate inflationary monetary and fiscal policies. Perhaps worse, foreign borrowing, at times, financed imports of consumer goods (food) to replace output which should and could have come efficiently from the domestic economy. Import priorities were often no longer related to development but to immediate social and political needs. Grant aid used for current consumption at least does not represent a direct charge against future output and future consumption (indirectly it may be a charge by raising definitions of tolerable consumption and expectations of achieving these levels). Borrowed money represents a charge against future output, savings, and consumption, which appears more obviously as a charge against the future foreign exchange availabilities of the country.

External borrowing to offset capital flight is another way to maintain current consumption at the expense of future growth and consumption. It characterizes the conditions of countries which then need debt renegotiations. The latest and most dramatic examples are Argentina and Mexico. It is a difficult choice for governments—to devalue the currency sufficiently to stop the capital flight may mean great overcompensation to earners of foreign exchange and excessively large increases in import prices damaging to industries requiring imported goods and further accelerating inflation. To impose capital controls is often an exercise in futility as illegal means are used to get funds out of the country. The need is to restore confidence in the currency of the country in difficulty. Yet, it is losing this confidence because of its management. Thus, it requires drastic changes simultaneously in a number of economic and financial policies, including major changes in exchange rates.

Another general cause of difficulties that lead to conditions which result in debt renegotiation is that actual public sector savings needed for investment often fall short of the government's budgetary estimates and plans, because current expenditures exceed current revenues. Frequently, public enterprises, because of chronic mismanagement, and subsidies in the form of pricing policies, need large-scale financial support of the central government. To cover the growing fiscal deficits, governments rely increasingly on domestic and foreign financing. In addition, wage increases often exceed by far improvements in productivity.

At times, it is argued that developing countries that get into external payments difficulties requiring debt renegotiations have grown too fast. In many countries which had to renegotiate debt, the growth in real output was not high by developing country standards, ranging from 3% to 6% per year. In years immediately preceding debt renegotiations, output was often declining in real terms. More relevant than growth rates was that investment levels had been comparatively high over a period of time. But increases in productivity from the investments were not large or did not come soon enough. Large investment projects with completion time stretching over many years did not bring returns needed to service loans even of a long-term character.

Impact of External Shocks

Ineffective financial policies were often aggravated by adverse changes in the country's terms of trade. World markets and prices for major export commodities declined and wiped out a major portion of total export earnings. International commodity agreements designed to put floors under export prices were exceptional and did not apply to commodities of countries in difficulties. Foreign spending had to be financed by drawing down reserves, which usually were modest to begin with and therefore quickly exhausted. International arrangements to help countries finance shortfalls in export earnings were relatively small, mostly concentrated in the IMF.

In addition, world recessions combined with world inflation meant less foreign exchange earnings while import prices continued to rise. The OPEC oil price increases meant drastic additional adverse changes of this kind. Moreover, interest rates in creditor countries, reflecting the persistent global inflation, remained high by historical standards. This increased the costs in foreign exchange of borrowing and reduced opportunities for refinancing more expensive debt with less expensive debt. This was especially true for countries perceived by the international financial community as likely to get into external financial difficulties.

Severe shortages of foreign exchange and the failure of governments to design in time appropriate economic policies made it very difficult, if not impossible, for the monetary authorities of these countries to provide sufficient foreign exchange in time to settle international accounts. In such circumstances, external payments arrears arise, reflecting delays in payments for imports and transfers of profits and dividends, as well as temporary delays in debt servicing. Once countries were in payments arrears, confidence in their economic management further eroded. Debt renegotiations became urgently needed when capital flight depleted reserves and foreign capital inflows ceased abruptly as creditors' confidence in a country's economic performance was severely shaken.* The loss of confidence in a country will lead quickly to a sharp decline in the inflow of new debt and equity capital from private sources.

In cases where debt was mostly or largely due to official creditors, the borrowing country wished to negotiate with its official creditors for some relief from the debt-servicing burden. If the official creditors agreed, the borrowing country had more time to correct the adverse effects of past poor economic management. It could do so without imposing as severe domestic austerity measures (increased consumption constraints and increased unemployment) or disruption of its investment programs as would otherwise occur.

In recent years, as debt servicing to private creditors became important and deb-

*Mexico is a vivid recent example, but this observation was made long before the events of 1982.

tor countries experienced difficulties in servicing loans from private creditors, they have increasingly approached private creditor groups to enter into debt renegotiations. They also hope to reduce the severity of needed adjustments.

Ability to Service Debt

Can we summarize the answer to the question: What determines the ability of a developing country to service its debt? Balance-of-payments analysis is useful because it reflects the outcome of domestic economic management, as well as the effect of external factors on the country's economic performance. The balance of payments is a mirror image of changes in the economy which may be caused by internal or external influences. Thus, an analysis of factors that determine the ability of a country to service debt can be organized within the framework of the elements constituting the balance of payments and the determinants of major changes in these elements.

The ability to service debt cannot, however, be judged by balance-of-payments behavior alone. It can be judged only by analysis of the domestic and external determinants of the elements that are conventionally recorded and labeled as the balance of payments. Relationships among different elements in the balance of payments are not fixed or unchanging. Historical relationships cannot guide judgments on the future, but an examination of the causes of behavior of the different elements may indicate what relationships are likely to prevail in the future.

The capacity to service debt is also related to its specific usage as well as general economic management. The relative roles of government and markets vary markedly, but, generally speaking, developing countries have given a larger role to government than usually found in a developed country. The keys to creating and maintaining debt-servicing capacity are the productive use of capital inflows through satisfactory economic management. If external debt is well employed, virtually every developing country is in a position to service its external debt. Well-used debt creates more than the capacity needed to service it. The delays in achieving increased output are often compensated for by persistent global inflation eroding either the real value of the debt or the real costs of servicing the debt.

Countries with good economic management have been able to borrow much in excess of any current debt-servicing requirement. Countries with past histories of sluggishness in economic growth and in exports can achieve more rapid increases in exports and debt-servicing capacity and to lay the basis for enhancing their creditworthiness. This is, however, never easy for a developing country nor can it be taken for granted that it will be able to do so.

Countries with governments that demonstrate the ability to manage their societies and economies well will attract new net inflows of capital. They thereby heighten their ability to service past and newly acquired debt even during periods of adverse external developments. The manner in which a number of developing countries maintained their creditworthiness in 1982, despite the dramatic events in Latin America and elsewhere, illustrates this generalization. The alternative for a country cannot be to eliminate or ignore those developments. It has no choice but to adjust to them. Foreign borrowing is not a viable alternative to adjustment. However, the adjustment process will be less burdensome if the country manages its economy so it has access to private capital markets and can increase net capital inflows. Whether this net inflow strengthens its future ability to service the newly acquired debt again depends on its productive use.

Against this background, we turn to examine the experience of developing countries in external debt renegotiations. Considerable attention is devoted to the institutional aspects and the discussions within the United Nations on these aspects. They shed light on the significance and likely outcome of such debt renegotiations and help in considering ways and means to improve our ability to minimize the inevitable risks in international lending.

7

Developing Countries' Debt Renegotiations With Official Creditors

Multilateral debt renegotiations have been initiated and conducted in various ways. Usually the first step has been for the debtor country to acknowledge a state of near emergency and approach its main creditors individually with a request for debt relief and avoidance of declarations of default. Usually the country has suffered a severe deterioration in economic performance and in its external balance-of-payments position, has fallen behind in its international payments, and has a severe weakening of its creditworthiness with external lenders. In some cases, debtor countries approach international organizations for assistance in convening a meeting of creditors or use already existing informal groups of institutions to organize a meeting within a multilateral framework (as opposed to bilateral negotiations). At times, debtor countries obtained help from outside persons or private institutions.

In the past, most creditor governments have responded positively to such initiatives from governments of developing countries and taken appropriate steps to prevent formal defaults. A loan is in default when a creditor declares that the government of the debtor country has failed to comply with some stipulations of the loan agreement. Entities within a country may be in default, but that does not mean the government of that country is also in default.

In general, it had to be evident to creditor governments that the debtor country's needs were real and urgent. Creditors normally have taken the position that they expect a country to meet its contractual obligations and turn to debt relief only as a last resort. However, in some instances, the debt relief was seen as a way of providing external development finance to a developing country.

In those cases where debt relief was considered, one of the main creditors usually called a preliminary meeting of creditors to discuss rearrangement of the debtor's service payments. Such meetings have been usually chaired by high government officials of a main creditor country or by an official of an international agency like the World Bank. The aim has been to have multilateral instead of bilateral arrangements between borrower and individual creditors. From the creditors' point of view, debt renegotiation in a multilateral framework has the advantage that the claims are treated more equitably. There is a more balanced sharing of the "burden" of debt relief among creditors than would be achieved through debt renegotiations on a bilateral basis.

From the debtor countries' point of view, the multilateral framework avoids simultaneous negotiations with a large number of creditors, all eager not to be treated less favorably than others—a very difficult and time-consuming process for dealing with an urgent situation on a bilateral basis. It also has the additional advantage that any corrective economic policy measures recommended by creditors would be based on an international consensus or made through an international agency. These policies, therefore, would be more easily acceptable to the government of the debtor country. Countries in financial difficulties are often especially sensitive to questions involving national pride.

Evolution of Institutional Framework

The institutional framework within which multilateral debt renegotiations take place has gradually evolved since the mid-1950s. Originally, informal groups, or clubs, had been formed within which debt renegotiations were discussed—taking their names from the meeting place. Although it is conventional to speak of creditor clubs—such as the Paris Club—as if they were well-defined institutions, in fact, such clubs existed only during particular debt renegotiations. They had no continuing existence, although they sometimes have an ex officio chairman, who belonged to the government of the country which hosted the club. They also did not have any continuing technical expertise of their own. They relied on assessments made by member governments or ad hoc reports from such groups as the IMF, World Bank, and Organization for Economic Co-operation and Development (OECD). Because of the ad hoc character of discussions within the clubs, publicly available information regarding these groups has remained sparse and rather incomplete.

The Hague Club was established in 1955 to move toward a multilateral system of dealing between European creditors and Brazil. The Paris Club was set up in 1956 to serve a similar purpose for Argentina. In the 1950s, during the period of nonconvertibility of major European currencies, Brazil and Argentina had accumulated large commercial and financial arrears vis-à-vis their major European creditors. These arrears were often the result of bilateral payments agreements between these borrowing countries and the European creditors which, for the most part, had not yet established the convertibility of their national currencies. Accounts were kept of international transactions, and net balances would lead to credits with contractually specified terms for settlement. The primary purpose for the clubs had been to deal with the complications from the diversity of the terms in the bilateral agreements. This particular need ceased to exist as bilateral payments agreements were eliminated when most developed countries established external convertibility. The clubs, nevertheless, continued to provide the most important mechanism for multilateral debt renegotiations. The complications were reduced but the need remained for collaborative, concerted action to achieve a common formula for debt repayment acceptable to a number of creditor governments.

The ad hoc creditors' meeting which convened in the early 1960s to discuss Brazil's debt-servicing difficulties may be considered an informal continuation of the Hague Club. These meetings resulted in the rescheduling of Brazilian debt in 1961 and 1964. The Hague Club has been inactive since.

Since the mid-1950s, the Paris Club has served as the most widely used instrument in multilateral debt renegotiations. The club meets in Paris and is chaired by a senior official of the French Treasury.

The London Club was convened for the first time in 1966 by the government of the United Kingdom to consider the debt-servicing difficulties of Ghana. It continued to serve for subsequent discussions that led to Ghana's multilateral debt arrangement in 1968, 1970, and 1974.

From the mid-1950s to the end of 1980, creditor clubs provided the mechanism for 32 multilateral debt renegotiations with 24 countries. In 1981, eight countries conducted debt renegotiations with government lenders under creditor club auspices. These countries included Liberia, Pakistan, Togo, and Zaire (which had debt reschedulings in earlier years) and first-timers the Central African Republic, Madagascar, Senegal, and Uganda. In 1982, five countries conducted renegotiations, with Malawi seeking a debt rescheduling for the first time (see Table 7.1).

Besides creditor clubs, other mechanisms such as creditor consultative groups and consortia have been used to renegotiate debt. Although these consultative groups and consortia usually have been chaired by senior officials of multinational agencies, the procedures to reach an agreement on a common formula for debt repayments were essentially similar to those instituted by the creditor clubs.*

Six debt renegotiations of India (1968, 1972, 1973, 1974, 1975, and 1976) and three of Pakistan (1972, 1973, and 1974) were conducted through consortia under the chairmanship of the World Bank. In the case of Turkey's debt renegotiations, the consortium was chaired by the Organization for European Economic Cooperation in 1959 and later by its successor, the OECD (1965, 1978, 1979, and 1980). The last three renegotiations were chaired by the head of the French delegation and resembled the Paris Club in the way in which they were conducted.

Special arrangements were made for the debt renegotiations of Peru in 1968 and 1969 and of Gabon in 1978. Although renegotiations of Peru's debt were conducted outside the Paris Club, with meetings in London and Brussels, the procedures were similar to those used by the Paris Club. Gabon presented a special

*Debt relief operations on debt related to official development assistance have been carried out under the auspices of aid consultative groups or consortia. Creditor clubs were formed to deal with debt arising from other official flows, including guaranteed supplier credits.

Table 7.1—Multilateral Debt Renegotiations of Developing Countries with Official Creditors, 1956-82

1956	Argentina	1973	India, Pakistan
1959	Turkey	1974	Chile, Ghana, India, Pakistan
1961	Brazil	1975	Chile, India
1962	Argentina	1976	India, Zaire
1964	Brazil	1977	Zaire (twice), Sierra Leone
1965	Argentina, Chile, Turkey	1978	Gabon, Peru, Turkey
1966	Ghana, Indonesia	1979	Sudan, Togo, Turkey, Zaire
1967	Indonesia	1980	Sierra Leone, Turkey, Liberia*
1968	Ghana, Indonesia, India, Peru	1981**	Pakistan, Togo, Madagascar, Central African Republic, Zaire, Senegal, Uganda, Liberia
1969	Peru		
1970	Ghana, Indonesia		
1972	Chile, India, Kampuchea (twice), Pakistan	1982	Sudan, Madagascar, Malawi, Senegal, Uganda

* Rescheduling sought but not undertaken before the end of 1980.

** Debt renegotiations were sought by Nicaragua but refused by the Paris Club as the country did not enter into a standby arrangement with the IMF.

situation as the 1978 renegotiations were undertaken by representatives of the creditor governments without a representative of the government of Gabon. The procedures to arrive at a common repayment formula, however, were similar to those used by the Paris Club.

Main Characteristics of Creditor Clubs

The main characteristics of multilateral debt renegotiations under creditor club auspices are summarized in the following pages.[7]

First, the type of debt considered in club renegotiations in the past has been official debt owed to creditor governments or commercial debt related to export credit financing guaranteed by official institutions in the creditor countries. It has involved debt exceeding one year in original maturity. Governmental creditor status can be derived from various government-supported export credit financing schemes available to exporters in the creditor nations. Once payments have fallen into arrears for a designated period of time, the private creditor is reimbursed by the export credit guaranteeing body for the insured portion of the debt which is usually most of the credit. The government agency then has the asset for collection or servicing. This leads to direct involvement on the part of creditor governments with the borrowing countries.

Second, the governments of the major creditor countries and the government of the debtor country, whose external debt is being renegotiated, are represented at

[7]Among sources of information for this chapter are the following United Nations Conference on Trade and Development, Trade and Development Board documents: *Present Institutional Arrangements for Debt Renegotiations*, TD/B/C.3/AC.8/13, Feb. 26, 1975; *Elaboration of Detailed Features to Give Guidance to Future Operations Relating to Debt*, TD/B/AC.28/2, Oct. 3, 1978; *Report of the Intergovernmental Group of Experts on Debt and Development Problems of Developing Countries*, TD/B/AC.28/3, Oct. 16, 1978.

the club meetings. The creditors seek a common formula regarding repayment terms. Since a number of the major creditor countries find themselves repeatedly involved in these separate clubs, the mechanism has achieved a similarity in approaches to various debtor countries.

Third, a case-by-case approach to multilateral debt renegotiations has been used, because the composition and number of major creditors represented usually varies in each case. The number of creditor countries involved has varied from 5 to 15 or more. Some creditor countries attend club meetings as observers rather than participants. Representatives of the IMF, the World Bank, OECD, and the United Nations Conference on Trade and Development (UNCTAD), as well as the relevant regional development banks, attend with observer status. Fortunately or unfortunately, these debt meetings often have been made literally grand occasions in international finance with widespread publicity.

Fourth, the case-by-case approach has the advantage of more negotiating flexibility as the seriousness of the debt situation and economic conditions differ widely from country to country.

Fifth, creditor club meetings have been inclined to segregate debt relief negotiations from the question of extending official development assistance to a debtor country. Debt relief is intended to improve the debtor country's balance-of-payments position in the short term, while development assistance has longer-term purposes. Some debt renegotiations by consortia under the auspices of the World Bank, however, have combined short- and long-term objectives of debt relief.

Sixth, in several instances, debt renegotiations under the auspices of the Paris Club were conducted within the setting of an economic stabilization program initiated by the IMF. Debt relief thus became dependent upon a successful implementation of the recommended stabilization program.[8]

Seventh, the creditor clubs continued to operate in a rather informal framework. No formal organization, based on internationally agreed criteria, has yet been established. Efforts to bring about a more formally organized approach by acknowledging and adopting certain basic concepts of multilateral debt renegotiation have been under way for some years and are discussed later in this chapter.

Procedures of Multilateral Debt Renegotiations

The procedures followed at creditor club meetings are essentially those described in the following pages.

At the first session, the creditors discuss their various attitudes to the requested relief and reach an outline of a common position. Once they have adopted a broad outline of their common position, the representative of the debtor country makes a detailed presentation of the country's condition and the extent of debt relief

[8]Irving S. Friedman, "The Role of Private Banks in Stabilization Programs," in *Economic Stabilization in Developing Countries* (Washington, D.C.: The Brooking Institution, 1981).

requested. The IMF representative usually explains the Fund's interpretation of the current situation and its views regarding the economic program needed by the debtor country. On occasion, a representative of the World Bank has been requested to present its views on the current economic problems and prospects of the debtor country.

After a session in which the debtor country's representatives respond to questions raised by the creditors, the creditors again meet to agree on a common set of proposals regarding the terms of the debt rearrangements. These proposals are then presented to the debtor country.

A final session is held in which the creditors and the debtor draw up an agreement containing the terms of debt relief to be recommended by the creditor representatives to their governments. Statements on economic policy measures which are to be implemented by the debtor country government are also included.

The terms of the agreement are put into the form of "Agreed Minutes." These minutes become the guidelines for the actual debt relief and spell out such details of the relief program as type of debt to be included, percentage of debt service to be relieved, consolidation period, and repayment terms. Recommendations on interest rates are included, but the interest rates are not specified in the Agreed Minutes.

The creditor nations almost always insist on the debtor country reaching a standby arrangement with the IMF. The adoption of new economic policy measures by debtor countries has been considered an integral part of a debt restructuring, although such obligations of the debtor are not spelled out in detail. In cases where standby arrangements have been agreed on or already signed by the debtor country, references to such standby arrangements are generally included in the Agreed Minutes.

The Agreed Minutes usually include a most-favored-nation clause. That is, the debtor agrees that in negotiations with nonclub creditors, the debtor's country will not agree to terms more favorable to any creditor than those accorded to creditors in the club meetings.

In the Agreed Minutes, the debt rearrangement is explicitly recognized as final. In some cases, a good will clause is added whereby the creditors indicate their willingness to review the debtor country's representation for debt relief at another time. The good will clause has often been very specific, referring to the credits which would be examined in any future meetings. Such a clause in multilateral debt rearrangements reflects the short-term nature of the relief usually accorded in club agreements. It also reflects the difficulties and uncertainties in evaluating the prospects of the debtor country's economy and in the perceived adequacy and feasibility of the measures agreed on. It is assumed that the short-term nature of the agreements will prompt debtor countries to pursue appropriate stabilization policies quickly in order to generate more foreign exchange earnings and improve servicing their modified debt obligations.

Bilateral Negotiations to Implement Agreements

These multilateral agreements provide the framework for debt relief. By themselves, they do not restructure old loan contracts or provide for new ones. The Agreed Minutes are expected to specify the terms of debt relief in sufficient detail to make possible their implementation on a bilateral basis. A more general formula of debt relief can be adopted when there are substantial differences in the legal requirements or institutional frameworks of the creditor countries. In such cases, specific terms are decided through bilateral agreements.

Agreements reached at creditor club meetings are followed by bilateral negotiations between the borrower government and the individual creditor governments. Debt relief is actually granted to the debtor country through a series of bilateral negotiations between the debtor and the individual creditor governments. These bilateral agreements specify the credits which are covered by the renegotiations and the terms of the renegotiated credits. These actions, in effect, postpone amortization payments and are frequently referred to as a moratorium.

Usually the moratorium interest rate is not specified in the Agreed Minutes but is expected to be settled in the subsequent bilateral agreements. For government credits, low concessional interest rates are generally continued. The multilateral agreements, however, may contain the provision that the moratorium rate of interest on officially guaranteed export credits will be derived by considering the appropriate domestic market interest rates at the time of the bilateral negotiations.

This provision reflects the view of creditors that relief of payments on officially guaranteed export credits is an ad hoc emergency measure and not a source of concessional assistance. Interest payments are normally due during the grace period which applies to the deferred payments of principal. It has been a cardinal lending principle that interest payments should be honored as originally agreed and rescheduling be confined to principal. This has not always been possible.

Various Forms of Debt Relief

Multilateral debt renegotiations result in various forms of debt relief granted by creditors to debtor countries. Debt relief essentially takes three forms:

1. Cancellation of debt payments.
2. Rescheduling debt.
3. Refinancing debt.

Cancellation of principal repayments, of interest payments, or of both can occur. This has rarely happened, although pure debt relief—forgiving interest payments on the original debt—has been granted to developing countries by official lenders. This is a form of official concessional aid or assistance.

Debt rescheduling has been the most widely used form of debt relief in the multilateral renegotiations of the 1960s and 1970s. Rescheduling involves rearrangements of maturities (amortization) so that repayments can be made according to a new deferred schedule, usually to begin after a grace period. New deferred amortization results in postponing foreign exchange transfers.

In the creditor country, the original lender is usually repaid on schedule under the normal export insurance arrangements, while the export credit insurance agency continues to hold the final claim on the debtor. On the debtor side, an official agency (usually the central bank) assumes responsibility for repaying the debt according to the new deferred schedule. Individual private debtors (including, at times, public enterprises) usually pay the full amount of their obligations on schedule to the official agency, which in turn transfers to the creditor country the nonrescheduled portion of debt according to the original contractual terms. The rescheduled portion is then to be paid according to the new schedule. As far as direct government debts are concerned, the local currency counterpart of the debt service is usually not transferred to the central bank in advance of the foreign exchange transfer. To this extent, debt relief also brings about a budgetary relief for the debtor country.

Refinancing, as distinct from rescheduling, normally implies that debt repayments are made under the terms of the original schedules by the debtor country. At the same time, however, the creditor country's government (or its export insurance agency) is extending new credits (to the country's government or central bank) equal to all or part of the amount consolidated by the debt rearrangement. The actual transfer of foreign exchange to the creditor country is expected to take place on schedule, either from the debtor's own resources, with a subsequent refund from the creditor, or by direct drawings on the refinancing loan. Often, the latter form of refinancing is preferred. The refinancing loans are to be repaid in accordance with the terms established during the debt renegotiation meetings and taken down in the form of the Agreed Minutes.

In some cases of debt renegotiations, the two forms of debt relief were combined, particularly when the final form of debt relief was left to creditors and debtors to decide on in the bilateral negotiations implementing the multilateral agreements. The choice of a particular form of debt relief is usually determined by the existing institutional arrangements in the debtor country and the creditor countries.

Extent of Debt Relief

Changing the specific terms of the contract under renegotiation determines the extent of debt relief granted in each individual case. The specific terms relate to the type of debt to be rescheduled or refinanced; the length of the consolidation period, the grace period and the repayment period; the proportion of principal and interest covered; and the rate of interest to be applied to the deferred amounts or to the refinancing loans.

As noted above, most renegotiations of official debt cover only credits granted or insured by the governments or by official export credit guarantee institutions in the creditor countries, although in some cases other types of loans have also been included. The consolidated credits are usually limited to those owed to creditors in countries participating in the multilateral renegotiations and falling due within a specified maturity range. The treatment accorded to similar debt owed to nonparticipating countries is usually limited by the nondiscrimination clauses included in the Agreed Minutes.

The proportion of eligible maturities rearranged usually varies with the nature of the debts and the amounts of debt service payments involved. In most cases of debt renegotiations, at least one-half or more of the country's total outstanding external debt has been covered by the consolidation proceedings.

The consolidation period is the time during which the original maturities of the debt covered by the renegotiation fall due for payment and are made subject to the rearrangement. Consolidation periods have generally extended over two to three years. A major exception was the 1970 settlement with Indonesia when the entire outstanding external debt was rescheduled over a 30-year period.

Short consolidation periods usually reflect the intention of the creditors to reexamine the debt service situation in the near future to review performance and need if the debt repayment profile projects high levels of debt service over several years. A short consolidation period means that debt service continues to exert unwelcomed pressures on the balance of payments of the debtor country. It prolongs the period during which the creditworthiness of the debtor country is questionable.

In such cases, of course, the benefit of the consolidation for the debtor country is reduced. The attitude of creditor governments is greatly influenced by their evaluation of the country, their desire to be helpful, and the precedent set for other debtors. In earlier years, creditors often emphasized the need for a "short leash" approach to reflect their general dissatisfaction with the use of the restructuring mechanism or, perhaps, more profoundly, with the borrower government's policies which resulted in the payments difficulties. The short leash keeps up the pressure on debtor governments to change their policies in a direction or manner approved by creditor governments.

Grace and repayment periods thus can be made to vary in length to achieve the desired aims of debt relief. The repayment schedule for rearranged maturities can stipulate smaller repayments in earlier years and a gradual increase in the amounts over the remaining repayment period.

In many cases, interest payments under the original contracts have been consolidated to be repaid simultaneously with the deferred principal. In some cases, they were excluded from the rearrangement. In nearly all cases, interest has been charged on deferred amounts during the grace period. As stated previously, recommendations regarding interest payments usually are included in the Agreed Minutes adopted by the negotiating parties. Recommendations that interest rates should be close to current market rates in creditor countries reflect the creditors' view that the rearrangements should be regarded as conventional refinancing operations. Interest rates in negotiations in the 1970s and early 1980s reflected the trends in rising international interest rates over the past decade.

Sharing the Burden

A difficult issue to be settled at the debt renegotiation table is a burden-sharing formula acceptable to all participating creditors. In most cases, creditors have agreed to share the burden of the consolidation on a proportional basis, that is, the same proportion of debt service due to each creditor would be rearranged. It has been suggested that creditors extending loans on relatively harder terms (shorter maturities and higher interest rates) should consolidate a relatively higher proportion.* Proportionate burden-sharing, however, has proved to be the simplest and quickest way of reaching an agreement.

Benefit to Debtor and Burden to Creditor

Debt relief results in a net benefit to the debtor on the one side, and possibly financial costs and a burden to the creditor, on the other. The net benefit of debt relief to a debtor country can be assessed by calculating its grant element. The net benefit (or grant element) equals the difference between the present value (in the base year) of the repayments stream before the debt rescheduling and the present value of the total repayments stream over the "consolidation period" following the rescheduling. This is expressed as a percentage of the present value of the repayments stream before the rescheduling.[9]

The formula can be expressed as follows:

$$\text{Net Benefit (grant element)} = \frac{\begin{array}{c}\text{(Present value of repayments before rescheduling)} \text{ minus } \text{(Present value of repayments during consolidation)}\end{array}}{\text{(Present value of repayments before rescheduling)}} \times 100$$

Present value calculations in past reschedulings were commonly based on a 10% discount rate, adopting the convention of the OECD's Development Assistance Committee. The grant element may differ substantially from case to case in debt agreements.

The financial costs of debt relief to the creditors depend on the amount and original terms of the rescheduled debt. As noted, a 10% discount rate was usually used to calculate the present value in the base year, but the moratorium interest (or rate of interest charged on the rescheduled amounts) can differ from case to case and vary with the level of market interest rates. However, financial costs are not

*On a proportional basis, countries lending on harder terms automatically receive a proportionately larger amount of future service payments. A 7% interest payment on $1 million is $70,000; a 2% payment on the same amount is $20,000. If one half is paid by the agreed common formula, the debtor pays $35,000 to the 7% lender and $10,000 to the 2% lender.

[9]Thomas M. Klein, "Economic Aid Through Debt Relief," *Finance and Development*, 10, No. 3 (Sept. 1973), p. 18; World Bank, *Possible Improvements in Techniques of Lending* (Washington, D.C.: World Bank Staff Study, 1970); Goran Ohlin, *Aid and Indebtedness* (Paris, France: OECD 1966); John A. Pincus, "The Cost of Foreign Aid," *Review of Economics and Statistics*, 45, No. 4 (Nov. 1963).

only a function of the moratorium interest rate but also of the maturity of the rescheduled amounts. Since the debt relief granted by the Paris Club from the payments due on officially guaranteed export credits predominantly carried moratorium interest rates equal to current market rates and short amortization and grace periods, the additional financial costs were minimal, even though in a few cases the amount of the debts was fairly large.

Differences in the relative burden on creditors can result from the following pre-conditions:

- The burden is heavier with a higher portion of rescheduled amounts in relation to the creditor's total loans outstanding.
- For the same amount of repayments due, the burden is heavier if the original terms were harder than the new terms, it is lighter if the original terms were relatively concessionary.

For the same amount of repayments due, the burden tends to be heavier if the creditor is in a weak bargaining position, and it is lighter if the creditor is in a strong bargaining position. These are all "financial" costs and do not include the costs of administration, personnel, and management, which can be substantial for all involved. Furthermore, the actual amount of debt relief provided can differ from that anticipated at the time of the rescheduling because of movements in the exchange rates of the creditors.

Case-by-Case versus Uniform Approach to Debt Renegotiations

The creditor countries believe that a case-by-case approach to multilateral debt renegotiations offers a larger degree of negotiating flexibility. This is because of the wide disparities in social and economic conditions, as well as institutions, in individual countries seeking debt relief. Solutions to debt servicing problems and relief measures are considered most effective if adapted to each debtor country's specific conditions.

The developing countries, through the Group of 77* (or the Group of 19 representing the Group of 77), over the past decade have repeatedly affirmed the position that multilateral renegotiations of debt should take place within an internationally accepted policy framework. They also argue that negotiations should follow agreed guidelines and procedures. Such guidelines, based on certain norms or features common to all debt renegotiations, are recommended to ensure comparable treatment to all debtor countries seeking debt relief. This uniform approach is said to provide protection to creditors as well. The Group of 77 has argued that the rights and obligations of all participants in such negotiations

*The "Group of 77" developing countries came into being in 1964 when 76 developing countries, along with New Zealand, signed a joint declaration at the conclusion of the first session of UNCTAD in June 1964. Although at present there are 125 developing country members of the United Nations, the group has retained its original name. The "Group of 19" consisted of 19 developing countries that participated in the Paris Conference on International Economic Cooperation from 1975 to 1977.

should be clearly spelled out. However, no formal international agreement has yet been reached on this issue.

Even so, certain institutional traditions have evolved over the years under which debt renegotiations have been conducted. The formation of creditor clubs, creditor consultative groups, and consortia to conduct debt renegotiations are major steps in achieving a more uniform approach. Since the late 1960s and early 1970s, increasing attention has been paid to viewing external debt renegotiations in the context of international cooperation. This is particularly true in connection with new initiatives by international agencies to accelerate development in Third World countries.

The developing countries have continued to pursue the issue of formulating meaningful and operationally relevant guidelines—and making appropriate institutional arrangements—for future debt renegotiations.[10] This has been done primarily under the auspices of UNCTAD's Trade and Development Board, as well as in consultation with various intergovernmental groups of experts. An ad hoc group of governmental experts, meeting in 1974 and 1975, was the first major intergovernmental attempt to derive common elements from past experience in debt rearrangements. They reviewed suggestions for the establishment of a continuing mechanism to deal with debt relief problems. The reason for convening this group of experts was the threefold increase in the less developed countries' public debt between 1965 and 1973.

Not New Concerns

An often-forgotten fact is that the external debt of developing countries is not a new concern. Those eager to maximize the net inflow of funds into developing countries have repeatedly stressed that larger magnitudes of debt servicing meant less net inflow of foreign funds. The UNCTAD emphasis was more on the developmental impact on developing countries than any dangers to lenders. Thus, advocates of concessional aid, either bilateral or through such institutions as the World Bank's concessional arm—the IDA—repeatedly stressed the debt-servicing burden throughout the 1950s, 1960s, and 1970s. No one had worried seriously

[10]The system of multilateral debt renegotiations has been studied by various intergovernmental groups of experts under the auspices of UNCTAD. An Ad Hoc Group of Governmental Experts on the Debt Problems of Developing Countries was formed in 1973 to "consider the debt problems of developing countries and the various possible international policy measures to be taken." The group assembled for three sessions (May 1974, December 1974, and February/March 1975) and submitted its report to the UNCTAD Trade and Development Board on March 7, 1975. This report was published as *Debt Problems of Developing Countries* TD/B/545 Rev.1. (New York: United Nations, 1975). The Intergovernmental Group of Experts on the External Indebtedness of Developing Countries convened two sessions (July 1977 and December 1977). The reports are contained in UNCTAD documents: TD/B/685, TD/AC.2/9, and TD/AC.2/10 plus addenda 1-3. The Intergovernmental Group of Experts on Debt and Development Problems of Developing Countries convened a meeting in 1978 to recommend to the UNCTAD Trade and Development Board detailed features for future operations relating to debt problems of interested developing countries. This report was released by the UNCTAD Trade and Development Board Oct. 3, 1978 as "*Elaboration of Detailed Features for Future Operations Relating to Debt Problems of Interested Developing Countries*," TD/B/AC.28/2. (New York: United Nations, 1978)

about the ability of developed countries to provide more development assistance if they wished to do so or thought it wise. Besides, in no country was foreign aid more than a very small fraction of the budget. Like any budget item, foreign aid can loom large if seen in isolation. History gives repeated examples of how creditor countries can greatly increase aid with a minor budgetary impact if it fits their national objectives.

Borrower concern has shifted in recent years to the ability of private banks to extend very large credits. Banks, in turn, are worried about the inability or unwillingness of their debtors to service debt promptly and fully. On the debtor side, the concern focuses on the ability and willingness of creditor governments to provide debt relief. Had an escalation of private lending not occurred, the debt renegotiation experience probably would not have received the close attention it now receives in creditor countries, nor would the prospect of debt renegotiation be raised to the status of high drama on the world stage. A play about what creditor governments will do for debtor governments is barely of world interest. But a play which raises the possibility of countries not paying their huge debts to foreign private banks is indeed high drama.

Agreement on "uniform" treatment of external debt is likely to evade the international community until private debt is distinctly separated from official creditor debt and agreements on public debt are not regarded as a model for private debt. Nevertheless, efforts by developing countries to achieve uniform rules for public debt renegotiation are noteworthy. They represent a possible area of cooperation between the developed and less developed countries which is much easier to accomplish because it is less costly to the creditor nations and less ideologically objectionable for the debtors.

Experts' Report

The report of the ad hoc group of governmental experts was released in 1975. At that time, the growing concern about the external indebtedness of developing countries coincided with the increase in the external deficits of many developing countries resulting from the oil price increase, the worldwide recession, and accelerating global inflation. Subsequently, at the fourth session of UNCTAD at Nairobi (May 5-31, 1976), Resolution 94 (IV) was adopted to invite an appropriate existing international forum to discuss the formulation of guidelines for future debt relief operations. The Paris Conference on International Economic Cooperation (CIEC) was chosen for this purpose and in 1976-77 various proposals regarding such guidelines were submitted on behalf of the developing countries, the European Economic Community, and the U.S. However, agreement could not be reached on these proposals.

Discussions continued at two sessions in 1977 of the Intergovernmental Group of Experts which met to prepare reports on the debt issue for UNCTAD's Trade and Development Board, after considering submissions from the developing and developed countries. Intensive negotiating efforts at the ministerial session of the

Trade and Development Board led to an agreement—Trade and Development Board Resolution 165(S-IX) of March 11, 1978—identifying four basic concepts common to the various proposals.[11]

These four basic concepts include:

1. International consideration of the debt problem of a developing country would be initiated only at the specific request of the debtor country concerned.

2. Such considerations would occur in an appropriate multilateral framework consisting of the interested parties. They would receive the assistance of the relevant international institutions to ensure timely action taking into account the nature of the problems. The problems may vary from acute balance-of-payments difficulties requiring immediate action, to longer-term situations relating to structural, financial, and transfer-of-resources requiring appropriate longer-term measures.

3. International action, once agreed by the interested parties, would take due account of the country's economic and financial situation and performance, its development prospects and capabilities, and external factors. Internationally agreed objectives for the development of developing countries would be considered.

4. Debt reorganization would protect the interests of both debtors and creditors equitably in the context of international economic cooperation.

Each of these concepts, described in Resolution 165(S-IX), needed to be expanded and elaborated on, in order to provide operationally meaningful guidance for future debt operations. As expected, many issues and questions have been raised in connection with the proposed formulation and implementation of detailed guidelines.

UNCTAD's Proposed Formulation and Implementation of Guidelines

The Trade and Development Board at its 21st session (Sept. 15-27, 1980) adopted Resolution 222 (XXI)[12] and endorsed a set of "agreed detailed features . . . which elaborate the basic concepts contained in . . . Resolution 165 (S-IX)." In this context, it was stated that ". . . finding a means through which debt servicing difficulties can be avoided was one of the most important tasks facing the international community. The avoidance of debt servicing difficulties under conditions that are consistent with an orderly development process in developing countries is in the interest of both the creditor and debtor countries." However, at the same time, it recognized that problems can arise, and it was important to have agreed on arrangements for timely action.

[11] *Report of the Trade and Development Board on the Third (Ministerial) Part of its Ninth Special Session*, Vol I, Part 2 (Geneva, Switzerland: UNCTAD, March 6-11, 1978) Annex I, p. 43.

[12] *Report of the Trade and Development Board*, Volume 2, 21st Session, (Geneva, Switzerland: UNCTAD, Sept. 15-27, 1980) A/35/15, Annex I, p. 8-13, Oct. 31, 1980.

International action, it was noted, may vary depending on the specific problems of the debtor country but "should be expeditious and timely; should enhance the development prospects of the debtor country, bearing in mind its socioeconomic priorities and internationally agreed objectives for the development of developing countries; should aim at restoring the debtor country's capacity to service its debt over both the short and long run, and should reinforce the developing country's own efforts to strengthen its underlying balance of payments situation; should protect the interests of debtors and creditors equitably in the context of international economic cooperation."

Resolution 222 (XXI) also dealt in more detail with the operational framework within which multilateral debt renegotiations should take place. International consideration of a developing country's debt problem would be only at the specific request of the debtor country concerned. That country could request consideration at an early stage when, in its judgment, the indebtedness problem existed or was likely to emerge.

Of interest for external debt analysis and country risk analysis are Trade and Development Board recommendations on what should be considered in determining appropriate international action. First, it recommended examination of the domestic economic situation of the country, including an analysis of its use of both domestic and external resources for safeguarding its development process. Second, the impact of external factors on the developmental and financial problems of the debtor country should be scrutinized. Third, estimates of short- and long-term developmental capital requirements and projected availabilities should be made. Fourth, the analysis should include projections of debt-servicing requirements and review the measures adopted by the country concerned to avoid debt-servicing difficulties. Finally, the structure and prospects of all items of the balance of payments, exchange rate, and monetary policies should be given particular consideration. In addition, the recommendation was made that in long-run problems, the analysis should give special attention to financing long-term investment and associated resource transfers.

Thus, the external debt analysis would reflect the complexities of a country's situation and outlook, with a strong flavor of concern with balance-of-payments behavior, but still not simplistic in how this should be approached. For acute balance-of-payments difficulties in which debt-servicing payments play a major role and which require immediate action, the debtor country would undertake an economic program designed to strengthen its underlying external payments situation, but maintaining focus on its development prospects. This program would include, where necessary, the reorganization of debts owed to or guaranteed by creditor governments. In the case of longer-run problems, the debtor country concerned should undertake viable domestic policies. These actions should be supported by donor countries and appropriate international institutions which would endeavor to increase the quantity of aid in appropriate forms and improve its quality.

Again, in more detail but still in rather general language, these resolutions reflected actual practice. Critical issues not yet resolved by practice remained to be resolved. For example, which multilateral agency (UNCTAD or IMF) should judge country conditions and adequacy of policies; the implications of official arrangements for private creditors; the treatment of official credits as part of development assistance; the treatment of credits or equivalent extended by multilateral agencies like the World Bank, European Investment Bank, the IMF, the Inter-American Development Bank, etc.; the short-leash vs. long-leash approach; the implications of renegotiations for new money from public and private sources; the existence, if any, of lenders of last resort; the importance of political relationships in decisions of individual creditors; reactions to debt renegotiations by bank supervisors and regulators, and so forth.

Such issues have to be confronted and resolved by the international agencies if marked changes are to be made by international agreement instead of international evolution resulting from experience with actual cases. There is much to be said for experience as long as there is continuing awareness of the broader context in which these issues are evolving and being resolved separately.

Issues on Improving Institutional Arrangements

Thus, attempts have been made to change the institutional arrangements for multilateral debt renegotiations and to improve the existing mechanism. As discussed previously, debt renegotiations have occurred under the auspices of either creditor clubs or consultative groups and aid consortia, including the World Bank, with the main donors or creditors being members of these groups. Thus, the framework for renegotiations comes from a creditors-to-debtors relationship. It is conceivable, as some developing countries have argued, that debt renegotiations within a multilateral framework and established by the international financial community might benefit from participation wider than the particular creditors and debtors concerned. An independent multilateral forum, consisting not only of creditors but others agreed on by both creditors and debtors, could be established. For example, an independent debt commission could be established by the General Assembly of the United Nations. It would be assisted in its work by relevant international institutions.

A related issue arises when a debtor country decides to avail itself of the expertise of appropriate international institutions to provide an objective and comprehensive analysis of its economic conditions. Traditionally, the World Bank and the IMF have assisted debtor countries in that analysis and in evaluating the debtor country's economic objectives and development prospects. More recently, the World Bank, the IMF, and UNCTAD were invited to propose, in consultation with each other, procedures for responding to requests from debtor countries for country economic evaluations. Other appropriate institutions with relevant developmental interests could also be invited to assist in country evaluations. However, such country evaluations would be submitted to the multilateral forum only at the request of the debtor country concerned.

In evolving appropriate institutional arrangements, three general principles were widely supported at the UNCTAD deliberations:[13]

1. The operational mechanism must have the confidence of both debtors and creditors.

2. Debt renegotiations should be guided by development considerations and support the debtor country's own efforts to pursue its economic recovery program, as well as providing a restructuring that satisfies the demands of the creditors.

3. The expertise of the international institutions involved in debt renegotiations should have the respect of all parties and should ensure timely and appropriate action to grant debt relief. (By invitation of the chairman of the Paris Club, the secretary general of UNCTAD would participate in the meetings of the Paris Club on the same basis and terms as the representatives of other participating international organizations.)

In addition, the recommendations and actions by the appropriate international institutions, including the multilateral and regional development banks, the IMF, and UNCTAD, should be largely consistent with the broader development objectives of the United Nations.

Thus, the international approaches to the external debt issues reflect the debate in recent years concerning Third World criticism of the IMF and Third World alternative support of UNCTAD or the formation of new international bodies. The developing countries have frequently emphasized the importance of considering simultaneously two different types of economic problems and of integrating two different objectives in multilateral debt renegotiations: overcoming short-term liquidity crises and fostering long-term structural change to accomplish developmental objectives.

In the past, debt renegotiations have been directed toward countries facing severe short-term liquidity problems. Creditors considered it satisfactory to respond to the external financial problems of the developing country by trying to assist the country in stabilizing its economy and in encouraging and supporting policies to alleviate the liquidity crisis. Such policies were designed by the countries with the help of the multilateral institutions. Creditors expected the debtor country to pursue policies appropriate to restore a substantial balance-of-payments equilibrium and the ability to service its external debt. No clear distinction was made between stabilization policies and the attainment of medium- or longer-term development objectives. The implicit assumption was made that the country could—or would—regain its long-term economic growth once its short-term balance-of-payments equilibrium had been restored. This philosophy had long been prevalent in institutions like the IMF.

The structural adjustment problems confronting the world economy and individual nations in the 1970s changed the perspectives of debt renegotiations, particularly from the viewpoint of developing countries. It became more widely

[13] Trade and Development Board, *Resolution 222 (XXI)*, (New York: UNCTAD, September 27, 1980).

recognized that debt servicing problems might well result from long-run structural imbalances. Therefore, the appropriate adjustment measures sought by debtors and endorsed by creditors might well be very different from those taken to overcome short-term liquidity crises. Again, the consideration of the external debt problems merged with the general debate in developing countries on the causes of their need for external finance and how such needs could be met. The outcome of this debate will greatly affect the content of country risk analysis and the views held by banks on economic management of borrowing countries. As lending is mostly done by private banks, such issues will become increasingly important in their considerations. Bankers will have to play a much more vigorous and initiatory role in these debates.

Objectives of Multilateral Debt Relief: Short Term and Long Term

In summary, the debate whether debt relief should be considered short-term or long-term assistance to a developing country has continued throughout the 1970s, and different viewpoints have been presented by developed and developing countries.[14] The developing countries, and others in developed countries, have argued that the usual first objective of debt renegotiations—the debtor country adopts short-term measures in the context of adjustment process primarily directed toward stabilization—has to be consistent with the second objective—the adoption and implementation of policies aimed at the country's longer-term development.

Development Objectives

To achieve this aim, development objectives need to be integrated in the adjustment process from the start. This view was embodied in study and proposals made to UNCTAD by the World Bank in the 1960s to deal with problems created for developing countries by unexpected declines in export earnings.* It was increasingly reflected in the application of conditionality of the IMF, as well as creation of special IMF financial facilities like the Compensatory Financing Facility. The integration of debt relief and development objectives was attempted in more recent years to the external problems of countries like Peru and Zaire. This approach to external debt renegotiations means development objectives should be given an operational significance in designing a policy package to assist the country in overcoming its problems. Such views have been well received when considered in the context of balance-of-payments support or development finance. They affect, but are not yet integrated, into debt renegotiations. The creditor countries still act on the premise that much of what is referred to as debt problems are essentially liquidity problems.

[14] Thomas M. Klein, "Economic Aid Through Debt Relief," *Finance and Development*, 10, No. 3, (Sept. 1973), pp.17-20.

*The author directed the study at the World Bank.

Economic and financial management in a developing country combines—not separates—domestic and international, monetary and developmental considerations. This is true conceptually and it is in practice everywhere among developing countries. It is useful to separate liquidity problems for analytical purposes, but debt problems require that the liquidity conditions and analysis be put back into their broader context. If this is not done there is great risk of the country's becoming a chronic repeater in debt renegotiations.

Type of Debt

Another important factor in multilateral debt renegotiations is the type of external debt incurred by the developing country. It can be either from official or private sources, and it is increasingly a combination of both.

For countries that depend primarily on official transfers to finance their external capital requirements, solutions to their external debt problems may include increased aid transfers in appropriate forms and rescheduling of their debt to official creditors. It may also involve balance-of-payments support by multilateral agencies and similar measures combined with domestic policy measures that are required by the assisting institutions. For countries with debt to official and private creditors, policy measures may also include rescheduling of debt owed to private creditors, and assurance that the domestic policies being adopted and implemented improve (or restore) the country's access to private capital markets.

It is tempting to advocate combining debt renegotiation with governmental and private creditors, since the debtor country is the same. There are those who would combine these governmental and private negotiations or come to the same end by insisting on common outcomes. Private banks can be aware of longer-term developmental considerations, but they must act in ways compatible with their profit-seeking private character. In a debt renegotiation, combining politically motivated debt granted by governments with economically motivated debt extended by private lenders is to mix oil and water. What is appropriate for a private lender in a particular debt renegotiation situation may be very different from official creditors who are guided by governmental considerations. To bring them together is to create the presumption that similar terms should be applied by official and private creditors. If done, it would run the danger of politicizing private lending or cause governments to lose the flexibility they need for their own governmental purposes, for example, to extend more concessional help to a debtor country.

Lending Terms

Thinking on the external debt question has, as noted earlier, been greatly influenced by thinking on development finance for developing countries. The terms of lending to developing countries have been widely and frequently debated throughout the past two decades.[15] This debate has been accompanied by a rich

[15] The author is indebted to the late Jo W. Sax of the World Bank's Development Policy Staff for making available his research and paper, "Concessionary Lending to Developing Countries" (Washington, D.C.: World Bank, September 19, 1980).

and changing variety of government practices, reflecting the differing attitudes of governments on this issue at any one time. The U.S., the largest single foreign assistance lender, fresh from the experience of the Marshall Plan in the late 1940s and early 1950s, strongly supported grant and other concessional assistance in the 1950s; by the 1960s, its support was lukewarm; by the 1970s, it was nearly hostile except on a highly selective basis for the "poorest of the poor."

As a result of the debate and governments' practices, it is widely believed that official development assistance to the poorest countries of the Third World (identified by the United Nations after the oil price increases in the mid-1970s as most seriously affected countries, least-developed, developing landlocked, and developing island countries) should be essentially in the form of grants.* Consequently, a number of the major creditor nations have adjusted the terms of their past development lending to the poorest countries. A number of creditors have decided to cancel all or part of their past official development assistance loan repayment requirements to some or all of the poorest debtor countries in favor of grants.

The Development Assistance Committee (DAC) of OECD was formed as a standing committee in 1961. It united the major industrial nations in a "common aid effort" to determine amounts and terms involved in official development assistance to developing countries. The discussion in the DAC on external debt has revolved around the debtor country's ability to service its debt, the equity of distributing the burden among creditors, and a multilateral approach to debt relief for individual debtor countries.

Thus, in donor or creditor institutions like DAC or in institutions most influenced by debtor countries like UNCTAD, the content and conduct of debt renegotiations have been major preoccupations. In the meantime, situations arise which require concerted action for governments and, more recently, of private lending to handle these matters in a manner acceptable to the parties involved. The driving force is the need of the developing country to reestablish its ability to obtain net inflows of capital; it cannot afford defaults. Within this context, creditors have reconciled their desires for full and prompt servicing of debt with the borrowers' desires for more extended maturities and lowest possible interest rates.

*The Development Assistance Committee of the OECD Recommendation adopted on February 28, 1978, states that "the average grant element" of all commitments from a given donor should either be at least 86% to each least developed country over a period of three years or at least 90% annually for the least developed countries as a group.

8

Developing Countries' Debt Renegotiations With Private Creditors

As of the end of 1981, private commercial banks had entered into, and concluded, multilateral debt renegotiations with six developing countries—Peru, Zaire, Jamaica, Turkey, Nicaragua, and Sudan. At some stage of their debt renegotiations with private commercial banks, five of them had implemented stabilization programs supported by the IMF. Four countries—Peru, Zaire, Turkey, and Sudan—obtained multilateral debt reschedulings with their official creditors. Jamaica and Nicaragua involved private creditors only. In 1981, debt renegotiations with official creditors were sought by Nicaragua, but refused by the Paris Club as the country did not enter into a standby arrangement with the IMF.

Private Creditor Involvement

In addition, in 1980-81, debt renegotiations were also conducted between private commercial bank creditors and Bolivia, as well as Costa Rica. A tentative, conditional agreement was reached with Bolivia in April 1981 (see Table 8.1). Furthermore, negotiations began in 1981 and continued in 1981-82 regarding modifications in bank debt maturities with Liberia, Madagascar, Senegal, and Togo. These four countries approached their private bank creditors after they had completed renegotiations with official creditors under Paris Club auspices.

The pattern has evolved that following a debt rescheduling with official creditors, a country may well approach private creditors for some lengthening of maturities. There does not exist, however, such a requirement under the Paris Club agreements and the development has not been especially encouraged by the private banks.

Although the history of borrowing and conditions vary greatly from country to country, certain generalizations can be made about bank lending to these countries, their general economic and debt management, and the debt restructuring process as such. As noted previously, bank lending to developing countries as a whole grew rapidly throughout the 1970s, particularly to the oil import-dependent countries after 1974. It also grew more rapidly than lending from public entities. The pattern of bank lending was fairly similar for those countries which had to approach their private creditors for a debt restructuring during this period.

Table 8.1—Debt Renegotiations with Private Commercial Bank Creditors, 1976-1981

Country	Bank Creditors Approached	Relevant Dates of Debt Renegotiations: Tentative Agreement Reached	Final Talks Started	Definitive Agreement Reached
Peru	Early 1976	July 1976	May 1978	Dec. 1978
Zaire	Mid-1976	Nov. 1976	June 1979	April 1980
Jamaica	Mid-1977	—	May 1978	Sept. 1978 and April 1979
	Nov. 1980	—	March 1981	July 1981
Turkey	Early 1978	Sept. 1978	April 1979	August 1979
	Jan. 1981	Aug. 1981*	—	February 1982
Nicaragua	Dec. 1978	April 1979	Dec. 1979	—
		Sept. 1980	—	Dec. 1980
Sudan	June 1979	Oct. 1981	Nov. 1981	Dec. 1981
Bolivia	April 1980	April 1981*		
Costa Rica	Sept. 1981			

*Conditional acceptance

For example, Peru's total public term debt more than tripled between 1972 and 1976 while debt owed to private financial markets increased eightfold and by 1976 accounted for nearly half of the total. Over the same period, Nicaragua's total public term debt increased about three times, while debt to private financial markets increased almost four times and, by 1976, it accounted for half of the total public term debt. The experience in other countries was similar, with Turkey a special case as official medium- and long-term borrowing from private financial sources began to grow rapidly after 1974. Table 8.2 shows the growth in public term debt from 1972 to 1981, for both the total amounts disbursed and those outstanding with private financial markets.

When these debtor countries met with serious debt servicing difficulties after the early 1970s, commitments and disbursements from private financial markets declined sharply. Domestic and international confidence in these countries greatly weakened. For example, capital flight persisted in Jamaica from 1976 through 1979 and in Nicaragua during the same period. Net borrowing declined sharply in the Sudan from 1977 to 1981, as well as in Peru in 1978, and Zaire after 1978. (Table 8.3 shows the net flow of funds from private financial markets to public and publicly guaranteed borrowers since 1972. These data cover term debt only; that is, loans exceeding one year in original maturity.)

The indebtedness of these countries to private bank lenders is much larger when short-term loans and private nonguaranteed borrowing are taken into account. Short-term bank claims—claims with maturity up to and including one year—can account for as much as one-third to nearly two-thirds of total bank claims.[16] The

[16]Bank for International Settlements, *Maturity Distribution of International Bank Lending* (Basel, Switzerland; BIS January 1982, and earlier releases). The results of the survey are published semiannually.

Table 8.2—External Public Debt or Publicly Guaranteed Disbursed Term Debt Outstanding and Private Financial Markets, 1972-1981* (millions of dollars)

Country	1972	1974	1976	1977	1978	1979	1980	1981
Peru								
Total, disbursed	1,055	2,221	3,666	4,711	5,402	5,934	6,168	5,974
Private financial markets	231	979	1,788	2,076	2,178	2,500	2,313	2,161
Percent of total	21.9	44.1	48.8	44.1	40.3	42.1	37.5	36.2
Zaire								
Total, disbursed	573	1,343	2,266	2,878	3,588	3,790	3,817	3,960
Private financial markets	204	650	1,022	1,265	1,502	1,576	1,219	1,101
Percent of total	35.6	48.4	45.1	43.9	41.9	41.6	31.9	28.2
Jamaica								
Total, disbursed	213	523	871	926	1,036	1,107	1,314	1,434
Private financial markets	130	359	475	469	475	414	433	447
Percent of total	61.0	68.6	54.5	50.6	45.8	37.4	32.9	31.2
Turkey								
Total, disbursed	2,450	3,126	3,588	4,299	6,356	10,993	13,477	13,809
Private financial markets	60	87	168	492	704	3,595	4,053	3,999
Percent of total	2.4	2.8	4.7	11.4	11.1	32.7	30.1	29.0
Nicaragua								
Total, disbursed	235	461	658	867	971	1,113	1,695	1,975
Private financial markets	88	244	336	397	400	398	743	746
Percent of total	37.4	52.9	51.1	45.8	41.2	35.8	43.8	37.8
Sudan								
Total, disbursed	396	942	1,762	2,036	2,383	3,334	3,714	4,595
Private financial markets	45	230	411	429	622	617	636	1,214
Percent of total	11.4	24.4	23.3	21.1	26.1	18.5	17.1	26.4
Bolivia								
Total, disbursed	618	696	1,024	1,375	1,649	1,828	2,124	2,422
Private financial markets	109	152	359	571	686	739	873	1,006
Percent of total	17.6	21.8	35.1	41.5	41.6	40.4	41.1	41.5
Costa Rica								
Total, disbursed	207	303	536	735	950	1,290	1,640	1,854
Private financial markets	40	96	194	301	388	623	813	905
Percent of total	19.3	31.7	36.2	40.9	40.8	48.3	49.6	48.8

*Private financial market debt includes funds raised from private commercial banks and other financial institutions and publicly issued and privately placed bonds.

Source: Debtor Reporting System, *World Debt Tables, 1982/83 edition* (Washington, D.C.: The World Bank, February 1983).

growth in short-term bank lending during the first half of the 1970s cannot be traced through available data. However, it is assumed that short-term lending also expanded rapidly during those years (see Table 8.4). Turkey provides a specific example as most bank lending was done short term prior to 1978.

Table 8.3—Commitments, Disbursements, and Net Financing from Private Financial Markets* to Public and Publicly Guaranteed Borrowers 1972-1981 (millions of dollars)

Country	1972	1974	1976	1977	1978	1979	1980	1981
Peru								
Commitments	$161	$586	$791	$162	$108	$863	$580	$909
Disbursements	126	624	443	446	174	572	365	800
Net flows**	98	490	392	269	20	357	−128	−38
Net transfers***	89	429	268	117	−168	109	−453	−340
Zaire								
Commitments	145	520	153	80	101	64	40	3
Disbursements	122	248	249	236	200	56	85	19
Net flows	111	208	239	225	182	38	33	2
Net transfers	103	169	212	185	126	−11	−17	−65
Jamaica								
Commitments	75	140	15	58	101	13	1	213
Disbursements	41	165	37	59	94	28	4	205
Net flows	28	142	−8	−12	2	−22	−23	25
Net transfers	20	118	−50	−45	−36	−71	−83	−31
Turkey								
Commitments	3	19	436	317	358	3,165	231	202
Disbursements	4	23	109	333	277	3,001	553	278
Net flows	−13	10	96	317	212	2,892	413	82
Net transfers	−16	6	84	282	175	2,807	−7	−331
Nicaragua								
Commitments	62	124	56	65	31	—	—	5
Disbursements	53	93	20	95	38	—	—	0
Net flows	38	82	−5	61	3	−2	−20	−10
Net transfers	33	60	−35	26	−28	−22	−20	−52
Sudan								
Commitments	23	184	234	14	59	101	61	62
Disbursements	20	161	196	15	19	46	36	66
Net flows	7	149	154	8	6	44	32	66
Net transfers	5	144	141	2	−4	42	29	66
Bolivia								
Commitments	33	71	220	252	309	180	151	80
Disbursements	32	48	156	252	319	113	198	42
Net flows	21	40	139	210	111	50	144	4
Net transfers	18	34	119	176	59	−27	38	−116
Costa Rica								
Commitments	22	67	127	147	286	352	305	79
Disbursements	23	49	72	136	232	375	240	124
Net flows	8	30	51	105	83	235	196	90
Net transfers	6	22	39	92	50	196	112	22

*Private financial markets include private commercial banks.
**Net flows equal disbursements minus amortization.
***Net transfers equal disbursements minus total debt service.
Source: Ibid.

Table 8.4—Maturity Distribution of International Bank Lending, 1978, 1981, and 1982 (millions of dollars)

Country	1978 Dec. 31	1981 June 30	1981 Dec. 31	1982 June 30
Peru				
Total claims*	$3,575	$3,931	$4,412	$5,216
Short term**	1,696	2,307	2,667	3,361
Medium & long term***	1,621	1,624	1,442	1,555
Credit commitments	518	1,756	1,384	1,443
Zaire				
Total claims	1,286	1,159	1,117	991
Short term	412	395	330	331
Medium & long term	501	764	498	419
Credit commitments	233	315	46	28
Jamaica				
Total claims	509	594	462	475
Short term	155	220	137	126
Medium & long term	331	374	265	312
Credit commitments	95	71	79	44
Turkey				
Total claims	3,777	4,038	4,235	3,956
Short term	2,655	1,081	1,044	1,111
Medium & long term	841	2,957	2,693	2,433
Credit commitments	877	435	508	420
Nicaragua				
Total claims	846	723	793	796
Short term	570	291	303	266
Medium & long term	273	432	482	523
Credit commitments	109	44	133	7
Sudan				
Total claims	925	949	1,124	1,146
Short term	491	581	765	631
Medium & long term	238	368	213	292
Credit commitments	224	181	83	62
Bolivia				
Total claims	1,042	1,064	1,121	1,053
Short term	453	375	440	374
Medium & long term	573	689	636	623
Credit commitments	390	95	93	80
Costa Rica				
Total claims	708	1,332	1,287	1,238
Short term	368	594	627	599
Medium & long term	327	738	633	602
Credit commitments	379	137	111	107

*Total claims also include unallocated amounts.
**Short term is used here to denote what the BIS identifies as loans maturing within one year.
***Claims exceeding one year in maturity.
Source: Bank for International Settlements, *Maturity Distribution of International Bank Lending* (Basel, Switzerland: BIS, December 1982).

The relative shift toward borrowing from banks, and consequently to shorter maturities and shorter grace periods, had a marked impact on the debt profiles of the debtor countries. The shortening of maturities in the mid-1970s resulted in a steep rise in amortization payments due to banks by the end of the decade. Bank lending also resulted in interest charges higher than would have been incurred if available by borrowing from official lenders, whether on a bilateral or multilateral basis. Interest rates were usually floating rates during a period when interest rates trended upward, thus adding to the debt-service costs. Almost all medium-term bank loans are based on a spread over market interest rates, either LIBOR or commercial bank lending rates to prime borrowers.

Economic Management

In all the cases requiring debt renegotiations with private banks, the economic management of the countries was poor. Large government expenditure programs were usually accompanied by expansionary monetary policies with rapid price inflation and by declining domestic savings rates and neglect of productive investments. Exchange rates were usually overvalued, creating an additional pressure on the balance of payments. Efforts made in the mid-1970s by these countries to bring domestic demand more in line with resource availability were not successful. In no case did the need to renegotiate debt arise suddenly or even quickly. A reasonably good country risk system would have made this need to reschedule evident well in advance.

Main Characteristics and Past Experience

Private banks have had to approach the question of a developing country's debt-service problem on the basis of:

- Fundamental distinction between the developing country's debt to official creditors (governments and official international financial institutions) and debt to private creditors.
- Assignment of the highest priority to servicing the private debt.
- Fundamental assumption that debts to private banks must be serviced as contracted.

The above distinctions and priorities stem from a basic characteristic of private capital: Its future availability will be heavily dependent on past debt-servicing performance and not on political and other nonfinancial considerations that may govern official credit. The conditions leading to the rescheduling of debt due to private banks are likely to damage seriously a country's creditworthiness with private lenders. The need to reschedule is likely to impair its future access to needed private capital, unless domestic policy changes are promptly taken and preferably endorsed by the IMF. This is much less true of debt owed to official creditors (or guaranteed by them).

New ground had to be broken in the second half of the 1970s to arrive at rescheduling agreements between private commercial bank lenders and some of the debtor countries. In the process, certain procedures evolved, and precedents were established for future multilateral debt renegotiations with private bank lenders. These private bank renegotiations profited much from the experience with public debt renegotiations. Banks favored rescheduling of debt of countries in balance-of-payment difficulties (changes in contractual terms to lengthen maturities or grace periods) over refinancings (extension of new credits to help finance the outstanding credits). Declarations of default were not practical alternatives. The private banks also opted for a multilateral negotiating framework.

Still, the negotiations were often lengthy and difficult, particularly when arrears in interest payments had to be settled. Private banks usually considered it important that a debtor country remain current on interest payments. In most cases where interest arrears had occurred, the banks insisted on a significant initial repayment of interest. It became usual for amortization payments to be stretched out and reduced, or even postponed, in the first years following the agreements, while interest usually continued to be paid. The reschedulings with banks have mostly involved market interest rates and interest spreads (over LIBOR) which were as high as or higher than those on the original loans.

The terms of private bank debt reschedulings, in general, have been more rigorous than those of official debt reschedulings. Furthermore, even after a successful rescheduling of bank debt, the debtor country did not necessarily regain its creditworthiness with private lenders. The banks were usually reluctant to make new commitments, or resume lending, until a turnaround in a debtor country's economic prospects was evident.

Multilateral debt renegotiations with private bank lenders have presented formidable organizational problems. In some cases, hundreds of individual banks from a large number of countries have participated or were represented in the negotiations. The lead creditor banks involved in the negotiations insisted usually on observing the so-called "fair treatment" rules. These are meant to ensure that if new funding is granted, or debt is rescheduled, the so-called burden is shared in proportion to each bank's existing exposure in the debtor country. The rules are also intended to prevent funds provided by one bank used to repay another bank. Observing the "fair treatment" principle, however, requires that the lead banks must have the cooperation of all the participating creditor banks.

Cooperative Efforts

Cooperation among creditor banks is even more essential in those cases where cross-default clauses have been entered in the original loan contracts and countries have actually fallen into arrears on their debt-service payments. Under cross-default clauses, all loans to a debtor country are automatically declared in default if just one bank, or a few banks, declared the government or a borrowing institution in default. Such action by a bank creates a chain reaction.

The experiences in the mid-1970s from the first two multilateral debt renegotiations (Zaire and Peru) with private banks shaped the institutional framework and the approaches taken in the later negotiations. In these cases, answers to the following issues had to be hammered out: Were debts to private creditors to be part of the multilateral debt renegotiation with official creditors? Was the treatment of official and private creditors to be similar? Were amortization and interest to be treated the same way or differently? Could interest payments be rescheduled? What were the preconditions, particularly in changes in domestic policies or agreements with the IMF? When did the new debt arrangements become effective, and for how long? How much debt was covered? Could any new credits be extended? How many creditor banks had to be involved and agree? What about other banks? How to obtain needed information? How to organize the meetings and what should the joint meetings aim to do? In the later cases of Jamaica, Turkey, Nicaragua, and Sudan, the procedures were progressively smoother because some of these questions had been more or less answered and agreed on in the earlier cases and more experience was gained.

In fact, a pattern developed over the years which has been followed more or less closely in subsequent private bank reschedulings, most recently in Argentina and Mexico. In the cases of Jamaica, Turkey, Nicaragua, and Sudan, the banks, early in the process, agreed on the necessity of debt rescheduling rather than the possibility of providing refinancing loans. Once the approach of rescheduling was accepted, steering committees of creditor banks were formed, representing creditors from the U.S., Canada, Europe, and Japan. Progress in each of the four cases, however, was quite different. The negotiations were more easily concluded on the countries that had remained current on principal and interest on public sector debt, and rescheduling of arrears was not an issue. The approaches taken by the banks were also influenced by the regulatory environment in which the banks operated. As was pointed out, the bank creditors have almost always insisted on the debtor country being current on interest payments. Suggestions for rescheduling of interest in arrears met with strong resistance.

Debtor Response

While the creditor banks had to cope with the organizational problems, the debtor countries had to become prepared for the negotiations and try to overcome difficulties arising from the lack of a centralized agency dealing with debt problems and the lack of adequate statistics and other relevant information.

The IMF also played a part in the debt renegotiations between debtor countries and private bank creditors, although the role was less clearly defined and more informal than in multilateral renegotiations of official debt. Usually, the banks have urged the debtor countries seeking debt relief from private creditors to initiate and carry out a stabilization program that would be approved and supported by the IMF. In almost all cases, a standby or extended arrangement was approved by the IMF and actually in place by the time the rescheduling agreement was signed with the banks. This pattern was also followed in the cases that arose in 1982. One exception was Nicaragua. In the case of Bolivia, the acceptance of the rescheduling agreement in April 1981 was made conditional on Bolivia's adopting and implementing an IMF-recommended economic stablization program.

IMF-endorsed stablization programs were of benefit to creditors as well as debtor country governments. Bank creditors had available to them an authoritative assessment of the debtor country's economic situation and also had the assurance of monitoring the reform programs. The debtor governments and the IMF staff obtained for themselves a realistic estimate of the potential debt relief from bank creditors. Important contacts between the bank creditors and the Fund staff existed in each of the rescheduling cases. In general, the role of the IMF staff consisted of reviewing the economic prospects of the debtor country, explaining the major elements of the stabilization program, and answering technical questions. In some instances, the IMF assisted the countries in preparing relevant statistical data and presentations to the banks.

In the 1982 Mexican case, an important precedent was established: The managing director of the IMF urged the banks that were rescheduling the debts to provide new incremental money. He went so far as to indicate that the IMF's program depended on this action. This was followed by the banks. There was great potential in this innovation to enhance the role of the IMF and its member governments in the rescheduling operations of private banks. Given the widespread need to reschedule, this innovation could also mean a much greater official role in the original lending of the private banks.

Commercial Debt Renegotiations Compared with Official Debt

Before reviewing the experience of specific countries that have conducted private debt renegotiations, let us briefly compare private commercial bank debt renegotiations with official debt renegotiations. The differences given may help illuminate the problems involved in dealings with countries wherein debt of both kinds is negotiated.

1. More nationalities are involved in private renegotiations ("creditor" banks can also be located in "deficit" countries which do not extend official assistance).

2. There are many more creditor banks than there are creditor governments or entities.

3. Aggregate statistics on commercial bank outstandings are only approximate; individual banks only have such statistics for themselves.

4. There is more proprietary information or confidentiality in the case of credits extended by private banks—public debt is more a matter of record.

5. Private entities involved are normally competitors and continue to be so during debt restructuring.

6. Leadership role is nearly thankless—frequently not competed for or even avoided by major banks.

7. No "neutral" outside private formal links or bridges exist among the private

banks. Often the borrowing countries have an investment adviser, but he is seen by the creditors as playing a partisan role, not a mediating role, like the World Bank or the IMF.

8. There is less presumption of private banks future lending into countries now in difficulties compared with official lenders.

9. More concern is felt with how financial settlements will have an impact on creditors because creditor banks are also borrowers and come under close market scrutiny.

10. Private banks are usually more concerned with public opinion—again because banks are also borrowers and are supervised or regulated by monetary or governmental bodies.

11. Private banks can act more quickly. They have need to act as efficiently as possible (can organize ad hoc action quickly, particularly with modern communication and transportation). Therefore, they are less likely to meet often. Moreover, negotiators are not subject to as much public scrutiny, and they operate with much more delegation of authority to negotiators.

12. There is more acceptance of ad hoc action—conversely, less pressures to be uniform in all cases, although precedents are important.

13. More ease of communication—particularly less formidable clearance procedures *within* creditor entities.

14. Can have outside links or neutral bridges if needed (probably more will be done in the future as banks find conflict of interest in leadership versus advocacy of own special interest).

The cases of developing countries which have had debt renegotiations with private commercial banks are given in the following chapters. The first deals with eight cases which arose before 1982. More precisely, these cases occurred between 1976 and 1981. In these cases, where appropriate, the history of past renegotiations with official creditors is also given.

In a subsequent chapter, country experiences of 1982 are given, including major cases not yet completed. In these additional cases, like Argentina and Brazil, no attempt is made to summarize their experiences with official creditors in prior years. As this book is completed, early 1983, these matters are in a state of flux and evolving. Before next year, other countries are likely to be added to these lists.

9

Case Studies of Developing Countries' Debt Renegotiations

From the material contained in chapters 7 and 8, we can see how debt renegotiations with official creditors and with private creditors have evolved for debtor countries. Both kinds of debt renegotiations have been undertaken by a number of nations. Following are case histories of debt renegotiations with official and private creditors for eight countries: Zaire, Peru, Turkey, Sudan, Jamaica, Nicaragua, Bolivia, and Costa Rica.

Zaire

Debt Renegotiations with Official Creditors

Zaire conducted four separate debt renegotiations with its official creditors during the second half of the 1970s. The first rescheduling of debt to official creditors occurred in early 1976; it was followed by two reschedulings in 1977 (July and December), and yet another in December 1979. These rescheduling agreements were made within the framework of the Paris Club and its member governments.

In the 1970s, Zaire experienced a rapid increase in debt-service obligations. The largest portion of the debt was contracted in the early 1970s, without due regard for the productive use of the borrowed funds and generating the foreign exchange required to service the debt in the future.

By the end of 1974, Zaire's total external term debt (public and private, nonguaranteed in the borrowing country) disbursed and outstanding amounted to $1.3 billion. The external debt then accounted for about 40% of GDP. By the end of 1979, the external debt had increased to $3.9 billion and accounted for almost 60% of GDP.

In 1974, about half of the external term debt was owed to official creditors, or guaranteed by creditor governments, less than 5% was owed to multilateral organizations and about 45% to private creditors without guarantees. The rest came from various sources. At the end of 1979, the official creditors and government guaranteed credits accounted for about 50% of the total, the multilateral agencies for an additional 10%, and private lenders for about 40%.

After 1974-75, Zaire's economic conditions deteriorated greatly, and Zaire lost its creditworthiness with private lenders. Despite the growing unwillingness to lend to Zaire on commercial terms after that time, the external debt outstanding with private financial markets still increased from $650 million at year-end 1974 to $1.3 billion at year-end 1977, and $1.6 billion at year-end 1979. Over the same period, the debt to official creditors rose from $300 million to $1.1 billion and $1.6 billion, respectively.

While private lenders became more cautious, concessional loans from governments and international organizations expanded their share in relation to bank lending and suppliers' credits. With the shift from private to official sources of funds, the average terms of lending improved. From 1973 to 1977, average maturities lengthened steadily by almost 50% to over 21 years, while average interest rates on new loans decreased from 7% to 4.5%. Contributing to this improvement in the debt profile was Zaire's more cautious attitude toward new borrowings under the standby arrangements of 1976 and 1977 with the IMF. Still, the maturity structure of Zaire's debt outstanding at year-end 1977 remained difficult, with almost half of the principal falling due between 1978 and 1982.

From 1975 on, the discrepancy between the country's debt-service obligations and its actual payments widened and arrears began to accumulate on a wide spectrum of payments categories. Total arrears at the end of 1978 exceeded that year's level of exports and would have been higher had Zaire not obtained rescheduling agreements from official creditors of 1975-77 maturities. An additional increase in arrears in 1979 was estimated at over $200 million.

Faced with considerable difficulties in meeting its debt-service obligations in 1976, Zaire approached its official creditors to have its debt problems examined at a meeting of the Paris Club in June 1976, subsequent to an IMF standby arrangement in March of the same year. Although the participants at the Paris Club meeting addressed themselves directly to the problems concerning debt owed to, or guaranteed by, creditor governments, the club participants also suggested a reorganization of the country's debt to private lenders, particularly debt owed to private commercial banks.

Under the Paris Club agreement of 1976, a substantial portion of the debt-service payments on official, or officially guaranteed, medium-term debt was consolidated. The combined amounts falling due in 1975, 1976, and 1977 reached $186 million. The terms of the 1976 rescheduling provided for a ten-year maturity, a three-year grace period, and a moratorium on interest rates to be negotiated bilaterally. At the rescheduling meeting, the creditor countries also took note of Zaire's request to consolidate maturities falling due after 1977 and agreed to assess its balance of payments and external debt situation within the framework of the proposed stabilization program. Further, it was agreed that a central agency in Zaire would be created to implement debt management policies.

The Paris Club meetings with Zaire in July 1977 took place as a follow-up to the understanding reached in June 1976. At that time, it was agreed that a consolidation of 1977 principal payments could be undertaken only following a new meeting of creditor countries and Zaire. This meeting would review balance-of-payments prospects and implementation of the stabilization program. This renegotiation also consolidated arrears on principal and interest accumulated during the first half of 1977. The total amount involved was $203 million, and the terms were similar to those of the previous rescheduling with a ten-year maturity and a four-year grace period. The interest rates were to be negotiated bilaterally, although the Zaire delegation requested that the moratorium interest rate be fixed multilaterally and at a lower level than that obtained by Zaire under the 1976 rescheduling.

Further agreements in December 1977 improved the terms of the previous agreement reached in July 1977 by consolidating unpaid interest due between July 1 and December 31, 1977, which was previously not consolidated. There were further negotiations in December 1979. The objective of these debt renegotiations was to agree on a rescheduling of Zaire's guaranteed short-term arrears outstanding on June 30, 1979 and not previously consolidated. These arrears were to be repaid in five graduated backloaded installments, with the first repayment, amounting to 10% of the total, due on September 30, 1980, and the fifth due on September 30, 1984, covering 25% of the total. The maturity was five years and two months, counted from the date on which arrears were outstanding, and the grace period was 14 months. Interest rates on the rearranged maturities were to be determined bilaterally. However, each creditor country agreed to make a maximum effort to keep the rate of interest as low as market conditions and legal and other considerations permitted.

The total amount involved in the consolidation of December 1979 was $1.3 billion. Even though the consolidation did not encompass previously rescheduled debts, the agreement allowed for a de facto rescheduling of arrears (outstanding on July 30, 1979 and due between June 30 and December 31, 1979) on already rescheduled debt by accepting Zaire's undertaking to settle such arrears over a period of one year and seven months. Zaire's government also made a commitment not to incur new payments arrears on rescheduled debt.

In December 1979, a further agreement was made that the Paris Club would meet again to consider rescheduling of debt service due in 1981-82. Such rescheduling was made conditional on a upper-credit tranche program with the IMF for a corresponding period and the observance by Zaire of provisions of current and previous Paris Club reschedulings.

At the Paris Club meeting of June 1976, the Zaire representatives stated that their government would seek reschedulings of service payments on debts to private creditors, notably of those to foreign commercial banks. These reschedulings were to be undertaken on terms similar to those arranged with official creditors as set forth in the Paris Club Agreed Minutes. At three subsequent Paris Club meetings in 1977 and 1979, the Zaire representatives confirmed their government's commitment to arrange for reschedulings of the country's external debt to private bank lenders under terms comparable to those provided for in the reschedulings with official creditors.

Debt Renegotiations with Private Creditors

Zaire was the first major developing country workout case faced by the private banks in the 1970s. From this experience, significant ground rules for future relations between private banks and developing countries evolved. By mid-1975, Zaire's ambitious development plan, which the banks were helping to finance, had been undercut by plummeting copper prices and economic mismanagement. These conditions, in turn, had exhausted Zaire's foreign exchange reserves and led to debt service interruption of $80 million in principal and interest due on the country's $2 billion in foreign debt.

Zaire moved in late 1975 to reestablish its credit in three stages:

1. It brought in the IMF to assist in establishing an economic stabilization program, signing a first tranche standby agreement of SDR 42 ($45) million with the IMF in February 1976.

2. In June 1976, it negotiated a ten-year partial rescheduling of the $1 billion it owed its government creditors.

3. In November 1976, it signed a memo of understanding with the private banks (the London Club) covering $375 million in consortium debt due to private banks. The memo was not a legally binding document but rather a gentlemen's agreement. It stipulated that the private banks would not declare a default, Zaire would keep up interest payments to the banks, and that one of Zaire's international creditors would undertake to raise up to $250 million in new credits to help get the economy back on its feet.

Use of this line would depend on Zaire bringing current the $80 million in principal and interest arrears; negotiating a new and stricter IMF standby arrangement in the higher tranches; maintaining eligibility to draw under the standby by meeting IMF stipulated economic targets; and suffering no further damage (material adverse change) to its credit rating.

Zaire's negotiations with private banks took the form of face-to-face meetings in London, Paris, and New York. The governor of the Banque du Zaire (the central bank) represented the Republic, and 13 agent banks represented 19 international loan syndicates involving more than 100 private banks.*

The IMF played a relatively informal role—present at the meetings as observer. The IMF worked to mesh the private bank-Zaire understanding into the new higher-tranche IMF standby. In contrast, the relationships between the private banks and certain of Zaire's government creditors were at times strained. The governments feared that the private banks would somehow induce Zaire to pay them off while leaving the governments holding the bulk of Zaire's debt. Indeed, as noted, in the Paris Club rescheduling agreement of June 1976, Zaire had to agree to obtain "comparable" terms from the private banks—a caveat that impeded private bank efforts to raise new incremental credits for Zaire afterward.

*The author played a leading role for the banks.

Over the 1976-77 winter, Zaire pursued its London Club obligations by paying $40 million in past-due interest and negotiating an SDR 45 ($54) million higher-tranche standby with the IMF. However, in spring 1977, Zaire's southern province of Shaba was embroiled in an invasion and rebellion, forcing the banks to postpone the syndication. Although the agent bank had nearly completed the $250-million credit syndicate by August, Zaire fell behind in its IMF stabilization program and lost its eligibility to draw under the Fund standby, thereby violating a key condition of the London Club memo of understanding. Moreover, Zaire's government creditors kept insisting that any new credit to Zaire had to be comparable to the government's ten-year rescheduling scheme as mandated by the Paris Club agreement.

In the fall of 1977, the agent banks designed a new five-year term loan facility acceptable to the Paris Club. By February 1978, they had received promises to participate in a loan amounting to about $220 million from a combination of American, British, Canadian, French, Belgian, German, Italian, and Japanese banks. It was notable that a number of these banks had no prior exposure in Zaire, while a number of the other banks committed themselves to amounts in excess of their past exposure. The basic approach of the private banks was to try to reestablish the creditworthiness of Zaire rather than just focusing on rescheduling debt. This effort failed because Zaire was not able to carry through a reform program and fulfill its standby with the IMF. However, it left the legacy of relating debt rescheduling by private banks to changes in economic policies and to IMF actions.

In late summer 1978, the government brought in foreign advisers for the Banque du Zaire and the Ministry of Finance. Also, Zaire continued to keep the banks current on interest. In spring 1979, Zaire started new negotiations for yet another IMF standby, which the Fund formally approved in the amount of SDR 118 ($142) million in August 1979.

New talks with bank creditors commenced in June 1979 when the lead bank approached Zaire with a new set of proposals regarding the consolidation of principal in arrears to all banks. In July 1979, the creditor banks considered accepting the lead bank's proposal of bilateral consolidation of principal in arrears and future amortization. In August 1979, Zaire retained the services of three investment banks as consultants to participate in debt renegotiations with private creditors, as well as official creditors, at the Paris Club meetings. In December 1979, the private banks finally accepted the proposed rescheduling terms, and an agreement was reached on the rescheduling of Zaire's outstanding uninsured syndicated bank debt of about $400 million (including arrears on principal in the amount of $287 million) over a ten-year repayment period. The definitive agreement was signed in April 1980 and became effective in May of that year.

The agreement of May 1980 did not provide for any new financing, but repayments of principal according to the agreement were to be made in relatively small amounts until 1984. However, as the consolidated debt was made subject to a LIBOR-based interest rate, the continuation of high interest rates over the years would result in large interest obligations. The interest rate spread on the consolidated debt was set to rise from 1.75% in the first five years to 2% for the remainder of the repayment period. These spreads were similar to those on most of the original loans.

Zaire was widely considered a test case. Its handling set several important precedents. Most important, the Zaire case forestalled two strong unfavorable trends in international finance that might have drastically curtailed private bank lending to the developing countries. First, by responding positively—that is, by refraining from declaring default and by trying to raise new incremental money—the banks helped forestall a strong movement among the developing countries to declare unilateral moratoria on their private bank debts. No one talks seriously of moratoria today.

Second, the banks forestalled a bias among some developing countries' creditors, specifically government creditors, to grant quick and easy reschedulings without the conditionality of reform needed to assure revitalization of a country's economy. The Paris Club often sets tough workout conditions. Had either moratoria or unconditional reschedulings become the rule of the day, private banks would probably have backed away drastically from developing country markets.

Peru

Debt Renegotiations with Official Creditors

Periodically, Peru has conducted external debt renegotiations with its official creditors. Economic developments during the second half of the 1960s prompted the Peruvian government to approach its external creditors in 1969 for a readjustment of the country's debt burden. A weakening in export earnings and the rising costs of imports led to trade deficits in 1966-1967. A deficit in the services accounts, as well as growing debt-service payments, resulted in a substantial current account deficit in all years except 1964. Pressure on the current account balance was temporarily relieved by the devaluation of the Peruvian sol in mid-1967, which helped reduce imports and stimulate exports. The devaluation was precipitated by massive capital flight from the country. Large government deficits and a rapid expansion in bank credits had fueled inflationary price trends for some years in the past.

In 1968, the government decided to put into effect economic reform measures and was aided in this effort by the IMF. In November 1968, a $75-million standby arrangement with the IMF was signed. The Peruvian government discontinued the authorization of new public external debt up to ten years' maturity (some credits required for large agricultural imports and for government banks were the only exceptions). Public borrowings were limited to 10-to-15 years' maturity. The government's fiscal and monetary policies under the standby arrangement were aimed toward gradually achieving financial stability. Since the government fulfilled the requirements of the standby arrangement, the IMF renewed it in 1969 and 1970.

The Peruvian debt servicing difficulties were mostly related to short- and medium-term suppliers' credits—including payments for military equipment from various countries and capital goods for infrastructure projects—and to commercial bank credits. Peru's total public or publicly guaranteed term debt, disbursed and outstanding at the end of 1969, was estimated at close to $900 million, approximately half of which was owed to suppliers and private commercial banks. Debt owed to governments on a bilateral basis amounted to close to $250 million, with the U.S. and West Germany the principal bilateral creditors. Debt to multilateral agencies, such as the World Bank and the Inter-American Development Bank, amounted to almost $200 million.

Suppliers' credits were mostly denominated in U.S. dollars, although these were also extended by Japanese, German, and non-American suppliers. The principal banking creditors were U.S. commercial banks, but some bank debt had also been incurred with Canadian and French lending institutions. Peru's debt-service obligations on this outstanding term debt accumulated rapidly in 1968 and 1969, with debt-service payments due over an 18-month period totaling $240 million. In 1969, the Peruvian government approached its creditors for a debt rescheduling.

The debt renegotiations of 1969 were not carried out in a typical Paris Club framework but were conducted individually between Peru's government representatives and its creditors. Rescheduling terms differed, depending on the individual deals concluded with creditor governments and bank lenders. While the process of bilateral reschedulings continued, the government of Peru attempted to coordinate the rescheduling effort by convening creditor meetings in Lima and in November 1969 in Brussels. When European and Japanese creditors could not agree to uniform terms, bilateral settlements were further pursued. In December 1969, agreements were reached with Belgian, Italian, Japanese, and Spanish creditors to defer 75% of the amounts due. A short time later, agreements with British, French, and German creditors were made.

Through these various settlements, amortization payments due between 1968 and 1970 were sharply reduced by agreeing to higher interest payments on the outstanding amounts. In 1968, effective amortization was reduced from $151 million to $95 million, and in 1969 from $197 million to $127 million, with the deferred amounts falling due between 1970 and 1975. In 1970, the German government agreed to reschedule 75% of the obligations to be repaid in 16 years from 1972 with interest at 8.5%. The French government rescheduled 75% of the obligations to French nationals at 9%, to be repaid from 1972 to 1976, and the Belgian government rescheduled credits at 9%, to be repaid from 1972 to 1975. Spanish credits were privately rescheduled at 8% and deferred until 1972-1976.

Not all the details of the debt that was effectively rescheduled were released by the Peruvian Ministry of Finance. But in February 1970, the government announced that no further reschedulings would be necessary. With part of the supplier credits replaced by longer maturity governmental credits and government guaranteed loans, the debt-service obligations became more manageable for the immediate years ahead.

In fact, from 1969 through 1973, real growth of the economy exceeded 5% per year (it reached 7.3% in 1970 and 6.9% in 1974), while inflation was fairly well controlled during the period. The external payments position improved for a while, but beginning with 1974, the balance of payments deteriorated rapidly. Export earnings dropped off sharply, while import costs continued to climb. As a result, the current account deficit increased from less that $300 million in 1973 to $1.5 billion in 1975 and $1.2 billion in 1976. It was close to $1 billion in 1977. The current account deficit amounted to 11% of GDP in 1975 and to 9% and 7% in 1976 and 1977, respectively.

Ambitious development programs by the government contributed substantially to climbing import payments, and the shortfall in domestic savings required external financing of these programs. In addition, current government expenditures were stepped up without adequate increases in tax revenues to cover these expenditures. Higher military expenditures and increased subsidies for imported food and oil products accounted for much of the increase in government expenditures.

Although initially Peru obtained adequate funds through external borrowings, by the end of 1975, the country's major creditors, particularly the commercial bank creditors, became more reluctant to extend additional credits. Discussions between the Peruvian government and its creditors continued throughout 1976, 1977, and into early 1978. In April 1978, when foreign exchange reserves were virtually exhausted, the Peruvian government announced its intention to seek a rescheduling of its debts with official as well as with private creditors.

The debt rescheduling efforts were preceded by a two-year standby arrangement in the upper credit tranches between the IMF and the Peruvian government, which was approved in November 1977. It soon became apparent, however, that Peru's government was not living up to the commitments incurred under the IMF standby. In May 1978, a new Peruvian economic team took office and a new standby arrangement with the Fund was formulated in July 1978 to extend through December 1980. This arrangement, as well as a compensatory financing purchase, was approved by the IMF board in September 1978. The amounts involved were SDR 184 ($234) million in the standby program and in the compensatory financing purchase, SDR 61.5 ($78) million. The arrangement also involved specific commitments in both the economic and financial fields by the Peruvian government.

It had become increasingly apparent that Peru had great difficulty in meeting its debt-service obligations since mid-1978. At a Paris Club meeting in November 1978, Peru's government proposed the rescheduling of 90% of the principal due to official creditors in 1979 and 1980, on terms similar to those that had been proposed earlier to bank creditors. This proposal was accepted by the Paris Club participants and the Agreed Minutes were dated November 3, 1978.

The agreement with the official creditors covered all principal due on officially guaranteed commercial credits and loans from governments or government agencies, contracted prior to January 1, 1978, with an original maturity of more than one year. The amount consolidated under the Agreed Minutes was $211 million, equivalent to 90% of the outstanding total debt to public creditors. Payment of the remaining 10% and payment of all interest was to be made as originally scheduled. Principal payments falling due between January 1 and December 31, 1979, were to be repaid in ten equal and successive semiannual installments; payments falling due between January 1 and December 31, 1980, were to be repaid in eight equal and successive semiannual installments. The grace period granted was three years, and the maturities (grace plus repayments periods) were extended to seven and one half and six and one half years, respectively. The interest rates on the re-arranged maturities were to be determined bilaterally between Peru and the individual creditor governments. A nondiscrimination clause was added to the arrangement to make sure any discrimination among creditor categories would be avoided.

The Peruvian delegation to the Paris Club meetings emphasized the strong determination of its government to reach the targets for the economic and financial program underlying the standby arrangement of the IMF. The reschedulings for 1980 were made conditional on Peru's reaching understandings with the IMF not later than December 31, 1979, on the policies and quantitative performance criteria for 1980 under the standby program. In fact, in August 1979, the then-existing standby arrangement was cancelled and replaced by a new standby, also through the end of 1980, but for SDR 285 ($370) million, using both ordinary IMF resources and its supplementary financing.

The Paris Club participants and the private commercial banks each made reschedulings conditional on Peru obtaining comparable terms from the other. The bank rescheduling was agreed on, in basic terms, before the Paris Club meetings, but it was signed only after the agreement had been reached with the official creditors. The two agreements were, therefore, almost identical. The official creditors adopted similar terms to those which had been acceptable to the banks. An important difference, however, was that the consolidation interest rate on the bank debt floated over LIBOR, rather than being fixed and concessional.

Peru's balance-of-payments performance improved dramatically in 1979, with a surplus on current account of almost $800 million. All arrears were cleared by the end of the first quarter 1979, and most of the swaps and short-term deposits, which the central bank had arranged during the earlier foreign exchange crisis, were repaid during the year. Peru's government, in light of these favorable developments, decided to cancel the 1980 Paris Club reschedulings with official creditors.

Debt Renegotiations with Private Creditors

Peru's experience with debt renegotiations with private creditors in recent years overlapped with Zaire's. These experiences interacted and together created many of the precedents for subsequent cases.

The Peruvian government requested and successfully negotiated two balance-of-payments facilities from the private banks during 1976-78. The first one, for $250 million, involved 19 U.S. banks and was fully disbursed by February 1977. The background to this first balance-of-payments facility was unusual in that the Peruvians made it clear from the outset that they did not want to go to the IMF, although they were strongly counseled to do so by the bankers involved. Instead, the government formally requested its principal bankers to review Peru's stabilization program as a basis for making a decision on the requested facility.

After reviewing this program, six U.S. banks in July 1976 expressed their willingness to constitute a steering committee and to proceed on a best-efforts basis to raise $200 to $250 million of the requested financing within the U.S. The financing was subject to the following stipulations:

1. Peru had to raise an additional $100 million from Canadian, European, and Japanese banks.

2. Participation by other U.S. banks having substantial exposure in Peru was mandatory. Because it was widely believed by the steering committee banks that the proceeds of the loan would be used to repay current maturities of term debt falling due during the balance of 1976 and 1977, the steering committee banks wanted to ensure widest participation in the balance-of-payments facility. This would assure that the risks were shared by as many lending banks as possible. The insistence on participation by the European and Japanese banks resulted in parallel negotiations between the Peruvian government and U.S. banks, on the one hand, and the Peruvian government and the foreign banks, on the other. The resulting inefficiencies in communication and coordination with respect to this first loan were later to influence the composition of the steering committee formed two years later for the second balance-of-payments loan.

3. Monthly information on the progress of the 1976-77 stabilization program was to be provided by the Peruvian government to the banks both during and following disbursement. Early in the negotiations and in the context of this third stipulation, the U.S. steering committee made the following key decisions. First, a special subcommittee chaired by the author was to monitor progress made under the stabilization program. Second, the eventual loan agreement would not list any specific numerical targets that Peru had to meet to qualify for the final loan disbursements in February 1977. Instead, 75% of the lenders (by dollar participation) had to agree that Peru was making satisfactory progress under the stabilization program.

During 1977, the program ran into difficulties, and by midyear it was obvious that the Peruvian program had failed. Reportedly, opposition to the program within the Peruvian cabinet had become increasingly vocal, with a faction committed to expansionary policy. A number of key moderate government officials resigned. At the same time, foreign exchange availability was severely constrained. This was due to first, a falloff in export proceeds from Peru's main commodities; and second, to a contraction in the level of short-term trade-related credits extended by both banks and suppliers. In their 1976 stabilization program, the Peruvians had assumed throughout that they would be able to maintain the same level of short-term trade-related credits, while using the proceeds from the balance-of-payments facility generally for international payments, including the servicing of current obligations on long-term debt.

After the failure of the 1976 program, the private bankers involved in the existing arrangement again urged strongly that the Peruvians go to the IMF to work out a new program that could be successfully implemented. Peru was informed that in the absence of effective stabilization measures, it must not assume that current levels (1977) of trade-related exposure could be maintained. Finally, any delays in defining a new coherent, well-integrated policy package, preferably in conjunction with the IMF, could create a most difficult, if not impossible, balance-of-payments situation.

By August 1977, the Peruvians had met in New York with their principal U.S. bankers and assured them that they were in fact going to work out a program with the IMF. Based on this intention, Peru requested its bankers to maintain short-term lines and outstandings at then-present levels until the IMF program could be negotiated and implemented. While they were successful in getting most banks to go along, some smaller lenders did not. The agreement with the IMF was reached in late 1977, but by December of that year some targets under the new standby had not been met. The Peruvians, however, initiated a new dialogue with the IMF to work out new targets.

By February 1978, the U.S. banks' steering committee had evolved into a six-bank international steering committee representing American, Canadian, Japanese, and European banks. To ensure that the IMF-Peruvian dialogue would continue under hopeful conditions, this international steering committee recommended to the banks that a cohesive and unified approach be taken with respect to the maintenance of trade-related credits. On the recommendation of the international steering committee, the banks also agreed to roll forward until January 3, 1979, approximately $180 million of current maturities of term debt owed to private banks and falling due in the second semester of 1978. These credits were to be refinanced if a satisfactory program with the IMF could be worked out.

Aside from these decisions, the Peruvians requested the banks to provide a new facility that would essentially refinance a substantial portion of maturities of central government or public sector entities owed to private bankers falling due in 1979 and 1980. The international steering committee recommended to the banks that the actions of the banks should be linked to an IMF Extended Fund Facility (EFF), which the Peruvians had indicated they wished to have.

A new EFF with the IMF for SDR 184 ($234) million was negotiated in September 1978. The IMF also approved a SDR 120 ($152) million compensatory financing facility to help offset the decline in the prices of Peru's main export commodities. In addition, the banks were encouraged by the fact that Peru had already restructured its debt with the Eastern bloc—obtaining relief for bilateral payments due over the following three years (that is, 90% relief for the following two years of payments; 65% for the third year), rescheduled over 11 years with a 3-year grace period.

Before triggering their own refinancing package, the private banks required the successful rescheduling of 1979 and 1980 maturing obligations on external debts owed to governments and official agencies as a formal precondition. This was done in a Paris Club meeting in early November 1978. Finally in December 1978, 285 private banks worldwide signed a restructuring agreement that rescheduled

50% of the 1978 roll-forward credits, deferring payment on the balance to year-end 1979; rescheduled 90% of 1979 current maturities on term debt to be paid in nine semiannual installments commencing in February 1982; and, subject to negotiation in the last quarter of 1979, made a provision which would allow 90% of all 1980 current maturities on term debt to be repaid in seven semiannual installments commencing in February 1983.

In view of the favorable economic developments in the country in 1979, the Peruvian authorities decided to forego the 1980 reschedulings which had been agreed with the banks and instead to seek a renegotiation of the terms of the 1979 bank rescheduling. The banks, however, were unwilling to renegotiate the 1979 terms. It was subsequently agreed that Peru would meet the 1979 rescheduled obligations in full in January 1980 and that the banks would reschedule 90% of maturities due in 1980 at a lower spread over LIBOR. Final consolidation into a medium-term loan was again conditional on Peru remaining eligible to purchase under its standby with the IMF. Peru had to meet the conditionality expressed in its arrangements with the Fund.

Turkey

Debt Renegotiations with Official Creditors

From 1959 to 1980, there were five multilateral debt renegotiations between the Turkish government and the country's official external creditors. The first multilateral debt renegotiation took place in 1959, the second after a six-year interval in 1965. In 1978, 1979, and 1980, three debt renegotiations followed each other in close succession.

The growth in the country's external indebtedness was very rapid in the 1970s. The public disbursed external term debt of Turkey increased from about $250 million in the mid-1950s to $4.3 billion by the end of 1977. This represented an average annual growth in external indebtedness of about 15% over a 20-year period. However, in the short span of three years, from the end of 1977 to the end of 1980, the public debt more than tripled to reach $14 billion. It remained close to $14 billion at the end of 1981. Similarly, the debt-service payments on external public debt in the mid-1950s amounted to about $11 million per year, had increased to over $360 million by 1977 and, even after rescheduling, amounted in 1980 to $1 billion and to $1.17 billion in 1981.

Official lenders have accounted for the largest portion, by far, of Turkey's public and publicly guaranteed term debt. In the 1950s and 1960s, over 90% of the total external debt was owed to official creditors, mostly governments on a bilateral basis. By the end of 1981, official lenders still accounted for almost 66% of the total public debt and 44% of the total debt-service payments were made to official creditors. As the debt included a comparatively large amount of concessional term debt, the debt service to official creditors in 1981 was somewhat lower than the debt-service payments to private creditors, even though the debt to official creditors was much larger. Of the total public and publicly guaranteed term debt outstanding at year-end 1981, about 45% was owed to governments, primarily the U.S., West Germany, and the United Kingdom; 19% owed to international organizations; 30% to private financial institutions; and about 6% to suppliers.

The first renegotiations of Turkish debt in the post-World War II period began in 1956 and 1957.[17] At that time, a number of specific obligations were rescheduled by the U.S. and some European countries. At the end of 1957, Turkey's total external debt—short term and long term combined—amounted to about $1 billion. These commercial debts were accumulated during the 1950s when Western European suppliers, supported by their official export credit insurance agencies, continued to extend large amounts of essentially short-term credits, even when serious repayment difficulties became apparent.

The payments due on this debt in 1958 were $371 million, an amount larger than total Turkish exports in 1957, or those expected for 1958. In 1958, Turkey suspended debt-service payments of about $500 million on its commercial debt outstanding at that time. It approached its creditor countries for a rescheduling of debt-service payments coming due within the next five years amounting to more than $400 million in commercial credits alone.

The debt renegotiations of 1959, as those of 1965, were transacted outside the framework of the Paris Club and involved arrangements quite different from those developed by the Paris Club. In 1959, the Organization for European Economic Cooperation, of which Turkey was a member, convened an international creditor meeting in Paris to negotiate a coordinated rescheduling of Turkey's commercial debts. The resulting agreement included both government-insured private credits and uninsured private credits and provided for rescheduling terms which were more generous than those previously granted to any country under Paris Club auspices. In addition, the debt relief by government creditors was associated with balance-of-payment loans on concessional terms. The rescheduling terms provided for repayment over a 12-year period in progressively larger amounts (to ensure greater relief in the critical earlier years) and an interest rate of 3% per year.

Despite the relatively generous terms of the 1959 rescheduling, Turkey's balance-of-payments difficulties persisted in the first half of the 1960s. In 1962, the OECD established a consortium of Turkey's official creditors which, in 1965, acted to extend debt relief to Turkey on payments due to member governments of the consortium. The terms of the debt relief, including some of the rescheduled debt of the 1959 agreement, were variable and were negotiated bilaterally. Some of the member governments, however, extended balance-of-payments loans instead of direct debt relief.

The second multilateral debt renegotiation of 1965 differed from the earlier renegotiations in a number of respects:

1. Some previously rescheduled debts were again rescheduled, a procedure which is opposed in principle by the Paris Club.

[17]Henry J. Bittermann, *The Refunding of International Debt* (Durham, N.C.: Duke University Press 1973); Albert C. Cizauskas, "International Debt Renegotiations: Lessons from the Past," *World Development*, Vol. 7 (1979), pp. 199-210.

2. Terms extended by government creditors were not uniform, although they were subject to review within the consortium.

3. Balance-of-payments loans, when disbursed on an emergency basis, were to be considered a substitute for debt relief.

4. Debt relief and official aid were connected with each other, although such an association was usually avoided by the Paris Club.

Turkey's economic difficulties began to increase during the mid-1970s, and by the end of 1977 the country was again unable to meet its debt-service obligations. Therefore, Turkey was granted substantial debt relief by its official creditors in a third rescheduling conducted by the OECD consortium in May 1978. At that time, the rescheduling terms were more typical of Paris Club arrangements. However, short-term official debt of less than one year, normally excluded from multilateral debt relief arrangements, was included as the country had accumulated very large short-term external obligations.

The Agreed Minutes, signed on May 20, 1978, provided for a rescheduling of principal and interest payments on officially guaranteed commercial credits and loans from governments and government institutions, contracted prior to January 1, 1978, and falling due from January 1, 1977 to June 30, 1979. The total amount involved in the consolidation with official creditors was $1.04 billion with 80% of the medium-term debt consolidated (covering arrears and scheduled payments) to be repaid in ten equal semiannual installments, after a grace period of four and a half years. Another 20% was to be repaid in four equal semiannual installments, after a three-and-one-half-year grace period. The final 20% was to be repaid in concerned, 80% of these was to be repaid in eight equal semiannual installments, after a three-and-one-half-years' grace period. The final 20% was to be repaid in four equal semiannual installments, after a grace period of one year and nine months. Interest rates on the rearranged maturities were to be determined bilaterally.

Turkey's external debt continued to accumulate at a rapid rate after 1977, reflecting the large current account deficits incurred by the country after 1975. In 1977, the current account deficit rose to almost 7% of GDP. Despite the rescheduling of 1978, the share of short-term debt continued to be very high. Consequently, debt-service obligations increased sharply, and the ratio of accrued debt-service payments to exports plus workers' remittances rose from 8% in 1974 to 29% in 1977 and 47% in 1979. (It was projected, at that time, to exceed 50% in the early 1980s.)

As debt-service obligations increased, external payments arrears also continued to accumulate. Various types of debts were involved in these arrears, including convertible Turkish lira deposits, suppliers' credits without official guarantees, overdue acceptance credits, and debt-service payments on bilateral and multilateral official credits.

The Turkish government, in an attempt to settle the problem of arrears, approached its official creditors for another debt rescheduling which was granted by the OECD consortium in July 1979. The debt covered by the 1979 rescheduling included principal and interest on officially guaranteed commercial credits and loans from governments and government institutions. Specifically it covered debt contracted prior to January 1, 1978, with an original maturity of more than one year, falling due between July 1, 1979, and June 30, 1980, and arrears, with an original maturity of one year or less, and contracted prior to January 1, 1979 (that is arrears that emerged between the May 1978 rescheduling and June 30, 1979).

The total amount involved in the consolidation was $1 billion, half of which consisted of medium-term debt and the other half of short-term arrears. In the terms of the renegotiation, 85% of the medium-term debt was to be repaid in ten equal semiannual payments, after a four-year grace period. The remaining 15% was to be repaid in three equal payments at six monthly intervals, after a grace period of nine months. As far as the short-term arrears were concerned, 85% of the amount was to be repaid in eight equal semiannual installments, after a four-year grace period, and the rest in three equal payments at six monthly intervals, after a grace period of one year and ten months. Again, interest rates on rearranged maturities were to be determined bilaterally.

In addition to the increase in arrears on suppliers' credits during the three-year period 1977-79, new arrears emerged on debt-service payments on official debt and on debt previously rescheduled. During the first three months of 1980, the accumulation of arrears was mainly caused by delays in debt-service payments on debt outstanding to official creditors, both on a bilateral and multilateral basis. Total arrears at the end of April 1980 were estimated at $2.6 billion. Consequently, in May 1980, the Turkish government approached its official creditors with another new rescheduling proposal.

The new proposal was adopted by the OECD consortium in July 1980. The debt covered by this rescheduling included principal and interest on officially guaranteed commercial credits and loans from governments and government institutions. Specifically, it covered debt *not* previously rescheduled and contracted prior to January 1, 1980, and debt *previously* rescheduled. The consolidation periods for debt not previously rescheduled were July 1, 1980, to June 30, 1983; for loans previously rescheduled but not in arrears, July 1, 1980, to June 30, 1981; and for payments of arrears, all arrears outstanding on June 30, 1980. The total amount involved in the consolidation was $3 billion. In respect of debt not previously rescheduled, and with payments falling due between July 1, 1980, and June 30, 1983, 90% of the consolidated amount was to be repaid in ten equal and successive semiannual installments, after a grace period of five and one-half years. The remaining 10% was to be repaid in five equal and successive annual installments, after a one-year grace period. Similar arrangements regarding repayment and grace periods were made with respect to debt previously rescheduled and outstanding arrears.

The interest rates on rearranged maturities were to be determined bilaterally. Each participating country, according to the Agreed Minutes, was to make a maximum effort to keep the rate of interest applicable to each bilateral agreement as low as possible, taking into account the market rate of the country concerned, and legal and other characteristics of each consolidation. For previously rescheduled debt, the interest rate would apply to principal and interest consolidated in 1978 and 1979, as well as to the interests resulting from these consolidations which had fallen due but were not paid by the time the bilateral agreements were signed.

Debt Renegotiations with Private Creditors

Turkey's repeated balance-of-payments crises since World War II and its extraordinary role in European and world affairs led not only to many debt reschedulings but to their being conducted in extraordinary ways. The Turkish experience completed the education of the private banks in debt renegotiations. What had been learned with Zaire and Peru was applied in Turkey, but new aspects led to greater sophistication and additional innovation.

Turkey's need for repeated debt renegotiations reflected the failure of successive Turkish governments to deal with Turkey's structural and monetary problems.

Turkey's balance-of-payments troubles began anew in the early 1970s, in part due to the government decision to focus its development program on domestic production to the neglect of exports. Three windfalls postponed the crisis: the 1973-74 world commodity boom, which temporarily boosted agricultural exports; growing remittances from Turkish workers in Europe; and the introduction of the short-term convertible Turkish lira deposit (CTLD) scheme,* which quickly attracted some $2 billion in foreign exchange, 90% from 250 foreign banks.

In 1976, the Turkish current account deficit reached $2 billion. Toward the end of that year, a major international bank concerned with the deteriorating balance-of-payments situation and mounting short-term external debt, offered to try to raise a Eurodollar standby credit. This facility, to be called on only in case of need, was to support the country's efforts to restructure liabilities under the CTLD. As the government did not at the time perceive any inherent problems in the CTLD maturity structure, the bank's proposal was rejected.

In early 1977, Turkey faced the consequences of its current critical payments imbalance. The country's international reserves reached near exhaustion, and after some emergency measures, reserves recovered to some extent. However, they fell again when import controls were relaxed in summer 1977 during a national election campaign. At the same time, the country's creditworthiness was seriously eroded.

That fall, as the current account deficit approached $3 billion and arrears $2.5 billion, the government started negotiations with the IMF for a standby arrangement that ended in disagreement over what stabilization terms to accept.

*Under the convertible Turkish lira deposit scheme, financial institutions, corporations, and individuals are permitted to deposit the lira countervalue of foreign currencies with commercial banks established in Turkey. Such deposits enjoy exchange convertibility guarantee and protection from exchange risk. Further, interest earned on these deposits tends to exceed that paid on deposits of similar amounts and maturities placed in the Eurodollar market.

Elections in spring 1978 gave a new government an uncertain mandate to negotiate a program with the IMF. An agreement for a two-year standby of SDR 374 ($486) million was signed in April 1978, with drawings conditioned on meeting IMF targets. In July, Turkey negotiated the rescheduling of much of its government debt. However, by September, the Turkish government, under political pressure to relax reform at home, had fallen short of several program targets. By November 1978, it became evident that the stabilization effort and the IMF agreement were not succeeding. By July 1979, the Turkish authorities and the IMF had agreed on a new financial program, and Turkey became eligible for a new two-year SDR 250 ($325) million standby.

Throughout this period, the private banks worked closely with the Turkish government on debt restructuring, encouraged because the Turks never went into arrears on their Eurodollar loans and kept the banks current on interest due in respect to CTLD and other debts. On the basis of the original standby arrangement reached with the IMF, eight international banks with major exposure to Turkey (three U.S., two German, two Swiss, and one British) formed an ad hoc steering committee. Its objective was to put together a financial package, including restructuring maturities under the CTLD, rescheduling existing commercial bank debt, and providing new money. Negotiations were long and arduous because the financial package was contingent on Turkey's compliance with the IMF's stabilization program.

The large number of banks involved (about 250 held CTLDs in something like 1,800 separate deposits) and the many types of debt created major organizational and administrative problems. It was estimated, however, that about 40 large Western banks were holding 65% of the total bank debt. Seven lead banks (three from the U.S. and four from Europe) negotiated on behalf of all participating bank creditors. The Turkish government retained the services of investment banking consultants to assist it in the negotiations. By September 1978, the lead banks and the consultants had arrived at a tentative agreement which covered the rescheduling terms of the bank debt. It also provided for syndication of a new bank loan which, the Turkish government hoped, would amount to $500 million.

However, the rescheduling proposals were accepted very slowly by the more than 200 banks holding CTLDs, as was the syndication of a large new loan. Progress was further slowed because the rescheduling terms and the syndication of a new loan had to be accepted as part of the rescheduling package. Negotiations with banks were temporarily discontinued in November 1978 when Turkey could not meet the performance criteria laid down in the IMF standby arrangement. They did not resume until the spring of 1979. By that time, the Turkish government had progressed in its discussions with the IMF for the standby arrangement. In July 1979, a rescheduling agreement between Turkey and the OECD consortium of official creditors was concluded as Turkey agreed to its new program with the IMF.

Meanwhile, the bank lenders had worked on solving a series of technical problems and in June 1979 reached an agreement on the syndication of a new medium-term Euroloan to Turkey. It was to cover the restructuring of bankers' credits and settlement of third-party reimbursement claims. The new Euroloan—a letter-of-credit facility—amounted to about $400 million, but its disbursement was conditional on meeting certain requirements, particularly complying with the stipulations of the IMF standby arrangement.

In addition to the new financing, bankers' credits in the amount of $430 million were rolled over.* Grace period and maturity for both the new financing and the rolled-over credits were three years and seven years, respectively. The rescheduling of about $300 million of third-party reimbursement claims (in arrears) was made conditional on immediate payment of past-due interest. Interest rate spreads were set at 1.75% over LIBOR. Not until August 1979 was an agreement reached between the commercial banks and Turkey on the restructuring of the CTLDs in the amount of $2.2 billion, with a three-year grace and a four-year repayment period, and an interest spread of 1.75% over LIBOR. In January 1980, the Turkish government introduced an IMF-agreed stabilization program. In June 1980, the IMF extended $1.65 billion to Turkey under a three-year standby arrangement, corresponding to the Fund's newly adopted more expansive lending policies.

In late 1980, Turkey's financial representative approached private bank lenders unofficially to obtain a modification of the rescheduling terms as set forth in the August 1979 rescheduling agreement. The Turkish proposal was aimed at extending the grace period from three to five years and at stretching out from four years to six years the subsequent repayment period of the principal of the loans (due to be repaid between 1982 and 1986). Turkey tried to lower the 1.75% interest rate spread over LIBOR. (At that time, the interest due on the debt had been fully paid up.) Having spent almost two years rescheduling Turkey's bank debt (from early 1978 to August 1979), the private banks did not want to embark on a new round of laborious negotiations involving 250 bank lenders. Some bankers felt it was premature to consider modifications, because the first capital repayments on the basis of the 1979 agreement were not due until July 1982.

In January 1981, the Turkish government invited 16 major international banks to a confidential discussion on the restructuring of the 1979 agreement affecting $3.3 billion in commercial loans. The purpose of the meeting was to get the bank lenders to accept an extension of the terms from the original 7 years to 10, or possibly 12 years and to reduce the interest spread over LIBOR from 1.75% to 1.25%. In addition, the banks were asked for a new medium-term loan of $400 million. The 16 bankers participating in the meeting acknowledged Turkey's difficult economic situation and the positive results of the economic stabilization program introduced in January 1980, and continued under the military government after September 1980.

The 16 banks individually considered the proposals and at the end of January 1981 decided in principle to extend the maturity from seven to ten years and the

*A refunding of debt by the replacement of existing debt with new debt is known as a rollover. It is used frequently by governments as a means of continuing debts, while normally incurring new debts as well.

grace period from three to five years. However, a reduction in the interest spread was turned down. The banks also informed the Turkish government that the implementation of their decision was conditional on complete acceptance of the new terms by all 250 foreign banks involved. From the outset, it was expected that negotiations would stretch over a considerable length of time. By August 1981, all but 5 of the 250 banks had accepted an extension of the terms of repayment, but it was not until February 1982 that negotiations were completed and all banks signed the agreement.

It should also be noted that in late 1979, the Turkish government proposed incentives to encourage foreign suppliers with outstanding claims in the form of nonguaranteed trade arrears to invest their money in Turkey. At that time, Turkey owed $1.7 billion to about 6,700 foreign suppliers but by year-end 1981, this amount had been reduced to about $1.3 billion. The creditors had been given two repayment options. They could either take repayment in Turkish lira and reinvest in Turkey, or if they wanted to be repaid in hard currency, they could wait four and one-half years and then begin collecting their loans over the following ten years. The plan also allowed companies to turn over the lira to third parties who want to invest in Turkey. Whatever option they chose, creditors had to make a decision by June 1982. Most of the estimated $400-million foreign investments made in Turkey in 1981 resulted from this suppliers' debt repayment loan.

The Turkish debt is an ongoing tale, and the final chapters remain to be written. At the end of 1981, it represented the largest and most complicated debt renegotiation case in the developing world.

Sudan

Debt Renegotiations with Official Creditors

The chronic gap between export earnings and import payments experienced for many years by Sudan continued to widen during the second half of the 1970s. While the current account deficit of the country amounted to about $90 million per year in 1977, it increased to over $240 million per year in 1979 and was about $640 million in 1981. The reason for this deterioration was that exports stagnated and commodity prices declined, while the costs of imports continued to rise. The deterioration in exports was partly caused by poor harvests but also by economic mismanagement, particularly in the country's agricultural sector. While exports paid for about 90% of imports in 1971, they covered only 56% in 1981. Although during 1978 and 1979 there was a net inflow of foreign capital into the country (mainly through the accelerated financing of ongoing projects and drawings on substantial cash loans from Saudi Arabia), this inflow was not sufficient to cover the current account deficit. Consequently, there was a large accumulation of arrears in external obligations. Because of the severe shortage of foreign exchange reserves, arrears on current payments for imports and on external debt service had accumulated to $1.2 billion by September 1979.

The outstanding disbursed public term debt at year-end 1979 was estimated at $3.3 billion, $1.9 billion of which was owed to official creditors on a bilateral basis, mostly the governments of Kuwait, Saudi Arabia, and the United Arab Emirates. About $530 million was owed to multilateral institutions such as the World Bank, the Arab Fund for Economic and Social Development, and the Arab African Bank. The remaining $865 million of loans consisted of suppliers' credits ($245 million) and loans from commercial banks and other private financial institutions ($620 million).

While loans from official creditors had mostly been contracted at concessional terms, loans from suppliers and banks had been extended at relatively hard terms. By year-end 1981, the country's outstanding disbursed public term debt had increased to $4.6 billion; of this total, $2.3 billion was owed to official creditors on a bilateral basis and $840 million to multilateral institutions. About $1.4 billion was owed to private creditors ($1.2 billion to private financial institutions and $200 million to suppliers). The total external term debt, including short term and nonguaranteed, amounted to about $7 billion at the end of 1982.

Sudan's first rescheduling of its external debt with official creditors was completed in November 1979, when an agreement was reached under the aegis of the Paris Club. The Agreed Minutes of the Paris Club rescheduling are dated November 13, 1979. The scope of relief granted by official creditors was wide. The debt rescheduled included principal and interest on officially guaranteed or insured commercial credits, or loans from governments and government agencies, contracted before January 1, 1979, with an original maturity of more than one year falling due between October 1, 1979, and June 30, 1981, as well as arrears outstanding on October 1, 1979.

The amounts involved in the rescheduling totaled $221 million of debt payments falling due in the period October 1979 to June 1981, plus $200 million of arrears. A grace period of three years and nine months was granted, and the repayment plus grace period was set at ten years and three months for payments falling due between October 1, 1979, and June 30, 1980. The grace and repayment periods on payments falling due between July 1, 1980, and June 30, 1981, were agreed to be ten and one-half years. The interest rates on the rearranged maturities were to be determined bilaterally by each of the creditor governments with the Sudanese authorities.

An effort to achieve a settlement of Sudan's arrears problem was initiated in 1979 by the IMF. Discussions took place regarding a standby arrangement. The Sudanese government agreed to adopt an economic stabilization and reform program, supported by a standby arrangement under the Extended Fund Facility (EFF) over a three-year period (April 1979 to March 1982). The IMF arrangement contained specific commitments by the Sudanese authorities regarding economic and financial policy measures, including ceilings on the country's external borrowing. The Sudanese government, at the Paris Club meetings in 1979, expressed its determination to comply with the targets of the economic and financial program. The creditor government representatives agreed to the consolidation of Sudan's payments due between July 1, 1980, and June 30, 1981, conditional on Sudan's observance of the policies set forth in the IMF standby arrangement.

When the country's economic conditions further deteriorated in 1981, the Sudanese government approached the IMF for an SDR 190 ($220) million emergency credit for 1982 to help the government in its financial crisis. In return for the IMF assistance, the government agreed to take some politically unpopular economic austerity measures, including a drastic reduction in basic food subsidies, a devaluation of the currency, and a ceiling on public sector borrowing. These measures were expected to lead to substantial increases in domestic prices of basic foods and in prices of imports, particularly oil products.

Despite political changes in the Sudan, the government had little choice but to implement a stabilization program agreeable to the IMF. Without emergency help from the IMF, the country would probably have lost all access to international credit. A standby arrangement with the IMF, moreover, could pave the way to a rescheduling agreement with private commercial bank lenders. In February 1982, the IMF decided to make available about $240 million over the next 12 months to support the country in its economic crisis. In March 1982, representatives of 13 Western nations, under Paris Club auspices, agreed to reschedule principal and interest payments on Sudan's public and publicly guaranteed commercial debts with a maturity of more than one year, falling due between July 1, 1981, and December 31, 1982. The creditors agreed to grant a four-year grace period and a ten-year maturity.

In January 1983, the government of the Sudan approached the country's official creditors to grant a second debt rescheduling within two years. The representatives of 13 creditor countries met in Paris in mid-January 1983 with representatives of the World Bank. In a communique issued in Paris on January 14, 1983, the country's official creditors expressed their support for a partial restructuring of $3 billion of foreign debt. The multilateral agencies pledged their continued financial and technical support to the country.

In early February 1983, the country's official creditors agreed for a second time in less than two years to accept a rescheduling of Sudan's official external debt. The actual amount rescheduled was not disclosed, but it was believed to have been about $200 million. Rescheduled were payments on principal and interest in arrears at the end of 1982 and all payments falling due in 1983. Under the rescheduling terms, payments were stretched out over a 16-year period, with a 6-year grace period.

Debt Renegotiations with Private Creditors

Sudan's balance-of-payments difficultires in the mid-1970s resulted from an ambitious agricultural development plan, declining commodity (cotton) export prices, and economic mismanagement. While Sudan was able to obtain long-term development financing from its principal bankers (Saudi Arabia and Kuwait), it failed to attract enough short-term capital for general purposes to bridge the gap before foreign exchange-generating projects came on stream. By 1978, Sudan was $600-$700 million in arrears on its $2-billion foreign debt to governments, banks, and suppliers.

During this period, Sudan had a weak government. In 1972 the president ended a 17-year rebellion in the south and in 1977-78 was still carrying out a program of national reconciliation. He feared that austere economic policies—particularly, curbing government food and fuel subsidies and a growing bureaucracy—would result in civil riots similar to those which had occurred in neighboring Egypt the year before. Hence, the Sudanese resisted IMF-suggested reforms and instead appealed to certain Middle Eastern sources for aid and debt relief.

Sudan also avoided formal debt restructuring negotiations with creditors, fearing tough reform conditionality would be demanded. Instead, the government dealt with individual creditors. In 1977 and 1978, it was successful in obtaining aid and debt rescheduling from some Arab and European governments. In 1978, it was one of ten developing countries which benefitted from post-World War II unilateral debt cancellations by concerned governments, including the United Kingdom, Sweden, and Denmark. Finally, while holding suppliers at bay, it obtained ad hoc relief from individual private banks through sporadic interest payments and short-term debt rollovers.

The commercial banks, which held only about 10% of the country's external debt, were prepared to be patient with the Sudanese. They realized that the bulk of the relief had to come from governmental sources, particularly the Arab nations that were the country's major creditors and also the prime beneficiaries of Sudan's development plan. (Sudan was to become the bread basket of the Middle East.) Furthermore, the banks knew that Saudi Arabia and Kuwait had encouraged Sudan to adopt IMF-supported stabilization and reform programs as conditions for new aid and credits. In August 1978, Sudan signed a SDR 27 ($34) million first tranche program with the IMF, thus reopening aid flows. While the Sudanese made reasonable progress under the first tranche program during 1978-79, the IMF and the Arab countries wanted further reforms before providing more aid.

In mid-1979, the Sudanese agreed to and signed a SDR 200 ($256) million three-year standby in the higher tranches, including the first supplementary financing granted an IMF member country under the new $10-billion facility. As the Sudanese predicted, severe rioting followed stiffer economic reforms. The government was forced to rescind certain measures, but was able, on balance, to maintain momentum in its economic recovery. In fact, on September 21, 1979, the IMF's board of directors approved Sudan's new liberalized exchange system.

Despite the debt crisis, the commercial bank lenders hesitated to ask for a rescheduling of the country's private bank debt and wanted official creditors to take the lead. An agreement was reached on the rescheduling of debt and arrears to official creditors under the Paris Club in November 1979. Meanwhile, the private commercial banks were holding preliminary talks with the Sudanese government and assisting it in compiling a record of all arrears to private lenders. Following preliminary talks, the first formal meeting between the Sudanese authorities and a steering committee representing commercial banks from the U.S., Europe, and the Middle East was held in London in October 1979.

According to the Sudanese rescheduling proposal put forward in December 1979, the government asked for a new bank loan of $500 million to be disbursed during 1981-82. By comparison, at the end of 1979, the entire outstanding medium-term bank loans of Sudan amounted to $500 million.

The commercial banks presented various proposals between December 1979 and February 1980. The banks intended during 1981-82 to reduce their external claims on Sudan by something like $200-$250 million. Actually, there occurred only a small net reduction in bank loans outstanding as of 1979.

After two new bank proposals in February 1980, the positions of the private commercial banks and the Sudanese authorities still remained far apart and the impasse lasted until the summer of that year. In August 1980, the Sudanese authorities retained an investment banking house as consultants for the debt renegotiations with private commercial bank lenders. In early November 1980, a group of five leading banks submitted a new proposal, according to which a rescheduling of 60% of the arrears of interest on medium-term debt and of all arrears on principal in respect to short- and medium-term debt was considered acceptable. The proposal also provided for a new loan of between $50-$100 million. Thus, the arrangement of November 1980 provided very substantial debt relief with respect to arrears. However, the proposed spread of 1.75% over LIBOR on the refinanced amounts was significantly higher than the spreads on the original loans.

Although the arrangement provided for the disbursement of a new loan, the net outflow of medium-term bank funds expected to occur in 1981 was large. Interest payments were also expected to be substantial during the consolidation period, especially if high nominal interest rates were to prevail during the repayment period. Despite these considerations, the proposal of November 1980 was accepted by the consultants acting for the Sudanese government. The arrangement with the banks in November 1980 was thus close to the Paris Club rescheduling of Sudan's debt with official creditors, which had been carried out exactly one year earlier. The banks were also prepared to accept a rescheduling of overdue interest payments. The banks' new loan was also intended to reduce the burden on the country's balance of payments in the period following the private debt rescheduling.

While the negotiations between the private banks and the Sudanese authorities were conducted, numerous informal discussions were held between the staff of the IMF and various commercial banks. In these meetings, the IMF staff discussed Sudan's balance-of-payments situation in detail and provided the consultants retained by Sudan with their outlook for the balance of payments.

Sudan's basic economic problems, however, continued to worsen throughout 1981, and toward the end of the year, the financial situation again reached crisis proportions. The gap between export earnings and import payments continued to widen, and the availability of foreign exchange was insufficient to even meet interest payments on the country's external debt of about $5 billion. By October 1982,

Sudanese officials were meeting with an IMF delegation to obtain emergency financial assistance from the Fund for balance-of-payments support during 1982. The IMF assistance was to total SDR 190 ($220) million and paved the way for additional financial assistance from private commercial banks and from the Saudi Arabian government.

At the end of December 1981, Sudan's private bank creditors agreed to reschedule about $600 million of the country's external debt due to private lenders, including $400 million in principal and $206 million in unpaid interest. The agreement was the result of extended, but fractious, negotiations between 115 commercial banks in the U.S., Europe, Japan, and the Middle East on the one side and the government of the Sudan, on the other. Approximately 25 U.S. banks were involved in the rescheduling.

Under the agreement, the commercial banks involved in the rescheduling would receive $106 million of unpaid interest by the end of March 1982. The remaining $100 million in interest arrears were to be repaid over a three-year period, beginning in January 1983. Repayment of the $400 million of the principal would begin after a three-year grace period in January 1985 and extend over seven years. The loans were to carry an interest rate of 1.75% over LIBOR effective March 26, 1982.

The Sudanese authorities, however, stated at the time of signing the agreement that their country would need additional outside financing to meet its obligations in 1982. It was expected that the government would approach commercial banks for new lines of credit and medium-term loans. In addition, countries with bilateral loans to the Sudan were to be asked for further debt relief. In January 1982, Western aid donor countries agreed to enter rescheduling talks on officially guaranteed commercial credits. In February 1982, the IMF decided to extend support in the amount of $240 million over a 12-month period, provided the stipulated economic performance criteria were met.

Throughout early 1982, Sudan's economic situation continued to deteriorate, and in January 1983 the country's government approached its official creditors for another round of debt renegotiations. When in early February 1983 an agreement was reached with the country's official creditors, the way was opened for a partial rescheduling of debt owed to foreign private creditors, particularly private commercial banks.

Jamaica

Debt Renegotiations with Private Creditors

Jamaica's debt renegotiations received much public attention. Interest in Jamaica was greatly heightened by sharp political disputes and social violence during the years before 1982.

The private banks played a role in the deliberations with the Jamaican government that was similar in some respects to the role they played in the Peruvian case. For example, during March and April 1977, bankers were counseling and urging the Jamaican government to negotiate a standby program with the IMF as a mechanism for getting access to additional private bank credits. Negotiations between the government and the IMF for the establishment of a standby had broken down late in 1976, presumably due to the Jamaican government's unwillingness to devalue its currency to the extent deemed appropriate by the IMF.

There were strong rumors in the financial markets in the spring of 1977 that Jamaica was about to default on its external debt. Poor performance of its commodity exports and tourism, the alarming decline in international reserves, and the impasse with the IMF worried key Jamaican government officials and private bankers. Jamaica quickly took the initiative, began a new dialogue with the IMF, devalued its currency, and initiated new discussions related to an IMF standby arrangement.

Once negotiations with the IMF began, the Jamaican government approached a few leading private banks. The government requested a facility to provide the funds to meet a substantial part of its medium-term public sector obligations falling due to private banks in fiscal 1979 (from April 1978 to March 1979). At the same time, government officials made it known to these private banks that eventually it would become necessary to address restructuring of current maturities of the public sector debt owed to private banks and falling due in fiscal 1980 and 1981.

Benefiting from the Peruvian experience, a steering committee of Jamaica's principal external bank creditors was formed to facilitate negotiations related to the first loan. The steering committee agreed to consider the first facility and to recommend approval to other potential participating banks, provided that the facility was linked to satisfactory performance under the IMF standby arrangement.

By mid-1977, the government had negotiated a two-year standby with the IMF for SDR 74 ($84) million. By December, however, the Jamaicans had failed to meet specified targets, and negotiations between the private commercial banks and the Jamaican government regarding the bank debts falling due in fiscal year 1979 were at a standstill. At that time, however, and separate from the refinancing negotiations, the Jamaican government approached the commercial banks for *new* funds. A consortium of seven banks indicated it was willing to extend a $32-million loan, conditional on Jamaica's acceptance of an IMF stabilization program. One bank agreed to provide a bridging loan of $27 million, if and when an IMF field mission would arrive in Jamaica.

In early 1978, the Jamaican government reopened negotiations with the IMF for assistance in the form of an EFF for SDR 200 ($244) million. These negotiations were successfully concluded in May 1978 and the standby approved in mid-June 1978. During that period, the commercial bank steering committee met to consider Jamaica's formal request for renegotiation of bank debts falling due in fiscal 1979.

Complications similar to those of Peru arose concerning the composition of the steering committee. Initially, the committee included representatives of U.S. and Canadian banks, but none from Japanese and European banks. This resulted in inefficiencies in communication and a delay in reaching an agreement. The lead banks agreed to put together a $70-million refinancing agreement with Jamaica, through which disbursements of the refinanced amounts would be linked to the scheduled purchases under the IMF program, a technique earlier envisioned for Zaire. The banks also provided a $15-million loan to bridge the first purchase under the EFF.

Shortly after the approval of the IMF loan in mid-June 1978, the commercial banks disbursed a $32-million consortium loan. This loan had been granted, in principle, the January before, while the $27-million bridging loan was repaid. The new loan had a three-year maturity with a one-year grace period and an interest spread of 2% over LIBOR. In July 1978, the first IMF drawing under the EFF was made, and the $15-million bridging loan was repaid to the commmercial banks.

Although the first disbursement under the bank loan agreement had been expected with the July 1978 purchase from the IMF, it was not until August that the major banks agreed on a refinancing package. Bank loans officially guaranteed in the creditor countries posed a particular problem for Jamaica because the government did not undertake a simultaneous rescheduling of debts with official creditors.

Following the Peruvian example in all essential elements, the major commercial banks agreed that 12.5% of the outstandings due to them in fiscal 1979 would be repaid, while 87.5%, or approximately $35 million, would be rescheduled over seven years with two years' grace and an interest spread of 2% over LIBOR. In late September 1978, the agreement was extended to include a number of smaller banks and to cover $55.5 million.

After signing the initial agreement, the first disbursement of $29 million was made. Some banks joined the agreement later, and in October 1978, the U.S. Export-Import Bank agreed to a deferral of payments on loans guaranteed by it and maturing between August 9, 1978, and April 30, 1979. The refinancing, therefore, totaled $83 million, with the remaining disbursements to be made after the scheduled IMF purchase in October 1978 and January 1979.

At the May 1978 steering committee meetings of the commercial banks, the Jamaican government had pointed out the necessity of a rescheduling of commercial bank debts due in each of three consecutive fiscal years—fiscal 1979, 1980, and 1981. Preliminary discussions on the reschedulings of amounts falling due in fiscal 1980 and 1981 were begun in September 1978. The commercial banks' steering committee was then expanded to include Japanese and European banks as well as North American banks, and subsequent negotiations among the banks were conducted much more efficiently.

In November 1978, the commercial banks agreed to reschedule 87.5% of the bank debts falling due in fiscal 1980 and 1981, with the provision that the agreement would become effective on April 1, 1979. It was intended to roll over the rescheduled portions on a short-term basis and on April 1, 1980 and 1981 to convert these into medium-term loans, conditional on the successful implementation of the IMF stabilization program, and compliance with the targets stipulated in the program. Under the agreement, each of the two medium-term loans would have a grace period of two years and a maturity of five years from the consolidation date. The interest spread was 2% over LIBOR.

During 1978 and 1979, the country conformed with the provisions as set forth in the IMF stabilization program. In January 1980, the government was unable to make the IMF purchase and asked for a waiver from the Fund until elections, scheduled for October 1980, could settle major political issues of the country. Then-Prime Minister Michael Manley was being opposed by the much more conservative Edward Seaga. On March 24, 1980, the government discontinued negotiations with the IMF.

The commercial banks were faced with a difficult situation when discussions with the IMF were broken off. The rescheduling of commercial bank debt on April 1, 1980, had been made conditional on continued financial support by the Fund. The medium-term consolidation loan was not signed. However, the banks did continue to roll over the amounts due on a short-term basis, as well as 87.5% of those amounts falling due after April 1, 1980. In September 1980, when the first payments on the fiscal 1979 rescheduling were falling due, the banks agreed to roll over the amounts due as well as 100% of all additional amounts falling due at that time. Throughout this period, Jamaica continued its interest payments on public sector debt.

The election was held in October 1980, and discussions between the newly elected Seaga government and the IMF were reopened in early December. At that time, the Jamaican government estimated its short-term financing needs at $300 million. Discussions were also held with the World Bank regarding a longer-term so-called structural adjustment loan of $45 million.

Although the Jamaican government did not seek a multilateral rescheduling with official creditors, the U.S. and 11 other Western donor nations, with the World Bank and the Inter-American Development Bank, agreed in March 1981 to give Jamaica a development assistance package of $350 million for 1981-82. This extended the assistance made conditional on the successful conclusion of negotiatins with the IMF for a three-year EFF. This assistance commitment was the largest that Jamaica had ever received up to that time.

By April 1981, the IMF and Jamaica had concluded negotiations, and the country was granted $698 million in financial assistance, consisting of $650 million drawings under a three-year EFF and $48 million compensatory financing. The EFF arrangement provided for deregulation of Jamaica's economy through progressive removal of import restrictions, price controls, and wage restraints. The main economic performance criteria stipulated by the IMF concerned limits on the expansion of the net domestic assets of Jamaica's central bank, and a minimum increase in the country's international reserves to be achieved in fiscal 1981-82. Measures required to satisfy the IMF criteria were crucial for the country's access to other credits, particularly those from private commercial lenders.

While negotiations between the IMF and the Jamaican government were still under way, eight major commercial banks agreed in March 1981 to a rescheduling of a portion of the total commercial bank debt estimated at nearly $490 million. The rescheduling covered loans of $120 million, of which $55 million were falling due in fiscal 1982 and the remainder in fiscal 1983. It also provided for a three-year grace period for repayments of principal, a six-year total maturity period, and interest spreads of 2-2.5% over LIBOR.

In addition, the eight lead banks agreed to arrange a new loan of $71 million to Jamaica at a spread of 2.25% over LIBOR, a three-year grace period, and a seven-year maturity. In July 1981, after about 100 smaller banks involved in the rescheduling of bank debt had accepted the terms, the agreement was signed. Again, in a manner which was becoming nearly commonplace, the new LIBOR margins were considerably above the original margins in the loan contracts being renegotiated. While publicists wrote as though the banks faced huge losses, in practice, they were proving quite capable of protecting their financial balance sheets.

Jamaica is now close to the third year of the three-year EFF arrangement with the IMF which became effective on April 1, 1981. The drawings available under the three-year standby total $520 million. As the second year of the arrangement expires in April 1983, negotiations between the Jamaican government and the IMF began in early 1983. These negotiations are conducted to reconcile the IMF stabilization objectives with the government's proposed fiscal and budgetary plans for 1983-84 and to determine the amounts of IMF drawings available to the country in 1983.

While negotiations between the IMF and the government were under way, the Jamaicans in early 1983 also approached a number of private commercial banks about syndicating a $25-million loan by the end of March 1983 to replenish the country's international reserve holdings. If this bank loan materializes, it would be the first private bank loan used to improve the country's international payments position since 1981. At that time, Jamaica raised approximately $70 million from private commercial banks. However, if Jamaica fails to meet the IMF's performance targets, it would be unlikely that private banks would extend further loans.

Nicaragua

Debt Renegotiations with Private Creditors

The issue of possible default was faced with Nicaragua. The fear of another country default, such as Cuba or the moratorium of North Korea, seemed more plausible because of the radical political changes taking place in that country.

During 1978, the banks had followed with increasing concern the civil disturbances and events leading eventually to the fall of the Somoza government in July 1979. The Somoza government had earlier agreed to a program with the IMF staff which, however, was not endorsed by the executive directors of the IMF. This was followed by another program which did receive endorsement, but it became inoperative with the outbreak of the civil war.

Before the change in government, the private banks had repeated discussions with the Nicaraguan authorities about servicing their external debt, particularly term debt owed by the public sector. It is noteworthy that in these earlier discussions, the Nicaraguan authorities emphasized they intended to meet fully and promptly payments due on short-term trade-related debts of the public sector, as well as all debts of the private sector. Eventually, interruptions were experienced in the payment to banks of maturing public sector term and all other debt.

As with Peru and Jamaica, a steering committee for the creditor banks was formed to conduct negotiations. Consideration was given to restructuring along the lines of the Peruvian and Jamaican examples and again tied to economic performance and IMF endorsement. With the civil war and the fall of the Somoza government, these discussions came to a halt.

Within two weeks of the Sandinists' takeover of the government on July 19, 1979, the new authorities discussed with Mexican financial advisors the country's external debt situation and decided, in principle, to meet the country's obligations. In August 1979, the Nicaraguan authorities and representatives of the largest commercial bank creditors began to catalogue the country's outstanding debts into three major categories. These three categories consisted of loans to the public sector of the former government, loans to organizations and entities which had been nationalized by the new government, and loans to private Nicaraguan entities.

Meanwhile, the private banks reformed the steering committee which included 13 of the largest creditor banks accounting for 52% of the outstanding bank debt. This committee represented the claims of about 115 banks. Lengthy negotiations with the new Nicaraguan government began early in 1980, with the first serious proposals and counterproposals made in March of that year. The Nicaraguans maintained from the outset that their country's case was a special one and that while they were prepared to honor the amounts owed to the banks, the debt-service burden should be low enough not to further weaken the economy. The Nicaraguan authorities proposed, at that time, a fixed interest rate of 7% on all rescheduled amounts. The total amount covered by the restructuring was estimated at $582 million, or over one-third of the country's total external debt of $1.6 billion.

The banks, on their part, insisted that all interest and principal had to be honored, including commitments made under the Somoza government, that full commercial interest rates would have to be paid, and the stretch-out would have to be restricted to a ten-year period. By the end of July 1980, the meetings between the steering committee and the government were temporarily adjourned when the negotiating parties were still far apart on the terms. When negotiations resumed later in the year, the gaps in the proposals began to narrow, and eventually a tentative agreement was reached in September 1980.

The terms granted, even considering the special circumstances, were unusually lenient. The rescheduling did not only cover the repayment of principal but also a substantial portion (more than three-quarters) of the country's past-due interest. Credits extended to the former Somoza government, including capitalized interest and all future maturities, were consolidated into one loan. Repayments were stretched out over 12 years including a grace period of 5 years. Repayment of the rescheduled principal, therefore, would not begin until 1986.

The debt-service payments during the first five years of the agreement would be very small, as only payments on past-due interest would be made during the period 1981-85. Furthermore, the amount of the past-due interest was recalculated at a spread of .50% over the 18-month LIBOR rate on July 19, 1979, when the Sandinists' government took over, and thus reduced from the amount based on the original spreads. (The rate used in recalculating the amount was 10.88% per year.) Although the total past-due interest was calculated at $90 million, lenders received only $20 million in 1980; payments on the remaining portion were deferred.

In addition, payments on the balance of the past-due interest during 1981-85 were to be made at a flat interest rate of 7% per year. The difference between the flat rate of 7% and the commercial rate (which would rise from 1% to 1.75% over LIBOR) would be capitalized and paid back over five to ten years after the signing of the agreement. Interest would be paid on the capitalized interest, preserving its present value. Thus, despite including a large amount of arrears in the debt rescheduling, actual repayments in the years from 1981-85 would exceed the original repayment schedule by a relatively small amount. The projected debt service, therefore, would represent a comparatively smaller burden on the country's balance of payments.

Although the agreement did not provide for any new financing by the commercial banks, short-term debt was consolidated into a medium-term loan. The agreement went into effect at the end of 1980. It is noteworthy that the private bank lenders did not insist on an IMF standby arrangement and stabilization program as a precondition for a debt rescheduling.

The question arising from the Nicaraguan experience was whether it would become the new precedent for settlements. If so, much of the confidence that the banks could defend themselves would not be warranted. It was rumored that the Nicaraguans had threatened default. In past cases, such threats had been treated with disdain.

In mid-December 1982, a group of foreign commercial banks (including one large U.S. bank) agreed to extend an amount of $25-$30 million in short-term trade credits as part of an arrangement to enable Nicaragua to meet a $40-million interest payment falling due at that time. This interest payment was the second payment falling due under the external debt restructuring agreement which had been signed in December 1980. (The first installment of $36 million on interest had been paid by the Nicaraguan government in July 1982.)

Nicaragua, under the 1980 restructuring agreement, must resume principal payments on its commercial bank debt by 1986. At present, Nicaragua is only paying a 7% interest rate, with the difference between current market rates to be added to capital to be repaid between 1986 and 1990. The new (December 1982) commercial bank credit was the first significant commercial bank loan granted to Nicaragua since the takeover by the Sandinist government in 1979.

The country's external debt amounted to $1.6 billion at the time of the restructuring. But it has since increased by an additional $1.3 billion, because of loans made available in the interim by multilateral agencies and governments on a bilateral basis. A $30-million loan to the country by the Inter-American Development Bank was expected to be approved in early 1983.

Bolivia

Debt Renegotiations with Private Creditors

Bolivia in recent years has experienced chronic political instability, greatly handicapping its ability to deal with serious economic difficulties. These conditions resulted in a drastic weakening of its external creditworthiness and consequent near crisis in its external financial position.

In April 1980, private commercial banks worldwide were approached by the Bolivian government for a rescheduling of debt to private commercial banks when it became apparent that the country could not meet its external debt-service obligations. At that time, Bolivia's total external debt was estimated at about $3 billion, and debt-service payments due in 1980 at $450 million.

In September, 1980—after a military government had taken over power in July of that year—private commercial banks accepted a "stand-still" agreement that postponed Bolivia's public sector debt-service payments due to private banks by three months. The amount involved was $172 million of principal owed to banks and falling due between August 1, 1980 and January 5, 1981. Bolivia intended to keep up interest payments. The interest rate was set at 1.38% over LIBOR for six-month Eurodollar deposits or at the level of the original loan instruments being negotiated, whichever was the greater. The negotiations on behalf of the private banks were conducted by a 10-bank steering committee representing 97 international creditor banks.

In December 1980, the Bolivian government approached the private banks again and was granted a second postponement of $180 million of principal payments falling due in the period through April 5, 1981. This postponement was an extension of the stand-still agreement granted in September 1980. The interest rate spreads remained unchanged. This extension by the private banks was intended to provide Bolivia with additional time to reformulate its economic adjustment program and come to terms in the government's negotiations with the IMF.

After protracted negotiations, the Bolivian government and the IMF finally reached agreement to implement an economic reform program. This program was designed to reduce the country's current account deficit; to limit sharply external borrowing, except for developmental purposes; and to stimulate savings, investment, and real growth of the economy. It consisted of a four-year development plan, with IMF assistance to be given in two successive, related phases.

At the outset, the IMF agreed to a one-year standby arrangement intended to improve the country's balance of payments. While investment levels were to be maintained, the necessary adjustment would have to be achieved by reducing consumption expenditures. The IMF's financial assistance during the first year of the program was to be $120 million. Provided the first phase of the program was successfully completed, the IMF would then provide a three-year EFF to sustain real growth in investment and output.

Although major economic reform policies as recommended by the IMF were adopted—including devaluation of the Bolivian peso, substantial increases in oil prices, and restrictions on domestic credit and public sector foreign borrowing—the program's targets were not met. Savings and investment as a proportion of GDP, declined in 1980 and real economic growth fell short of expectations. The country's poor economic performance in 1980, however, did not prevent the IMF from disbursing the largest portion ($103 million) of the $120 million standby. While this assistance was forthcoming during 1980 in three quarterly installments, the IMF refused the fourth installment in December 1980 when the Bolivian government exceeded the stipulated spending limits of the public sector and raised $200 million in freely disposable credits from Argentina.

During 1981 and 1982, the Bolivian government made several attempts at reviving the IMF standby arrangement. Meanwhile, negotiations with private bank creditors continued. In March 1981, Bolivia's new financial authorities under the military government approached the banks for a renegotiation of external debt-service obligations. In April 1981, 128 of Bolivia's private creditor banks, mostly American, accepted a tentative agreement to reschedule $460 million in foreign debt-service payments falling due between August 1, 1980, and March 31, 1983. On short-term obligations, the grace period granted was two years and the amortization period three and one-half years. On medium-term obligations, the grace period granted was three years and the amortization period seven years. The interest rates agreed on were 2% over LIBOR on the short-term debt and 2.25% over LIBOR on the medium-term obligations.

Any definitive rescheduling agreement with the banks was made conditional on Bolivia's government coming to terms with the IMF on an economic stabilization program. Although the standby arrangement with the IMF did not materialize either in 1981 or in 1982, until September 1982 Bolivia met its financial obligations to the private banks, as if the rescheduling agreement had actually been signed and put into effect. In early September 1982, however, Bolivia informed its foreign bank lenders that the country could not meet its external debt-service payments due by September 30 and asked for a deferment of September-October 1982 payments.

On October 10, 1982, Bolivia's military government handed over power to a newly elected civilian government, and shortly thereafter the new government approached the country's private commercial bank creditors for another round of debt renegotiations. At year-end 1982, about $1 billion of the country's external debt was owed to a consortium of 128 foreign banks. For the purpose of negotiations, the syndicate appointed a 12-bank steering committee.

While negotiations with the bank steering committee were under way, Bolivia also applied to the IMF for a $300-million, three-year EFF credit. Both the IMF and the bank syndicate made the extension of credits conditional on the Bolivian government's acceptance of an austere stabilization program.

In early 1983, the private commercial banks had yet to succeed in working out an acceptable formula to refinance Bolivia's principal payments that fell due from 1981 through 1983 which totaled $460 million. In addition, the country owes $600 million in interest payments for that period. A refinancing package was proposed by the banks, in which bank debts would be stretched out over seven years with a three-year grace period. However, the banks now insist that Bolivia come to terms with the IMF on an economic reform program before a definitive restructuring agreement with the private banks can be reached.

Costa Rica

Debt Renegotiations with Official Creditors

The Costa Rican government, late in 1982, approached the country's official creditors and asked for a rescheduling of a portion of official, bilateral credits. It was estimated that, at year-end 1982, bilateral credits totaled $350 million.

In mid-January 1983, at a Paris Club meeting between representatives of ten major lending nations, the official government creditors agreed to rescheduling a portion of Costa Rica's bilateral debt. Although the actual amount rescheduled by the Paris Club meeting was not disclosed, banking sources indicated that the rescheduling involved about $100 million and affected debt-service payments due from July 1982 through the end of 1983. Under the agreement, payments will be extended over the next nine years, with a four-year grace period. The nations represented at the Paris Club meeting included the U.S., West Germany, Britain, Japan, Mexico, Sweden, France, Italy, Spain, and Austria.

Debt Renegotiations with Private Creditors

In early August 1981, the government informed 150 of its foreign private creditors that the country had been experiencing serious foreign exchange difficulties and that payment of principal on short-term debt, coming due before September 30, 1981, would have to be delayed. The government also stated that temporary delays in debt-service payments were likely to continue. Foreign creditors were asked to submit details of loans so that the Costa Rican government could prepare an external debt profile.

At the time when debt-service payments were interrupted, the country's total external debt (including short term) was estimated at over $4 billion. Of this total, about $2.9 billion were public sector obligations. The external term debt to private commercial banks (debt exceeding one year in maturity) was estimated at about $1 billion. In September 1981, the Costa Rican government approached its private commercial bank lenders for a meeting to begin renegotiations of the public sector's external debt.

The country's economic difficulties had mounted with the rising trade deficits incurred in the late 1970s, which had been financed through heavy foreign borrowing. A crisis developed in 1980, however, caused by the sudden drop in coffee prices on the world market and the continuing rising costs of oil imports. A year before, in 1979, coffee had contributed as much as one-third to the country's total export earnings. The crisis worsened when three successive standby arrangements with the IMF were broken in the course of two years. A three-year EFF arrangement (the last of the three), signed in June 1981, was suspended by the IMF in August 1981 when the Costa Rican government failed to comply with the agreed economic policies and did not meet the prescribed performance targets. Only after the election of a new government in February 1982, and its inauguration the following May, could negotiations be resumed with the IMF regarding a new (possibly one-year) standby credit.

Meanwhile, debt renegotiation meetings with private commercial bank creditors continued through the winter 1981-82, with the Costa Rican government submitting various proposals for rescheduling of the outstanding bank debt. It also attempted to raise additional bank credits of $1.9 billion. The meetings conducted by a 12-bank steering committee representing 148 private banks ended inconclusively. Any rescheduling agreement with the private banks was felt to be contingent on Costa Rica fulfilling the terms of an IMF stabilization program requiring the implementation of severe austerity policies.

Since a new government took office in Costa Rica in May 1982, however, the country has introduced economic austerity policies designed to improve its financial condition, and it has been able to resume some "symbolic" interest payments on its external debt.

In late November 1982, Costa Rica reached an agreement with the IMF regarding a $100-million standby credit. In early December 1982, the U.S. government provided a $70-million loan conditional on IMF approval of Costa Rica's austerity program. The U.S. also agreed to support the government's efforts to obtain a rescheduling of the country's external debt owed to private commercial bank creditors and to foreign governments on a bilateral basis.

Of Costa Rica's $4-billion external debt, $1.2 billion is owed to private commercial banks. In the rescheduling negotiations, a 12-bank steering committee represented about 180 private creditors. At year-end 1982, the arrears in interest payments amounted to about $260 million and arrears in principal payments to some $360 million.

On December 15, 1982, an agreement in principle was reached between the government of Costa Rica and the leading creditor banks. The agreement reportedly covered overdue interest, as well as interest falling due in 1983. It also provided for a revolving trade facility to give Costa Rica sufficient funds to repay the interest. International banks used the trade facility concept for the first time during the renegotiation of Poland's debt in February 1982. As applied to Costa Rica, the trade facility would mean that for every dollar in interest Costa Rica pays, the banks would put 50 cents in a facility to finance imports. Banks normally insist that interest payments are up-to-date before they agree to reschedule principal repayments.

However, rather than accepting the bankers' proposal, the Costa Rican government offered a set of new terms. The banks' steering committee did not accept those terms, and the negotiations were suspended. When the IMF approved a one-year standby loan to Costa Rica at the end of December 1982, one obstacle to the successful debt renegotiations with private banks was removed. Foreign bank creditors had made the agreement with the IMF a condition of the bank debt restructuring. An almost $100-million standby loan in December 1982 was expected to be followed in 1983 by a three-year EFF that could be as high as four and one-half times Costa Rica's quota at the IMF, or some $450 million at current values.

Conclusions from Country Experience

The country cases reviewed herein demonstrated that commercial banks have made much progress in creating common understanding of how to deal with debt renegotiation and, for the most part, common understandings on new terms. Provisions for new money were becoming frequent with extended maturities of varying lengths and liberal grace periods. Agreements covering different periods were found in all renegotiations. Interest rates were to be profitable for lenders, often more profitable than the original terms on the renegotiated loans. Nicaragua came close to being an exception. Another strong precedent, starting with Zaire and implemented in all cases but Nicaragua, was the insistence by the banks on prior agreement with the IMF and fulfilling the terms of standby agreements.

Thus, experience was converting the renegotiation situation into nearly a routine—making it more acceptable and more likely to be used. Experience also demonstrated that the first rescheduling was likely to be the first of a series. Countries in difficulties and needing to restore creditworthiness did not do so in a lasting fashion by having an agreement with the IMF. Performance was sought and often not achieved. Moreover, renegotiating debt could be helpful but was only temporarily. Rescheduling did not tackle fundamental causes of a country's problems, and the IMF agreement often proved too difficult to implement. Repeated reschedulings were typical. The events of 1982 summarized in the next chapter introduced major innovations and complexities. Most important was that reschedulings now encompassed some of the largest developing country debtors in the world, with foreign debts even larger than those of Poland.

10

New Debt Problems: Argentina, Brazil, Mexico, and Chile

A number of major borrowing countries needed to reschedule their external debts in 1982. They were regarded as uniquely strong borrowers, particularly Brazil and Mexico, and their need to reschedule came as a surprise to many. The causes of the payments difficulties and the methods used by the banks to reschedule were not totally unique. However, the actions of the IMF and the reactions to these 1982 events could be lasting, and important innovations in methods and terms of rescheduling were introduced. Unlike earlier renegotiations, the IMF made commercial banks' agreements to supply new funds part of the conditions required before the IMF would allocate its own resources. The following focuses on the most important rescheduling exercises as of early 1983.

Argentina

At the end of 1982, Argentina's total external debt was estimated at over $38 billion, of which short-term funds accounted for more than $18 billion. Forecasts of Argentina's debt obligations by year-end 1983 have ranged up to $45 billion.

In late 1982, the government of Argentina released an 11-page document detailing a new financing plan designed to deal with the country's external debt problem and liquidity crisis. The document states that the plan would involve $11.75 billion, consisting of either new loans or refinancing existing external debt. The assumptions of the financing plan were that *new* loans from private banks would provide $2.6 billion, IMF loans would total $2.15 billion of new funds, and the rescheduling of principal payments on bank credits coming due before December 31, 1983, would account for $5.5 billion. In addition, official exchange-guaranteed debts or "swaps" of $1.5 billion would be renewed for a term of two years. Furthermore, as announced on January 12, 1983, Argentina sought a $500-million loan from the BIS which was granted at the end of January 1983. These events in 1982-83 sent shock waves throughout the international banking system, which resulted in greatly increased restraints in lending to developing countries, particularly those in Latin

America and Africa. The events brought into serious question the entire future of private bank lending to developing countries. Countries, such as Mexico, with outstanding reputations for their ability to manage their economies, instead pursued policies which temporarily disrupted or destroyed these reputations.

Private Bankers Response

Private commercial bank creditors were presented a three-point plan:

• A $1.1-billion short-term bridge loan.

• A $1.5-billion medium-term (five year) loan.

• Refinancing arrears on principal due in 1982 and on principal that would be due in 1983 on publicly guaranteed debt. The amount involved was given at $5.5 billion.

On December 31, 1982, 260 private commercial banks worldwide signed an agreement with the government of Argentina to extend a $1.1-billion short-term 15-month bridge loan. The bridge loan carries an interest spread of 1.62% over LIBOR, or 1½ points over the U.S. prime rate; it is intended to be repaid by March 1984. This means that the bridge financing would be repaid when the medium-term loan becomes available. The first part of the bridge loan, $600 million, was disbursed in the first week of January 1983, an additional $400 million in the third week of January. The bridge loan was needed in its entirety to settle arrears on Argentina's foreign debt-service payments. At year-end 1982, the arrears were estimated at $2 billion. Private commercial banks were concerned with agreeing to the bridge loan before year-end 1982 because, without settling arrears, some banks might have been forced to carry part of the Argentine loans on the books as nonperforming.

Private banks also accepted a commitment to extend a five-year $1.5-billion syndicated loan to Argentina that would be signed at a later date. Banks participating in the syndicated five-year loan would be offered an interest rate of 2.25% over LIBOR, or 2⅛ points over the U.S. prime rate. Each of the participating banks was asked to contribute an amount proportionate to its current exposure in Argentina to both the bridge loan and the longer term credit. Citibank, acting as agent for both syndicated loans, stated that both credits were oversubscribed.

IMF Concerns

Cooperation by private commercial bankers was a prerequisite for Argentina's request to the IMF for a $1.62-billion standby credit. The IMF had asked private banks to provide a written assurance before the end of December 1982 that banks would participate in Argentina's new financing plan.

On January 24, 1983, the IMF's board of directors approved a $2.18-billion loan to Argentina. Of this total, $1.62 billion consists of a 15-month standby credit to assist in the country's economic adjustment program; $561 million are granted under the IMF compensatory financing facility to help offset a decline in Argentina's export earnings from the sale of agricultural products and manufactured goods in the year ending September 1982. As a condition of the IMF loan approval, the Argentinian government late in 1982 introduced a number of austerity measures, including new tax measures and cuts in public spending. The government intends to reduce the budget deficit from 14% of GDP in 1982 to 8% in 1983, and 5% in 1984.

However, the first part of the IMF financial assistance was not expected to be available before May 1983. Quarterly disbursements of the credits are dependent on Argentina meeting the targets of the government's austerity program. By the end of January 1983, total credits supplied to Argentina were estimated at $1.72 billion. It was expected that these credits would be sufficient to meet the country's debt-service obligations for the first quarter 1983, which amounted to about $2.2 billion (or between $700-$800 million each month).

While the Argentinian government was negotiating with the private banks for a $1.5-billion syndicated loan, the country's central bank in March 1983 suspended the repayment of all foreign loans taken out in currency swaps or foreign exchange forward contracts. Such short-term debts in a total amount of $1.4 billion, falling due within a few weeks following March 4, 1983, would be refinanced over a 36-month period.

Brazil

In order to tide Brazil over its current (1982-83) liquidity crisis, financial support was given by the U.S. government. BIS, the IMF, and private commercial bank lenders around the world. At the end of 1982, Brazil's external debt was estimated at $87 billion (according to recent OECD statistics) and is said to be the highest overseas debt of any nation. Of the total amount of $87 billion, about $44 billion are reportedly owed to private commercial banks.

The support operations started at the end of November 1982 when President Ronald Reagan announced that the U.S. Treasury would provide $1.23 billion in short-term lines of credit, repayable in 90 days, to assist Brazil in solving its immediate liquidity problems. In mid-December 1982, the central banks of major industrial nations agreed to extend an additional emergency loan of $1.2 billion to be channeled to Brazil through the BIS. Of this total, $500 million were disbursed before the end of December 1982.

Furthermore, the Brazilian central bank succeeded in raising $1.5 billion in short-term private commercial bank credits to ease the liquidity shortage during the month of December 1982. The so-called bridge loan was arranged to provide Brazil with foreign exchange until other credits became available. Banks participating in the bridge loan were given the option either to be repaid in January 1983 with cash or to roll over their participation into the expected new large bank credit. Brazil asked 40 of the world's largest banks—15 of them in the U.S.—to take part in the bridge financing.

IMF Contribution

On December 15, 1982, Brazil and the IMF reached a tentative agreement to provide about $4.9 billion of loans to the country. Under the terms of the letter of intent, the credit could rise to $6.7 billion over the next three years, provided the IMF member nations agreed to increase their contributions to the IMF by 50% later in 1983. In return for the IMF credit, the Brazilian government agreed to continue an earlier instituted austerity program.

In December 1982, Brazil's quota in the IMF amounted to about $1.09 billion. Under IMF rules, there is a limit of 4.5 times for an EFF credit. Such an amount is usually disbursed by the IMF over a three-year period. The first installment of the IMF facility, $546.5 million, was approved on December 22, 1982. Purchases are repayable in five years and the interest rate was set at 6.6% per annum. A $1.02-billion compensatory financing loan was also approved of which half was immediately drawn down. The $4.9-billion EFF was approved on February 28, 1983.

It is possible that a substantial portion of the total EFF credit would be drawn during the year 1983. However, the remaining portions of the IMF loan carry considerably higher interest rates. Interest will be calculated at variable rates depending on rates charged by commercial banks in major industrial nations.

Private Commercial Credits

As far as private commercial bank credits are concerned, Brazilian officials in December 1982 presented 125 creditor banks with a four-point financing plan. (The meeting between the Brazilian government officials and the representatives of the private banks took place in New York on December 20, 1982. Also present were IMF representatives who endorsed the country's financing plan.) The plan consisted of:

1. A *new* medium-term money facility of $4.4 billion.
2. Rescheduling medium-term bank credits falling due in 1983 in the amount of $4 billion.
3. Continuation of $8.8 billion of short-term trade-related credit lines.
4. Renewal of $10 billion in money market credit lines to foreign branches of Brazilian banks and restoring these lines to the June 30, 1982, level.

The Brazilian government considered the four points of the plan as interrelated, equally important, and to be simultaneously implemented. Both the new bank loan and the rescheduled credits were to have an eight-year repayment schedule including a three-year grace period. Current LIBOR rates and U.S. prime rate spreads plus fees would apply to these credits.

The participating 125 creditor banks together hold 90% of the $59 billion of credits outstanding with private commercial banks. Each bank's share in the new financing had been allocated on the basis of its Brazilian claims outstanding at the time. U.S. banks were expected to provide 34% of the $4.4-billion total of new financing and Japanese banks about 17%.

The 125 creditor banks were split into four coordinating groups, with Morgan Guaranty the agent bank for the new money facility, Citibank the agent for the rescheduling operation, Chase Manhattan the agent for the trade-related debt, and Bankers Trust the agent for the money market lines to overseas branches of Brazilian banks.

By the second week in January 1983, private bank creditors had committed more than $2.5 billion toward the $4.4-billion new money facility. It was expected that the total required would be committed before the end of January but it took slightly longer. At the same time, Brazil offered more generous terms to induce the banks to restore credit lines to the government and private financial institutions. In a wire to creditor banks in early January 1983, Brazil's central bank informed bank creditors that higher commitment fees and higher interest rates will be offered to those banks that agree formally to extend so-called interbank lending to Brazilian financial concerns. Lending banks also had the option of making their own arrangements with borrowers if the lenders did not want to accept the general terms the central bank offered. By adding a slight premium to borrowing terms, the central bank believed lending banks would be more willing to keep money market lines open.

Central Bank's Action

However, uncertainty arose about the success of the refinancing plan when the central bank announced on December 29, 1982, that all debt payments falling due in the first week in January 1983 would have to be made by private borrowers through the central bank rather than directly to foreign creditors. The move alarmed some of Brazil's creditor banks because it started rumours in banking circles that the country was declaring a moratorium on its foreign debt payments. The governor of the central bank, however, clarified the situation by stating that the new central bank ruling affected only payments on the rescheduled amounts and that implementation of the new financing plan required establishing a mechanism at the central bank.

At the end of February 1983, the IMF approved a $5.4-billion credit for Brazil, including the $508-million credit it had approved in December 1982. The credit terms require Brazil to continue with a stabilization program. As part of the IMF arrangement, commercial banks had to agree to renew existing credits and to provide new loans. The banks are involved in the following provisions:

1. Restoring credit lines of $7.5 billion.
2. New bank loans of $4.4 billion.
3. Refinancing loans of $4 billion and falling due in 1983.
4. Maintaining the short-term trade credits in the amount of something like $9 billion.

The IMF did not approve the $4.9-billion EFF until banks had signed agreements for points 2 and 3. This was done on February 25, 1983.

Mexico

The Mexican liquidity crisis came to a head on August 23, 1982, when the Mexican government first asked for and received a postponement of amortization payments on debt falling due to lending banks in the following 90 days. The country's total foreign debt at that time was estimated at $80 billion. In November 1982, private commercial banks agreed to a further 120 days' postponement. At that time, the government of Mexico stated that it would soon present a more permanent debt rescheduling plan to bankers.

On Friday, December 10, 1982, the Mexican government sent a telex to all commercial bank lenders proposing a debt rescheduling plan that would allow the postponement of all amortization payments falling due prior to December 31, 1984. In addition, the Mexican government asked the commercial banks for new financing of $5 billion.

Government's Request

In the telex, the Mexican government asked that each bank restructure separately the debt it was owed, but that the debt restructuring terms be substantially identical. As the rescheduling was intended to cover all principal payments falling due between August 23, 1982, and December 31, 1984, the total amount to be rescheduled was estimated by the banks at $20 billion. Mexico also proposed that the principal payments be repackaged as new eight-year loans. The debt's principal payments would, according to the proposal, begin with the first quarter 1987 and end in the fourth quarter 1990. The loans would carry interest floating 1.75% above the U.S. prime rate, or 1.87% over LIBOR. Banks would also receive an upfront fee of 1%. (At the time of the Mexican government's proposal, the U.S. prime rate was 11.5% and LIBOR about 9.75%.)

The rescheduling involved more than 1,400 commercial banks worldwide and would cover all commercial bank debt. A 13-bank advisory committee, with Bank of America as global coordinator, was appointed to act on behalf of the creditor banks. The rescheduling, however, does not include certain types of debt, such as that owed to the World Bank and other multilateral agencies or the obligations of the foreign agencies and branches of Mexican banks.

The Mexican government's proposal, moreover, does not guarantee rapid repayment of interest falling due or interest arrears that accumulated since August 1982. The proposal calls for Mexican companies to deposit pesos in Mexico's central bank in an amount equal to their unpaid interest, converted at the prevailing government controlled exchange rate. The dollar obligations then would become obligations of the Mexican government, with an interest rate of .87% over the U.S. prime rate or 1% over LIBOR.

According to the Mexican proposal, on January 1, 1983, the central bank would have paid about 10% of the balance outstanding on interest payments to foreign banks, with the remainder to be paid in monthly installments contingent on foreign exchange availability. Any amounts still owed on September 30, 1983, would be refinanced by the foreign banks as a term loan on conditions to be determined.

Private commercial bank lenders were not given much time to respond to the government's proposal. The banks had a December 15, 1982, target date to produce the necessary assurances from the international financial community to accept the rescheduling proposal. Their response was needed in a short time since the IMF standby agreement with the Mexican government was contingent on its acceptance.

By December 15, 1982, more than 1,000 banks worldwide with Mexican loans outstanding had responded favorably to Mexico's request for a rescheduling and for $5 billion in new credits. As proposed by the IMF, each creditor had been asked to contribute the equivalent of 7% of its Mexican exposure to the new loan. To the extent that small banks faced with a difficult decision would not participate, the bigger banks were prepared to pick up the slack.

The new bank loan would, according to bank sources, be disbursed in four tranches over the course of 1983. In 1983's first quarter, Mexico received $1.7 billion from the banks with an additional $1.1 billion to be disbursed in each remaining quarter. According to bank sources, the new loan is to bear interest of 2.25% over LIBOR (compared with spreads for Mexican loans as low as .38% over LIBOR just a year earlier) or 2.12% over the U.S. prime rate. Mexico will be given six years to repay, including a three-year grace period. With the $5-billion new loan signed, the bankers turned their attention to rescheduling the old loans.

IMF Actions

The acceptance of the rescheduling proposal and the request for a new loan opened the way for the final approval of an IMF standby credit. On December 23, 1982, the IMF formally approved a $3.96-billion loan to Mexico, after the IMF had received assurances from private commercial bankers that they would provide about $5 billion in new financing needed for 1983.

The IMF loan to Mexico (amounting to $3.96 billion) will be disbursed in three approximately equal tranches over the next three years, with the first tranch disbursed in January 1983. The first tranche had interest of about 6.6%, while the next two will be repaid at a rate reflecting the prevailing commercial lending rates for the IMF's basket of major currencies. Mexico was given six years for repayment, including a three-year grace period.

As outlined in Mexico's letter of intent formally requesting the IMF loan, the government pledged to keep the 1983 *net* increase in the country's foreign debt to $5 billion, lift most retail price controls, boost taxes and interest rates, restrain wage increases, and cut the government's budget deficit to 8.5% of GDP in 1983 from its current 16.5% level. Moreover, a cutback in government subsidies and a freeze on government hiring is planned. This austerity program was designed to extend over the next three years. But the program, introduced to conform with the IMF's credit conditions, has come increasingly under political attack.

Political Aspects

Of political significance is that Mexico's largest labor federation has openly disapproved of the austerity program, particularly the use of sales taxes to increase government revenues. Conservative opposition parties, backed by some business associations, have argued that some of the other proposed fiscal policy measures—such as requiring the legal registry of stock ownership and raising corporate tax rates—would act as disincentives for private investment.

The financial rescue package for Mexico also includes an additional $2 billion to be raised from government lenders on a bilateral and multilateral basis. U.S. officials have been instrumental in assembling this loan package from about ten major industrial countries. The funds would be extended as agricultural credits and export financing. For example, it was announced on December 29, 1982, that 25 private commercial banks had signed a 3-year, $450-million credit agreement with 5 Mexican banks for the purchase of American farm products. The participating creditor banks are located in the U.S., Australia, France, West Germany, Greece, Italy, Japan, South Korea, and Spain. The loan would be guaranteed by the U.S. Commodity Credit Corporation under a program established two years before. The Mexican banks participating are Banco Nacional de Mexico, Banco Internacional, Bancomer, Banca Serfin, and Multibanco Comermex. The agricultural commodities covered include feed grains, oilseeds, and wheat. With the First National Bank of Chicago acting as lead bank, the interest rate was set at .12% above First Chicago's corporate base rate.

Miguel Mancera, governor of the central bank of Mexico, stated on January 11, 1983, that interest payments of $90 million, owed to banks by private Mexican companies, would be made by the end of that month. These interest payments would be part of a previously announced repayment plan for companies to repay interest to foreign banks, most of which has not been paid since August 1982. Under the plan, companies deposit pesos in the central bank in an amount equal to the unpaid interest at a government-controlled exchange rate. The dollar liability would then become an obligation of the Mexican government. The government was supposed to pay about 10% of the balance outstanding on these debts on January 31, 1983, with the remainder to be paid in monthly installments. Mancera also expressed his confidence that Mexico would have sufficient funds available for the rest of 1983 to cover all interest payments falling due on the country's $80-billion foreign debt. Those payments are estimated to total about $12 billion.

Mancera reportedly considers an undervalued peso an important economic policy instrument of Mexico's new foreign exchange system. Under the new administration's exchange system, the country has three exchange rates. A floating rate determined by the free market and used for most transactions, which is currently (May 1983) close to 150 pesos to the U.S. dollar. A controlled rate which is kept lower than the floating rate and is designated for importing raw materials and making interest payments, currently standing just under 106 pesos. A special rate to repay "Mexdollar" loans (loans in dollars made in Mexico) which is even lower than the other rates at about 73 pesos to the dollar was discontinued in mid-March 1983.

Important for borrowers and lenders is the controlled rate, which opened at 95 pesos to the dollar on December 20, 1982, and recently has been depreciating by 13 centavos a day since then. However, on January 12, 1983, the central bank announced a new plan to assist privately held companies to pay foreign creditors, provided the creditors cooperate by extending repayment schedules. For making debt payments, Mexican companies may obtain dollars at the rate of 70 pesos, if the companies' foreign creditors agree to a stretched out repayment schedule. This plan was put in operation in April 1983.

Chile

Chile's total external debt at year-end 1982 was estimated at $18 billion. Of this total, the private sector debt was estimated at $12 billion, and public sector debt at $6 billion. Of the $12 billion, the amount of external debt outstanding by private banks in Chile totals $6.35 billion.

External Debt

Principal payments falling due on external debt to private commercial bank lenders were estimated at $1.765 billion in 1983 and $1.743 billion in 1984. The Chilean government is seeking a stretch-out in principal payments over a five-to-seven-year period. Interest payments on the country's external debt would amount to $1.648 billion in 1983 and to $1.381 billion in 1984. The Chilean government has declared that all interest payments falling due in 1983 and 1984 will be met in full.

The interest charges include the interest owed by private sector borrowers, including the three financial institutions* put into liquidation by the Chilean authorities in a series of emergency measures announced by the minister of finance on January 13, 1983. These liquidated institutions owe $410 million to foreign private banks.

In addition to the three liquidated banks, the Chilean government also intervened** in five other financial institutions, and two more banks were put under government inspection. These institutions together owe foreign private banks an amount exceeding $3.4 billion.

Initially, the government had the position that the public sector does not share responsibility for the affected banks' debts. But on January 20, 1983, the central bank informed foreign banks that it will stand behind the debt owed by the eight Chilean banks that were either liquidated or taken over by the government.

*Banco Hipotecario de Chile, Banco Unido de Fomento, and Financiera Ciga S.A.

**Intervened refers to action taken by the Chilean government to temporarily take over management control of a private bank.

Private Creditors

On January 30, 1983, the government approached private bank creditors to request a 90-day extension of all public and financial sector external debt (with some minor exceptions), which would fall due in the 90-day period commencing January 31, 1983. At the same time, the government requested that all private corporate sector debt coming due during the 90-day extension be deferred.

Previously, Chile had signed a standby agreement with the IMF. This was interpreted as an endorsement of Chile's fiscal and monetary program to keep a normal flow of trade and permit Chile to fulfill its foreign debt-service commitments. The IMF program assumed a 1983 current account deficit of $1.6 billion, down from a deficit of $4.8 billion in 1981. It is expected that by 1985 the country's current account deficit would be eliminated. The agreement with the IMF allows for a total borrowing of $860 million; $500 million of the purchase is extended as a standby arrangement and $360 million as a compensatory facility. On January 10, 1983, Chile drew down $451 million, while the remaining $409 million will be drawn in equal installments of $58 million at the end of each quarter over the next 21 months.

A key assumption of the IMF program is the rollover of all short-term outstandings as well as medium- and long-term amortizations. However, Chile has been unable to obtain the refinancings as originally programmed within the context of the IMF agreement.

Government Actions

The government of Chile, as stated in its telexes to the private creditor banks, has undertaken a series of policy measures to reactivate the country's economy. The first step was a significant devaluation of the Chilean peso, from 39 pesos per U.S. dollar (at the beginning of 1982) to 74.50 pesos per U.S. dollar at the beginning of 1983. This devaluation was supposed to bring about a substantial surplus in the country's trade balance in 1983. Further steps included implementation of a moderately active monetary policy, restructuring of fiscal expenditures to provide for a doubling of public works outlays, and, in January 1983, the intervention into the domestic banking system. The last step was explained by the government as necessary due to the magnitude of anticipated loan portfolio losses by some commercial banks.

The government set forth its main macroeconomic objectives for 1983 as: 4% growth in real GDP, a reduction in the unemployment rate from approximately 21% to 14%, a rate of inflation below 25%, and a foreign reserve position of $2 billion. Furthermore, the government stated its intention to return the "intervened" banks to private management as soon as possible. The government also stated its commitment to make all reasonable efforts to assure the continued normal operation of all private corporations.

Details of the 90-Day Extension

Public Sector

External debt falling due in the 90-day period commencing January 31, 1983, will be extended for 90 days. Interest will be paid on a current basis by the public sector. The margin over prime or LIBOR for determination of the rate of interest will be the higher of either the current margin on such external indebtedness or at lender's option, 1% over prime or 1.12% over LIBOR.

Chilean Financial Sector

External debt falling due in the 90-day period will be extended for 90 days. The ministry of finance, Banco Central de Chile, and Banco del Estado de Chile will support the Chilean financial sector. This includes taking all necessary measures in order that all interest payments due on financial sector external indebtedness will be made.

The government also reconfirmed that the Banco del Estado de Chile will purchase the outstanding foreign obligations of the Banco Hipotecario de Chile and Banco Unido de Fomento as of January 13, 1983. The government intends to have these obligations refinanced as part of the agreement to be negotiated under its financial plan for 1983.

Private Corporate Sector

The government requested private commercial bank creditors to roll over all advances with the original obligor for 90 days. It was further stated that Banco Central will sell at the prevailing rate of exchange all foreign exchange necessary for private companies to meet interest payments on duly contracted external indebtedness.

Exceptions

The proposed 90-day extension in all three sectors of the economy will not include direct and guaranteed loans from government export agencies, loans from official agencies such as the World Bank and the Inter-American Development Bank, certain trade-related financings, and publicly offered securities. As trade-related financings are repaid, the banks are expected to open new credit accommodations for an equivalent amount, if requested.

Refinancing Plan for 1983

During the 90-day extension period, the Chilean government expects to negotiate its 1983 financing plan. The plan anticipates a refinancing of certain maturities as well as a new money credit. In order to facilitate communications with creditor banks, the government formed an advisory committee of banks. The member banks are Bank of America, Bank of Nova Scotia, Bank of Tokyo, Bankers Trust, Chase Manhattan, Chemical Bank, Citibank, Credit Suisse, Deutsch-Suedamerikanische Bank, Manufacturers Hanover, Midland Bank, and Morgan Guaranty. The members of the advisory committee supported the 90-day extension and consider its acceptance by all banks to be essential.

Current Status

Given the difficulties, these efforts have been remarkably successful thus far. But difficult periods still lie ahead. Many debt reschedulings are in process in 1983. Settlements will be negotiated and agreed on. Their durability will vary, greatly influenced by the world economic situation. For most people, the details of such settlements will not be important. But what is important is that despite great complexities and adversities, efforts are made by borrowers and lenders to find ways and means to continue the process of international lending to developing countries.

11

International Lending: Country Risk Perspective

We have reviewed international lending in general and specifically for certain developing countries. We have examined how international lending resulted in greatly raising the levels of external debt and debt servicing. In a number of countries, this culminated in debt renegotiations and in increased concern with international lending to developing countries. Before turning our attention to methodologies in evaluating country risk and management processes, let us look at international lending from a country risk perspective.

Background

It was in the 1950s and 1960s that many borrowing countries, and many advocates on their behalf, began to argue that the foreign assistance they were receiving was not sufficiently concessional. Some countries even argued that these debts to official lenders could be forgiven, recalling the then-recent experience of the Marshall Plan and its grant mechanism. A number of lending governments took a similar view, although the World Bank insisted on its so-called preferred creditor position—it would be paid fully and promptly irrespective of how other creditors were faring. It indeed became nearly fashionable to be apologetic about the need of developing countries to repay promptly and fully their external debt to governments.

In the 1950s and 1960s, many bankers and development economists, including myself, who were devoted to promoting more rapid economic and social progress in the developing countries, looked on concessional terms for development finance as the appropriate way to finance development. Private bank lending, with its inevitable use of commercial terms of lending, was widely regarded by many, including private bankers, as not suited for developing countries. An exception was made for short-term trade-related and similar short-term financing needs. It became conventional wisdom to regard substantial private bank lending for other purposes to developing countries as inappropriate for borrowers and dangerous to private lenders. Trade-related financing expanded rapidly in the early 1970s, but it was in response to the large expansion in world trade during those years. On the other hand, governments of creditor countries did not discourage lending to developing countries. Instead they, in effect, encouraged such lending.

Developing Countries

This was the prevailing philosophy and attitude toward development finance when the world was hit in the mid-1970s by the combination of persistent global inflation and falling primary product prices. While inflation brought higher prices for capital goods and food stuffs, industrial countries actions to fight inflation by inducing lower rates of growth and more unemployment caused a drastic fall in primary product prices. Then the world was hit by unexpected large increases in oil prices. Developed and developing countries alike reeled under the impact of this combination of adversities. The developing countries were confronted by the choice of slowing down growth in their already underdeveloped countries or trying to maintain momentum by borrowing from abroad.

Such countries were not fussy about from whom they borrowed. Indeed, they sought grant aid as much as possible. They did receive additional assistance from various multilateral agencies, including the IMF, the World Bank and the regional development banks, the United Nations, various OPEC governments and institutions, the European Community, and so forth. These official responses, however, fell far short of the needs of developing countries for external finance. For many developing countries, the previously avoided private banks with their commercial terms now became an acceptable alternative to fill the large requirements not met by official sources. The countries which already enjoyed the confidence of private lenders found quick responses through the existing efficient intermediation capabilities of the private banks. The Brazils, Koreas, and Mexicos soon found that they could obtain the external credits they needed on terms acceptable to them as well as to the private lenders.

Country Limits

A process began in 1974 which will last at least through the 1980s and even 1990s, if not longer. Private banks will be used to intermediate to a major extent the world flow of savings to help finance the socioeconomic advances of many, if not most, developing countries. Private banks have become the most important single source of development finance for many developing countries at almost all levels of output and income.

The novelty of this activity for private banks is illustrated by the fact that the words "country risk" came into vogue only in 1974-75. The term describes the conditions in a foreign country that could cause losses to external private lenders. Until then, risks of losses in lending to developing countries were not deemed general or serious in official or private circles. Now risks of lending to such countries are seen everywhere. Country limits were now introduced to designate total exposure of a lender in a country, including all foreign currency loans of all its branches and subsidiaries. The use of country limits as a management tool was a major innovation in bank management.*

*These are merely examples of many innovations that characterized the latter part of the 1970s. Reference should also be made to some of the more technical innovations like floating rates, large international loan syndications, and co-financing, which became a familiar part of the international banking scene.

The record of the late 1970s in international lending to developing countries was particularly remarkable in light of these fears. There were no repudiations or defaults. There were some countries that required debt restructuring but these totaled only a small fraction of total lending. In no case, did it seriously threaten individual banks or the international banking system. In every case, the rescheduling exercises were accompanied by efforts of the countries, often with IMF help, to strengthen their economic and financial management.

As noted, it became a cardinal principle of debt renegotiation that debt rescheduling by private banks must be related to specific performance criteria by a borrowing country. What had been a novelty when it was suggested for Zaire in the mid-1970s was accepted practice by the end of the 1970s. Private banks acted on the principle that the servicing of such debt to lenders should and would be of the highest priority to the borrowing countries.

Experience

In the IMF and World Bank, experience taught the content of, as well as the need for, country evaluations. The methodology used was a response to the experience. The capability developed only after the need was clearly perceived. Nothing happened without advocacy, resistance, debate, and compromise. The present capabilities of these institutions are outstanding. Their activities are institutional responses to fulfilling the responsibilities of their respective institutions, but they did not evolve instantaneously. They combined abstract thinking and theorizing with the fruits of rich experience over years of practice.

How has that differed from the experience of private banking? Did the IMF and World Bank have more need to know countries? Did they have more capability? Were they more responsive to countries' needs and more willing to develop the capability? Do the international institutions have built-in advantages to do this country work which private banks do not have?

All these financial—official and private—institutions lend to countries in one form or the other. All of them, therefore, are concerned with the assessment of country risk. Nevertheless, these institutions differ greatly in purposes, sources of funds, membership or ownership, management, and so forth. They approach the very same countries at any given time with different content given to the concept of risk.

The Perspective of the IMF

In the IMF, the chief responsibilities are to create and maintain a system of international payments for goods and services based on the convertibility of currencies at a unified rate of exchange. Another responsibility felt keenly in the 1950s and 1960s was to try to achieve a world of exchange rates which were economically realistic but essentially stable and changed only with international agreement. These definitions of purposes have changed, particularly in the acceptance of floating exchange rates, but much of the IMF's basic purposes remain largely unchanged.

With regard to the serious balance-of-payment repercussions sparked by the huge increases in the price of oil, the focal point for the IMF was how countries could best adjust to the changed conditions. Adjustment was to be in a manner which fulfilled their obligations under the IMF's Amended Articles of Agreement. The Fund focused on how it could best assist in this adjustment process and if necessary provide member countries access to its financial resources.

The IMF's judgment as to the magnitudes of finance to be provided to a country and the period of time before "repurchase" is required—the equivalent of the maturity period of a loan—is determined by its perception of the adjustment process and the IMF's role in that adjustment process. A country in weaker economic conditions might well be given a longer period to repay—now it can be as much as seven years, as in the recent case of Turkey—while stronger countries might be expected to repurchase in considerably shorter time, say three years. In other words, whereas a private bank tends to lend for longer maturities to stronger countries and shorter to weaker countries, the IMF may well do the reverse.

Liquidity Concerns

The IMF is concerned with maintaining its liquidity, which is its ability to sell to member countries needed foreign exchange in required amounts. Were it to become illiquid, this would mean that it no longer would have sufficient amounts of hard currencies to make available to countries with balance-of-payments deficits. It could then no longer fulfill its function of assisting its member countries to avoid governmental restrictions on international payments without resorting to prolonged and severe domestic restrictive policies leading to lower income and output and higher unemployment.

Such IMF liquidity problems, however, were manageable in the 1950s and 1960s. Increases in Fund quotas and borrowings from member countries were modest, yet sufficient to preserve the effectiveness of the IMF. The only way liquidity could have become a major problem in those years would have been if a number of economically large member countries made very large-scale simultaneous use of the Fund's resources. This would be particularly true if heavy use were made by countries that did not have the prospect of being able to repurchase, or repay, with so-called hard currencies. The IMF normally had the opposite problem—a very large amount of funds to lend but relatively small usage despite existing large balance-of-payments deficits in many countries. Nevertheless, the need to defend its liquidity was and remains a paramount consideration for the IMF and a critical need during periods like the oil price increases. Repurchase is essential for the IMF's survival.

Country risk analysis in the IMF consists of evaluating the dangers that a country will not be able to fulfill its international monetary responsibilities. This invites concern over the domestic and external conditions and policies which lead to such undesirable actions. Use of IMF resources after 1950 was related to helping counries avoid such conditions. Consultation with countries, adoption of standby agreements, and use of the approved jurisdiction of the IMF over exchange rates and capital restrictions were tools designed to evaluate country risk and deal with it. The Fund expertise on countries and its analysis and approach to country problems and solutions were conditioned by this special institutional content of country risk.

IMF recommendations for policy changes were designed to create conditions of improved balance-of-payments behavior and management because then countries could avoid increased reliance on exchange restrictions or avoid excessive exchange rate devaluations. Because the roots of current balance-of-payments difficulties are frequently found in domestic inflationary policies or overvalued exchange rates, these issues often loomed large in IMF conditionality. Successful changes along these lines would strengthen the balance of payments, improving the ability of the country to pay for its goods and services and to meet its external debt obligations. Thus, the fact that IMF analysis and conditionality became useful to banks was not because the Fund was particularly concerned with banks, rather it was the coincidence of common interests.

The IMF and Country Risk

The experience of the IMF in country analysis is particularly pertinent because of the important role of the Fund vis-à-vis private banks. Let us summarize this experience.

• For a number of countries, much information has been collected and sifted by scholars and experts and digested by government officials, publicists, and communicators. No one can read all that is available on such countries. Avalanches of new material—historical and current—overwhelm conscientious users. Nevertheless, information is sparse, unreliable, out-of-date, or sporadic about many countries. Even where substantial available material has existed (in the United Kingdom, India, Brazil, and Japan), the IMF has had to create its own capability to describe and evaluate countries. Other international lenders have the same experience.

• Country reports and judgments in the IMF have to be changed often and, at times, drastically. These changes resulted from changes in country conditions or changes in Fund policies and activities which altered the needed content of the country study as well as its conclusions and recommendations.

• Much of the IMF's country studies must be highly confidential. An elaborate system, involving various departments within the IMF and many departments within governments and central banks of member countries, was required to achieve the needed expertise and objectivity and earn credibility with the country being analyzed and judged, as well as all other members. Countries have been very sensitive about what the IMF writes and who reads the reports. What starts as a technical exercise, ends as a diplomatic exercise. The content of the IMF consultation reports soon became unique, designed to serve the general purposes of the Fund, but reflecting the ever-changing conditions within a country and its ever-changing relations with other countries. As the IMF's experience with countries grew, its own sophistication and views on appropriate policies also changed, adding other dynamic dimensions to these country analyses. It soon became clear that country reports of even the previous year could not simply be updated.

• Every step in the evolution of these procedures for country evaluations was controversial: headquarters versus field; new investigation versus updating; size of IMF missions; composition of missions; distribution of reports; nature of Fund decisions; relation to other IMF policy issues, like changes in par values and use of Fund resources; relation to other international reports; frequency, etc. Governments, as well as staff, sharply disagreed. It took years to sort out, and the process has not yet ended.

• The reasons for these controversies were that these reports were part of the IMF's management process in deciding matters within the Fund. These reports are the basis of staff judgments and policy recommendations which go to the executive directors with the endorsements of the managing director and chairman and, finally, became binding decisions of the executive directors. They are practical reports, not theoretical or academic exercises. The recommendations and decisions are important to member countries. Therefore, the very role of the IMF in world affairs is involved in how country analyses are made. The Fund reports are not comprehensive in the encyclopedic sense, not scholarly in the academic sense. They are designed to serve IMF needs—no one else's needs. They are not even designed to educate the public anywhere. They are intended to be confidential. Governments cannot be expected to agree to frank exchanges of view on sensitive policy issues otherwise.

• Country analyses had to be periodic and scheduled as such. It meant also having enough qualified staff.

• Periodicity had to be combined with continuity. Country conditions would not stand still until the IMF got around to its next scheduled annual consultations. Therefore, the country assessment system included flows of information on a daily basis to desk officers—again not all information, but information deemed relevant to the IMF's obligations. The studies were not designed for any other purpose or the needs of other institutions. Others, however, did use the IMF studies. Other users had to be aware of the limitations of those country reports for their particular purposes.

• Country evaluations had to serve specific purposes. They had to be done by people sensitive to these purposes and eager to fulfill them. The quality of the evaluation could be judged only by their specific usefulness. They could be prepared well only by people with specialized experience and understanding of the institutions' needs. The experience of the IMF was very similar to the experience of the World Bank in country analysis and risk.

The World Bank's Perspective

The World Bank exists to help the less industrialized countries accelerate their social and economic development, primarily through financing development projects. In assessing projects, the World Bank carefully analyzes financial costs and benefis. A project with anticipated financial benefits outweighing its costs meets lending criteria similar to those which guide a private commercial lender. The World Bank, however, does not stop with financial cost-benefit analysis: It goes on to consider social costs and social benefits. It is concerned with how its project financing activities affect a country's overall development strategy and its implementation. It becomes involved in such related social questions as demographic changes, family planning, rural rehabilitation, and patterns of income distribution.

These nonfinancial considerations can weigh heavily in the World Bank's judging risk in lending to a country or for a particular project. The ability of a country to service World Bank debt is not as important as the usage to which the borrowed funds have been put. The long-term improvements, directly or indirectly, in human resources and quality of life, as well as in productivity, efficiency, and output, can readily justify lending to a country whose ability to service debt over the years is uncertain, at best. For the World Bank, risk is closely related to improper usage of funds or changed conditions which invalidate the original financial and social cost-benefit analyses.

These criteria mean that the World Bank can enter into investments in countries and for purposes outside the scope of the IMF, on the one hand, and private commercial banks, on the other. The World Bank's perception of economic risk must be different from the IMF and other lenders or it will not fulfill the functions for which it was established by its member countries.

The new oil price situation understandably created concern that development strategies and the momentum of development in many poorer countries would be disrupted. Instead of becoming more cautious about lending to its member countries, the response of the World Bank was appropriately the reverse. Instead of retreat, it tried to find additional ways and means of lending more to such countries—and to do so in a manner that protected their development efforts. Most recently, the World Bank has departed from project lending to more general balance-of-payments support. This differed, however, from the IMF support because the World Bank emphasized the need to support structural change which is at the core of the development process. It did not focus on short- or medium-term stabilization, adjustment, and balance-of-payments improvement which is stressed by the IMF. Questions of repayment of World Bank balance-of-payments loans are important. But, as with project loans, repayment is secondary to the usage of loans, technical assistance, and their combined beneficial effects on the development process.

The World Bank could not fulfill its function if repayment were of primary concern. It is noteworthy that the World Bank has tried to manage its international asset acquisitions to create a portfolio which is relatively attractive to the investor in World Bank bonds, despite the noncommercial purposes for which the World Bank must itself borrow the money which it lends. The World Bank has succeeded in harmonizing its developmental purposes with its need to defend its own creditworthiness.

On the other hand, the World Bank cannot expect the same ability as commercial banks to leverage its asset acquisitions over its capital. The primary protection of the World Bank comes from its capital subscriptions by the strong creditor countries of the world. This has been reinforced by the fine repayment record of its borrowers and worldwide acceptance of the preferred creditor position of the World Bank. The repayment record, however, reflects more the perceived willingness of borrowing countries to give the highest priority to servicing debt owed to the World Bank. This contrasts with the discipline found in commercial banking where there is a selection process by which economically weaker countries find themselves much less capable, if not unable, to obtain funds.

In short, the World Bank is primarily protected by its capital and to some extent, by its preferred creditor position. A private commercial bank is primarily protected by its asset portfolio quality, earnings, and diversification and secondarily by its capital. Servicing of debt is a contractional obligation enforced in courts of law but essentially dependent on the financial viability of the borrowers. The commercial bank enjoys no preferred position as a creditor.

In light of their distinct purposes, the World Bank and the IMF are guided by the *political* wishes of their member countries in the broadest sense of the word. Every case of borrowing by a country must be judged separately, even though general rules or criteria of lending must be applied. Perhaps the greatest single difference between the IMF and World Bank, on one hand, and private lenders on the other, is that *all* member countries of the IMF and all developing countries in the World Bank can expect to have access to their resources. In the case of private banks, however, the process is highly selective. All countries are potentially qualified to obtain private loans. But, in practice, many countries do not qualify for substantial borrowing from such private sources. Countries unable to borrow from private banks have no legal or constitutional right to borrow.

Private Bank Lending

Country risk in private bank lending, accordingly, is very different from country risk in the World Bank or the IMF. Private banks lend private funds in response to demand for loans; they are owned and managed by private individuals. Their purposes are profit-making which also implies avoidance of losses. Their managers have no authority to waive these objectives. They cannot take excessive risks because it serves the political objectives of their country. Domestic and international politics are watched closely by private bankers to see how they might impinge on the economic management of a country and thus affect economic and financial risk for the bank. Private lenders, however, have no choice but to be guided at all times by the simple principle that borrowed funds of their institutions must be serviced fully and promptly and that the agreed terms of lending and borrowing guide lender and borrower alike.

The private banker must try to avoid reacting to political changes within a country from a personally preferred political or social philosophy. The primary concern must always be with how changes will affect the portfolio or balance sheet of the institution. Private bankers have no authority to alter business judgments because of political ideology. If they do, they are likely to prove poor bankers or poor investors.

On the other hand, the private lender must look at such questions as whether a domestic political change will enhance or diminish the likelihood of disruption of debt service; whether some international political change will impinge on the ability of the borrower to service debt; and whether a changed international environment will make the government of a country more or less likely to interfere with the servicing of external debt. Indeed, the political questions go much beyond debt servicing. They cover such topics as nationalization, expropriation, indigenization, taxation, and safety of individuals.

Because private banks depend on full and prompt servicing of their loans for their financial profitability and viability, they (in contrast to the IMF and World Bank) understandably tend to focus their activities on the best managed countries. Within these countries, they concentrate on the best managed firms in the most modern sectors of the economy. Even in many of the developing countries generally classified as the poorest because their national income per capita is very low, there are relatively advanced sectors, or "islands of modernity." These may be manufacturing plants or modern facilities for producing or processing primary commodities for export.

As these islands of modernity attract financing, their growth and the development of other advanced sectors play a vital role in the structural transformation of the developing economy. These islands of modernity generate relatively high incomes despite the general low level of income in the country. As the islands expand, the per capita income of the entire economy rises. The vast bulk of private lending to developing countries, for example, has been concentrated in high-income countries not because of the national income level per se, but because these are generally the countries with a larger number of these islands of modernity. Private lenders also lend to islands of modernity in the poorest countries. This process will continue, as more and more developing countries continue to modernize more sectors of their economy, increasing their access to private sources of finance.

Increase in Activity

Events in 1981-82 (Poland, Mexico, Argentina, and Brazil) constrained international lending to developing countries. Many banks decided to avoid further exposure and even to reduce existing exposure. Nevertheless, international private bank lending may be expected to increase markedly in the foreseeable future, both with developed and developing countries. There is also a possible expansion of other forms of international lending, such as the Eurobond market, to entities in developing countries which will enjoy such a degree of confidence from institutional investors that they can move from commercial bank lending to the bond markets or to private placements with institutional investors like insurance companies and pension funds.

This increase in international private bank lending will encompass banks from all over the world, including banks from developing countries themselves. In the banking sense, there are no simply deficit countries and simply surplus countries. International lending takes place from entities in countries whose balance of payments are in overall deficit and from those whose balance of payments are in surplus. More lending takes place from entities in industrialized countries since there are more savings and more institutional capabilities.

International private bank lending will continue to be highly selective. The industrialized countries can borrow very substantial funds either directly as governments or through government-owned or private entities. Skepticism will occasionally arise about the country risk in lending to some of these industrialized countries. Nonetheless, it is likely that the industrial countries—in Western Europe, Japan, Australia, New Zealand, Canada, and the U.S.—will continue to have the financial standing internationally that will make them acceptable borrowers for whatever balance-of-payments financing they may require. Such countries may, of course, choose to go in whole or in part to the IMF instead of to private banks or to the bond market. They do have a wide range of options. Indeed, they may go directly to the OPEC surplus countries, as some already have. The developing countries do not have the same range of options. For them, the main sources will continue to be the private banks, official development assistance (be it bilateral or multilateral), and export credits guaranteed by creditor governments.

Countries in balance-of-payments difficulties which interfere with debt servicing, including countries which need to renegotiate debt, may well experience temporary interruptions in their ability to borrow from private sources. Still even many of these developing countries will continue to be able to borrow very large sums from the private banks—sums much larger than their external debt-servicing requirements. Countries in this category include: Brazil, Mexico, the Philippines, Korea, Taiwan, Venezuela, and Indonesia which already have this option, despite the need of some to reschedule. Such countries will be continuously analyzed and monitored from the viewpoint of country risk. But most, if not all, can continue to maintain or reestablish their acceptable country risk with the private commercial banks of the world. Continued creditworthiness with the private commercial banks will enable such countries to have the critically needed net inflow of real resources which they require for their social and economic development.

These countries, and others like them, have achieved their standing in the international financial community because of the way they have managed their affairs, met their obligations, and the productive usage they made of borrowed funds. These actions include avoidance of defaults and acceptance of renegotiated terms of external debt acceptable to private lenders. These countries became strong borrowers and enjoyed the ability to borrow at spreads over LIBOR which some individual banking institutions have regarded as too narrow at times to be acceptable.

As world conditions become adverse, these countries may well have to pay more for borrowed funds in terms of wider spreads, but the impact on a country's total cost of money will be small indeed. No developing country is going to deny itself credit to finance needed imports of goods and services because of a change in market spreads. Even if the change means another 1/8%, 1/4%, 1/2%, or even 2% or more in the spread. Developing countries, of course, will be concerned with what happens to interest rates. Even high interest rates may be accepted because of the high return on capital in a developing country. Nevertheless, borrowers in developing countries, as borrowers everywhere, will carefully watch interest rates. From time to time, they may refrain from borrowing if they anticipate that in relatively short periods of time the same borrowings can be accomplished at considerably lower rates of interest or depressed world and national conditions discourage investment.

Parallel to the expansion in the number of lenders, there will be an expansion in the numbers of borrowers, particularly in the developing countries. Country creditworthiness with private financial institutions is not a function of national income, gross or per capita. Nor is it a matter of political and socioeconomic systems. As this is realized, more and more developing countries, including those at the low income scale, will evaluate whether they can pursue economic management policies which could make large-scale international borrowings from commercial banks a real option for them. An increasing number will reply positively, particularly as the world economy grows again and as their absorptive capacity for savings improves more rapidly than their ability to generate domestic savings for productive investment. They will be further encouraged because they perceive that the lending criteria of the banks do not involve fundamental changes in political, social, and economic systems or institutions, although they may involve important changes in policies.

Implications for Country Risk Assessment and Management Systems

Because of the continuous storms and strife of political and social disturbances and chronic uncertainties and risks globally and within countries, lending banks will give increasing attention to strengthening their country risk systems. A principal responsibility of a private bank lender is to ascertain whether the country will continue to be a creditworthy borrower, despite the chronic existence of risk. The bank is likely to give great weight to the effort of the developing country to maintain its external creditworthiness to avoid otherwise-intolerable domestic conditions. More and more developing countries see the need to pursue economic and financial policies which experience has shown are successful in maintaining or reestablishing external creditworthiness, irrespective of the political and social disturbances of the moment.

Even so, the banker dare not reach favorable conclusions on individual countries and loans without the most careful analysis of country conditions. This evaluation should combine available information with the richest possible practical experience. The need to reconcile rigorous and logical economic and financial analysis with political, social, and institutional realities can lead to muddles in our thinking, between what is desirable for coping with the difficulties of countries and that which is politically feasible. The most that can be feasibly done often becomes acceptable, even though it leaves the problems unsolved. The tests of success become temporary amelioration, like reducing rates of inflation or reducing balance-of-payments deficits, rather than eliminating the causes of the domestic or external difficulties.

Commercial Banks' Views

Another lesson learned from my IMF and World Bank experience was that the purposes, policies, and procedures of institutions are the principal determinants of the content and quality of their country assessments. The use of country assessments in decision making acted as the discipline to improve steadily the quality of the country assessment. Evaluations by commercial banks of countries has to reflect certain key aspects of commercial banking, which may be worth stating briefly because of their relevancy to the design and execution of country risk evaluations.

• Commercial banks are usually privately owned and profit-oriented. But even when government owned, they are managed by the same criteria as privately owned lending institutions. They usually have responsibilities to private shareholders and private depositors and must make profits unlike governmental entities.

• Commercial banks lend to governments and government enterprises, as well as to entities in the private sector. Guarantees are often given to private sector loans by government institutions, like central banks, in the borrowing countries. A portion of international lending is guaranteed by governmental institutions in the creditor countries, but most international lending does not have such guarantees by creditor government institutions.

• Much of the international lending is in currencies foreign to the borrower and in part at maturities which can only be regarded as medium or long-term, say 5 to 12 years. Nearly half of international lending is at shorter maturities of one year or less. Some commercial banks have branches within the country which engage in local currency lending. Concern with country risk has usually focused, however, on the foreign currency lending, particularly in maturities over one year.

• Private banks which operate in countries outside of the headquarters country regard themselves essentially as entities of the countries in which they are operating. The banking laws, supervision, monetary policies, taxation, wage policies, ownership limitations, etc., provide the framework within which the commercial banks operate. At the same time, these entities in the different countries are closely linked with headquarters and with other entities within the bank's family.

• Commercial banks must regard full and prompt servicing of their loans as an unqualified obligation of the borrower. In this sense, commercial banks implicitly expect to have a preferred position in the use or allocation of the foreign exchange earnings of a country. Commercial banks aim at minimizing losses. But they also must be prepared for payment arrears, renegotiations, and even defaults, and where possible to recapture investments even in the case of defaults. Borrowers which go into default must expect to suffer enduring loss of creditworthiness. Borrowers which have to reschedule or restructure outstanding debt because of the inability to make full and prompt payment must expect to be regarded as weak borrowers at best for a significant period of time.

• Banks will look more carefully at individual credits in countries outside of their own than they do for loans made inside their own country.

• A private bank will increasingly want to know a great deal about the country before it accepts significant foreign currency exposure. And even then it will follow well-known principles of portfolio management such as the avoidance of concentration and the achievement of asset diversification.

12

Key Terms in Country Risk Analysis and Management

The previous chapter provided the background for a more formal approach to country risk analysis and management. Key terms in country risk analysis and management process are emerging and becoming common to practitioners. As in other areas, new approaches create the need for a new vocabulary, and new terminology in country risk analysis is still developing. The three main tasks in country risk management are country risk assessment, country exposure measurement, and control. Most of the key terms refer to aspects of each of these banking functions. The key terms defined in this chapter include sovereign risk, country risk, country risk assessment, transfer risk, political risk, country exposure, country exposure limits, cross-border exposure, and foreign currency exposure.

This chapter examines a few critical concepts in depth. A more comprehensive glossary is presented in a report compiled by the Association of Reserve City Bankers[18] and in Appendix A of this book, which contains approximately 75 of the more technical terms in the report.

Country Risk

Country risk is incurred by lending into another country, irrespective of the causes of the risks or their particular forms. It is a generic category, which encompasses a multiplicity of subcategories. Such subcategories include sovereign risk; transfer risk; economically, socially, or politically induced risk; and risk inherent in specific international banking functions, such as funding risk, foreign exchange risk, and other less tangible risks.

Some of these risks result from the nature of the borrower or obligor—private or government. Some of these results are attributable to causation—political, social, economic, country policies, business cycles, international events, etc. Some directly effect the ability of lenders to receive payments in foreign exchange, like restric-

[18]*Country Exposure Measurement and Reporting Practices of Member Banks* (Chicago: Association of Reserve City Bankers, 1977). The author chaired the committee which prepared this report.

tions on payments by the monetary authorities. Others are more indirect, such as increases in the local currency needed by a borrower to service external debt because of devaluations of national currencies. Some are actions taken by individual borrowers.

Lending in local currency and commercial or credit risk are typically excluded from the definition of country risk, particularly when local currency lending is based on local currency funding. Country risk itself, however, can be regarded as one subset of *credit* risk, the risk that a specific loan will not be serviced fully and promptly in accordance with contractual terms, irrespective of cause. The separation of country risk analysis from credit analysis is in some sense artificial. But it is justified when different professional skills are employed or a new country risk process is initiated in a bank.

Sovereign Risk

Many analysts still use the words country risk and sovereign risk interchangeably but this may be misleading. Sovereign risk has a more restricted usage that should not include everything relating to the sovereign activities or powers of a national government or subgovernments. However, under the broader definition, still followed by many, sovereign risk includes:

- All bank loans and other financial transactions made with sovereign governments along with all other loans made to private residents bearing the guarantee of the host government.
- The full gamut of policy decisions a sovereign government has at its disposal to affect loan servicing by private debtors. Not only are governmental actions included here which, in effect, lighten its own loan servicing burden but also all measures which impede the repayment of loans made to private borrowers domiciled in that country, by such actions as imposing exchange controls.

Sovereign risk in this broad sense emerged as an acute concern of international bankers and bank supervisors. Not until the later 1970s was country risk coined and assumed much visibility. However, with the common usage of the country risk concept, the phrase sovereign risk should be limited to governments or to loans guaranteed by governments. Country risk should include sovereign risk and government actions which affect loan servicing by private debtors. In addition, country risk refers to many other obstacles to loan servicing and profitability. The scope of country risk applies to that whole class of possible adverse events which may arise from being in a foreign country and that would not arise if loans were made domestically. Thus, country risk applies also to external as well as internal adverse causes, such as drastic price changes in international markets for export commodities or the aftermath of natural calamities like earthquakes which would affect the foreign loan but not the domestic loan.

Uncertainty

What is called risk—country risk or sovereign risk—is a type of uncertainty. There is a subtle distinction between the meanings of risk and of uncertainty, at least in their strictly economic usages. The two terms differ with regard to the amount of information known by the observer. Risk implies that the observer has firm knowledge about three separate things:

1. More than one possible outcome is associated with a particular event.
2. In what form each of these outcomes is likely to manifest itself.
3. The approximate probability of each identified contingency actually arising.

On the other hand, the distinguishing mark about a situation of uncertainty is precisely the absence of knowledge about the probabilities associated with each specific outcome. While risk can legitimately be overcome through an insurance scheme, uncertainty cannot be so handled.

It is worth emphasizing that although the terms country risk and sovereign risk serve quite well in every day usage, they are commonly misapplied to situations which, strictly speaking, are better characterized by the term uncertainty. In other words, country risk practitioners are often confronted with potentialities, the nature of which imply that little can be determined about their probabilities of occurrence. A case in point is the great uncertainties surrounding so-called political risks like revolutions.

These semantic distinctions can have an important operational impact. Analysts feel compelled to assign probabilities when doing risk analysis—how else? But in many country situations, there are no bases for assigning probabilities, not even logically or historically. They are guesses which, like any other guesses, lead to misleading precision. They can give rise to a false sense of security and confidence in the country judgments derived from these arbitrarily assigned probabilities. Incredible errors have been made in reaching conclusions on countries based on probabilities that simply should not be used. Perhaps the use of the word risk strengthens the tendency to use these often dubious analytical techniques. With this strong caveat, the familiar usage of country risk and sovereign risk is retained throughout this volume.

Definitions

Next, we examine our key terms in somewhat greater depth.

Sovereign risk refers to the foreign borrower as a national government (or one of its subdivisions) or to other loans fully and unconditionally guaranteed by that government. It refers to claims held by banks against governments and government agencies or enterprises which are backed by the full faith and credit of the foreign government. Governments and government enterprises have become increasingly important as borrowers from commercial banks. Methodologies suitable for normal credit evaluations for borrowing by private entities are helpful but inadequate for borrowing by governments. As long as the borrower can be evaluated on the capability of servicing a particular loan, the credit process can work reasonably well.

In the case of loans to governments, however, it is the entire performance of the country and the government's management that are being evaluated. The clearest example of this type of lending is for general balance-of-payments purposes. Country risk evaluations have been specifically designed to scrutinize loan requests of government bodies. In this special case of sovereign risk, country evaluations play a comparable role to the traditional credit review of the private or individual corporate borrower. Thus, it may be called credit assessment of countries.

Lending to government entities is also a major form of sovereign risk. In many countries, government-owned enterprises engage in activities much beyond such public utilities as power, sanitation, and urban transportation. They also include automobile and steel factories, oil production and distribution, chemicals, aircraft production and transportation, and other business activities. Loans to such entities can be scrutinized by the normal credit procedures. They can be separated from other loans of the private and public sectors. At the same time, they involve directly the full faith and credit of the government.

Loans to these entities are too intimately related to government policy to stop with normal credit examination procedures. They have to be examined both as loans to corporate entities and loans to governments and meet tests suitable to both. There is a temptation to treat such loans without close scrutiny of their own means and purpose. But this can lead to serious difficulties for a lender if subsequent governments change policies. For example, if a government entity relies on government budgetary subsidies for adequate cash flow, a subsequent government may reduce or eliminate the subsidy, making the entity unable to service its debts fully and promptly.

Country risk refers to elements of risk inherent in doing business in the economic, social, and political environment of another country. A bank's foreign exposure is affected not only by the individual financial circumstances of the entities with which it deals but also by general factors that affect the country environment in which they operate. The latter—their totality referred to as country risk—can have an adverse (or favorable) impact on the quality of assets and other types of exposure that foreign lenders or investors may have in that country. These risks are incurred from corporate activities undertaken in a foreign country and are distinct from the more traditional concerns about the creditworthiness of individual firms. Thus, country risk refers to a spectrum of risks arising from the economic, social, and political environments of a given foreign country (including government policies framed in response to trends in these environments) having potential favorable or adverse consequences for foreigners' debt or equity investments in that country. The multidimensional concept and definition of country risk is perhaps best explained by simply listing various types of country risk.

Events which may adversely affect profitability or recovery of *equity* investments in a given foreign country include:

- Confiscation.
- Nationalization.
- Branching limitations.
- Restrictions on earnings remittances.
- Higher local taxes levied on earnings.

- Market conditions.
- Devaluation.

Events which affect profitability of *debt* investments in a given foreign country include:

- Withholding and other special taxes which affect existing outstandings.
- Interest rate management.
- Government-imposed delays on the liquidation of private or public sector external obligations.

Events which affect potential recovery of debt investments include:

- Certain types of foreign exchange controls, including government-imposed restrictions on the liquidation of public-private sector external obligations.
- Domestic policies which may be imposed in a sudden, unpredictable manner which affect clients' ability to generate the necessary cash flow to repay loans. Examples: fiscal policy (increase in taxes), restrictive monetary policy or price/wage controls, and exchange rate changes.

Besides these factors, more subtle country risk causative factors include:

- Inadequate banking data in borrowing country (central banks as well as other banks).
- Ignorance of magnitudes of debt and of debt-servicing obligation because of lack of data.
- Excessive or unsound borrowing by entities facilitated by lack of adequate banking supervision in borrowing country.
- Governments borrowing for consumption purposes.
- Corruption of governments.
- Denial of access to money markets.
- Changes in government attitudes toward foreign borrowing.
- Availability of work permits for employees of foreign bank agencies and representatives.
- Indigenization—government regulations requiring employment of local nationals.
- Personnel—problems of safety, remuneration, career training, collaboration of staffs of mixed nationalities.
- Adverse impact of inflation—opportunities and dangers of inflation hedging that affect costs of funding and profitability.
- Unfriendly attitude toward foreigners and foreign institutions, for example, personal terrorism directed against foreign businessmen.

Among the continuing risks in lending abroad is the so-called **transfer risk** arising from balance-of-payments difficulties. This is the risk which dominates nearly all discussions on country risk evaluation. Transfer risk describes the potential that an unguaranteed private borrower will not be able to make timely and full repayment of the loan in accordance with contractual schedule due to host government policies which make foreign exchange unavailable. This can happen through exchange controls or other means, irrespective of the causes of such policies, including developments external to the borrowing country.

A long list of exchange control practices can be cited. The transfer problem must be seen in much more detail than is normally implied by the question of whether the needed foreign exchange will be available. For example, if a country introduces an advance deposit requirement which requires local currency to be deposited in advance for, say, six months before the foreign exchange can be available, then this requirement increases the cost of the transaction. The local currency deposit must be financed and this can have a major impact on the borrowing entity, even though nothing has been done directly to limit the foreign exchange transfer. Similarly, exchange controls can distinguish among different markets for purchasing foreign exchange depending on purpose and borrower, leading to multiple exchange rate practices. Exchange controls may affect the permitted timing of international payments, etc.

Political risk involves primarily the likelihood of political continuity or discontinuity and whether there is danger of economic and financial disruption due to political instability or fundamental political upheaval.

External indebtedness denotes the sum total of foreign borrowing of a given country, taking *all* sources into account and all maturities including public and private.

Country exposure is a term of measurement which refers to the total volume of assets held and off-balance-sheet items considered subject to the country risk of a foreign country by an individual bank. In practice, one important aspect of this measurement is based on identifying the country of domicile of the entity ultimately responsible for the credit risk of a particular transaction.

Country exposure refers to aggregation of assets in the *broadest* sense and includes foreign currency exposure.

Two simple relevant formulas are CBE + IFCE = FCE and FCE + LCE = CE. CBE is cross-border exposure; IFCE is intraforeign currency exposure; FCE is foreign currency exposure; LCE is local currency exposure; and CE is country exposure.

It is useful to define country exposure in the broadest sense, even though concern with country risk is focused on foreign currency exposure. Bank supervisors have become insistent on usage of the broadest possible (that is, most cautious) definition of the term.

Country exposure in a given country is not homogeneous as to country risk. This complicates the evaluation of country risk by bank managers. In practice, this lack of homogeneity entails distinguishing risk associated with the following factors:

- Local and foreign currencies underlying that exposure.
- Maturity schedules for balance-sheet and off-balance-sheet items.
- Classes of borrowers involved—government agencies, multinationals, own branches and subsidiaries, etc.
- Usage—trade-related letters of credit, bankers' acceptances, correspondent bank lines, balance of payments, project finance, hedging credits, budgetary financing, etc.

• External guarantees—full and unconditional, letters of comfort, other types of protection commonly associated with specialized shipping transactions.

Greater disaggregation of foreign country exposure would be a valuable step in the development of more sophisticated country evaluation methodology.

In the ARCB report,[19] over 100 banks were asked about their treatment of individual assets and off-balance-sheet items involving foreign obligors when computing the total level of the exposure in any given country. Fairly uniform treatment was reportedly accorded to balance-sheet risk assets, such as loan advances and overdrafts and certain types of off-balance-sheet items. These included contingent liabilities, such as clean and standby letters of credit, formal (but unutilized) commitments to lend, etc. Less consistency, however, was evident in the treatment of balance-sheet items, such as minimum risk transactions, placements with foreign branches or subsidiaries of third-party banks and certain specialized off-balance-sheet items. These included contingent liabilities arising from forward exchange contracts and intrabank placements.

The basic decision necessary to devise a method for analysis is the determination of just what assets are identified as subject to country risk. Here again, different types of institutions vary markedly, and multinational corporations with large fixed direct investments will differ fundamentally from international lenders on just what is at stake. For most private international lending institutions, the assets which need to be monitored most closely in relation to country risk are those contained in the term "cross-border exposure."

Country exposure limit—a form of credit administrative control by which a bank sets a maximum amount of permitted aggregate loan exposure in a given country for its individual bank (and possibly affiliates and subsidiaries). More than one limit or sublimit can be set, for example, different usage, maturities, or borrowers. These limits can be for designated time periods or subject to change at any time. Often a sublimit is set for term loans. Term loans are usually loans with a maturity of more than one year, usually from one to ten years repayable according to a specified schedule (for the most part in periodic installments) under a legal agreement between the bank and the borrower. Exposure limits are sometimes set for whole geographic regions or even total international lending by the bank to *all* countries. Some international banks have added refinements to their country risk control systems by constructing multiple country limits to reflect the increasing complexity of their international business affairs.

Foreign currency exposure is a term of measurement for the volume of assets and other nonbalance-sheet items that are deemed subject to the country risk of a given country and denominated in a currency other than the currency of that country. Foreign currency exposure exists when any subsidiary or branch of the bank holding company or bank (including any other entity of the holding company or bank), irrespective of location, lends to, invests in, places with, or other-

[19]Ibid.

wise extends any form of credit or credit commitment to any bank or nonbank entity that is located outside the bank's national borders, irrespective of currency. Across the national frontier is the critical consideration.

Exhibit 12.1 defines graphically what is included in foreign currency cross-border exposure. This is distinguished from intracountry foreign currency exposure which exists when a creditor lends, invests, or otherwise extends credit to borrowers located in the same country but in a currency foreign to the country where the borrower or lender is located. For the most part, intracountry foreign currency asset acquisitions, like local currency assets, are funded by deposits gathered from third-party sources in the country.

Both kinds of activities create less concern about country risk for several reasons. To the extent that a branch is nationalized or confiscated, the government presumably takes over not only the assets but also the liabilities of the branch. The resulting loss of such an event is limited to equity and reserves. By the same token, if a country imposes restrictions affecting the manner and means of the repayment of intracountry foreign currency assets, these same restrictions would generally apply to the intracountry foreign currency liabilities gathered from third parties. Again, the net effect can be a wash. If an intracountry foreign currency asset is funded with corporate resources from outside the country, the funding will usually be caught and included in the cross-border exposure to that country.

Country risk assessment is a recent area of systematic risk analysis. It refers to specific methods and information-gathering activities used by banks to monitor and evaluate risks associated with cross-border loan exposure and other country risks. It evaluates the risk elements that arise when a private bank lends, places, or invests funds across a country border. Whereas local currency lending overseas is fundamentally the same as U.S. dollar lending domestically, foreign currency lending (lending in a currency other than the borrower's local currency, i.e., cross-border lending) typically involves country risk. Cross-border exposure can be monitored by a proper country exposure reporting process and managed to avoid exposures beyond limits regarded by the private bank as acceptable for the country. But these processes and procedures involve a strong commitment to country risk evaluation as the prerequisite for sound business judgments in lending to entities in foreign countries.

Country risk evaluations are designed to assess the likelihood of these risks materializing and the probable response of the government in the country if they do materialize. For example, it is useful for a commercial bank to have available a balance-of-payments forecast that lays the basis for the judgment that a country might experience difficulties in fully and promptly servicing its external debts to commercial banks. It is then important to have a judgment on what the government is likely to do about this situation, either to prevent the difficulties from arising or to cope with them if they do arise. Country evaluations need to be designed not merely to set forth alternative scenarios but to help select the one that should guide the bank in making precise decisions.

Exhibit 12.1—Definition of Foreign Currency Cross-Border Exposure

Assets All assets, for example equity investments, loans, discounts, leases, and placements.	**Except**	Transactions involving obligors domiciled in Puerto Rico or U.S. territories. Shipping transactions. Local currency assets. Externally guaranteed assets.*
Contingent Liabilities Formal, unused loan commitments. Opened, confirmed commercial credits, etc.	**But Not**	Unused lines of credit not governed by formal commitments. Externally guaranteed contingent liabilities.*
Liabilities To majority owned or managed units.	**But Not**	To nonbank entities.

* Equity investments, loans, discounts, leases guaranteed by official entities, or acceptable private entities in headquarters country.

Conclusion

Country risk analysis is linked with credit analysis and other banking functions. Good country risk management must go hand in hand with good credit risk management. The most important single action in defending a bank against the risk of being in a foreign country is good credit risk analysis and a good credit risk monitoring system. That means that the credit mechanism must be able to serve a variety of loans and credits to a great variety of entities in many different countries.

The value of understanding these key concepts lies primarily in improved communication. A common conceptual framework must first be established within a bank. Ultimately, an international understanding will be needed on the meaning of key terms similar to the understanding evolving on common statistical definitions and reporting requirements in international lending and external debt.

13

Methodologies of Country Risk Evaluation

The basic premise in the determination and management of country risk is that risk in international lending by private banks or by any private investor cannot be eliminated—just as it cannot be eliminated in lending within the U.S. Bankers are involved in a risk-taking business. Risk, however, can be managed in such a way as to strengthen the private banks that do international lending. Lending overseas is a potential source of strength for the bank, not an inevitable source of weakness. The view that it is inevitably a source of weakness is based neither on knowledge of countries nor on experience in modern times.

The key is anticipating change, not simply reacting afterward. The need is being able to react quickly to change and avoid excessive losses caused by failure to anticipate what could have been anticipated or to react quickly enough. The key is to react in such manner as to protect the lending institution from eventual loss, even in case of disruption of debt servicing causing temporary losses.

Bankers always have been concerned with conditions in countries in which they operated. Awareness of country conditions, however, was essentially a byproduct of individual lending activities and decisions. What is novel is the perceived need for country risk evaluations on a periodic or continuous basis as a precondition for deciding the magnitudes and composition of a bank's investment in any country. For certain banks, the process needs to apply to many, if not all, countries, because private bank lending has become global.

Different Approaches

In this chapter, we cover the first stage of this country risk management process—the intelligence-gathering activities, country review and assessment. A major underlying theme is that, while it is useful for individual private banks to be cognizant of country assessments and judgments of other private, public, and multilateral banking institutions, these cannot substitute for their own. The orientation of each institution's country assessment must be custom-made and unique, given the diversity in institutional purposes and characteristics in operating policies, in lending criteria, in size, and in geographic spread.*

*This chapter has benefited importantly from the 1976 survey of 37 banks conducted by the Export-Import Bank on country evaluation practices.

There has not yet evolved any standard approach to country evaluation among the major private international banks. A study of U.S. banking practices in 1976 by the U.S. Export-Import Bank surveyed existing practices. In most banks, country evaluation was undertaken at headquarters by the bank's line personnel, without critical review by another group in the institution. The analytical approaches were reported to vary greatly, with a small number of banks using quantitative techniques, generally with more qualitative systems. In addition, a number of banks used either a letter or numerical rating to summarize the results from the country evaluation system in setting maximum exposure limits. Few banks used their results to help analyze the quality of their portfolios, and none used the results in fixing interest rates or fees. Each bank's own optimum manner of carrying out its responsibilities was determined by its own institutional structure, the extent of its resources, and its particular needs.

It is not surprising that private banks differ in the process of analysis. Each bank has different concerns resulting in part from different implications of the changes in the world economy and concomitant changes in the demand for international banking services. Many banks initiated their international activities in a very limited way, for example, servicing the overseas needs of domestic multinational customers. Many have not gone beyond this stage. Other banks, however, eventually began to concentrate on building a portfolio of high-quality international loans. From this base, still others now maintain a foreign branch-affiliate network. In addition, a relatively few of the more mature international banks have developed specialty market segments (ranging from geographic specialities to such individual customer segments as government agencies and enterprises, multinational insurance companies, correspondent banks, shipowners, aerospace, etc.). Thus, even international banks differ from each other in fundamental ways. Some banks are organized along holding company lines while others are not. The former may own diverse overseas subsidiaries engaged in merchant banking, real estate, consumer finance, leasing, and other specialized asset acquisition activities.

Operating and lending policies differ as well. Some banks extend term credit to overseas entities only when exposure is fully and unconditionally guaranteed by the central bank (or some other central government agency) in the borrower's country. Some participate in credit extensions that are only short-term trade-related while others have significant term exposure.

Despite the differences, banks need to refuse to invest in risk assets in any given country that have attractive income returns but do not meet institutional standards and judgments on country conditions and outlook. In addition, banks need to ensure that there is an adequate, independent internal monitoring process—both external and internal to the country—designed to provide advanced warning of difficulties and possible losses. A cautious attitude to possible losses means that they are anticipated by way of loan loss provisions or offsets against current earnings or reserves, if warranted. Thus, each bank's own manner of carrying out its country assessments is importantly determined by its own objectives, institutional structure, operating and lending policies, as well as by the character of its own resources.

The existing state of the art of country assessment is well summarized by Professor Ingo Walter:

> The conflicting demands of country assessment—ranging from high levels of usability, auditability and comparability and the need to capture exceedingly complex and country-specific qualitative judgments over extended periods of time, to the need to avoid abuse of the results in decision-making—probably means that there is no such thing as an "ideal" system. "Appropriate" systems will certainly differ for different banks. The key may reside as much on the "human resources" side as on the "technology" side.[20]

Banks as Borrowers

Banks and bank holding companies are often perceived by the public more as lenders of funds than as borrowers. Bank deposits, however, can be thought of as a form of borrowing. Traditionally, demand deposits and personal savings deposits have provided a significant portion of bank funds. Loans (only a small portion of which are on a demand basis) and investments are thus partially funded by liabilities payable on demand. Increasingly, however, banks obtain their funds by borrowings on which they pay interest, and the maturity periods are likely to be quite different from maturity periods on loans. Such activities create mismatching between asset and liability maturities. In contrast to demand deposits, however, the repayment date of these instruments is known in advance. Unanticipated outflows are therefore minimized.

A bank holding company is not a bank and may not accept deposits. Citicorp, for example, has had to utilize or develop other funding sources, including commercial paper, intermediate-term notes, long-term debt, and floating-rate notes, in order to ensure as stable a resource base as possible in support of its worldwide asset acquisition activities.

Private bank funding needs and practices are heterogeneous. They depend on full and prompt servicing of their loans for their financial creditworthiness and viability. Private banks (in contrast to the IMF and the World Bank) understandably tend to focus their activities on the best-managed countries and, within these countries, the best-managed firms in the most advanced sectors of the economy. Good country risk analysis is of critical importance in this process.

Small-Size Banks

Let us look, finally, at the special situation of a small-size bank in terms of total assets with substantial international exposure. Although banks in this category may not be able to afford or need anything like a country risk assessment system of a medium- or large-size bank, this does not mean such smaller banks can be any more lax in monitoring and controlling their international portfolios. The same quality standards of country risk management apply, although the ways of achieving these standards are very different—less complicated and less costly.

[20]Ingo Walter, *Country Risk, Portfolio Decisions, and Regulation in International Bank Lending,* Mimeo., New York Univ., June 1980.

Many small banks may wish to supplement their own limited resources by using the assessments of larger institutions to which they have access through correspondent bank relationships or participation in loan syndications or clubs. Thus, some private banks take the view that they cannot themselves marshal adequate personnel and instead rely on the judgments of others. They say, "We are in this or that country because we have found that if we participate in loan syndications headed by a Morgan, over the years that they make good judgments and therefore, our experience of being a partner in syndications with Morgan has been a good one." This approach may be quite sensible.

It means, of course, that the smaller bank relies on the record of the syndication leader. A smaller-size bank may not be able to afford the kind of analysis that is essential before the big decisions are made. Someone, however, must undertake a comprehensive analysis, and it is reasonable to assume that it is done by a medium- or large-size bank. Yet it is crucial that these smaller banks have someone on staff (or as a continuing consultant) who can meaningfully link them with the syndication leader. The bank should be able to question and cross-examine the leader until the bank is comfortable about participation in any syndication, including the significance of the amount involved for the participating bank.

Three Major Country Assessment Methodologies

Three basic country evaluation systems are commonly used by commercial banks and may be categorized as follows:

1. Delphi/expert opinion.
2. Quantitative/econometric.
3. Integrated and comprehensive.

The Delphi/expert opinion approach consists of a panel of experts who rate each country's performance on a predetermined set of elements assumed to be influencing a nation's future. A scorecard approach is used in which responses to elements are weighted, aggregated, and the higher the overall score, the lower the potential country risk. The information obtained using the Delphi method, however, is too generalized to be significantly useful in making specific business decisions.

The second method, quantitative/econometric, focuses on a transfer risk or on the potential of a country's having balance-of-payments difficulties. The first step is to identify countries with potential balance-of-payments difficulties. Reliance is placed on econometric models which highlight selected economic variables believed to have value in predicting balance-of-payments behavior. To assess a country's likely response to balance-of-payments difficulties, initial model results are often overlaid with qualitative data before judgments became final. As a logical initial step for analysis, this second method has merit. But it should not exclude looking at other less obvious potential sources of significant risk, of which there are many.

Third Method

This leads us to a third method—integrated and comprehensive in scope. This approach has three distinct layers of analysis:

1. Likelihood of balance-of-payments difficulties (like the quantitative/econometric approach).

2. Likely country responses to possible balance-of-payments difficulties.

3. Outlook for risks other than payments and likely country responses where appropriate.

This approach involves:

- Use of quantitative elements which aid in arriving at judgments.
- Use of qualitative data or information.
- Analysis of quantitative and qualitative data in the form of country evaluation.
- Application of experience and accumulated knowledge of bank officers, including identification of banks' business interests and possible related country risks.
- Adequate sources of information both in the field and at headquarters.
- Preparation of country risk assessment giving conclusions on risks for business activities of bank and recommended business practices.

Delphi Approach

The Delphi/expert opinion approach has four specific drawbacks:

1. It is difficult for private banks to give confidential business information to panels and relate business decision-making to panels.

2. It is difficult to transform this into an approved method of continuous assessment of changing situations. Therefore, it is not well designed for *anticipating* risk, which is an essential feature of any country risk assessment and management system.

3. It is difficult and costly to assemble competent groups of experts with rich experience, knowledge, and seriousness of purpose required for high-level professional opinion on countries for which very few experts exist. There are other ways to obtain top level experts' views.

4. It obscures responsibilities for country evaluations.

Econometric Method

The econometric approach is also limited in reliability and usefulness, even if expanded to include noneconomic factors, for the following reasons:

1. For many countries, needed reliable data for such methods are not available.

2. Even if available, relevant historical experience is limited or can be misleading as a basis for anticipating the future.

3. The predictive quality of such models has repeatedly proven weak.

4. Facts used in country evaluations are restricted too narrowly in order to fit

methodology. For example, they do not include qualitative aspects which do not lend themselves to quantification.

5. The method underestimates the importance of policy responses to balance-of-payments difficulties.

6. There are relatively too much economic and insufficient political, social, and cultural factors.

7. It is too simplistic in representing domestic and international factors and trends.

8. It becomes a crutch and substitute for hard, responsible thinking needed for important business decisions.

9. It separates country assessments from banking functions and thus does not train bank staff to incorporate country concerns into their own judgmental business processes.

Emphasis needs to be placed on the difficulties or pitfalls inherent in excessive reliance on quantitative indicators because some banks are relying on quantitative indicators to give them virtually automatic judgments about countries. This approach is well intentioned but professionally inadequate for practical business decisions. Quantitative indicators are essential elements in country risk analysis, like rates of inflation and money supply. Such quantitative indicators have the advantage of being more accurate and up to date than others because banking and monetary statistics in a country are usually among the best and most up-to-date information available in a country.

Other data, however, may well be much more profoundly important, including wages, productivity, employment, investments, savings, export and import movements, inventories, demographic trends, etc. The countries themselves often do not have satisfactory data in these areas. Monetary indicators are often chosen not because they describe best and sufficiently what is the state of the economy but because other data are not available. They provide only a partial indication of the state of the economy. Monetary aggregates and other monetary indicators are useful, but only if they are used with sophistication based on a general knowledge of the country, its institutions, managers, and past experiences. The wisdom acquired from dealing with many different countries under varied circumstances helps in interpreting a country, despite the inevitable handicap of data gaps.

Few indicators have the same meaning for one country that they have for another. There is simply no labor-saving device yet invented that can spare us the effort of painstakingly examining each country individually—and repeatedly or even continuously—since changes of significance can occur rapidly. The process of knowing how to assess a country takes years to mature.

An Integrated and Comprehensive Assessment Method

Of all country risk evaluation systems, the integrated and comprehensive approach is highly regarded as the most reliable. It aims to be comprehensive enough to cover all significant identifiable risk factors, and integrated enough to reach conclusions. This approach can be effectively meshed with the rest of the bank's activities. As noted previously, it involves three layers of analysis along with other supportive activities.

It benefits the bank to have a comprehensive view of what it has to know about a country. If concern is limited to foreign exchange payment (whether the country will have the foreign exchange capability to service debt over a certain period of time), the bank will focus on the set of variables, qualitative or quantitative, which would give reasonably good projections of the outlook for foreign exchange income and expenditure. The bank, however, cannot be satisfied with this, even if it can be done satisfactorily, which often is not the case. It will need a judgment on how the country will control or restrict payments, particularly in case of difficulties. This requires country knowledge much greater than forecasting balance of external payments and income.

Our notion of risk, as broad as it is, drives us into a methodology that is broad and complicated. A bank must include all potential significant risks in doing its country assessments, and not simply confine itself to those which have appeared in the past or in other countries or for other banks. It is important to anticipate the way changes in country conditions will occur and not simply to react to current events. This is obviously a demanding professional task.

Analytic Layers

The comprehensive and integrated approach of analyzing country risk usually involves the following analytic layers. The *first* is the likelihood of balance-of-payments difficulties. Is the country likely to have balance-of-payments difficulties over the next five years? Many factors (external and domestic) must be looked at to answer this question. This analysis should be based on historical and current trends as well as future prospects. Quantitative forecasts can be useful if the data exist but are never sufficient by themselves.

External factors range from the likelihood of war and hostile or discriminatory acts short of war to economic conditions and outlook in major trading partners, terms of trade or prices of critical commodities such as oil, food, and capital goods. Other international factors may have an impact on actual or potential access to foreign exchange. These might include protectionist measures adopted in other countries limiting access for exports, or measures adopted by monetary authorities and bank regulators in the U.S. and other industrialized countries which limit international lending to the country under review.

Domestic factors which affect the balance of payments must be considered. These extend well beyond the obvious. Obvious are conditions in export industries, tourism, need or demand for imports, etc. Less obvious but necessary for balance-of-payments outlook judgments are the political and social environment including likelihood of revolution, extended civil unrest, labor policy, policies toward domestically domiciled U.S. and other multinational firms, etc. Such analysis leads to a judgment on the quality or adequacy of present domestic economic and balance-of-payments management. For developing countries, great weight is attached to the ability to manage long-term development and accompanying changes in political and social environment, as well as to current conditions, needs, and uses. This is important because in most cases deterioration in country conditions and management precede balance-of-payment difficulties. This type of country analysis is the genesis of a true *early*-warning system.

The first layer of analysis is anticipation of balance-of-payments difficulties. The *second* layer is likely governmental responses to such difficulties. Does the country have the political, social, and institutional ability or willingness to introduce balance-of-payments stabililization measures (exchange rate change, export promotion, import and service payments restrictions) to ward off an impending balance-of-payments crisis? Is the country likely to meet its balance-of-payments difficulties with an interruption or delay in debt service, default, repudiation or a formal moratorium, or rescheduling? What are the implications for banks' activities of identified likely responses to possible balance-of-payments troubles? For example, is the country's management able and willing to give highest priority to servicing external debt? If unable or unwilling to do so, what are the country's servicing priorities by type of borrower (public vs. private) or by type of creditor? In these ways, the bank is helped to reach a conclusion on whether it runs excessive risk in lending into a country.

Last, the *third* layer is to gauge the outlook for other risks. What other country risks are there which potentially affect bank income or equity? This diverse residual set of risks includes the likelihood of various measures that affect the income stream by affecting the bank's individual borrowers. These other risks include changes in corporate tax rates; in branching regulations; in asset acquisition constraints; exchange rate impact on dollar values of local equity or ability of local borrowers to service debt; interest rate ceilings; domestic regulatory climate, such as permission for local borrowers to borrow abroad; and the impact of monetary and fiscal antiinflationary policies, etc. It is impossible to give an exhaustive list applicable to all countries at all times. Bank officers, however, are experienced in many of these matters. It cannot be overemphasized that many country risks exist in addition to the transfer problem and that country risk analysis must go far beyond balance-of-payments analysis.

Data Needed

Many quantitative elements are useful in arriving at objective judgments in each layer of analysis, although not all the indicators described herein need to be followed in each and every country. The quantitative factors include debt structure, profile, and debt servicing ratios; exports; external debt outstanding in relation to exports; exports to imports; imports; compressibility of imports; terms of trade; changes in level of reserves; international reserves ratios; inflows of equity; per capita income; fiscal indicators; monetary indicators; investment and savings ratios; social indicators like health and housing; economic indicators like food consumption, income distributions, demographic trends, and other quality of life indicators, etc. At times, indicators need to be especially constructed for individual countries such as ratios indicating degree of government ownership of productive sectors.

Econometric methods also can be enlisted to improve country assessments. For example, the possibility of constructing a composite index of creditworthiness of a less developed country has been explored. The results of our efforts thus far indicate that this technique does not give conclusive and reliable results but does highlight conditions in countries which may require more careful attention than in other countries.

Many sources of information are available which country assessors can productively tap, both at the bank's headquarters and in the field. Information sources in the field include central banks and other government or municipal agencies; embassies; international agencies located inside and outside the U.S.; business and academic contracts; journalists and correspondents; newspapers, journals, and periodicals; and last, but not necessarily least, rumor and gossip. At the bank's head office, potential sources of information include information received from external branches and affiliates obtained by head office officials; the breadth of experience and knowledge of bank officers; internal bank reports; other bankers; inflow of current newspapers, journals, and periodicals; business contacts; consultants to the bank; and rumor and gossip.

As far as the collection of information is concerned, some international banks receive large masses of data, qualitative and quantitative, on an individual country basis. A large part of the information comes from representatives or officers stationed overseas and is supplemented by data obtained from national and international organizations. The information is evaluated on an individual country basis. Banks now are able to determine what their share of exposure is in a given country in relation to all other U.S. banks, thus helping the lending decisions.

Need for Global Framework

An important need is a useful worldwide framework within which the performance of individual countries can be assessed. It is not enough to know a country in isolation. It is necessary to be cognizant of factors exogeneous to the country which may have an impact on that country's creditworthiness. Some factors to focus on include world inflation, world trade, rise in protectionist sentiments in key countries, changing magnitudes of bilateral assistance, and growth rates in industrialized countries. All these have major effects on any given country's performance.

The integration of individual country information into a much larger framework presents a number of problems. The most basic one is lack of comparability of quantitative data collected in more than 100 countries. It is difficult to compress the multitude of information into a global framework of manageable proportion. But given these limitations, a knowledge of the world economy—within a global framework—will help a great deal in doing better country assessments.

Checks-and-Balance Process

A comprehensive and integrated approach to country assessments is greatly aided by the full cooperation and collaboration of different officers in the bank, in the field or branches, and at headquarters. It can be done by a separate group concentrating on country risk analysis. This group, however, is likely to be chronically understaffed and not as well informed as it could be unless it makes use of other bank staff. No one person, or few people, can combine the knowledge, experience, and wisdom that is desired if the bank's international lending is to be of significant proportion for the bank. Not only do others add information but they add other perspectives and interpretations. They also add to the likelihood that the country conditions will be assessed in light of the needs of the bank. An intellectual checks-and-balances process makes possible a richer and better country assessment for the bank.

Evaluation System

The following gives the broad outlines for such an evaluation system.

• A system is established for making information available to a relatively wide group of designated responsible bank officers. Such information includes internal reports prepared by bank officers and consultants, economic databases, review of current publications, news media, etc. One mark of a good country report is that it contains highly specific information and confidential analyses for use of the bank only and not written for public circulation.

• Evaluations and conclusions by bank officers in the field and at headquarters are circulated and reviewed at different levels directly—a system of checks and balances.

• Judgments by a responsible country risk official (or officials) are given (and if necessary, become the final judgment).

• Judgments are checked with other outside experts, if needed.

• Final country assessment is decided in light of the bank's business needs. This judgment is then used to make business decisions, but it is changed when conditions affecting country or business change.

• Formal procedures exist to assess the accuracy of past judgments and evaluations. If country evaluations do not anticipate events which have adverse consequences for that bank's activities in a given country, the system has failed. To the extent that a system can anticipate events in a country in adequate time, the bank can take appropriate defensive action to protect its interests. The key, as noted elsewhere, is successful anticipation.

• Finally, the responsible bank officers must continually refine their understanding of the linkages between a country's expected performance and the bank's specific business objectives in that country. Trying to understand the links between the country's macroeconomic performance, on the one side, and the outlook for specific economic sectors and individual public and private sector enterprises on the other, help provide the understanding the bank needs in arriving at business decisions.

In the years ahead, all banks doing significant international business will seek to introduce or improve existing methods for assessing countries and the processes for applying these judgments to the management of their portfolios. No institution can afford to see this work done badly, and increasingly the rewards will go to those banks which do it well.

Personnel Selection and Training

There are some clear implications for personnel selection and training—particularly for the larger banks that are heavily engaged abroad and need to dedicate substantial resources to these activities. Banks will become increasingly aware of the professional nature of country analysis and broaden their search both within and outside their institutions to find the most qualified persons. The same applies to assignment rotation and promotion policies within such banks. It takes years to develop the professional skill to evaluate countries and time to learn any country in depth.

Another implication is that this kind of analysis is a professional discipline which requires specialized knowledge and skills beyond those normally taught in graduate schools, in credit training, or acquired through a loan officer's normal on-the-job experience. Action must be taken by management to ensure that those entrusted with this responsibility are properly equipped. This requires a combination of formal education, general banking experience, and specialized training after the individual is employed by the bank to do country risk assessment or to help manage country risk.

The ability to have an outlook about the country on a continuous basis means a commitment on the part of the institution to doing this kind of work. It takes qualified personnel. At the bottom line, it takes money for staff, computer time, data banks, and so forth, depending on the size of a particular bank's international loan portfolio. An inadequate budget for these purposes signifies that the bank has not yet appreciated the difficulty of doing the job well nor does the bank believe it is important to do so.

Assessing the Economic Management of a Country

Assessing a country's economic management is a crucial element in country risk assessment, and therefore some further observations are in order.

Appraising the risk from changes in a country's conditions during the term of the loan derives from a banker's need to judge whether repayment will occur fully and promptly as scheduled according to contract. A nation's financial, economic, and political horizons, thus, must be continuously scanned for signs of impending vulnerability. As emphasized repeatedly in this book, an analysis of a wide range of qualitative and quantitative indicators is required to reach valid conclusions about a country's economic management and outlook.

Many of the key political and social variables are not quantifiable in any useful manner. Monitoring political risk is impossible unless numerous sources of information are tapped. Objectivity, however, remains the basis for business decision making, even though many factors are qualitative and cannot be quantified usefully. It is suggested that an appraisal include overseas visits and discussions. This is a tested way to improve ability to make reliable country judgments. Intuition is valuable and needed, but intuition should be based on knowledge, experience, and self-confidence that comes from successful past judgments.

The ideal approach to the analytical process is to know the individual country, its uniqueness, its vulnerabilities, its longer term historical development, as well as the most detailed statistical data available on its past and present performance. One must know who is really running the country (it is not always the political party in power) and whether the government has the political will and ability to carry out needed economic changes. The economic management of the country and its consequent policies and outlook are principal objects of study.

A bank's criteria of good economic management in a country is reflected in its lending criteria and vice versa. These criteria are greatly influenced by such other factors as the actuarial principles of balance and diversity of risk assets by geography, maturity, and borrowers. They are also determined by the economic management criteria by which banks judge whether or not a country deserves to enjoy their confidence in placing funds at risk in a country. The need to judge economic management becomes very clear when a bank evaluates how a country is handling an external payments crisis caused by persistent inflation, overvalued exchange rates, inadequate reserves, and a history of unsuccessful monetary and fiscal policies.

Government Response

Private banks judge economic management for countries in such difficulties by evaluating the following government actions:

• Removing governmental interference in the marketing mechanism, particularly that which interferes with the efficient allocation and use of resources.

• Correcting overvalued exchange rates and otherwise strengthening the international competitive position of the country.

• Improving monetary and fiscal policies by use of market-determined interest rates; reducing fiscal expenditures, particularly for unproductive investment and subsidized consumption; and improving tax collection.

• Strengthening international monetary reserves.

• Maintaining good relations with the IMF, World Bank, regional development banks, and most recently the BIS.

• Encouraging more efficient government administration including administration of exchange controls, if used.

• Maintaining or strengthening the productive capacity and efficiency of enterprises; encouraging more efficient management of productive enterprises—private and public.

• Encouraging more domestic savings and more sophisticated and nondiscriminatory money and capital markets to distribute savings.

• Eliminating or reducing regulations and laws which discriminate against foreigners.

• Implementing the principle that external debt to private lenders must have top priority in foreign exchange allocations, if exchange controls are used.

• Strengthening the central bank's position within the government and within the country in general.

• Creating conditions which give a country the option to borrow externally from both private and public sources and attract equity investment.

• Improving statistical services to enable better awareness and evaluation of country conditions in the future.

• Pursuing clear-cut and decisive management of a country's balance of payments, as well as of the domestic economy, and thereby reducing the uncertainty of banking business with and within the country.

Unpredictability

These are criteria which are rarely met in toto. The combination of pluses and minuses which adds up to acceptable country management can be calculated if knowledge and experience are brought to the task. Our methodological footing becomes more shaky when we try to monitor elusive risks and uncertainties, like political risks which are, nevertheless, very important for assessing country risk. Predicting future actions by governments, for instance, is exceedingly difficult, if not impossible, if we literally mean predicting. One can simulate what the economic response to different policies would be. From this, some idea can be formed of the implications of one set of policies as opposed to another. For example, we can test the implications of hypothetical changes in monetary targets, interest rates, or even an expansion in fiscal deficits financed by monetary expansion. Bankers do this all the time.

This, however, does not predict what will happen. It does not indicate what will be the domestic economic and social forces which at any given time determine government responses. Moreover, the context of international developments and responses of other governments cannot be known or predicted. However, these responses precipitate changes in domestic and international conditions and outlook. Bankers can try to give intellectual order to this terrifying complexity by making simplifying assumptions. But unlike a cyclotron, we cannot separate out what is moving and place it within a constrained and more controlled environment. When we do simplify, as we must to some extent, we run the risk of destroying the realities with which banks must deal successfully most of the time.

Assessing Balance-of-Payments Management

Balance-of-payments management is one area in which it is relatively easy to demonstrate the quality of national governments' macroeconomic management, particularly as it impinges on servicing external debt. Perhaps this is why it is frequently used as the central mode of country risk analysis. It is often tempting to approach balance-of-payments analysis and management as analogous to corporate cash flow analysis. Balance-of-payments statistics can be interpreted in an effort to foresee the availability of foreign exchange to service outstanding debt similar to cash flows within a corporation. The limitations of equating the analysis of the financial strength of a country with that of a corporation are at least twofold. The first is that a country will continue to exist, despite current difficulties, even crises and disasters. Companies go bankrupt and even disappear, but countries do not disappear because of financial difficulties. The second has to do with the much greater ability of governments to manipulate and monopolize cash flow.

Governments can decide to create and commandeer sufficient funds to repay foreign debts, either in domestic currencies or in foreign exchange. The foreign exchange position may be made favorable by using monetary and fiscal policies to equilibrate the balance of payments, adjust the exchange rate, or impose restrictions on the payments of imports. Resources realized in local currencies may not be transferable across national boundaries at any given time if such causes as prolonged inflation or chronic balance-of-payments deficits make foreign exchange unavailable. But the country can and usually will create the conditions needed to obtain the foreign exchange at some future time.

Balance of payments refer to the offsetting of foreign exchange earnings with foreign exchange expenditures. It amounts to a nation's exports net its imports in the current accounts section, plus net transfer payments and long- and short-term net capital flows. Changes in a country's net foreign exchange reserves, along with long-term and short-term capital transfers, usually offset deficits and surpluses registered in current accounts. Thus, capital movements including external borrowings do not finance particular items in the balance of payments. They finance the collective deficits which include the expenditures on interest but also include many other items. The cause of a deficit may be attributed to any portion of external expenditures or shortfall in earnings, depending on the focal point of the analyst.

Exports and imports of goods and services typically make up the bulk of the balance-of-payments statement. In some countries, services represent a substantial part of the foreign exchange income and expenditure mix. One component of services most relevant here is servicing interest on external debt and income on equity. Tourism and trade-related shipping costs and insurance are other services included in the data.

Data on balance of payments and international reserves are published by the IMF for member countries. Figures on official capital transactions are generally of reasonable reliability, whereas private capital transactions are less reliable and tend to be understated by the data, except in the case of a small number of countries.

Import trends need to be scrutinized closely, since imports are the chief user of foreign exchange. Essential imports should be separated from the nonessential because under economically stressful circumstances, a nation may choose to ration available foreign exchange to pay for essential imports at the expense of less essentials. This is referred to as the compressibility of imports. "Essentiality," however, is not uniform among countries and, indeed, varies within a country over time. This reflects not only changes in a country's production and distribution facilities (finding new sources of energy, for example) but also cyclical conditions affecting stocks and changed price relations influencing substitution possibilities.

It is quite normal for less developed countries to encourage considerable net inflows of foreign capital for the sake of achieving rapid economic development. This implies the accumulation of both private and public debt and thus a correspondingly larger future obligation to find enough foreign exchange to service this accumulating foreign debt, in addition to the other items in the balance of payments. A profile of a nation's external debt structure allows one to spot peak periods of debt servicing with higher associated risk of delays in debt servicing during such periods.

Central Bank Activity

It is also important to monitor those changes in a nation's international liquidity due to central bank actions. Banks with credit exposure in various countries should obtain statements of their central banks on a regular basis to gain an understanding of their monetary policies and their management of both foreign and domestic assets and liabilities. What is, literally, the bottom line of the balance-of-payments statement is a central bank's net foreign exchange position, that is, its liquid assets minus current liabilities. This occurs because nations do not usually voluntarily accept the currency of a less developed country in settlement for international payment. Thus, central banks do not have the occasion to acquire assets in the national currencies of debtor developing countries. The IMF accumulates such national currencies of members when it sells them needed foreign currencies.

By careful analysis of the details of the balance of payments, professional judgments can be made on the likelihood of balance-of-payments difficulties or strengths. The weaknesses in balance-of-payments management, if any, and the significance of possible, or probable, international changes can also be seen. We are then ready to judge the likelihood of changes in internal policies. Each policy has a different likelihood of change and different impact. We cannot assume that because a policy change will help correct a weakness, it will be done, or if done, that it will occur in sufficient magnitudes or in time. In addition, most policy measures require other measures to make them effective. But this does not mean that they will be taken.

We have seen numerous cases of countries not correcting overvalued exchange rates which were damaging their balance of payments. Consequently, these countries increased external debt much more than warranted and lost foreign exchange reserves. This encouraged capital flight, hurt income profitability and employment in export industries, encouraged imports, and discouraged efficient import substitute industries, and so forth. Yet, the needed change does not take place, is long delayed, or, when taken, is insufficient in magnitude.

Mexico in 1982 was simply the latest and most dramatic example. Many, if not most, developing countries committed such errors sometime during the past two or three decades. In other cases, the change was made, but other related measures in monetary and fiscal areas needed to gain the benefits of the change were not taken. For example, an inflationary credit policy continues to encourage domestic consumption and discourage exports, despite the improved competitive position for exports gained by a devaluation. Pricing policies keep down food production, although the new exchange rate encourages food production. A similar litany can be described for failure to react adequately to changes in international conditions.

Understanding the difference between what could be done to deal with difficulties and what is likely to be done is essential for country risk analysis. If we *can* forecast the likelihood of balance-of-payments difficulties, that is, deficits that increase significantly the possibility of delays or interference in servicing loans fully and promptly, we *cannot* predict policy behavior. Yet we must decide for reasons of business decision making what we think is likely to happen. Although confronted by uncertainty, we cannot avoid deciding based on our judgment of what is likely to happen and what is not likely to happen. Wisdom becomes the desired, though rare, ingredient. By managing uncertainty, it is possible for a bank to perform its function internationally as it does domestically.

Country Rating and Ranking System

The virtue of reducing uncertainty by country risk work is further highlighted in considering the proper uses and abuses of country rating systems. Although we prefer to integrate information on individual countries into a global framework, this should not be confused with a method of ranking countries by any type of sequential numerical method.

A rigid or precise ranking system is arbitrary and unrealistic. It cannot take into account the fundamental proposition that exposure in a given country is not homogeneous as to risk. Take the client base of large banks. Some clients, like shipowners and airlines, have access to foreign exchange independent of the foreign exchange availability of the country in which they reside. Other customers may have much less favored access to a country's foreign exchange income or available reserves in the event of foreign exchange shortages. Loans from the IMF, the World Bank, and regional development banks are given preferred creditor positions compared with loans to other creditors. Correspondent bank loans usually have special status. Banks vary greatly in their loan composition in any country and therefore in the country risk in any country—leaving aside magnitudes, maturities, and borrowers and focusing on purpose. Focusing on other aspects reveals other dissimilarities in country risk.

Specific Risk Ratings

Specific country risks vary from country to country. Some countries have balance-of-payments vulnerabilities; in others, equity investments might be confiscated. In still others, we are concerned with specific government measures which adversely affect the cash flow generation capability of private sector clients (and their ability to service foreign *and* domestic debt), and so on. No simple ranking system can cope with such a diversity of concerns. Ranking or rating systems have two major faults. The first relates to their statistical and economic validity; the second, to their usefulness for a private bank.

Countries can be distinguished by broad categories—minimal country risk, acceptable risk, or unacceptable risk. A minimal risk category means a willingness to lend to all creditworthy borrowers at acceptable spreads in virtually any amounts compatible with the bank's definition of portfolio diversity and avoidance of concentration. In such cases, country risk in a particular country still needs to be carefully identified and evaluated at close to zero. General reputation for acceptability cannot be a substitute for hard thinking. In addition, country assessments can sensitize credit officers to changes in economic or financial conditions or in government policies particularly those which are likely to hurt potential borrowers to the point of impairing their ability or willingness to service debts. Experience indicates that an overall favorable impression of a country from a banker's viewpoint does not mean neglecting the "surprise" possibilities for individual business sectors and firms. Moreover, there is some country risk in all countries.

A crude category of acceptable risk can be used to indicate willingness to lend, but in limited amounts or on a selective basis as to usage, maturities, and portfolio mix within the country. Each country within the category and each loan within a country still has to be considered separately and carefully. It will be important, however, to have a mechanism or method of country assessment which gives a basis for this crude categorization, as for any other. It is an anticipating judgment—a judgment on expectations without the benefit of the usual basis for probability decisions. Historical experience and knowledge of the country will probably be weak for such needs by normal statistical standards. Judgment will be very important.

The danger is to disguise weakness in hard information by precise probability numbers, including weights. These are forms or methodologies of science. Without the necessary knowledge of the country, such forms or methodologies can give a sense of false comfort to decision makers. They can lead to major mistakes which could have been avoided by recognizing that the problem is how to reach a good business decision without having the desired reliable information for better analysis. Intuition and wisdom based on experience and available knowledge become the ingredients of successful analyses on which business decisions can be based.

Similarly, another crude category can be established like unacceptable risk. This means no increases in total exposure but possibly with changes in assets allowed as amortization runs down leaving room for others as business opportunities materialize. Another possible refinement is whether a particular new loan portfolio mix should be sought deliberately that might include more government loans (or less), more shorter-term (or longer), more bank lines (or less), more local firms (or more multinational). Or should the portfolio simply address business opportunities as they arise.

Another possible category is simply no exposure wanted. Again, there can be refinement—no exposure wanted, except for . . . . This opens the possibility of exceptions but only within the framework of a strong presumption of no lending to the country. Exceptions will arise like financing energy and food imports with bank lines. A danger, however, is following the market leaders. A bank can make poor loans or lose acceptable opportunities for market penetration by imitating others, particularly a bank that is relatively new in a country or new to the particular service it has the opportunity to provide. Market opinion is influenced by the past experience of banks, as well as current conditions. Each bank has its own constraints but also its own potentials. A red warning light for a country market may well be warranted for a particular bank by existing conditions, but the implications for another bank of the same conditions should be made by the bank for itself.

Countries Not at Risk

The concern does not include, of course, countries in which a bank is simply not interested for reasons other than country risk—too remote or too small to be worth an effort. In practice, many developing countries, particularly in Africa and in the Caribbean are in this red category for such nonrisk consideration. Yet analysts and commentators wrongly put them in the same category as countries in which banks could find business and would be glad to have business, but turn down such opportunities because of perceived country risk.

Thus, the use of crude categories is much less objectionable than precise country rankings. In modern societies, precision is often valued more highly than accuracy. "Rather precise than right" is often a good motto for those advocating a quantitative approach. Precision in country risk analysis is very hard to achieve. Furthermore, it is much harder to achieve when countries are compared with others. It is again even harder when their relativity is expressed in a numerical rating order rather that grouping by broad categories. When available, such precise numerical ratings can be used as points of departure for further analysis or as another check on views among others, not as a substitute for such analysis or other judgments.

Unlike the use of country ratings in numerical or letter rank of some sort, it is preferable to use country assessment directly and separately in the management of cross-border exposure and other business activities. Country ratings can be misleading, not only because they imply unrealistic precision, comparability, and homogeneity where there is none but because their use can damage a bank's relations with a country unnecessarily and with little or no benefit to the bank. It can increase the likelihood of failure to identify risk or failure to identify a profitable opportunity which could have been otherwise anticipated. Country risk is not homogeneous either within or among countries and a country ranking system tends to treat all assets alike within a country.

A loan to a central bank in a high-risk country can be less risky than a loan to a politically vulnerable person or entity in a low-risk country. A loan to a multinational customer in a foreign country has a different country risk than a loan to a domestic company—not necessarily less risk, perhaps more.

To quantify a country correctly in relation to others is virtually impossible. Take Uganda as an example. After a bloody destructive civil war, it had very poor country risk. It probably needed to reschedule its debt. It was in grave balance-of-payments difficulties—obviously not a country for private bank lending. On the other hand, it agreed to a program with the IMF, which endorsed its new economic program and provided substantial financial resources. It has a strong agricultural basis. It has domestic violence inherited from the previous regime, but is getting help to eliminate it. Private banks are reluctant to lend. How does it rate numerically with Nicaragua? Nicaragua also has a very poor country risk—with complex international relations, uncertain political future, no meaningful relations with the IMF, but a much higher per capita income and export earnings, and many more connections with the international financial community. How does Uganda compare with the Ivory Coast, Costa Rica, etc.? How do these countries compare? Which ranks higher or lower? What countries rate higher or lower, in what order? What is the use of this ordering? What does a bank learn from the relative ranking? Are the rankings related to the portfolio composition of the bank?

If the ranking systems are examined, the results are often preposterous—completely at variance with knowledge, experience, and wisdom. What about the countries the analyst does not know? Are they better judged and ranked? Is ignorance bliss? Is ranking as a good risk justified or do methods which give silly results for the more poorly managed give better results for the better managed?

What is fundamental is that country risk is not homogeneous or internationally comparable, except in a very crude way. If the ranking or rating is merely one input among many in the bank's country assessment system, then little harm is done or even good may be gained. The danger is that the ranking or rating is obtained by simplistic methods or formulas which lend themselves to such methods. They are quick, cheap, and nearly painless and therefore a tempting alternative for methods which are relatively laborious, time-consuming, and costly.

Country Classifications

The use of country rankings is, at times, related to the use of country classifications. Some comments on country classifications may be useful. Country classifications differ from rankings and ratings in that they may be seen as a mechanism for evaluating an existing portfolio, while ratings are usually reserved to make decisions about new loans and other business activities.

With respect to individual loans in a bank's portfolio, classified loans indicate how the bank should view existing assets. Should they be regarded as income-earning assets or should they be put on a nonaccrual basis, that is, nonincome earning because debt servicing is falling behind the contracted schedule? How long are delays before loans are so considered? Should they be written off or should loan loss reserves be increased by the bank to meet contingencies after agreed periods of delay?

These practices clearly derive from bank practice with respect to worrisome or weak individual credits, but the system of classification is also applied to countries. It seems a logical step to move from the familiar practice of classifying individual credits to classifying countries.

Examiners' Views

The views and practices of the U.S. bank examiners and regulators are important to understanding existing views of ranking and rating. The comment from practitioners is often that their use of country rankings or ratings seemed justifiable since bank examiners also used classifications for individual credits. If a bank regulator can classify a loan or a country, why not rank a country? Bank examiners and regulators are seen as greatly influenced in their views of banks' country risk systems by their credit classification systems. Moreover, each bank may have its own classification system, which often closely parallels the system used by the bank regulators. Internal auditors prefer to anticipate the bank examiners and classify loans which merit classification before the bank examiners do so. It is much easier to do this when the system and the criteria within a bank are very close to what the bank examiners will do.

Before summarizing the system of the U.S. bank examiners, it is noteworthy that the classifications of bank examiners are confidential. This is in line with a long tradition of respecting the bank-customer relationship. Borrower and lender have a common interest to preserve this confidence, and the bank examiner shares this interest. When the system is applied to countries it tends to break down. Leaving aside the intellectual validity of classifying a country, it is newsworthy, at times dramatically newsworthy, on the first page of a metropolitan newspaper. The classification is done by a U.S. government agency. Classified countries have no choice except to be indignant and protest officially. It is always a leak or a speculation, but it hurts in any case. Apologies are always in order but inadequate. Banking becomes even more politicized and this is not necessary to achieve the aims of regulators. These comments are *not* addressed to classifying individual credits, but the application of this method to countries and the use of country classifications, ranking, and rating systems.

Classified Loans

In their inspection of individual loans in loan portfolios, bank examiners are trying to pinpoint particular loans which need strengthening and careful management if they are to be collected. Such assets are assigned separately a quality rating, "based on the examiner's best judgment concerning the degree of risk and the likelihood of orderly liquidation . . . No formula covers all the various types of loans made by banks."[21] Thoughtful guidelines are given to examiners. Short-term credit is essentially related to the inventory to cash cycle. When the loan is not repaid at maturity, problems are indicated. But examiners look for other factors that also can explain difficulties in making payments, like the seasonal nature of the business. Term loan repayment is closely related to projections of future operations. Failure to meet projections is a credit weakness but does not necessarily mean that assets should be classified. Failure to generate sufficient cash flow to service the debt would in most cases justify classifying the loan. However, not all delinquent loans are necessarily classified. Other factors, like the presence of guarantors, influence the severity of the criticism. Criticized loans are categorized into the four following classifications, with increasing severity indicated by higher numbers.

1. *Other loans especially mentioned (OLEM).* These are loans judged to be currently protected but are potentially weak credits. They are "an undue and unwarranted credit risk" but not to the point of justifying a substandard classification.[22] An adverse trend in the borrower's operations or an imbalanced position in the balance sheet which has not reached a point where the liquidation is jeopardized may best be handled by this classification.

2. *Substandard loans.* These have a well-defined weakness or weaknesses that jeopardize the liquidation of the debt. They are characterized by the distinct possibility that the bank will sustain some loss if the deficiencies are not corrected.

3. *Doubtful loans.* In these cases, collection or liquidation in full is regarded as "highly questionable and improbable. The possibility of loss is extremely high."[23] In some cases, examiners are instructed to determine a reasonable carrying value for a distressed credit and request a writedown through a charge to the valuation portion of the loan loss reserve. Examiners are told to "avoid classifying an entire credit doubtful when collection of a specific portion appears highly probable."[24]

4. *Loss loans.* Such loans are considered "uncollectible and of such little value that their continuance as bankable asset is not warranted, even though partial recovery may be effected in the future. Banks should not be allowed to attempt long-term recoveries while the loan remains booked. Loan losses should be taken in the period in which they surface as uncollectible."[25]

Examiners are admonished that they must submit comments which support the classifications. Methods used to present a criticized loan may vary, but certain categories of information have to be covered, including actions taken or proposed by borrowers to rectify existing financial failures.

[21]*Comptroller's Handbook for National Bank Examiners* (Washington, D.C.: Comptroller of the Currency, 1977 and supplements).
[22]Ibid.
[23]Ibid.
[24]Ibid.
[25]Ibid.

The issue for country risk management is not whether to classify individual loans. One can accept this as a healthy precautionary technique. The issue is whether all assets in a certain general category in a country (loans to governments or government entities or private entities with government guarantees) should be classified uniformly. Again, the issue is treating different assets as though they were homogeneous. Giving the same classification to different countries (or to the same country at different times) or to a broad group of assets assumes a comparability which is often not real. With individual credits, each credit is considered separately as something unique. These are common in rules on repayment—elapsed time after payments are due. It is a limited guide for a country rating because only rarely are all external debts delayed simultaneously for the same periods of time. It could happen and when it does, the same result is achieved by classifying all the individual loans by the same rule. If it does not happen and a country is classified, it can mean similar treatment for dissimilar payments situations.

Indeed, these classifications are like rankings or ratings when they are used to indicate the country risk in an existing portfolio. Under such circumstances, efforts emerge to recognize diversity among countries by such devices as measuring total assets in a country in relation to the capital of the lending bank, as though the larger the exposure, the more capital is at risk, irrespective of the composition of the assets. Again, assets are treated as homogeneous when they are not, except when made homogeneous in such extreme cases as repudiation and default.

Conclusion

The response of the private banks to the world's interminable series of uncertainties and difficulties cannot be paralysis of decision making and action. In appreciating the realities within which they act, banks can reduce risk to acceptable proportions by applying actuarial principles and by country evaluations which employ all sources of information, all known methodologies and analytical tools, all feasible judgments based on experience and sophisticated intuition. These two assessments combine the insights which can only be gained on the spot by firsthand continuous and maturing experience with the fruits of careful and systematic scholarship.

The preferred approach to country evaluation is the opposite of oversimplification and annual exercises. It tests itself by continuous monitoring and reviewing of past judgments. It avoids inadvertently harming countries by oversimplified and unrealistic rankings and ratings. It avoids the diplomatic tensions that arise when countries see their names in print as poor country risks or classified by criteria which must seem arbitrary and inequitable.

It helps in the management of unpredictability and uncertainty. It allows country assessment to become an integral part of the bank's business process and gives bankers the experience needed to make country risk analysis part of the banking profession.

14

Country Risk Management Process

Country assessments are of little value unless they are integrated into a bank's business process. Whatever assessment methodology is used—even merely going along with the views of syndication lenders—the country assessment must be a vital part of the business decision making. Indeed, it will be much easier to determine what kind of country methodology is best suited to the business of the bank and how it can be used most effectively after deciding decisively that country assessment should be linked to all business decisions which would benefit from such links. Banks of medium and larger size will find the comprehensive integrated approach most suitable.

Management Considerations

This chapter examines various aspects of the design and implementation of management systems and processes which create appropriate linkages between a bank's country evaluation and its international business activities. It does not provide a manual or form for the design or implementation of a country risk management system. It aims to provide a broad perspective that will be useful in such tasks.

Since a bank's country exposure is subject to manifold types of country risk, the bank needs to establish a number of both formal and ad hoc institutional arrangements or linkages so it can assimilate sufficiently country risk evaluative information into its decision-making process. If establishing such linkages does not become a central priority, the country evaluative function (as outlined in the previous chapter) may well become simply an isolated, useless, and hence cosmetic organizational appendage.

This appraisal of current country risk management practices profited by two separate surveys of U.S. banks, each with large samples of U.S. banks. The Association of Reserve City Bankers' survey of 119 banks in 1977 used a questionnaire to elicit detailed information on the country exposure measurements and reporting practices of respondent banks. Seventy banks were surveyed by Robert Morris Associates in 1980 on how they manage the diversification of their international loan portfolios. The second survey corroborated and brought up to date the findings of the first.

Lenders Decisive

The rapid growth in overseas lending and other banking activities has caused the need for country risk analysis to be included in business decision processes. From the viewpoint of country risk analysis and use, it is noteworthy that although the process is demand driven—borrowing entities, private or official, create the demand—the lenders determine the magnitudes and terms on which they will supply. Thus, the obvious is of central importance—country risk administration is done by lenders which is the focus of this chapter. In this chapter on country risk administration, there is no attempt to analyze how the borrower should organize itself and achieve its objectives as a borrower.

The creditworthiness of the individual borrower is decided by the lending banks on the basis of the normal credit criteria. The decision also must be made whether the total or proposed increased foreign currency exposure in a country is acceptable to the private lending institution in light of country conditions and outlook. Topflight professional expertise is needed as the overseas foreign currency loans become important in the bank's total lending to any one country and the country portfolio needs to be changed as conditions and outlook change. Portfolios must and can be carefully scrutinized from the viewpoint of country risk.

Many bankers have felt they do not have the necessary experience and discipline to make judgments about countries. They can judge markets, they can judge funding, they can judge exchange risk. They can, of course, do individual credit assessment. To assess a country in any comprehensive way, however, is new. In exceptional cases, if they had visited a country or were stationed there, they may feel they know the country well enough for their business purposes. Normally, bankers have turned eagerly to others to provide the missing expertise on countries. Demand became strong for methodologies which bankers could use to assess country risk. Less attention was paid to linkages within the bank to business decisions.

New Assessments

International banking is hundreds of years old. Bankers, however, had dealt with countries with which they were familiar.[26] There was an intuitive, undescribed, and inarticulated process when dealing with entities within a country about which they knew a great deal. They automatically embodied the country risk elements in their banking business decisions. The new situations of a new group of countries with which bankers did not have this experience led to a desire for more formal, structured, professional country assessments, rather than a process based essentially on experience. This is novel.

What is the importance of country risk analysis? How can it be used to reduce the risks in international lending to acceptable levels or to identify acceptable

[26]F. John Mathis, ed., *Offshore Lending By U.S. Commercial Banks*, 2nd ed. (Philadelphia: Bankers' Association for Foreign Trade and Robert Morris Associates, 1981).

profit-making opportunities? How does country risk analysis relate to other safeguards taken by lenders? Can it be truly effective in avoiding risks? Is it really a major element in business decision making or is it an ancillary peripheral kind of interest? Does one have to invent something else and take a different approach? Such questions cannot be quickly resolved; they are likely to continue to challenge international bankers for some time to come.

Increased Safeguards

The management response to risks in international lending has essentially been more safeguards to constrain international lending. A brief look at other safeguards may be useful. In this respect, there is an increasing emphasis on the importance of portfolio diversification, particularly geographically, in addition to evaluation of country risk. Diversity in maturities is also sought with the assumption that shorter maturities reduce country risk. Diversity of borrowers is also sought, with government and government entities given high credit standings. Purposes of borrowings are also diversified, although not as a separate factor but related to other considerations.

Lending to newer and troubled countries has also resulted in increasing emphasis on capital adequacy. Everywhere, capital has become a lower and lower proportion of the total assets and total liabilities of banks. The question of capital adequacy, however, tends to be raised most avidly when discussing international lending as compared with domestic lending, especially lending to developing countries. Those concerned worry more about the possibility of losses, or write-offs, when they consider the potential adversities of lending outside their countries. They believe it is much riskier. Limitations on total loans to one borrower have long existed. It had not, however, been commonplace to limit total exposure in one country because of capital adequacy considerations. In the headquarters' country, capital has always been important. Managers, depositors, bank security analysts, shareholders, possible new investors, boards of directors, regulators, and correspondent banks regarded capital as a major element in their assessments of the bank's own creditworthiness. Nevertheless, the fact that capital was an increasingly lower proportion of total liabilities and assets did not prevent the expansion of bank business, though this trend was frequently a cause of comment and concern.

Capital Adequacy

Increasing attention was given to asset quality and portfolio management as well as funding strategies, policies, and practices to protect the liquidity of the lending bank and build capital. As long as banks were lending either in relatively small amounts, either absolutely or in relation to total domestic and foreign assets, or to well-known countries with strong standing in the financial community, like Canada, the Western European countries, and Japan, capital adequacy was a general question not related particularly to country risk. As international lending expanded, both to the well-known countries enjoying the confidence of international lenders and to countries acceptable as borrowers but without the same sturdy reputation, capital adequacy was seen as segmented and particularized to individual countries. In the U.S., assets/liabilities could be 20 or even 30 times capital for U.S. banks. The same banks with the same capital with loans in Germany or Japan would be thought excessive at two, three, or four times capital. The banks would be thought excessive at one or two times capital in Brazil or Mexico and excessive at 50% of capital in most borrowing developing countries. Variants in country risk greatly influence, and at times dominate, thinking on capital adequacy. In most industrial countries, lending internationally continues to be regarded as riskier than lending domestically.

What about the record of loan losses in the past five years of write-offs by banks or write-offs against capital? By such criteria, lending to developing countries, as a group, has been no more risky than other categories of lending. The bulk of write-offs for U.S. banks has come from lending to U.S. entities and entities in other industrial countries.

This is not to argue that lending to developing countries is not risky. It is risky. There probably has been an exaggeration of the risks involved because there has not been a sufficiently long historical experience from which to draw. If banks had been lending for much longer periods, firm conclusions could be drawn. It is, however, difficult to have firm conclusions based on a relatively short historical experience. The experience with these countries as major term borrowers, especially by governments and government entities, from private banks is relatively brief.

Country Assessments

In addition to the safeguards of portfolio diversification, asset and liability management, and capital adequacy, there are also considerations of country assessments. The criteria by which banks judge whether a country deserves to enjoy their confidence in placing their funds at risk in a country are important. In general, banks recognize the need to integrate the country risk evaluation system with other banking functions. Specifically, these dimensions should be covered in the integration of:

- Credit assessments.
- Comptroller function.
- Preparation of annual business budgets.
- Longer-term strategic planning.

Although many banks have begun to do this, it needs to be strengthened. Banks that have not yet started should start as soon as they can.

Given the basic creditworthiness of the individual borrower, judgments on country risk, currency risk and institutional policies on magnitudes, acceptable spreads, and appropriate maturities become major elements in private bank decision making. Country risk assessments, effectively used, can help in nearly all these decisions to reduce risk, lessen losses, and identify business opportunities. In these various ways, it can increase the profitability of the bank while defending its liquidity and strengthening its solvency.

Private bank lenders have different strategies in international lending because they differ in such key policy areas as capital and reserves, leveraging, profitability prospects, structure of portfolios, geographic and customer dispersion, and so forth. The application of a general strategy new to a particular borrower, even a prime European government, is a business decision the wisdom of which only time will tell.

Cross-Border Exposure Management

Officials of a bank must take adequate precautions in managing their international lending or cross-border exposure. It is their skills and commitments which constitute the most important elements of any country risk management process and system. The bank will probably wish to establish ceilings and subceilings for each country's foreign currency exposure. Responsibility for establishment and changes in ceilings must be designated. A control function and reporting system must become operational as precursors to even minimally managing country risk contingencies. The reporting system is comprised of the following aspects—content, frequency, personnel, distribution, monitoring, review, and re-appraisal of business decisions.

Cornerstones of Decisions on Ceilings

The following four cornerstones underlie decisions on exposure ceilings:

1. Judgments on potential in-country business opportunities.
2. Analysis of the varying shades of risk inherent in the patterns of exposure in any one country.
3. Anticipating or analyzing national and international events, including governmental policies and measures which affect exposure.
4. The development of *quantitative* and *qualitative* techniques applied to information potentially available to banks.

Private banks find it useful to establish ceilings on the total amount of exposure they are prepared to have in any one country. Subceilings are also often set according to maturities or types of borrowers. Country loan limits (or ceilings) are generally established periodically (once a year) and altered as conditions warrant. The setting of such ceilings is directly related to the country assessment. This relationship can be firmly established by placing the responsibility for the establishment and the amendment—either the raising or the lowering—of self-imposed ceilings on exposure in the hands of the loan officer. He or she should be the same officer who makes the determination of the acceptability of proposed business activities in a country from the viewpoint of country risk as set forth in the country assessment.

Heterogeneity

The concept of country sublimits derives from the important tenet that country risk is not homogeneous within any economy. Different sectors, in which borrowers of differing characteristics are present, are affected in different ways by both the domestic and international events included in our definition of country risk. A bank can better recognize this heterogeneity by the use of subceilings for different maturities and types of transactions and borrowers which can be managed separately in anticipation of—or in reaction to—changing country conditions.

The kind of mechanism used to set country ceilings (if any), implement ceilings, report exposure, evaluate countries, and assess country risk must be tailor-made to suit the individual bank. The main determinants include:

- Size of operations abroad.
- Geographical spread.
- Business-segment spread.
- Relationship of field to U.S. head office—degree of decentralization and delegation of authority.
- Extent of physical presence abroad.
- Kind of presence—branches, subsidiaries, consortia, representative offices, visits, and so forth.
- Professional capability in evaluating countries and international development.
- Head office management style—degree of differentiation of functions—marketing, credit evaluation, auditing, foreign exchange operations, and personnel policy.

Managing Exposure

It is important that the exposure identified be managed in a way that best uses the results of country risk analyses. We are still in the process of evolving more and more promising ways of accomplishing this, and there will probably never be any single system compatible with the needs and purposes of every institution. The step-by-step explanation presented here is a procedure for managing exposure which experience indicates can be effective. It is generally designed for a private bank with branch networks or other business presence in foreign countries:

1. Establishment of cross-border ceilings and subceilings at the beginning of the year for each country into which the bank books business. Where appropriate, procedures may include:

- Recommendation by the senior officer in the field or at head office responsible for preparing the country business budget.
- Review by senior management of proposed ceilings at the head office.
- Approval by executive authority within the bank ultimately responsible for establishing ceilings or subceilings.

2. Procedures for allocating and re-allocating agreed exposure ceilings and subceilings among different lending units within the bank at home and abroad.

3. Procedures to ensure total outstandings of the bank worldwide do not surpass established ceilings.

4. Reporting of actual worldwide exposure on a periodic basis.

5. Procedures for changes in ceilings and subceilings during the course of the year as country conditions and outlook warrant.

6. Ongoing assessment and monitoring of country conditions and outlook from the viewpoint of banks' activities in the country. Where appropriate, this is a combined activity of:

- The field staff.
- Senior management at head office.
- Final responsibility rests with the executive authority responsible for establishing ceilings or subceilings.

7. Identification of potential country risks—a byproduct of ongoing assessment and monitoring of country conditions and outlook. Where appropriate, this is a combined activity of the field and the head office.

The country officer in the field, marketing officer for the bank, or the executive officers in charge of country risk must propose changes in country judgments whenever country circumstances change sufficiently to warrant adjustments in country limits or sublimits. The content of written submission for recommended action regarding the setting or changing of exposure ceilings and subceilings is comprised of an analysis of key elements, economic, financial, social and political; conclusions and judgments on country outlook; and recommendations on exposure, or other business activities.

The nature of ceilings and limits can have many facets:

- By maturities—one year or less, more than one year (one to two years, to five years, over five).
- By categories of borrowers—government, government entities, private domestic firms guaranteed by governments, private domestic firms not guaranteed by governments, multinationals, etc.
- By principal country category of borrower—world ceilings, developed countries, developing countries (for example, in terms of oil exporters, higher, middle, and lower income countries) and Eastern Europe.
- By purposes or usage—general purpose lending, project finance, balance-of-payments support lending, leasing, shipping, trade-related correspondent banking, and co-financing.

A comprehensive country risk management system aims to ensure that country risk assessments are also used in other banking tasks. These include deciding to open or close branches, booking centers, affiliates, investments, hedging capital, funding, exchange risk, visits to countries, receiving delegations from countries, public relations such as speeches and press interviews, checking the creditworthiness of each individual borrower, and improving overall portfolio dispersion and balance. The country risk management system also can play a major role in credit inspection and portfolio review activities, either by external or internal controllers or regulatory bodies.

Defining and Monitoring Country Exposure

For country risk analysis to be useful to the bank's business decisions, the scope and content of this analysis must be framed with an eye on the specific (actual or contemplated) foreign assets (or liabilities) at risk and other business activities of the bank. The volume and maturity of such assets must often be measured and efficiently and timely reported as an integral part of managing an international portfolio, so that the responsible officers can respond to the new streams of information. Reporting forms and instructions need to be clear and specific; automation should be used to ensure timeliness.

Even allowing for the heterogeneity of risk to which different kinds of assets or balance sheet items are exposed, the total volume of assets nonetheless must be diligently monitored and aggregated. The total volume of assets at risk in a country usually gives the single most important piece of information on what the bank has at risk in a country. A bank's total exposure level is needed to evaluate the significance of current trends and anticipated difficulties. It also helps regulators as these totals are important elements in their attitudes. Total exposure figures need to be accurate and available virtually instantaneously. Efficient exposure measurement and reporting schemes, and efficient interbank communication, are needed to arrive at this larger aggregate picture in time to be operationally useful. Using such country exposure limits, the bank applies the results of country risk analysis to advance specific business goals. The harmonizing of country exposure limits with the other banking functions enables diversifying risk as well as maximizing long-term profits.

Country exposure applies to the risks associated with the geographical location of a bank's business activities. Depending on the scope and magnitude of its overseas portfolio, a bank's balance sheet is not immune to risk of incurring losses stemming from adverse political or economic events which could jeopardize the quality of a bank's loan portfolio. This exposure is often of a cross-border (or foreign currency) nature. These cross-border aspects can increase the difficulties in loan repayment. Accordingly, bank management must meticulously identify the maximum number of balance sheet elements subject to country risk.

Country exposure and risk may be summarized in the following manner. First, the ability of a borrower to repay debts can be undermined by actions of a sovereign government affecting international payments or transfer of funds internationally, tax incidence, interest rates, and other policies of general application. Second, if the bank has branches or subsidiaries interested in a foreign state, these are not only exposed to the kind of general governmental policies mentioned but also are exposed to direct actions. These specific actions include nationalization or restrictions on branching or personal financial services which can be marketed, pricing, capitalization, and remittances of bank earnings. Third, the legal loan contract can be unilaterally altered due to default, rescheduling, or refinancing. Even rescheduling a loan is a serious problem for a commercial bank due to the opportunity cost of tying up funds and personnel time in the activity.

The size of a bank and the extent to which it is involved in international activities have a considerable impact on the number and type of items which create country exposure. Generally speaking, the larger the bank and the greater the scope of its international operations, the more likely it is to have a wide variety of balance-sheet and off-balance-sheet components. The smaller the bank and the narrower the scope of its international activities, the more likely it is to have its exposure limited to traditional balance-sheet items.

Survey Results

The principal vehicles used to communicate data for the Association of Reserve City Bankers (ARCB) survey were two questionnaires. The first questionnaire solicited information about the size and scope of the responding banks' international operations and about their general reporting procedures. The second sought to define the treatment, for exposure measurement purposes, of the various types of asset acquisition and off-balance-sheet transactions. The survey brought many interesting facts into focus.

One empirical finding was that the larger the bank in total assets, the larger the percentage of assets in international activities. This was particularly significant because most banks in the survey group of money center banks were not large, particularly compared with the few truly large banks. While only 9% of the banks had total assets in excess of $10 billion in 1975, 66% of the respondents possessed assets of less than $2.5 billion.

Turning to the percentage distribution of international assets as a percentage of total assets, only 15% of the 119 responding banks had more than 25% of total assets in their foreign operations. In contrast, 38% of the responding banks had less than 5% of their assets tied to international activities (plus 37% with between 5% and 15%). It could be expected that these small percentages would be more typical of the smaller regional and local U.S. banks. At the other extreme, only 3% of the responding banks had the more awesome statistic of greater than 45% of assets involved internationally.

With regard to the *dispersion* of foreign country exposure, the larger the percentage of international assets in total assets, the more dispersion of exposure among foreign countries. Fully 23% of the responding banks had a foreign asset exposure in over 50 countries representing a broad international dispersion. On the other hand, 8% of responding U.S. banks had no reported foreign country exposure whatsoever. The majority, or 51%, reported such exposure in between 11 and 50 foreign countries.

Because so many banks had a very high diversification of foreign country exposure in numerous countries, it is surprising that proportionately few banks had a significant number of foreign branches or subsidiaries. Only 3% of respondents had full service branches in more than ten countries. Two or more foreign subsidiaries were reported for 13% of the respondent banks, while 28% had two or more foreign affiliates.

In contrast, 24% of respondents had no foreign branches, while 47% only had branches of the Eurocurrency kind, such as exist in Nassau or the Cayman Islands. Similarly, 72% had no foreign subsidiaries and 57% had no foreign affiliates. As a result, questions relating to local currency exposure were not applicable to many respondents. The lack of a foreign presence also appears to facilitate frequent and less cumbersome reporting procedures for these banks. For banks with the most extensive foreign branch networks, the reporting procedures were clearly more burdensome.

A substantial majority of the responding banks surveyed by the ARCB used formal country exposure reporting procedures. Only 12 banks with foreign exposure did not prepare country exposure reports on a regular basis. These banks had international assets of less than 5% of their total assets.

The majority of responding banks (54%) prepare country exposure reports monthly. Generally, frequency of reporting is inversely proportional to the size or relative scope of international activities for any given bank. Over 90% of the banks that have formal reporting systems include the aggregate exposure incurred in foreign countries by their head office (whether holding company or bank), their foreign branches, or subsidiaries. A substantial majority of banks, however, did not include either their investment in or the assets of their foreign affiliates. It is interesting to note that of the 59 banks having one or more Edge Act Corporations, 21 banks did not include the country exposure created by their Edges in their reporting systems. Possible explanations for not including such foreign country exposure are that such vehicles are often minority owned or used primarily as investment vehicles.

There is a strong correlation between the number of countries in which the ARCB-surveyed banks have exposure and the number of countries which are included in the regular exposure reports of responding banks. For example, of those with exposure in 25 or more countries, 51% include all countries in which they have exposure in their reports.

The questionnaire responses and interviews conducted with the 30 largest ARCB member banks suggest that the determination of what is included as country exposure, and how this exposure is disaggregated, is very much a function of two principal factors. First is the significance in volume terms of particular types of assets and off-balance-sheet transactions to a given bank's operation. What one bank may consider of great importance in the measurement of foreign country exposure may be ignored by another bank simply because the relative volume of such items in its operations may be negligible. The second, and more important, factor is the need to include certain types of country exposure (regardless of volume) in bank management information systems to respond to information requests from regulatory authorities, boards of directors, and internal auditors.

The principal categories in which exposure data are presented include:

• By booking unit—56% of the responding banks' disaggregate exposure on the basis of the location in which the exposure was booked. In addition, 83% of those so doing, also present the data on some other basis.

• By type of exposure—67% of the respondents describe their exposure in terms of its type, such as loans, acceptances, deposit placements, etc. In addition, a significant percentage of the banks using this format disaggregate the exposure on more than one basis.

• By maturity—Recording the exposure in terms of its maturity is the most frequently used manner of disaggregation; 67% of the responding banks use this method of presentation. Most of these banks use two maturity classifications: one year or less and more than one year.

• By cross-border and intracountry foreign currency exposure—This method classifies foreign currency exposure into that which is booked outside or that booked inside the country of the obligor; 22% of the banks report their foreign currency exposure on this basis.

The need to have country exposure aggregates presented in more than one way is reflected by 70% of the responding banks using at least two of the above reporting bases.

Robert Morris Associates' (RMA) survey of 70 banks published in 1980 demonstrated a fair consistency between the way banks define exposure in the ARCB survey and the RMA survey. Two-thirds of the respondents in the RMA survey have not instituted an overall limit on international assets as a proportion to total assets. Those that have such limits tend to be the smaller banks and they determine their limits by the following criteria: credit market conditions, percent of total assets, or percent of capital.

According to RMA, 80% of respondents have diversification strategies and 90% set country limits on the maximum loan exposure allowable. Sublimits on the government sector are used by 40% of the responding banks; 25% use sublimits for multinationals operating in the country. Country limits are typically set by the international banking department or a senior loan committee. Only 10% of participating banks established a separate country exposure committee.

Defenses Against Country Risk

Banks have a number of defenses against country risk. These safeguards are related but the following categories may be separately identified:

1. Monitoring of country developments through the banks' informational network.

2. Managing and monitoring of international exposure.

3. Use of collateral held outside country of obligor.

4. Guarantees received from creditor institutions or governments such as U.S. multinational firms, Export-Import Bank, Overseas Private Investment Corporation, U.S. Department of Defense, Non-U.S. multinational firms, or non-U.S. official agencies, for example, COFACE (France), ECGD (U.K.), Hermes (Germany), EXIM Bank (Japan), NCM (Netherlands), Ducroire (Belgium).

5. Guarantees received from governments of borrowing entities.

6. Other measures, like diversification of booking countries or duplicate recordkeeping.

Having focused on the country risk management and summarized the reported practices of U.S. banks, it may be useful to provide some conclusions on how banks can defend against country risk.

Good Management

These defenses are not easy to select and manage on a country-by-country basis. It takes a combination of varied skills, backgrounds, and responsibilities. Thus, good bank management is the key element in defending against country risk. Some of the main elements of good management—from the viewpoint of country risk—are as follows:

1. Knowledge of the country in which risk assets are acquired.

2. Avoidance of magnitudes of acquisition of risk assets in any country that are in violation of the actuarial principles of avoidance of concentration, balance, and dispersion.

3. Avoidance of unacceptable risk should not be a pro forma qualification of earnings targets. Earnings should always be subordinated to avoidance of excessive risk.

4. Careful, effective, and current control of acquisition of risk assets to stay within limits deemed acceptable in light of country evaluations. Exceptions are possible but should be made thoughtfully and with full accountability. Mechanisms are needed to ensure that portfolio composition also reflects possible adverse impact of country environment or governmental policies on the individual borrower's continued ability to generate the necessary cash flow to meet its commitments.

5. Awareness of the flexibility of the bank's portfolio by having machinery in place so that a bank can act to reduce exposure if deemed desirable as quickly as loan contracts permit.

6. Refusal to acquire risk assets that have attractive income returns but are not in accord with country limits and sublimits dictated by country conditions. Avoid limits which become market targets instead of constraining devices.

7. Perception that country risk is a combined staff and line function but not a marketing function and preferably separate from other management control processes, such as credit evaluations and general economic publications functions.

8. Adequate auditing procedures, loan documentation, and legal structuring of loan contracts. Such aspects as waiver of sovereign immunity and legal systems applicable in case of dispute are important elements in defending against country risk.

9. Continuously monitor the international environment to assess possible impacts on borrowing countries.

10. Recognize that a good credit to an individual borrower may be transformed into a bad credit with potential losses by adverse economic, social, and political

developments within a country subsequent to the original credit decision. Countries must be continuously monitored to assess the impact of actual and potential country developments within a country subsequent to the original credit decision and assess the impact on a bank's portfolio of loans outstanding.

11. Strict accountability of responsible officers for all country risk decisions, no freewheeling even by top management. No changes in country evaluation or application in business decisions except after deliberation in accordance with agreed procedures.

12. Mechanisms that enable banks to respond profitably to changing country conditions but not in a manner which weakens the control process.

All private banks are acutely aware of the possibility of losses. Special reserves, as well as capital, are available for such purposes. Judgments must be made regarding acceptable ratios of risk assets and earnings to capital. U.S. banks, as well as those in other industrialized countries, still live in the shadow of the bank failures of the 1930s. Potential calls on capital and reserves need to be limited and manageable, although profits in a single year can be significantly impaired by charge-offs without serious loss of a bank's liquidity or creditworthiness.

Worst Case Event

A constant challenge to the banker is how much attention should be paid to the worst case event, even if it is deemed most unlikely to occur. A worst case approach simply assumes that a foreign government repudiates all the outstanding external financial obligations to commercial banks of all entities within its country. From the viewpoint of the commercial lender, the country disappears beneath the waves with no prospect for salvage! In any country, the probability of this happening is slight. Wars and revolutions can, at least temporarily, create such situations. However unlikely such events may be, prudent bank lenders are ever on the alert. If signs appear that such an eventuality may occur—a minor disturbance of potential significance—the banks can take defensive measures as they would in other cases of anticipated country or credit deterioration. Such events do not occur quickly; they are not true surprises. They can be anticipated.

However, country portfolios should be continuously scrutinized, and measures taken to reduce excessive risk. If anticipated, exposure can be run down quickly, in most cases because of the large proportion of short-term assets. Loans with maturities of over one year decline much more gradually through amortization, but they do decline. Banks need not renew loans which mature or replace paid-off debt with new credits. The bank can simply choose to be paid.

It is conceivable that an individual bank could so manage its affairs as to cause it serious financial difficulties. From past experience, such difficulties are unlikely to arise simply because of the nature of the borrower's country—lending to developing countries. The cause is just as likely, if not more so, to be in the private bank management rather than the borrower. Nevertheless, the bank must act on the assumption that difficulties and losses will not be avoided, but rather can be kept to acceptable low levels.

Thus, in defending against country risk, as in so many other aspects of banking, diversification is usually prudent. Policies of diversification by lenders lead borrowers to rely on more lenders to satisfy their total needs. Neither the U.S. banking system nor a U.S. bank are necessarily made vulnerable to disruption because of the overseas lending by a number of private banks. Indeed, short of the worldwide holocaust scenario, more countries in a bank's portfolio may well reduce the country risk aspects. Individual banks must always be realistic about their financial strength. They must be continuously aware of their available capital and reserves, earnings, profitability, liquidity, risk assets, and standing in financial markets. Risk assets must be carefully scrutinized on a one-by-one basis to determine chances of loss. Risk assets include those acquired internationally as well as domestic. In this context, professional judgments can be made, and are being made continuously, on whether a particular bank is prudent in managing its assets and loans in relation to capital and reserves.

Guarantees

It has been repeatedly emphasized that adequate knowledge of a country in which a commercial bank has, or plans to have, significant exposure is the principal safeguard against the risks involved in lending to entities outside national borders. It is also a necessary background for reaching decisions on acceptable borrowers, magnitudes, maturities, grace periods, and other loan conditions and characteristics of a loan portfolio in a country. No other safeguards can free the bank from the responsibility for the soundness of its country assessments in the business decision-making process. If this is kept in mind, other safeguards can be considered without diverting attention away from the importance of the country assessment and its links to business decisions.

Guarantees by government entities in the lender's own country. These are fairly obvious defenses against country risk and need little comment. If the lending private bank finds an export/import bank or other official agency in its own country willing to assume all or most of the country risk without ambiguity and delay (and at an acceptable cost), then the country risk effectively can be greatly reduced and nearly eliminated. Ambiguities can arise from the dual character of the transaction—private lending combined with comprehensive official guarantee. In case of difficulties in debt servicing, it must be clear that the guarantor agency is taking all the country risks for the guaranteed portion of the loan. In case of governmental rescheduling which includes the officially guaranteed debt, then the private bank must be serviced by the official guarantor as originally agreed.

Private guarantees. Since part of overseas lending by private banks is to overseas branches, subsidiaries, or affiliates of multinational firms, it is also possible in gray cases to request the headquarters company to guarantee fully the debt incurred by its branch, subsidiary, or affiliate. This reflects a country risk concern which is greater than can be met by a comfort letter from the firm. A comfort letter is not a guarantee. Comfort letters are good enough when the concern is mild. Guarantees, however, may be needed to meet adequately concerns about the country risk in any particular country. Care needs to be taken that the company headquarters meets the normal criteria of creditworthiness with no ambiguity as to its responsibilities and no delays in meeting its guarantee obligations. The headquarters must itself also be located in a country that is judged to be an acceptable country risk.

Guarantees by official debtor agencies. Guarantees of loans to private sector entities in developing countries are often underwritten by the governments or central banks of such countries. Whether it reduces the country risk depends on the judgment of whether that country's government will give a higher priority to providing the foreign exchange necessary to service the private sector debt it has guaranteed than to debt it has not guaranteed. It can do so, and this can be a formal undertaking with the lender. Thus, country risk can be reduced.

Central bank guarantees can be especially useful because the central bank normally administers the foreign currency income of the country. This is particularly important where there is a tradition that the central bank gives the highest priority to safeguarding its own creditworthiness with foreign lenders, including honoring its guarantee. It cannot be forgotten, however, that central banks are official agencies of the government and subject to government instruction and domination. Thus, government guarantees may be as useful in reducing country risk as central bank guarantees and in certain cases, even more so. If, however, a government or central bank is not obligated or expected to give preference in allocating foreign exchange to its guarantees, then such guarantees are of minor importance in reducing country risk.

Collateral. Country risk can, of course, be reduced by provision of collateral (gold or foreign currency deposits) of adequate character, magnitude, location, and legal protections. This is more likely to be acceptable than guarantees when a country is beginning to establish its creditworthiness with private banks.

Credit control and auditing procedures. Credit control and auditing procedures are time-honored practices of banks. These activities are recognized as vital for the bank. Credit officers are bankers who have earned their spurs by their professional competency. They are likely to be former loan officers who understand the conditions under which the loan officers in their bank operate. They know who are the enthusiastic salesmen eager to expand their profit centers. They know who are likely to be very cautious and reliable in enforcing the intent of the decisions on country risk. They know the intellectual caliber of the decisions involving country risks. They are the defenders of the liquidity of the bank. They are likely to enjoy the confidence of regulators and other bank supervisors and are likely to be eager to have their high regard. They know and understand the portfolio strategy. They know undue concentration when they see it and they know the costs of mistakes in judging creditworthiness. They are likely to have been involved in workout cases in their banking history or contributed to avoiding such cases. They know what a default is and what are the implications of default and cross-default. They can be strong allies to those given the responsibility for managing the country risk process if encouraged by the bank's top management to so regard themselves.

Overseas lending, including lending to developing countries can, and often does, involve a number of layers of auditing:

1. Auditing all overseas credits by the banks' internal auditors at headquarters.
2. Separate auditing of the credit review process in any borrowing country by resident auditors of the private bank.
3. Review of accounts at headquarters by independent certified accounting firms.
4. Review of accounts within branches in borrowing countries by resident internal auditors.
5. Inspection by official regulatory authorities in the headquarters country.
6. Inspection in the borrowing countries by official regulatory authorities from the headquarters country of loans booked in overseas branches or subsidiaries.

Loan classifications employed by any of these groups are designed to ensure advance warning of difficulties and possible losses to the banks. A cautious attitude to possible losses means that they are anticipated by way of loan-loss provisions or offsets against current earnings or reserves, although there may be reasons to believe that such declared losses will ultimately prove collectible. International loans require the close scrutiny of those auditors as do domestic loans. A novel country location for the auditor is no excuse for less severe or cautious scrutiny of a credit; indeed, it may readily argue for the reverse.

Portfolio diversification and actuarial principle. Portfolio diversification within a country is of essential importance. Maturity diversification is essential in defending against country risk. A diversified portfolio with more of the portfolio at shorter term is easier to run down when the signals become unfavorable. This is not to argue against the acceptability of important amounts of medium- and long-term maturities but rather to stress the need for maturity diversification, as well as diversification of borrowers and purposes. The danger is not that an entire country sinks under the waves, but that adverse developments will strike particular sectors within a country and that the bank will be more heavily exposed in these particular sectors as compared with others or overexposed to a particular borrower.

If all short-term credit, for example, is to one correspondent bank, defensive rundowns may be very difficult to accomplish. Country analyses help to implement policies of avoidance of concentration by shedding light on the potential scope of the market for financial services. It is only necessary to remind the readers briefly of the great variety of possible banking activities to demonstrate this point: trade financing of exports and imports; project financing; balance-of-payments support; co-financing with official multilateral agencies; letters of credit; and performance bonds. There may also be diversity among borrowers: banks, private industrial and trading firms, governments, government entities, multilateral agencies, other institutional borrowers like insurance companies, and individuals. There are at least 60 countries, developed and developing, that are important potential markets for some or all these products. The achievement of diversification may be constrained by lack of sufficient administrative and professional skills and costs—

specialization can result in economies. But whatever the constraints, the achievement of a highly diversified portfolio with the needed flexibility to deal with adversities and avoid excessive losses is feasible.

In-depth country analyses designed for such uses enable banks to assess more accurately whether they are prudently applying the actuarial principle. It is not always obvious or even true that diversification is preferable to concentration. In some countries with minimal country risk, for instance, a much higher percentage of total lending to a few borrowers may be safer and more acceptable than a highly diversified portfolio which includes riskier individual credits. This would not be true in a high-risk country unless borrowers were giving guarantees or offering acceptable collateral.

When banks look at lending from the point of view of portfolio management and country risk, they are naturally led to take a global view. One of the easiest ways to diversify is to examine the bank's portfolio to judge what potential business can be done in a wider group of countries and with more and more entities. If a bank finds another country where it can make attractive returns at an acceptable risk, then the bank is strengthening its portfolio. Therefore, more and more banks will reach out to a larger number of countries because diversification can provide a strong defense against the uncertainties and risks that exist today and tomorrow. Business decisions will continue to be made from the point of view of potential expansion of profitable business in a country. Opportunity cost will continue to be a dominant factor in making choices. No region or country will be ruled out in advance without analyzing profitability and country risk. All in all, this will strengthen banks' portfolios.

Diversification is harder to achieve if in advance of careful analysis a bank arbitrarily rejects countries to which it could be lending prudently and profitably. It is not a matter of underestimating risks. All countries in which the bank has foreign exposure should be considered as subject to country risk. Nor can any country risk analysts and managers be expected to be infallible. Country risk assessments are no substitute for portfolio management; similarly, diversification is no substitute for good country assessments.

Centralization of authority and responsibility. Mistakes in country judgment are going to be made but their impact may be softened by portfolio diversification. But how can country judgment be improved? Diversification itself depends on good country analyses and effective application to choose markets with acceptable country risks as well as attractive profitable returns.

In many banks, improvement can come from giving absolute authority to someone who can say no to loan officers at any and every rank level. That executive must not be in charge of a profit center. And the loan officer for the country should not be the officer who has the final country risk authority. The final country risk authority must be given to someone who has a corporate view of the bank's business, who is located at headquarters, is concerned with the performance of the entire parent corporation, and whose overview is not biased by any particular market, or region, or country. In this kind of country risk work, one officer, rather than a group of officers, should be given the needed authority, responsibility, and accountability. There should be appeals to the bank chairman or president to change country risk evaluations, but the chairman or president should not be able to overrule the decisions in the first instance. He can ask for reassessment with the expectation that the bank will follow the decision given by the country risk officer. Frequent need for reassessments or reversal of decisions indicates that the country risk officer does not enjoy the needed confidence to have the needed authority to do the job.

At the same time, the country risk management system needs to be one of checks and balances. Every officer in the system should sign off on the country judgment and recommendation as he or she would on a credit or a loan. Thus, responsibility for their country views must be accepted by all officers involved in the process. This is the reason why, however, either one person or possibly a committee accepts the responsibility for the country decision and its application. By having strict accountability, and having the authority to exercise that accountability, the responsibility for decisions is clear-cut. If serious mistakes in judgment are repeatedly made in a particular institution, the responsible officer is probably miscast. Even the portfolio diversification method is not immune to the onslaughts of too many mistakes.

When country conditions change, the officer in charge of country risk evaluations and application must be prepared to change his or her views if warranted. The officer must be fully aware of what the bank is trying to achieve in a country and should be helping to achieve these objectives as long as they are within the decided country risk evaluation parameters. When country risk work is done in this way, country risk management becomes an integral part of the bank. This authority must be given to the country risk officer by the chairman and the president of the bank. Therefore, it is their perception of the importance of the activity and what needs to be done that establishes the function and the authority. In turn, the country risk officer must know how to convince the chairman and the president of the usefulness of the system and the necessity of its implementation. The functioning of the system depends largely on the confidence in the country risk officer who is given the country risk management responsibilities.

Risk/Reward Equation

A concise review and analysis of the country risk assessment literature has been done by Professor Ingo Walter of New York University.[27] Professor Walter's paper provides a useful beginning of a theoretical approach to identifying the facets of country risk in the context of a bank's risk/reward equation.

While the original application of modern portfolio theory focused on optimal investor decisions in stock markets, it has been extended to other fields, such as the

[27]Ingo Walter, "International Capital Allocation: Country Risk, Portfolio Decisions and Regulation in International Banking" (New York: Conference on Internationalization of Financial Markets and National Economic Policy, April 1980, mimeo.).

management of international loan portfolios. Without pushing an analogy between optimal international loan portfolios and the conventional stock market investor too far, Professor Walter points out that the basic management task, the risk/reward equation involved in both business decision-making situations, is the same. The objective is the maximization of the "real economic value of their assets subject to various types of risks."[28] This risk/reward equation is expressed in the form of a conventional present value equation, by which the future stream of returns of a bank's entire loan portfolio is incrementally discounted according to a constant term representing a bank's cost of funds plus a country risk premium. This is represented by the following equation:

$$PV_j^o = \sum_{t=0}^{n} \frac{E(F_t)}{(1+i_t+a_t)^t}$$

PV_j^o is the present value of returns to the bank related to exposure in a particular country j.

$E(F_t)$ denotes the expected value of that future stream of returns over time t.

i_t is the risk-free discount factor representing the bank's cost of funds.

a_t represents a country risk premium which depends on the covariance of returns on the bank's total portfolio.

Both the $E(F_t)$ and a_t, the *means* as well as the *variances* of the probability distributions associated with these returns are affected by country risk factors. Expected returns $E(F_t)$ for international lending portfolios is a complex relationship of several factors: repayment of principal, repayment of interest, front-end management fees for syndicated loans, and less tangible benefits such as maintaining a business relationship with the borrower in expectation of further lucrative business. All these factors are said to make both $E(F_t)$ and a_t into highly complex composite variables. Country risk assessment, according to this view, involves making accurate scenarios of all political and economic risk factors potentially unstabilizing to $E(F_t)$ and a_t.

This notion of risk as a variability of returns is amplified by H. Robert Heller of the Bank of America:

> Risk in its technical sense can be understood to mean "potential loss" or increased variability and can impact the bank in several ways. For instance, the incapacity of a borrower to repay, regulatory constraints, or other external events may affect the bank's profit and loss statement through loss of principal, interest income, management time, stability of earnings, and leverage capability. An even broader view might encompass the bank's market standing, security ratings, and general perception as they are affected by risk.[29]

[28]Ibid.

[29]H. Robert Heller, "Bank of America's New Country Evaluation System," Conference on Country Risk Assessment (New York: AMR International/Euromoney, October 1980).

Various adverse contingencies may be represented in terms of this framework. Returning to Professor Walter, events reducing the value of PV_j^o include prospective defaults of rescheduling of debt which show up as corresponding declines in $E(F_t)$. Quantum jumps in political risk, owing to assassination of a country's president, is likewise reflected in increases in the value of a_t. Thus, Professor Walters underscores the complexity of these two variables.

A last aspect about a bank's risk/reward formula and the significance of country risk assessment is identification of a threshold when the benefit of the country assessment in the form of decreased risk vulnerability no longer exceeds the costs of providing this function. At this hypothetical point, any more effort into country assessment ceases to make economic sense.

Prerequisites of Adequate Management

In summary, the main aspects of a risk management system include:

1. General purposes or aims of lending institutions.
2. Current business strategies.
3. Country-by-country business activities, particularly lending.
4. Identification of risks to bank in doing country business.
5. Evaluation or assessment of country conditions.
6. Application of assessment to business decisions for coming period(s).
7. Relation to regulatory or supervising authorities.
8. Mechanism for monitoring and reporting business decisions affected by country assessments.
9. Mechanism for reviewing and if warranted changing business decisions in light of changing country assessment.

The key lessons learned from my experience with the IMF, the World Bank, Citibank and other banks include:

1. It is essential that the country risk system be part of business decisions.
2. Clear accountability by all involved for their judgments on countries and resulting business recommendations must be assigned.
3. Clear location of final authority and responsibility for country risk decisions must be indicated.
4. Clear responsibility for leadership within the bank in analyzing countries must be established.
5. Clear responsibility for management of the system must be assigned.
6. Conformity of the system to needs, capabilities, and potentials of banks is also a necessity.
7. Reliance on "system" of management rather than "evaluation" of countries to make possible significant international lending in a world of chronic uncertainty and risk.

The following chapter describes in some detail how these country risk processes are carried on in various banks.

15

Country Risk Management in 11 Banking Institutions

Previous chapters provided a general approach as a framework for analyzing the country evaluation systems of different financial institutions. This chapter draws on the experience of specific institutions,* including Citibank, Bank of America, American Security Bank, Continental Illinois, Bankers Trust, Chemical Bank, First National Bank of Chicago, Morgan Guaranty, Chase Manhattan Bank, Security Pacific, and Bank of Montreal.

It is hoped that descriptions of the systems of several banks give the reader a perspective on the diversity of approaches used in practice. Some are given in detail; others are included to broaden the perspective. They illustrate the seriousness of purpose with which these major international lenders approach country risk, as well as the possibilities of further improvements and strengthening.

Citibank

This section describes Citibank's system for reporting and managing country exposure. The system is used as the principal illustration because of the author's involvement in establishing the Citibank country risk management system and because this system reflects the needs and capabilities of large international banks which account for the bulk of international lending today.**

Citicorp is a diversified financial services organization whose principal subsidiary is Citibank, N.A. In addition to general banking, Citicorp's subsidiaries and affiliates are engaged in asset-based financing, merchant banking, consumer businesses, and investment management and trust services. Altogether, Citicorp and its subsidiaries and affiliates have over 2,000 offices in 103 countries around the world. By 1975, the organization's international earnings were about 70% of earnings.

Country exposure management/country risk evaluation has become an essential part of the business decision-making process at Citicorp. It is essentially a *control* function for the bank. Decisions on cross-border exposure are made in a separate

*Banks differ on the amount of information on country risk which they have made public. More details are given for those banks for which more information has been publicized.

**The country exposure management and the country risk evaluation function were the author's delegated responsibility (1974-80) as senior vice president and senior advisor for international operations.

and independent fashion from decisions on marketing. It was recognized that the profit motive conflicts with country risk considerations. The inevitable tensions between risk-taking and profit-making were to be resolved by providing the best possible information base and by mustering and applying the best in management judgment.

The key instrument for managing the bank's exposure in a particular country is ceilings on the amount of country exposure permitted. The use of ceilings leads to a need for a mechanism to measure and report exposure, as well as to review and change ceilings when conditions warrant. Country risk judgments which are used to determine country ceilings are also used in other types of banking decisions, such as in long-range strategic planning of the bank's international portfolio or in credit review decisions.

Only a small proportion of U.S. banks are large enough and have sufficient international exposure to warrant as elaborate a system as Citicorp's. Roughly 75 large banks situated around the world probably account for 90% of all international bank business and thus represent the dominant mode of international banking practice. Thus, the more important prototypes for international lending are the large-scale, internationally oriented banks with substantial overseas presence, either through overseas branches with local currency deposit business or overseas offices established for other business reasons or overseas affiliates or subsidiaries. The more simplified approaches which smaller-size banks would prefer are discussed later. Before presenting a detailed analysis of the Citicorp system, a few general remarks may be useful.

Guiding Principles

Several guiding principles were identified that should facilitate proper usage of the country risk function by the rest of the bank. The function was seen as an early-warning system and was designed with this in mind. One of the guiding principles was that an adequate network of intrabank communication had to be set up for monitoring and reporting country exposure on a frequent basis.

A second guiding principle was to guarantee the direct use of country risk judgments in setting specific ceilings (and subceilings) to the total amount of exposure which the bank was willing to undertake in a particular foreign country. Specific ceilings for various countries serve as a management mechanism for achieving greater diversification of the loan portfolio. Equally important, they give focal points for acting on information on changing country risk developments if particular country ceilings need to be altered (whether raised gradually or decreased) in the course of the business period for which the ceiling is set, which is one year in Citicorp.

An early-warning system will be ineffective unless a certain flexibility exists for changing country exposure limitations when appropriate. The need to do this carefully is underscored by the poor quality of data published for a majority of nations often with long time lags. Poor and delayed data make even more vital a tight monitoring system managed by experienced and knowledgable bank officers. Monitoring is best accomplished on a continuous basis with a steady flow of information generated and circulated within the bank and reviewed by those with the needed background to absorb the information or substitute their judgment for the lack of current information.

A third guiding principle was never to permit a country ceiling to be raised without careful deliberation. The existing level of a country ceiling is often indicative of the current extent of creditworthy business contacts. A system that too easily raises a country ceiling brings about a temptation to lower one's credit standards and eventually the quality of one's loan portfolio. A deliberate relationship, moreover, must be established between how fast a country ceiling should be increased and the overall growth of a bank's total assets. Therefore, the need for flexibility had to be built into the Citicorp management system, recognizing that to be effective it had to be a living behavioral system, rather than a preconceived mechanistic system.

Influence of Field

At Citibank, the focus of country risk decision making was the world headquarters. Frequent exchanges of ideas and information between field offices and headquarters were seen as vitally important and encouraged. As time went on and experience gained, the whole process became more and more field-driven. Field resistance to the burden of country assessment and reporting declined as the process proved useful in enabling the field to expand business and earnings attractive fashion, that is, profitable and without excessive risk.

Citicorp operated both as a national and international intermediary. It made loans in national currencies financed by deposits or money market sources in the same currency. It also made loans in foreign currency. Thus, although concern with country risk tended to focus on foreign currency lending, analyses of countries and business applications of these analyses included all loans made by the bank holding company, irrespective of currency. However, local currency lending was seen as not involving exposure across country borders and therefore not involving country risk, while lending in currency foreign to the borrower was seen as typically involved in country risk. This view gave particular importance to the fact that over half of Citicorp's loans abroad involved lending within a country to a borrower in his or her own currency. The local currency asset was seen as not involving country risk because the local currency asset was generally offset by a locally acquired liability in the same currency. This was perceived as limiting exposure to normal credit factors, rather than country risk.

In 1975, Citicorp put into place its country risk management system which reflected its business needs and its organization, structures, and capabilities.* Management of country and cross-border risk was made an important function for two key groups:

*Citicorp's philosophy and approach were explained in its annual report for 1975.

1. Officers in the field. The officers of Citicorp managing the business in their respective countries would be expected to provide the knowledge of local conditions. By being actively involved professionally and socially, these officers would be better able to anticipate and respond to changes in local conditions. More than 99% of Citicorp's total loan outstandings at year-end 1975 were to borrowers located in countries in which the firm had its own officers on a full-time permanent basis.

2. Head office management. Top and senior management were to add both perspective and experience to the judgment and recommendations made by the field. The evaluation and administration of Citicorp's country risk and cross-border program worldwide were made the primary responsibility of the author.*

Systems Objectives

Citicorp put into place a systematic process of establishing limits on country exposure and of monitoring outstandings under its limits. A reporting system was established that aimed to give management quickly and accurately outstanding cross-border exposure by country. The objective was to anticipate national and international developments within or outside the control of the country's government which might adversely or favorably have an impact on each country in which Citicorp did business. The ability to respond rapidly to changes in local conditions was critical to avoid loss, exploit business opportunities, and enhance profitability.

The management process provided for ceilings to be established for cross-border exposure subject to country risk in any given country. Subceilings existed for different maturities as overall exposure had to be broken down because country risk was believed to vary with tenor, obligor, and other factors.

Cross-border exposure was to be reported quarterly for all countries, and additional statistical and qualitative information was required monthly (in practice at times daily) for countries experiencing rapidly changing conditions. The aim was primarily to defend against adversity but also to spot favorable business opportunities.

Checks-and-Balance System

To ensure that the cross-border management system worked well to achieve its purposes, a checks-and-balance system involved the field and headquarters, with responsibility and needed authority for its management given to the author.

The control mechanism required that all Citicorp entities outside the country of the prospective borrower needed credit approval from the senior officer in the field

*Citicorp's Vice Chairman G.A. Costanzo was given top management responsibility. Part of the management system was the support given by experienced international bankers, most of whom had served many years abroad. Frequent visits by the author to overseas countries and continuous communication with senior officers overseas were integral parts of the management process.

responsible for the borrower's country of residence. This approval was required before cross-border transactions were consummated by the Citicorp entity outside the borrowing country. This was done to ensure that outstandings in the country would be maintained within established limits. No exceptions were made to this rule, and senior officers were not authorized to delegate this authority to juniors. Requests for permission were to be answered precisely and quickly.

The authority to establish and decide changes in ceilings and maturity subceilings was kept in headquarters. It was feared the field could be excessively driven by profit center motives, although it was hoped that experience would teach the field officers how to reconcile profit motive with country risk considerations. The success of the system was dependent on the top management unequivocably supporting the administrator's delegated authority.

The procedure also provided for ceilings and subceilings to undergo continuing review and adjustment. This part of the management process was, in a way, more difficult to administer and implement. The original ceilings were related to business expectations, that is creditworthy loan opportunities foreseen by field officers in the coming business budget period, say one year. Our view was that it was no use to have theoretical notions on how much cross-border exposure might be acceptable, if desirable business was not to be found in any case. This approach could lead to ceilings or limits much in excess of business needs and greatly weaken the control aspects of the ceilings. There would be the danger that field loan officers could misinterpret such excessively high limits. They might see them as business targets instead of ceilings and see them as hunting licenses instead of constraints.

The answer given to the tension between marketing and control was the ceiling related to appropriate loan business which was seen by the field to be reasonably attainable. It meant bringing ceilings into line with business expectations. Conversely, it meant business expectations defined in terms of acceptable credits which met individual credit criteria and acceptable in terms of country risk assessments as reflected in agreed ceilings and subceilings. In this way, loan officers could commit themselves in a manner familiar to them to try for a certain volume of creditworthy business and achieve certain agreed earning targets as profit centers, without exceeding limits related to country creditworthiness. The loan officer tended to be cautious in promising business or profit results which were unrealistic because failure to achieve budgeted targets might well be taken as failure as a business manager.

Judgments Used

The judgments used to establish cross-border ceilings were critical to the whole management process. Four principal factors form the basis for these judgments needed to establish cross-border ceilings:

1. Evaluation of the needs and capabilities of Citicorp's client base in each country.

2. Analysis of the various business characteristics, such as classes of business, investments, guarantees, transactions, and accompanying tenor, in any one country.

3. Anticipation or analysis of national and international events which might affect Citicorp in any one country.

4. Application of quantitative and qualitative techniques to the information available to Citicorp worldwide.

At the time, very high standards of information-gathering, professional analysis, and application of these analyses to business decision making were being set. These standards could not be reached quickly in all business sectors in all countries. Much would depend on Citicorp's activities in a country and its personnel there, as well as the information available. However, by enunciating these factors, they not only became standards or targets to achieve but also the framework for education and experience. Perfection was not expected, but it was hoped that with experience and a growing awareness of the benefits, both standards and performance would rise world wide, and they did.

Citicorp monitored country conditions and other elements needed for country assessments and judgments and compiled, if necessary, a large variety of statistical indicators of national creditworthiness. It analyzed domestic economic conditions, outlook, and policies; balance of payments and management thereof; other international economic and financial aspects; principal economic sectors—trends and prospects, flow of funds, and financial intermediation—actual and potential. Other factors included political conditions and outlook; social conditions; international positions and relations; and impact of world events—economic, political, and military. All these factors were brought together and joined into a single comprehensive country risk assessment.

In addition to information about the statistical indicators of national creditworthiness, people were told that reliance on debt-service ratios was inadequate and could be misleading in country risk analysis. While other debt-service ratios of rather sophisticated forms like changes in debt service to changes in gross national product were examined, emphasis was also placed on the need to examine other statistical relationships like compressibility of imports and consumption and investment goods, or variability in export earnings or foreign investment in relation to total investment. Citicorp developed its own databank, particularly regarding developing countries, and constantly sought and examined new statistical or functional relationships which might give deeper insights into country conditions and policies. Considerable time was spent describing the great variety of sources used and in efforts to consult with experts in the IMF, World Bank, or the Inter-American Development Bank.

Because the concern with widespread country risk was novel for this post-World War II period, Citicorp attempted to explain how to reduce country risk. Acting on the premise that country risk generally increased with the length of the obligation, Citicorp thought short maturities usually permitted relatively rapid reduction in exposure if conditions changed and such reductions were desired. Therefore, maturity scheduling was an integral part of asset management. The majority of Citicorp's loans outside the U.S. matured in less than a year, longer maturities were specifically and closely controlled and limited to stronger borrowers.

Risk was also seen as significantly reduced, regardless of maturity, where the financing was directly related to self-liquidating transactions. Most international trade financing was directly related to self-liquidating transactions and commercial credit was in this category. A large proportion of Citicorp's customers were engaged in such trade transactions.

Guarantees

Guarantees by official entities in the borrowing countries could help reduce country risk, although the benefits were more likely to be in reducing credit risk. For example, Citicorp had never experienced loss where the loan had been guaranteed by a central bank. A central bank guarantee is particularly useful to reduce country risk if the borrowing entity is given preferential access to foreign exchange needed to service external debt. The central bank can command the foreign exchange resources of a country and honor an obligation to give preference to a particular borrower. On the other hand, the central bank may be reluctant to do this on a very selective basis for a particular borrower or lender. The more generalized the central bank's willingness to give such guarantees, the more it approximates a weak guarantee showing intention, but with questionable ability to fulfill its intention in case of a general foreign exchange shortage. The experience of the central bank of Turkey which found itself unable to honor its commitment to convert Turkish lira holdings into foreign exchange is a case in point.

A guarantee by an official agency in the creditor country or by the parent company in the creditor country can virtually eliminate country risk. In all cases, risk to lenders can be reduced or eliminated by provision of sufficient readily marketable collateral. Collateral in foreign exchange held in the legal jurisdiction of the creditor can nearly eliminate country risk, although questions can arise in enforcement in case of failure to service the debt fully and promptly or default. The variety of protective devices are many, and new ones can be investigated. The lender always wants to be paid fully and promptly. But when difficulties occur, the private bank lender is likely to attach special importance to payments of interest and be willing to consider rescheduling amortization. Country risk was also perceived to be reduced by increasing local currency financing. Some argued that this eliminated country risk, and this view prevailed in the practice of setting ceilings. But while local currency lending does reduce country risk greatly, it does not disappear. Compensating for loss of local currency assets by release from local currency liabilities may not always prove feasible.

It is also important at this point to stress that whatever is done to reduce country risk by the bank's management system, the bank's own financial backstops continue to remain important. It is important to have adequate capital for ultimate contingencies and adequate reserves to absorb future loan losses. Comparisons of net loan losses to earnings streams and to stockholders' equity must be tracked continuously, and international exposure examined from those viewpoints. With these kinds of safeguards, Citicorp felt able to continue its policy of expanding overseas lending, although not eager to increase its proportion of earnings from overseas assets. Thus, total assets were increased and the percentage of earnings from overseas assets reduced, even while total overseas lending increased.

Measuring Exposure in the Citicorp System

The Citicorp system began with its own definitions of exposure. No legal definitions existed, and as the regulatory authorities have gained experience, uniform procedures have been encouraged for reporting to these authorities. In turn, internal procedures within banks have tended to conform to these general banking procedures. Attention is drawn to the detailed country exposure reports and instructions for preparing them now required by the U.S. banking regulations set forth in the next chapter. Citicorp's original definitions evolved as a result of discussions within the bank and with the regulatory authorities. The present reporting requirements are close to the original procedures.

Country exposure as now reported includes both foreign currency and local currency exposure to residents of each foreign country. The term indirect exposure is now used interchangeably with contingent liabilities. Foreign currency exposure is defined as (a) all cross-border direct and indirect claims on residents, including Citicorp-related residents of foreign country, irrespective of currency, *plus* (b) all intracountry foreign currency direct and indirect claims on residents, *minus* (c) all Citicorp (offshore) to Citicorp (resident) intercorporate flows in foreign currency, backing up the intracountry foreign currency exposure.

In the original system, Citicorp foreign currency exposure to residents of each foreign country was broken down into two main components: cross-border and intracountry foreign currency exposure. Each component was separately identified and reported. In the new system, foreign currency exposure was consolidated. Citibank requires this information from the field in its reports of country exposure. But it also goes on to require sufficient detail to enable a breakdown of loan exposure by meaningful groups of countries like low- and medium-income developing countries to be presented in its annual report.

The reporting system requires maturity breakdown into four categories as required by the regulatory authorities. All continue to be governed for cross-border management purposes within Citicorp by cross-border exposure ceilings (one global, and for most countries two maturity subceilings) governing the total magnitude of exposure which is permissible at any given time in a country. Special reporting requirements are added for international financial centers or offshore banking units to govern the maximum permissible level of exposure flowing into the country in support of the offshore bank. Intercorporate exposure would usually consist of placements or loans in support of intracurrency, foreign currency assets, and placements in support of local currency assets, equity, and nonequity reserves which have not been insured.

The categories under which country exposure is reported distinguish between maturities and types of entities and also between differing categories of borrower (monetary authorities, bank, nonbank, and multilateral organizations) and ownership—private sector, public sector and Citicorp-owned. Thus, with the help of these reports, Citicorp tries to monitor its exposure in all countries throughout the world.

Assets and contingent liabilities are included as cross-border exposure subject to country risk. They are tallied and reported by the branch in the country where the borrowing entity is domiciled. For assets, most equity investments, loans, discounts, leases, and placements are included, except for transactions involving U.S. obligors, shipping transactions, local currency assets, or externally guaranteed assets. For contingent liabilities, formal, unused loan commitments as well as opened, confirmed commercial credits are included as cross-border exposure. Left out are those unused lines of credit which lack formal commitments and externally guaranteed contingent liabilities. Last, the only liabilities included are to Citicorp, majority-owned or managed units.

In addition to these balance-sheet items, it is emphasized that cross-border country exposure ceilings are typically much greater than the sum of those items which actually end up in the balance sheet. Two items—intrabank cross-border and contingent liabilities—are also included as country exposure, although these do not appear on the balance sheet. These off-balance-sheet items could well be in the same order of magnitude as the balance-sheet items themselves.

Procedures for Establishing and Changing Foreign Currency Ceilings

Three flow diagrams are presented to illustrate the various procedures and the sequence of the decision-making process which was developed in 1975 by Citicorp to manage its cross-border financial exposure. Exhibit 15.1 shows the yearly sequence whereby Citicorp established annual foreign currency ceilings and coordinated these with drawing up the annual business budget. The aim was to keep the business budget within ceilings that had been agreed on. The new country ceilings were recommended by all senior country officers at the time the budget was formulated each year. Where increases in country ceilings were contemplated, senior country officers were required to submit appropriate recommendations to headquarters for approval to be obtained prior to the final business budget ratification. Moreover, if during the year, the senior officer in a particular country decided that the ceiling should be increased, this officer would notify the country desk officer giving recommendations, which in turn, would be relayed to the senior country risk officer at headquarters. Justifications for raising country ceilings consisted of a comprehensive analysis of country economic, social, and political conditions.

Exhibit 15.1—Citicorp Procedures for Establishing Foreign Currency Ceilings, 1980

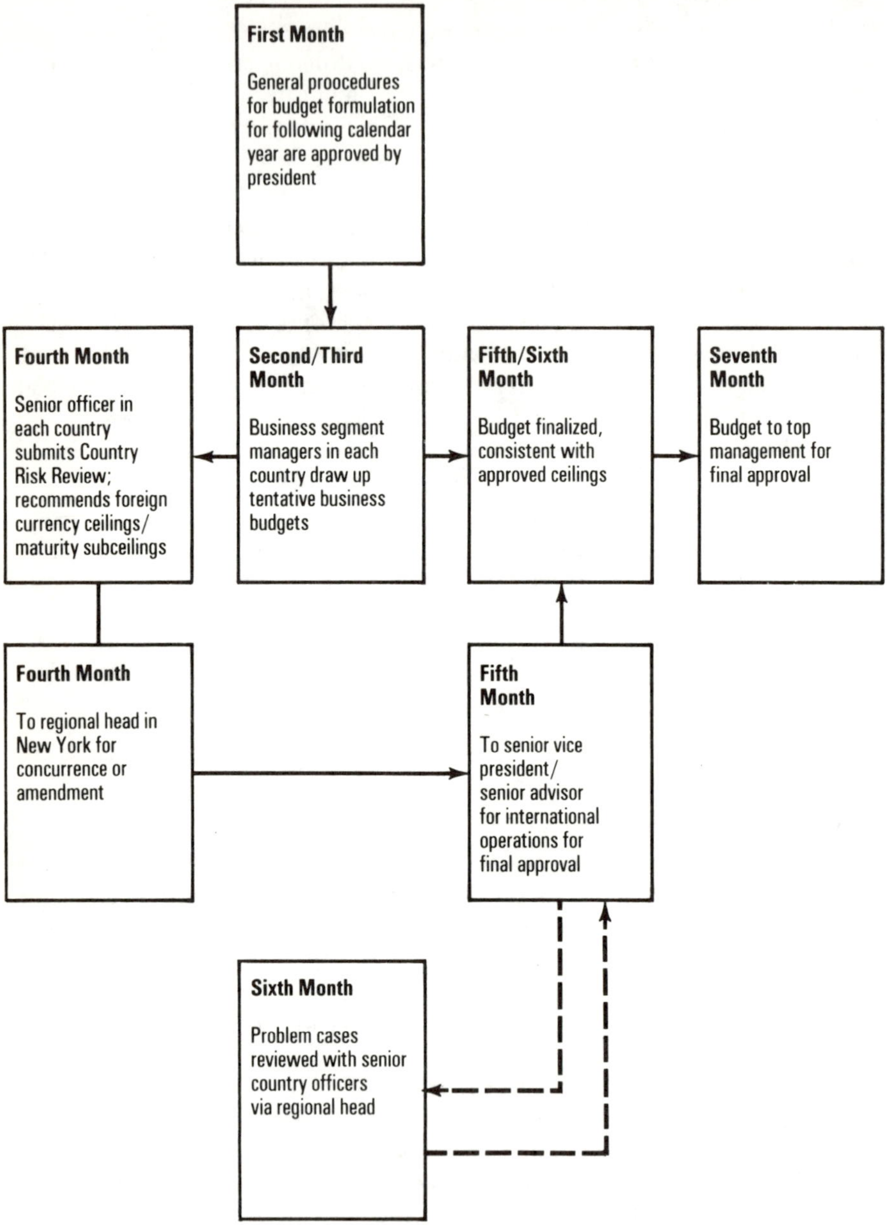

Exhibit 15.2—Ongoing Country Evaluation and Changes in Foreign Currency Ceilings and Subceilings during Calendar Year 1980

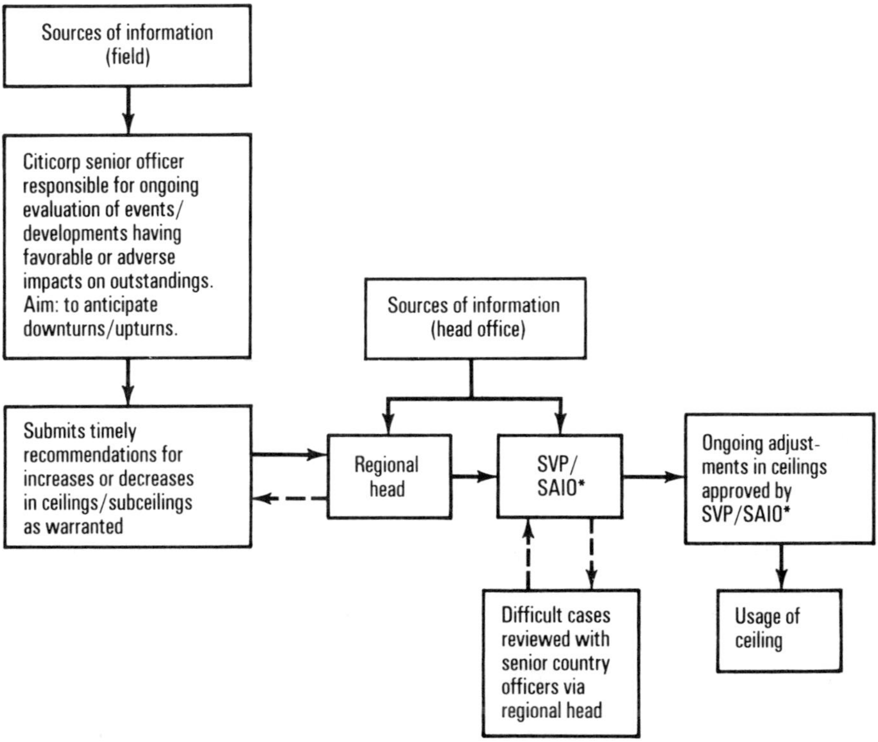

* Senior vice president/senior advisor for international operations.

When the senior country officers made recommendations about country ceilings (or subceilings), they were largely guided by business opportunity considerations but within a framework of what seemed acceptable country risk to them. Business opportunities referred not only to those at hand or foreseen but also to the potentials within the year ahead.

It was my responsibility as senior country risk officer at headquarters to review the formal recommendations for ceilings and subceilings for final approval after they had been scrutinized by others at headquarters. This multistep process of establishing country ceilings, depicted in Exhibit 15.1, had a system of checks and balances built in to lessen the possibility of egregious error.

Exhibit 15.2 outlines the arrangements set up at Citicorp for conducting ongoing country evaluations and for changing, if warranted, foreign currency ceilings during the calendar year. In addition to the senior country officer recommending changes in ceilings, the officers at headquarters also could and did initiate changes in ceilings, particularly when crisis situations arose which required a stop to further asset acquisitions or initiating rundowns from existing levels of financial exposure in a country. At the opposite extreme, as noted earlier, country risk evaluations not only tried to anticipate adverse developments but looked out for opportunities for increasing exposure. The flexibility afforded by this control device of country ceilings (and subceilings) allowed for a quick response mechanism to manage a bank's loan portfolio in a foreign country.

With the advent of the Eurocurrency market, cross-border bank placements had been normally monitored by Citicorp's London Placement Control Center. Under this system, New York headquarters determined bank placement ceilings for each participating country, while London monitored actual bank placement exposure against the approved ceiling for any one country. Other Citicorp European treasurers were free, in practice, to make cross-border placements in response to business opportunities, with the proviso that, at the end of each working day, they cabled the London unit with basic data concerning each day's executed placements. London was to alert all participating treasuries to "cease and desist" placements into any particular country whenever actual exposure approached 80% of the established ceiling.

The local Citicorp branches were now expected under the comprehensive country risk management system introduced in 1975 to control and manage all cross-border exposure, not merely bank placement lines. To enable them to do so, the following rules were observed. Before *any* form of credit was extended that would create cross-border exposure to some foreign borrowing entity, a cross-border exposure allocation had to be obtained from the branch in the country where the borrowing customer was domiciled. Similarly, a cross-border allocation had also to be obtained for any drawdown on any and all credit lines, except when such an allocation had already been requested and approved by the appropriate branch beforehand. While these rules were appropriate for credit-related transactions, special expedited procedures were instituted to accommodate fast-moving money market cross-border placements by Citicorp entities. For intracountry foreign currency exposure, control was easy for the local branch since the branch had no difficulty at any time in determining the amount of direct and contingent obligations due Citicorp from borrowing entities located in that branch's country.

Exhibit 15.3 traces how these country ceilings are used in relation to another key banking function, that is, reviewing loan repayment under three different circumstances. These circumstances are normal repayment, problem (classified) loans, and problem countries. Countries which have fallen into difficulties and are in arrears in servicing their debt to a foreign commercial bank must expect a relatively long period of recovery. Special actions are needed to shorten such periods, for example, standby arrangements with the IMF and successful rescheduling of debt. Moreover, banks dare not encourage countries to believe restructuring of debt is an easy available way out or expect to be bailed out by the actions of governments or international agencies. For the country risk management process to work, it is

Exhibit 15.3—Usage of Ceiling and its Relationship to Other Institutional and Noninstitutional Review Processes, 1980

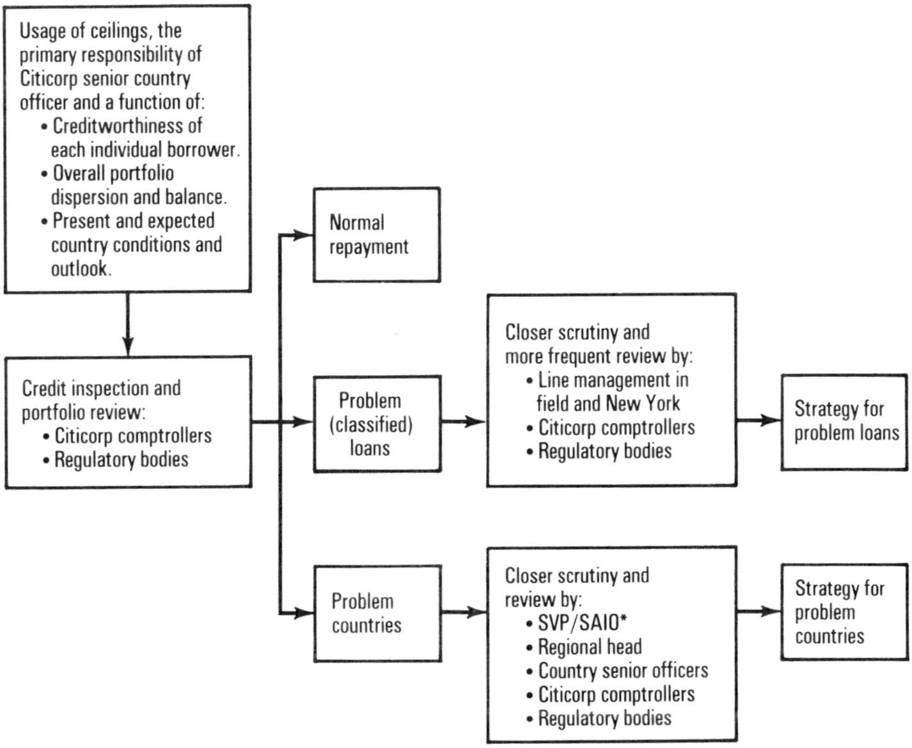

*Senior vice president/senior advisor for international operations

necessary for borrowers to realize that every bank must be a prudent lender and will act to protect its interest as a lender without recourse to outside assistance like the Federal Reserve or other central bank.

If the borrower, even a government, has destroyed its creditworthiness, it has to go through a workout period. Again, this may be a difficult position to pursue, when other banks with a different role in world lending seem to be eager lenders, even to countries which have only recently lost the confidence of the financial community and are only beginning to rebuild this confidence through changes in economic policies. Difficult cases need to be handled separately from ordinary business and probably by different people, not encumbered with other responsibilities. In the Citicorp system, the senior advisor for international operations was kept fully informed from the earliest stages of perceived problems, and a procedure for consultation with other officers agreed on as soon as it became clear that extraordinary action could be necessary.

General Reporting Practices Involving Cross-Border Exposure

The reporting system is computer assisted and utilizes standardized forms to provide management with the information needed to monitor, as well as manage, cross-border exposure.[31] In practice, this meant that every Citicorp (majority-owned or managed) entity within a country had to prepare a report which listed each country in which exposure had been incurred. These separate reports were sent to the senior officer of the country in which the exposure existed. The officer used these separate reports to prepare an exposure report for the country.

The country exposure reporting system emphasized and required all booking units to report all assets and contingent liabilities of all borrowers in any one foreign country to the local Citicorp branch, to keep the branch up to date. The reporting system of exposure was so orchestrated that the senior country officer in the country of the borrower's domicile was responsible to report to headquarters, rather than the officer in the country where the loan was booked. The senior country officer was to be able to determine immediately the maximum amount of Citicorp's cross-border exposure by referring to the allocations made out of the cross-border ceilings. When senior management wanted to know what outstandings were in any particular country, the local country branch could obtain the information quickly by contacting each booking unit which had been allocated part of the cross-border ceiling.

Senior country officers granting cross-border or intracountry foreign currency allocations were required to keep a special log indicating the recipients of their allocations and other essential information. Meanwhile, booking units receiving these foreign currency allocations had to maintain proper files on all transactions within their purview.

With information provided by the consolidated reports received from all countries, the senior officer of each obligor country then prepared two reports for distribution to the head office. One report detailed cross-border exposure in the country, broken down by tenor, nature and the asset/contingent liability, and types of obligor (business segment) involved. Copies of these forms were sent to headquarters, the senior advisor for international operations, and the appropriate division head.

The second report dealt with intracountry foreign currency exposure. Procedures involving the consolidation and reporting of intracountry foreign currency exposure could be and were less intricate. Intracountry foreign currency exposure in a particular country, nevertheless, was disaggregated by tenor, nature of the asset/contingent liability, and types of obligor (business segment) involved. Copies of this report were also sent to the senior advisor for international operations and the appropriate geographical division head. The principle applied was that in those few unusual cases where the exercise of individual judgment was

[31]Citicorp, *Annual Report 1981*, pp. 26-27.

unavoidable, it was preferable to report greater exposure rather than to understate Citicorp's position.

Field and Head Office Roles in Managing Exposure

The head office was greatly assisted by the field offices in determining country risk and ceilings.* The field had better access to on-the-spot information which often is of an enlightening nature. At any time, it was the role of the senior country officer in each country to have a highly expert opinion on that country and its outlook from the viewpoint of Citicorp's country risk. These judgments could be expressed briefly but well. It was literally impossible for anyone to give all the factors entering into a country judgment. It was not large reports that were asked for, but succinct expert judgments that could guide the actions of the local branch and were of crucial value to the head office.

At the head office, a group of people was developed who were capable of following, reviewing, and independently judging country situations. These people had an experience base in Citibank. They were instructed to emphasize acquiring knowledge which was not readily accessible to the field. In this way, the views of the field could be checked against other expert judgments based on other sources of knowledge. Differences between the head office and the field would then point clearly to the need for further thought by both, while the independently achieved agreement of the two would be mutually reinforcing and reassuring.

The purpose of activity at the headquarters was not to substitute or second guess the field but rather to exercise an independent judgment and in the process link the thinking in the field with the general experience, policies, and objectives of Citicorp. In this way, the inevitable risks involved in very large-scale operations in over 100 countries could, it was believed, be reduced to levels acceptable to prudent managers.

Country desk officers at headquarters were expected to be in continuing contact with the field and were discouraged from proposing changes in recommended actions originating in the field without consulting the field. Senior management was made aware of any differences in views between the field and the headquarters. A specific procedure for handling proposed changes in cross-border exposure guidelines was established to assure that both the views and recommendations of the field and the independent reviews and judgments of the headquarters staff became part of the decision-making process.

One of the ways to develop a broad capability in officers at the head office was to have them deal with actual country problems—requested increases in country exposure guidelines. Another typical case was evaluation of a country without exposure to judge whether opening business was warranted or assessing international

*This author's responsibilities at Citicorp included, in addition to the judgment on country risk and ceilings, the development of a corporate view on any country outside the U.S. I was greatly assisted in this work by Citicorp's far-flung network of bankers in branches, affiliates, and subsidiaries, as well as officers at the head office.

developments which might bring into question existing attitudes on increasing or decreasing cross-border exposure. The dramatic change in Iran and the implications for Citicorp of political changes in Portugal and Angola were discussed for example. Possible participation or management of loan syndications in a number of countries was also considered. The emphasis was always on the actual problems of Citicorp entities and how these country desk officers could participate in the decisions.

Creation of a headquarters management process and capability was done in a number of different mutually reinforcing ways:

1. Preparation of memoranda giving recommendations of suggested changes in guidelines.

2. Close work between individual country desk officers and top headquarters staff.

3. Development of relationships with country experts in Washington, D.C., particularly in the IMF and World Bank.

4. Frequent meetings of the senior country risk officer with country desk officers, along with participation of other special groups in Citibank to discuss country risk developments. Minutes of such meetings were kept and disseminated to the field.

5. Encouragement of all groups within the head office to look to the country desk officers as sources of information and judgments.

6. Encouragement of all groups within the head office to include desk officers in policy discussions and decision making on their countries.

The staff had prior valuable banking experience, but on-the-job training, including suggestions for further education, was essential. The effort would not succeed, it was felt, if inadequacies of training and perspective of many of the desk officers were to lead to their exclusion from discussions or the policy-making process at the head office. Morale-creation efforts were equally important, so that all individuals assigned to this new function understood clearly that they were in the mainstream of Citicorp activities, doing a job which was highly valued. If they believed that these assignments were waiting rooms for future assignments or sidetracks, the needed top flight staff would not be created.

Visits of senior foreign country officers to New York and visits to the field by country desk and other staff, as well as myself, provided opportunities for important exchange of views. These field meetings were most helpful in identifying problems and increasing awareness of the importance of this country exposure/country evaluation work. Priority was also given to setting up contacts between Citibank people in the field, as well as at the head office, with experts in central banks, governments, international agencies, etc. Other possibilities explored for strengthening country risk work were relating country desk work at headquarters to future field assignments and vice versa.

My views can be summarized as follows: "Once corporations searched available domestic markets before looking abroad. Increasingly, the scan is simultaneously worldwide. In the same way, procurement, allocation of materials, personnel, finance, marketing, and so on are being developed with a global perspective to obtain maximum efficiency in all markets. In light of the emerging role of the multinational corporation, we require a new breed of corporate and government executive to cope with the world of tomorrow. We need executives who can deal with their specialties in terms of the larger whole. We need people who can move from one field to another, who perceive the interrelatedness of varied functions, who can function efficiently in a constantly changing, unpredictable, and often disrupted and even threatening environment. The successful corporate manager must have a large dose of Sir Francis Drake or Daniel Boone in his or her character and experience. These new executives must appreciate the requirement for global economic strategies. They must be globalists in every aspect."

Bank of America

This system merits special attention because of the major importance of the Bank of America as an international lender and the differences in its evaluation and management process compared with Citibank. The country evaluation system developed by Bank of America may be broadly characterized as a numerical rating system that blends qualitative and quantitative data sources. Its management style encourages substantial delegation of authority and decentralized decision making. Insofar as decision making is decentralized, a strong and integrating framework of portfolio management becomes critical to ensure that the sum total of the individual decisions taken will add up to a total bankwide portfolio that is satisfactory and consistent with the bank's objectives.

With a very large international loan portfolio, the Bank of America has long been involved in most facets of international lending with foreign branch and subsidiary business on a global scale. How to cope with country risk problems has been a major concern of the bank's management as is evinced by the elaborate approach developed for country risk assessment and portfolio management.

The Bank of America's country risk assessment techniques combine quantitative indicators, where proven useful, with a judgmental component determined by a consensus-building process of rating the creditworthiness of many countries. The requirements of Bank of America's country evaluation system are shaped by the great diversity of its financial business abroad and its highly decentralized organizational structure. The bank has believed that its purposes are best served by calculation of country ratings. The approach used is said not to be static, but has reportedly evolved with the changing international environment, new staff capabilities, or new emphases like the examining the consequences of political upheavals on country creditworthiness.

Risk Management

The Bank of America's system aims to manage effectively a whole spectrum of risks inherent to global banking: asset quality, liquidity, interest rates, foreign exchange, and country risk. Country risk also plays an indirect role often in what happens in these other risk categories. Several facets of these primary risks are worth recalling, so that the complex role of country risk in a bank's overall risk management may be better highlighted.

Notwithstanding Bank of America's safeguards for asset quality and credit risk of detailed credit analysis, proper documentation, timely re-evaluation of outstanding credits, and prompt follow-up of identified problems, some uncertainty of loan repayment always remains. The bank is reported to look for protection against this potential adversity both by including risk premiums on interest rate charges to different major loan categories. It also adds sufficient loan loss provisions to reserves to cover expected future losses for each major loan category plus additional reserves maintained against less predictable losses. Net loan losses from nonperforming loans in a particular year are charged off or deducted from loan loss provisions. One major loan category is foreign loans, for which roughly a quarter of total loan loss provisions are held.

Second, Bank of America conducts its international liquidity management to meet multicurrency needs of borrowers by trying to secure deposits in the Eurocurrency market or elsewhere, by maintaining additional sources of liquidity in the form of marketable securities, and by setting shorter limits on the funding of each currency. Third, overseas interest rate risk is seen to be less difficult to manage than its domestic counterpart because international loans are typically priced at prearranged spreads which remain constant regardless of subsequent interest rate movements. Maturity mismatching, the major type of interest rate risk remaining, is handled by limiting the amount of mismatching permitted for each currency.

Fourth, foreign exchange risk arises from volatility in rates of exchange between currencies. Bank of America's more than 30 currency trading units worldwide manage foreign exchange risks both by limiting the size of acceptable trading positions and by the great decentralization of trading activities and the many currencies involved.

Even though these categories are all influenced by country risk issues, the Bank of America country evaluation system is quite distinct from these risks.

Country Assessment System Culminating in Ratings

The Bank of America's methods of country assessment evolved over time in response to long-term developments like the internationalization of banking over the past two decades. They began from a largely judgmentally based transfer risk rating system in the 1960s to a computer-assisted system. This system combines an analytical formula with judgmental factors to arrive at a comprehensive country risk rating. The country evaluation system consists of three major elements:

1. A country assessment method which culminates in numerical ratings.
2. Setting overall country lending limits and sublimits.
3. Frequent monitoring of actual country loan exposure levels.

The country rating is mainly used as one of several determinants for adopting an overall country lending limit.

While the bank's approach begins on the basis of quantitative and statistical information, it is refined by the inclusion of two distinct judgmental letter ratings: a judgmental economic indicator and a political indicator. These are arrived at by having the appropriate staff and line officers and economists filling out questionnaires and then negotiating a consensus on various country ratings. The two judgmental ratings serve as the distillation of the results of the overall country assessment.

Adherence to a country numerical rating system, accordingly, does not necessarily imply a naive belief in the objectivity and sufficiency of only information that lends itself to statistical and quantitative expression. The bank's model recognizes the absolute importance of assimilating judgmental information in addition to quantitative analysis when assessing a country's relative creditworthiness. The search for a reliable set of statistical lead indicators of debt-service difficulties has been tried numerous times but is beset with basic difficulties. Finding a precise enough definition for the dependent variable (debt-service difficulty) is the main obstacle cited. Many other similar problems arise. How can a satisfactory dividing line between acceptable and unacceptable delays in payment be determined, when short delays are common and often for innocuous reasons?

The relatively small number of countries which typically experience debt-service problems in a given year is another reason for statistical estimation problems, particularly when the real aim is to measure fine gradations of country creditworthiness and not merely a simple bipolar classification scheme. Moreover, seemingly good proxies of country creditworthiness (IMF standby agreements or actual Euromarket spreads paid by borrower countries) are prone to ambiguous interpretations on reflection. Market spreads are neither easily nor validly compared partly because of the diversity of actual loan agreements (tenor) and partly because of the less visible front-end fees to syndicated loans and other devices which may be used to mask the real size of the spread paid.

Therefore, it is Bank of America's belief that sole reliance on statistical indicators for country evaluation is apt to be misleading. This results in the need to supplement and illuminate such quantitative analysis by factoring in judgmental information.

Quantitative Point of Departure

Salient factors in any country risk assessment are grouped under four broad headings: external liquidity, economic policy, economic structure, and sociopolitical factors. The quantitative point of departure is development of an analytical data matrix, which was constructed in the mid-1970s as sets of equations made to approximate a set of subjective country ratings that were agreed on by a number of senior line officers and economists.

Even though external liquidity factors in the analytical data matrix were at first separated from those of economic policy and economic structure so as to calculate two composite indices (the debt-service rating and the so-called adaptability index), it was soon found preferable to combine these into what then became the debt-service capacity index. The original debt-service index had four weighted components: debt-service capacity ratios, import coverage index, debt-burden index, and the compressibility index. The original adaptability index had eight weighted subindices, including gross domestic product, inflation, exports, product concentration, and savings patterns.

A statistical estimation procedure was soon undertaken to correlate the economic characteristics of a country in a base year with the debt-servicing record of the country during the next one to five years. It was found that a country's external liquidity situation is a good statistical predictor of a country's *short-term* ability to service its external debt punctually, whereas economic structural variables tended to be dominant in the long-run perspective of five years. The best three-year medium-term debt-service index proved to be a balanced composite of liquidity, policy, and structural variables. This became the basic debt-service capacity index.

Judgmental Indicators

A relatively informal method was used to gather less readily quantifiable economic and sociopolitical information, partly by tapping Bank of America's global network of economists. Influential factors not adequately covered in the debt-service index are the focus of a questionnaire filled out initially by the bank's country and regional managers. Flexible enough to encompass possibly unique environmental factors, the questionnaire has a consistent enough format to allow comparison between countries. Questionnaire responses are sent to divisional headquarters, at which point preliminary ratings are assigned to each of 80 countries. These are then sent to Bank of America's world headquarters in San Francisco, where they are consolidated and checked for global consistency. The worldwide ratings are then reviewed by senior management.

Recent changes in the Bank of America's country evaluation system suggest that more emphasis is now placed on incorporating judgmental factors in country risk assessment. The country rating process is described as moving up the organizational hierarchy and is based on consensus-building along the way. Any disagreements in proper ratings are resolved, and other ratings are reviewed by the bank's world banking division executive council. This is composed of executive officers of regional and divisional units and representatives from headquarters. By implication, these divisional executive officers are delegated many responsibilities over international lending occurring in their respective geographic areas. The division centers are located in London, Tokyo, Caracas, and Los Angeles.

The results of the debt-service capacity index displayed little change on average during the 1970s. This is true for all country groups stratified by per capita income level. For example, the index finds that the nonoil-developing countries changed only slightly in rating as a group from 68 out of a possible 100 in 1973 to 64 in 1981.

Yet, 1981 was a threshold year before a number of countries ran into serious debt-servicing difficulties, for example, Mexico, Brazil, and Argentina in 1982. The author remains highly skeptical of the use of such indices, however carefully constructed, because they do not reflect reality and encourage excessive reliance on them, despite repeated caveats by their creators.

Country Ratings in International Portfolio Management

The country rating process is recognized to be little more than an academic exercise when abstracted from how a bank uses this information. Given the size and diversity of Bank of America's international assets and liabilities, country ratings, as well as more discursive country reports, are generated for numerous purposes. While the role and nature of the country rating system is well documented in published information, its integration into the annual budget process as well as more informal uses of country assessment is not published in detail.

The three most important uses of country ratings are in setting country lending limits, overseas investment of bank capital in advance of opening a new foreign branch, and in setting loan loss reserves. The setting of country lending limits is regarded by the Bank of America as a key to managing country portfolios when coupled with an elaborate computerized monitoring system which provides current information on actual cross-border exposure levels of the bank. Actual risk exposure levels must stay in compliance with lending limits. The country ratings serve as one of a number of inputs which are consulted when deciding on country lending limits. Other criteria are the profitability of country markets, the size of the country, its external debt position, whether the bank has undue concentration of business in a country, and occasionally long-run strategic goals and complementary business relationships.

Specific lending limits are attributed to different ratings, so that all those countries with the same ratings are assigned a common maximum permitted exposure level. Treating all countries with the same rating in a similar fashion for macroportfolio management is said to make sense from the standpoint of finding a logical procedure for diversifying risks through the portfolio. Country lending limits together with the country evaluation system are intended to serve both as top management and line tools. Both macro- and microapplications exist in the myriad decisions that add up to an optimal bank portfolio.

A second major use of country rating is in the authorization of overseas investment of bank capital. Most countries stipulate in law or regulation the magnitude of capital required to set up a branch or subsidiary. Country risk difficulties may affect the profitability of the invested capital. Moreover, the absence of forward markets in many currencies has precluded hedging this capital exposure in foreign exchange markets.

Loan loss provisions also are made to reflect the country risk ratings as one criterion of asset quality because of a policy that greater reserves be set aside for lower rated countries. Having loan loss provisions correspond to primary risk factors is believed to help create proper incentives for individual bank units to take all relevant cost factors into account in making a lending decision. Management can better gauge the risk-adjusted profitability by allocating costs properly to each profit center of the bank. Hence, risk factors can be assimilated into business decision making by being converted explicitly into a type of cost.

Monitoring Country Exposure

Bank of America continuously monitors actual loan exposure in many countries and tabulates fairly detailed information with the aid of a computer. This information consists of the agreed country lending limits, commitments made by all bank units, and the actual exposure level. This is further disaggregated according to tenor (short, medium, long) and sector (government, banks, commercial). Such management tasks as checking compliance with country lending limits or identifying opportunities to expand loan business are facilitated greatly by this monitoring system.

American Security Bank

American Security Bank in Washington, D.C., although much smaller than Citicorp and the Bank of America, has given considerable attention to international lending because of its location. Washington, the center of official world finance, is the headquarters of the IMF, the World Bank, and the Inter-American Development Bank. American Security has total assets of about $2 billion, but its international assets are expanding and total about 30% of the bank's total loans.

Economic and Political Factors

American Security defines country risk as the elements of risk in the economic and political environments of a given country. It starts from the assumption that events taking place within a country can adversely affect the collectibility of debt investments, irrespective of the financial conditions of the borrower.

In its corporate manual, the bank notes the following factors as those which may adversely influence debt collectability.

1. Economic: special taxes imposed on the lender or borrower; interest rate management; government imposed delays or liquidation of external obligations; devaluation or foreign exchange controls; and domestic policies, often imposed in a sudden unpredictable manner, which affect the borrower's ability to generate the necessary cash flow to repay debt.

2. Political: nationalization, confiscation, wars, embargoes, revolutions, etc.

The management system is designed to measure total country risk in all countries, segregated into maturities of under one year and over one year. Exposure is divided into direct and indirect as follows:

- Direct exposure—loans (including overdrafts and acceptances), placements, investments, guarantees and standby credits, legal commitments to lend, and letters of credit.

• Indirect exposure—unused portions of lines of credit, including placements and foreign exchange lines.

Country risk is defined in relation to the entity which bears the legal responsibility and ultimate credit responsibility. Unsecured facilities which do not have binding legal support from a third party are considered to be exposure in the country in which the borrower is domiciled. Facilities which have legally binding support from third parties, principally guarantees and insurance, are reported as risk in the country in which these third parties are domiciled. If facilities are secured by cash, marketable securities, or real estate, the risk is placed in the country where the security is physically located. Branches of banks are considered as exposure to the head office of that bank regardless of where that branch is located. Majority-owned subsidiaries of banks are generally (after careful study) reported as exposure to the bank that has majority interest.

Any division within the bank originating a country risk transaction must obtain the concurrence of the international division. The head of the international division (a senior vice president) is directly responsible for monitoring country risk and recommending changes in country limits. These recommendations are reviewed by the bank's consulting economist, the chairman of credit policy, the president, or the chairman of the bank. American Security policy is to monitor and evaluate risk in countries where the bank has exposure, even though the countries are not among the group of countries selected for new business solicitation. Country limits are established and approved at least annually.

On country conditions, each geographic group head in the international division is responsible for maintaining current knowledge of each country assigned to the group. Any developments that might affect country risk must be brought to the attention of the division head and the chairman of credit policy via written memorandum. Monthly reports are sent to the chairman and president of the bank and the head of the credit policy committee on outstanding exposures; quarterly reports are sent to the loan policy review committee.

The two basic inputs into establishing country limits are the country risk assessment and the marketing strategy of the bank. Other factors considered in establishing maximum lending limits are credit risk, profitability and other benefits, capital, tenor, and impact on rating agencies.

Country Studies

A country studies format is used for most countries in which the bank does business. The study calls for details similar to Citicorp's. The study aims at judgments used to establish country limits. Two key aspects are identified for those preparing these studies. First, an assessment is made of a country's ability over time to generate a sufficient amount of revenue from the export of goods and services or financing to service the principal and interest on its foreign debt obligations. Second, assessment is made regarding the willingness of a country's political leadership to fulfill its international financial obligations. Thus, the study format recognizes that a country's debt-service ratio must be assessed within the context of a wide range of economic and political factors. After these assessments, the head of the international banking division after consultation with respective area officers recommends limits.

Continental Illinois Corporation

Continental Illinois has integrated the use of exposure limits into its planning process, as well as asset and liability management. In the planning process, the general direction of the corporation is determined by projecting an international loan portfolio growth consistent with prudent risk levels and long-term profit growth. The plan is then used to guide geographic division goals. Attention is also focused on the cost of funding international loans, as well as on the interest rate spreads and fees accompanying the making of loans.

To examine country exposure, Continental Illinois has a committee composed of senior officers from the international and multinational banking departments and from the economic research division. The committee meets every two weeks, with the calendar of countries to be reviewed determined by a country's risk rating or special developments that demand attention. Committee members receive three inputs: first, an economic risk evaluation and forecast; second, a political risk evaluation and outlook; and third, the recommendation from the geographic lending division. The subsequent decision to increase, reduce, or hold constant the exposure limit for a country is then subject to final review by top management.

The country exposure committee has the responsibility not to make any decision based on the profitability of particular loans. The management of profitability of loans is the general responsibility of the geographic division head under the direction of the senior officer responsible for the international or multinational departments. Each credit extended by the bank is subject to review by a separate credit review group which evaluates the quality of the individual loans.

Limits on Exposure

Exposure limits cover all extensions of credit by the bank and its branches, as well as by all its majority-owned subsidiaries. Several sublimits within these overall limits also are established. The most important of these include sublimits on term credits by amount and years of maturity for each country, as well as limits on extensions of credit of less than one year. The normal maximum on term credits is seven years. The limits apply to aggregate exposure encompassing unused lines and commitments in addition to outstandings.

In defining exposure, location of the borrower is generally the determinant of the country of exposure. Certain industries have overall limits, irrespective of any country. Branches of a borrower are generally considered to be the responsibility of the borrower's head office, and credit exposure to the branch of a borrower in a country other than that of the head office is counted as exposure in the country of the head office. Borrowings of a subsidiary located in a country other than that of the parent company are considered to be exposure in the country in which the subsidiary is located. Credits that are supported by guarantees are considered exposure in the country of the issuer of the guarantee.

In determining the maximum exposure allowable in any one country, the impact of a potential loan loss on capital funds is regarded as of paramount importance. The impact of such a write-off varies from country to country depending on the tax structure of a particular country. It also may vary from bank to bank within any given country. Such analysis has contributed significantly to Continental's thinking as to the maximum exposure allowable in any country.

An economic risk rating for all countries is provided by the economic research division, which administratively is separate from the international and multinational banking departments. The economic risk rating, updated regularly, is based on the present situation and outlook for about 30 criteria for each country. It not only deals with the current situation but also is designed to identify economic risk and vulnerability in the medium and longer term. Economic analysis focuses on determining a country's foreign borrowing requirements, the achievability and sustainability of the nation's growth targets, and the ability of the economy to generate hard currency earnings to meet its debt-servicing obligations now and in the future. Consideration is given to a country's natural, human, and capital resources and how efficiently and effectively they are or might be employed. The ability of government officials to manage the economy also is appraised.

A number of factors have been identified as closely correlated with debt-servicing difficulties. They include debt-service ratios and maturity profiles, international reserve adequacy measures, selected macroeconomic variables, and government policy indicators. These factors are monitored very closely. Much attention is given to the current status of a country's balance-of-payments components as well as to their future prospects. Key early-warning indicators have been developed to flag significant changes in countries' international financial conditions. In addition to these various economic risk indicators, more detailed written reports on future implications of recent developments also are regularly scheduled for each country. One of five ratings of creditworthiness or economic risk is applied to all countries, and Continental refers, for example, to a given country as having a group II or group III economic risk rating.

Political Analysis

In the political risk rating system, the country analysis is provided by the loan officers responsible for each country and includes information from Continental Illinois officers overseas. Regular reports are prepared that provide an estimate of the willingness and political ability of the government to continue to honor its foreign obligations. Also, attention is given to the possibility that any change in political conditions might interrupt the normal process of meeting obligations if the existing government is replaced. Attention also is given to the risk of expropriation or nationalization without adequate compensation.

Included in the political analysis is an evaluation of the stability and strength of the political institutions created for governing and of the individuals holding various power positions. The objective is to identify potential conflict among the centers of power inside the country as well as with other nations. Criteria have been established to calculate the effect that any internal or external change could have on the government's attitude toward foreign debt or foreign investment. The analysis not only focuses on the current situation but also is designed to measure risk factors in the medium and longer term. Countries are placed in one of five grades of political risk. Exposure to countries is monitored very closely, and any excess over the limits can only be authorized by senior management.

Other Banks

Considerable detail has been presented on Citicorp, Bank of America, American Security, and Continental Illinois. Rather brief highlights follow for other banks, which point to some of the differences in practice. These highlights are based on information obtained from annual reports of these banks and public statements of senior officers, complemented by personal talks in most cases. The choice of banks for inclusion was essentially made on the basis of the available authoritative information. Only a few banks have chosen to publish the details of their country risk management systems. It would be most useful if more banks were to do so.

Bankers Trust

In managing its international loan portfolio and considering opportunities for new business, Bankers Trust emphasizes that the prime consideration is prudent risk management. Over 85 countries are reviewed on a regular basis by relevant geographic groups and the bank's international credit group of the international department, in concert with its world corporate department credit personnel. The expertise of the bank's international economists, political scientists, and senior credit officer of the risk management group is combined in its evaluations.

The strategy of the country risk system is to bring the qualitative judgments of the professional economists and bankers to bear in a well-defined manner on two kinds of decision making: establishing country limits and ratifying specific loan proposals. Country risk meetings are held several times a month to review a small subset of a total of about 80 countries. At these meetings, an adversarial relationship has been encouraged between the political-economic analysts and the country lending officer.

The country risk meetings serve to update senior management on current conditions in each country and for reaffirming or altering country limits. The basis of discussion is a country risk review which follows a structured format and is disseminated prior to each meeting. Part of each review consists of written assessments prepared by economists and political analysts plus tables of germane economic data and projections. The country lending officer contributes the remainder of the review through an independent assessment and record of current country loan commitments and outstandings.

Three distinct sublimits are determined in these meetings for each particular country on the agenda: one for short-term credit of less than one year's maturity, another for term loans of longer maturity than one year, and a third one for contingent exposure. The size of the gap between the country limit and actual outstandings is reviewed in light of expected near-term acceptance of additional credit. But if appreciable unexpected credit requests accumulate, an ad hoc country review is presented with new written or oral updates presented. Finally, the performance of different lending divisions is checked by credit wings of both the international and world corporate departments.

Unhappy with the initial handling of political risk assessment and lacking a structured way of reasoning for social and political determinants that was anything like that for economic variables, management first sought a "magic formula." But two basic requirements had to be met: an adequate information-gathering system and an assessment mechanism to provide the basis for bank policy in a given country. The hallmark of Bankers Trust's revised country risk system is its dual system of information-gathering and assessment. The pattern of checks and balances developed in the adversarial relationship between the staff analysts and the line country lending officers has reportedly proved valuable.

Chemical Bank

Chemical Bank, like other banks, controls the various degrees of country risk through continuing evaluation of economic and political trends and through a system of predetermined exposure and maturity limits for each country. For some countries, sublimits are established and, in most such cases, with varying maturity limits by sectors—government, banking, and private.

As a refinement of its methods of dealing with political risk, Chemical Bank has made use of an analytic technique called a political spread sheet. This technique tries to determine the probable disposition of various political "actors" in a particular country with respect to a specific country lending strategy. Weighting and aggregating this information aims to give a useful benchmark for the likelihood of potential adverse political events.

The complementary elements of Chemical Bank's country exposure system are the country review format and the country rating categories. The latter is said to stress an approach of grouping countries according to their similarities, whereas the former focuses on the uniqueness of each country. Financial, economic, and political parameters are combined to arrive at a particular country's rating. Specific maximum capital ratios are assigned to various country risk categories, although these are indicative rather than binding implications for the setting of country limits.

First National Bank of Chicago

The First Chicago's country risk system bears a strong resemblance to the way it does a credit assessment of an individual company. Countries are explicitly classified—in definition and use, just as individual problematic credits are—according to each one's short- and long-term creditworthiness as determined by First Chicago's country risk management committee. This committee makes the vast majority of decisions relating to country risk. Its membership is comprised of most of the bank's senior management; its chairman is also chairman of the credit policy committee.

Risk ratings, exposure limits, and country marketing strategies are all decided by the committee. The chairman of the committee must ratify any proposals for large exposure in high-risk countries. The two major inputs to the deliberations of the country risk management committee are country risk reports done by analysts in First Chicago's country risk division and a country marketing strategy.

The country risk classifications used by First Chicago are similar (both procedurally and functionally) to credit classifications applied to individual credits. Credit classification, of course, is a long-standing practice and requirement of all banks and regulatory authorities. The bank uses a 1-4 range country classification scheme, and countries are assigned both a short-term and a long-term classification. Many banks, as we have seen, shy away from such explicit classifications.

The First of Chicago management has stated that the explicit classification of countries is the main reason a significantly smaller proportion of its international loan portfolio is located in those countries classified in high-risk categories, as compared with the average international exposure distribution of other largest U.S. banks. Country limits are set for over 100 countries, both in terms of the size and the composition among competing product areas of lending activities in a particular country. If the circumstances change in the risk or marketing opportunities between regular country reviews, additional reviews are scheduled as needed.

The country analysis forms one basis for setting country limits. It focuses on seven factors:

1. External balance sheet of the country.
2. Foreign exchange earnings capacity and financing needs.
3. Access to capital market.
4. Quality of economic and political management.
5. Analysis of major political actors and institutions.
6. Resources available to government and other power centers.
7. International context.

Analytic forecasts are revised when different circumstances arise. Where uncertainty is great, several alternative country scenarios are constructed and the implications of each potential contingency with respect to First Chicago's business are examined.

The second important ingredient is the country marketing strategy (along with country limit proposal) written by each country manager. This limit proposal reflects the bank's overall strategic planning. Each proposal is accompanied by details about the country's current and proposed portfolio structure, which is divided by sector, product, and currency. The country manager coordinates the requests of product specialists in each country in the following product lines: trade finance, energy, transportation, multinational, merchant bank, and financial institutions. Potential customers and projected usage of the proposed limits are delineated. Whereas marketing ideas filter up through First Chicago's hierarchy, the setting of country limits and sublimits is done at the top of this hierarchy by the country risk management committee. This committee examines all countries annually, but countries deemed high risk are scrutinized two or more times a year.

Morgan Guaranty

Country exposure is measured according to Morgan Guaranty's concept of credit risk. Risk is assigned in the country which best reflects the location of the entity having ultimate legal responsibility for repayment of the obligation. Two limits have been set: maximum country exposure and exposure over one year. Loan officers attached to the international banking division have the initiative on an ad hoc basis to request changes in country limits. Country evaluation reports must accompany all such requests for countries in which the bank has appreciable exposure. Review of country limits occurs with greater frequency for countries undergoing major changes. Even countries regarded as safest are reviewed on an annual basis.

Morgan Guaranty's standard country evaluation procedure comes to a focal point in a meeting called by the senior credit officer of the international banking division. The area manager, the loan officers, and the international economist who has written the most recent report of the country to be discussed also attend. Subsequent to the economist's elaboration on how the future of the country should be viewed, the area manager outlines the bank's current and contemplated position in that country. Country evaluation reports examine policy factors, basic economic factors, external finance, and political factors. The division senior credit officer determines the new country limit magnitudes on the basis of the information assembled at that meeting. For particularly sensitive countries, further consultation with more senior bank officials is stipulated. Country risks are anticipated by means of shifts in the composition of exposure toward less risky options, such as accumulating a higher proportion of short-term financial instruments.

Chase Manhattan

Chase Manhattan operates on the principle that international lending requires not only the normal credit risk analysis associated with extending financing to a particular customer but also an assessment of country risk. Attention is focused on availability of foreign exchange to permit timely repayment of foreign currency loans. In addition, country risk can be the result of government decisions or unforeseen events which interrupt normal business activities in the country and affect a borrower's ability to repay its loans.

Chase continually monitors the political and economic climate in each country so that management can structure its exposure in each country in accord with the risks which are identified. In structuring its exposure, Chase focuses on these major considerations:

- Currency of exposure.
- Maturity profile of the exposure.
- Underlying types of business which are being financed.
- Political and economic outlook for the country.

Security Pacific

Security Pacific, a large-size bank with a large international portfolio, has procedures for assessing country risk and achieving portfolio diversification. The corporation analyzes the international and domestic economic and political factors which influence the quality of a nation's economic performance. Based principally on data from the recent past, short- and longer-term assessments of the future of a country's economy are developed. Embodied in these analyses are studies made by the bank's economic staff and reports from the corporation's offices located in many countries. The final product is an evaluation of the economic and political factors which are expected to influence future growth and therefore the prospective economic performance and risk potential of a given nation. The loan portfolio has tended to be concentrated in countries regarded as having higher future business potential.

Ultimate country exposure limit responsibility is found in the vice chairman and executive vice president of international banking and the vice chairman in charge of credit. The day-to-day administration is coordinated by the chief credit officer. Lending officers play a major role in assessing countries, as well as administering country limits and exposures.

Bank of Montreal

The Bank of Montreal's overseas lending activities reportedly take into consideration elements of risk associated with the social and political environments of countries where borrowers reside and those countries' future capacity to honor foriegn debt commitments. Internationally, as within Canada, the Bank of Montreal follows a policy of risk diversification. A high percentage of loans is to borrowers in the industrial countries. Economic and political developments in other countries are constantly monitored. The bank maintains lending guidelines based on procedures similar to those used to set credit limits for individuals or business accounts.

The decision process involves field and headquarters line and staff officers. It considers each country's liquidity situation, its ability to service foreign debt burden, and the nature of marketing opportunities presented. Country limit proposals are presented for approval by the credit policy committee and changes in the country lending limits are placed before the board of directors.

A checklist of important factors and causations is used as a convenient format for quantifying country risk. This checklist method is regarded as a minimally adequate technique to use in lieu of other assessment method. Considerable attention is given to the chain of causation by which debt-servicing problems might arise. The specific type of probable debt-servicing problem is identified, and countries are ranked according to relative risk. The occurrence of country risk is associated most frequently with economic, political, or social disruptions. Hence, the narrower concepts of economic risk, political risk, and social risk are seen as constituent parts of country risk.

The Bank of Montreal aims to assimilate country risk consideration into its everyday lending decisions. Country risk information is cited as a critical ingredient in four distinct types of decision making: setting exposure limits, strategic planning, portfolio management, and evaluation of a bank's international performance.

The world's complexity is seen as not permitting a straightforward application of the results of country risk analysis for the setting of country exposure limits. However, the country risk analysis helps set approximate guidelines. Avoidance of loan concentration—whether geographical or maturity—is another principle that is stressed. Another important use of country exposure policy is in placing restrictions on specific types of lending. Judgments on country risk, together with spread and maturity, are used to assess the bank's loan quality.

Conclusion

These bank examples have not been compared or criticized. The purpose has been to illustrate the state of the art of country evaluation and country risk management systems. As can be seen, there is no uniformity of views, preferences, and practices. Many aspects are coming together—the need for country risk assessments and the need for country risk management systems—which include definitions such as measurement of exposure, reporting, monitoring, and setting of foreign exposure limits.

Each bank, however, differs importantly in format of country assessments, professional background of analysts, sources of information, and frequency and detail of analysis. Each has different system administration, location of ultimate responsibility, accountability for fixing and changing country limits, use of sublimits, ways of linking to business decisions, and so forth. Each bank believes it is responding to its own needs and capabilities. And within the same bank, officers of similar background will differ sharply on these issues. Banks are still in the formative stages on country evaluation and country risk management.

More and more bankers believe that a practical, efficient country risk system is essential for the managers, shareholders, investors in the bank, and bank regulators and supervisors. All have much to learn from each other and in so learning can spare themselves unnecessary costly mistakes or more quickly obtain better systems and processes.

The area in which further improvement can be sought and profitably found include:

- Integration of country risk assessment with business decision making.
- More sharply defined country risk management systems with clearer responsibility and accountability.
- More firsthand knowledge of countries and experience in evaluating countries.
- More self-reliance in judging countries' policies.
- More focus relative to portfolio management.
- Less use of committees.
- More involvement of all engaged in international lending.
- More awareness that country risk evaluation and management are a part of banking, not a separate analytical skill or function.

In short, the problem should be looked at as one of bank management not primarily as one of analysis.

16

Regulatory Aspects of Country Risk Management

Apart from its role in buttressing the depositing public's trust in a nation's banking system, the government has long been recognized as a major determinant and constraint in patterns of international lending and often as a catalyst of innovative changes in banking. One of the latest extensions of banking regulation has been the greater scrutiny given to the adequacy of a bank's country risk assessment methods and cross-border exposure management system. This chapter focuses on those banking regulations which are designed to respond to novel anxieties about country risk in banking.

These anxieties have been heightened by the events of 1982-83, and bank supervisors have been reviewing their policies and practices vis-à-vis international lending to developing countries. In the U.S., these concerns have been tied to proposals to increase the U.S. contribution to the IMF. As a consequence, the U.S. Congress may mandate changes in rules governing international lending. These changes point to more severe constraints on the lending practices of private banks, with the danger that lending to developing countries will be limited beyond the needs or requirements of prudent banking. In other countries, bank supervisors are also taking similar restrictive actions, including the discounting of bank assets held in designated developing countries.

Only in the past few years have bank supervisory authorities in the U.S. and other developed nations perceived the need to impose the following types of regulations or supervisory techniques.

- Examination of a lending bank's capabilities to cope with country risk, specifically focusing on two areas: One, evidence of an adequate diversification strategy for avoiding undue concentrations of country loan exposure as judged by various capital ratios; two, greater uniformity in assessing a bank's approach to country risk analysis, monitoring its foreign exposure, and the adequacy of human and organizational resources allocated to this task.
- New requirements are contemplated by bank supervisory authorities to ensure that banks maintain an adequate liquidity cushion to cover unexpected earnings

shortfalls. For example, the setting aside of a loan loss provisions may become less discretionary and sought at an earlier stage.

To ensure adequate diversification of a bank's assets and liabilities, bank supervisors inquire how country loan exposure limits are established and modified by management. Some countries, furthermore, have adopted legal large-loan limits. These stipulate the maximum amount of money that can be lent to individual debtors or interrelated debtor groups usually as a proportion of a bank's capital resources. Large-loan limits are expressed as a constant proportion of bank capital. Definitions vary among countries. For example, while U.S. banks must observe a maximum loan limit to any debtor of 10% of capital, Italian banks may lend a customer up to 100% of capital.

Aside from the relatively few country risk-related regulations, other more general areas of regulatory involvement influence international capital flows and lending by private banks.

International Regulatory Frameworks

Each country's regulatory framework, which impinges on international capital transactions, may be compared by use of the following classification scheme. It was designed by the OECD to assemble the first fairly comprehensive survey of such regulations in Western European countries and Japan. Such regulations and policy instruments are put into one of the following six categories.

1. Exchange control measures, whether of legal or administrative origin.
2. Minimum reserve requirements.
3. Interest rate control.
4. Prudential regulations.
5. Tax regulations.
6. Other miscellaneous regulations of similar purpose, such as central bank swap agreements.

These six categories indicate how wide the universe of international banking regulations is. The role of national regulatory authorities from the viewpoint of country risk centers on category four—prudential regulations. From an even wider perspective, however, regulators are preoccupied with general issues affecting international lending such as effects on domestic monetary policies of international credit flows, risk to financial soundness of banks, and reciprocity in treatment of foreign branches.

Hence, supervision of country risk is only a small part of the responsibilities of central banks or other bank supervisory authorities. A change in the application of reserve requirements to deposits held abroad by banks or changes in tax regulations can be more significant for international lending than those directly related to prudential aspects. Indeed, because the regulatory response to country risk is of such recent origin, published information about the latest changes in regulatory treatment of country risk in various nations is sparse in relation to more conventional areas of banking regulations.

Examiners' Concerns

Before focusing on what U.S. bank regulators do, let us examine what might be the appropriate content of their exercises. Bankers tend to look at their activities in a manner quite similar to bank examiners. They have similar reviews and tests. Nevertheless, regulators obviously concentrate on the contingency of shades of payment difficulties in their examinations and are less concerned with other business considerations. A regulatory system for examining a bank portfolio from the country risk viewpoint can be divided into two issues: standardized procedures for conducting a bank examination; and suggested procedures for keeping a bank's board of directors informed.

Bank examiners need to be thoroughly briefed on country conditions to conduct exchange of views with banks examined. Preparation may well include field visits as well as use of all information available to regulatory authorities, including information obtained from other government agencies. Country briefing would involve preparation of country studies for such countries deemed needed by the regulatory authorities.

Regulatory country briefing would identify two main areas of possible questions: country conditions, outlook, and policies as they affect possible risks faced by banks; and the impact of changes in the national and international environment on individual credits.

With this general preparation as a guide, bank examiners could better examine the particular banks assigned to them. Examination of a bank's portfolio could be done simultaneously or separately from the bank's credits for the well-established credit review purposes. Examiners should probably *not* expect to need to review the same countries with all banks or to identify the same risks in each bank. This would be done on a bank-by-bank basis, but their common country briefing could help avoid important oversights.

Several findings could prompt an examiner to make recommendations. First, if an examiner feels country knowledge is inadequate, he or she could so inform the bank's management or the board of directors of this condition. Second, an examiner should discuss and exchange views on any countries for any reason the examiner feels sufficient. An examiner should be prepared to examine individual credits for the impact of country and international environment on these credits. If the examiner believes that country conditions may or will adversely affect a credit, he or she could classify individual credits accordingly, using the agreed regulatory criteria for classifying credits as summarized in an earlier chapter as a guide. This process might well lead to a credit being classified, even in strong countries, if the examiner feels that certain aspects of the environment will cause adversities.

Board of Director Involvement

The examiner could inform the board of directors of his or her opinion of the bank's country risk management system. The examiner should ensure that the board is kept current on the following matters:

• Ceilings and subceilings and exposures for *all* countries.

• Country reviews of those countries whose total exposures are significant for the bank's earnings or capital.

• Countries in which exposure has grown much faster than did the bank's average growth during the past six months or is projected to grow much faster over the next six months. The aim is to help the board focus on the countries which are becoming more important for its bank. It would have *no* implication for creditworthiness or country risk.

• Countries with individual credits which have been classified because of country reasons.

In this process, the board will learn more about what guides the staff's thinking on countries and how it goes about defending the liquidity and profitability of the bank in its international lending. The board can satisfy itself that the information flows, management processes, and results are reasonably satisfactory. It can satisfy itself with respect to countries about which it is hearing various views which may be causing concern. Such views, even market gossip, should be aired with the bank's management.

Board members also have sources of information and bases for judgments which may help the bank management improve its own judgments on individual credits within a country. The board can also hear the views of invited experts or of an advisory committee it may have established.

The danger is that such bank exercises can become academic and devoid of significance for bank decisions. It is also necessary to avoid diluting the staff's sense of responsibility and accountability. Nevertheless, such procedures may improve the caliber of staff work and hasten the process of improving the professional qualities of the bank's work in this area. In this way, the regulatory authorities would be exercising their responsibility to safeguard banks and the banking system without falling into the pitfalls created by mechanical and simplistic approaches.

Regulatory Supervision of Country Risk

In the mid-1970s, U.S. bank supervisiory agencies—principally the Comptroller of the Currency and the Federal Reserve—became leaders in improving country risk supervision. The Comptroller of the Currency did not have an international division until 1965 and began examining branches abroad in 1967. By 1973, however, the accounting standard of full consolidation of worldwide activities in the bank's reported balance sheet was in place.

In 1974, the Comptroller of the Currency expanded its activities in country risk. To assure greater uniformity in the judgments of bank supervisors about the acceptability of large foreign *public* sector loans, the Comptroller of the Currency set up a committee to focus on country creditworthiness. This early committee was a forerunner to the one established by all three U.S. bank supervisory agencies in 1978, at which time the Interagency Country Exposure Review Committee

(ICERC) was formed, representing the Comptroller of the Currency, Federal Reserve, and the Federal Deposit Insurance Corporation.

The approach prior to 1978 left bank examiners wide discretion in evaluating country risk which lead to inconsistent treatment of banks by different supervisors. This inconsistent treatment was most noticeable when entire country-specific classes of loans were occasionally classified as substandard according to perceptions of risk of some bank examiners, but not by others.

The new uniform U.S. supervisory approach to foreign lending has been publicized. However, the criteria employed by bank supervisors in arriving at their conclusions, particularly criteria used in assessing specific borrowers, are kept confidential.

Foreign Countries' Ratings

The specialized function of the ICERC is to rate foreign countries according to country risk. The committee makes its decision on the basis of briefing notes prepared by Federal Reserve economists. The briefing notes stem from what is indeed two types of country risk analysis:

1. A preliminary screening technique creates a priority list of countries warranting more detailed investigation. Countries are flagged as falling above or below a composite quantitative proxy of debt-servicing capacity. Quantitative formulae are used as a preliminary screening device despite acknowledged limitations of this approach.

2. A fairly conventional country analysis of the selected countries, the results of which are distilled into summary ratings of different countries according to perceived political and economic risk.

Thus, the U.S. has made country risk assessment an integral part of the bank examination process. Since the aim of the bank examination process is to double-check the decisions of bank management, supervisory authorities have built an analogous set of mechanisms to those of the commercial banks. It serves three functions: country risk assessment, country exposure measurement, and control.

Periodic supervision and auditing of the portfolio quality of individual banks are accomplished by on-site inspection of a bank's books by bank examiners and by sending a record of foreign exposure to the appropriate authorities. Bank examiners are trained to be the responsible principals in investigating a bank's business practices and have opportunities to acquire rich experience in these practices. Thus, in the special area of country risk-related activities, bank examiners play a key role in judging the adequacy of a bank's program of managing its international portfolio, according to minimum standards of diversification of assets, information-gathering, and assimilation into business decision making.

The interagency committee is composed of nine bank examiners, three each for the three U.S. bank supervisory agencies. This committee reviews assembled information on a specific country and takes a position on its creditworthiness. The committee meetings are held three times a year usually for a week. The agenda of each meeting is typically composed of a series of discussions about several specific countries, either in a routine sequence or as the committee deems appropriate. The deliberations of the committee are confidential.

Several economists from the Federal Reserve System sit in on the meetings as ex-officio members. In addition to preparing periodic country screening procedures or detailed country risk reports on specific countries on the committee's agenda, these staff economists present their evidence and recommendations at these meetings. The committee is then free to solicit other information and take testimony from others as it wishes.

Summary Ratings

It was once standard policy for bank examiners to classify as problematical all cross-border loans to specific foreign countries when these were deemed at risk. Instead, the committee attempts to grapple with and relate relative risk judgments in different countries and the ratio of a bank's exposure in a country to its reserves and capital. The result of this committee process is a summary rating of various countries to serve as a benchmark for bank examiners to consider when auditing an individual bank's capital adequacy. Banks receive special comments on examination reports when a bank's loan exposure in a country is deemed excessive in relation to the bank's capital and reserves, according to a set formula with the risk rating decided by the committee.

The bank examiner, like the banker, is the principal who must apply the results of country risk analysis to make recommendations about a bank's decision-making process and observations about the quality of its loan portfolio. The bank examiner's emphasis on country risk is viewed as a logical extension of his or her accustomed role in the valuation and classifying of loans experiencing debt-servicing difficulties. The country risk examination is only one facet of a bank examiner's responsibilities.

By focusing on the quality of a bank's loan portfolio in relation to its capital, the bank examination aims to identify banks with financial difficulties, namely those with a disproportionate amount of substandard loans. The examiner's estimate of probable default is reflected in the terminology of classification—the gradation of substandard, doubtful, and loss.

Nonperforming loans are placed on a so-called nonaccrual basis, that is, net interest earnings are no longer expected or projected as part of the bank's earnings stream. If the judgment is made that the borrower is not likely to repay the debt, then the loan is written off or charged off against existing reserves or capital. A bank's capital is available to meet its own obligations. Minor write-offs or charge-offs are not serious, but major write-offs bring the viability of the bank into question. Moreover, they hurt the financial standing of the bank as a borrower. The bank must be able to borrow at reasonable costs if it is to be a viable lender. To do so, it must have profitable earnings net of losses and indeed net of taxes.

Some developed countries have made important strides in including country-specific risk factors in bank examinations. However, some countries, like Japan, place much less emphasis on bank examinations, relying instead on uniform rules of accounting and strict enforcement of a number of capital ratios. Moreover, bank supervisory authorities in most nations do not rely as much on bank examinations as a way to exert their authority but seem to prefer more informal techniques such as moral suasion. This is due to the much greater market concentration of banking organizations in virtually all developed nations, except the U.S. The British, the West Germans, the Japanese, and the Swiss are making efforts to improve their supervision of international lending. More countries are following the U.S. example of having their banks consolidate earnings of branches, wholly owned subsidiaries, and affiliates with those of headquarters. More attention is being given to country risk assessments, and many non-U.S. banks reportedly already have elaborate systems.

International Cooperation

Impetus for cooperation among the banking supervisors of many nations arose in the wake of the financial concerns and crisis of the mid-1970s. It was recognized that the proliferation of international lending by private banks was a major innovation. Moreover, a supervisory vacuum arose from the jurisdictional cracks among the various national authorities.

To cope with these new concerns, representatives of major industrialized nations met to work out a common response. The main forum for discussing such cooperative initiatives and for exchanging information among the governors of the world's major central banks (the Group of Ten advanced industrial countries) was created in 1974. A new standing committee, called the Committee on Banking Regulations and Supervisory Practices, has convened regularly (usually three times a year) at the headquarters of the BIS in Basel, Switzerland. Since its inception, this committee of supervisors has been chaired by Peter Cooke of the Bank of England.

In response to the growing internationalization of the banking environment, the committee first had to reach an understanding of the appropriate division of responsibility between national authorities for the supervision of a bank's foreign establishments. The objective was to ensure that no foreign banking establishment escaped supervision. A general statement of the committee's views on jurisdiction was issued and endorsed by the BIS governors in December 1975. Known as the Concordat, it sets out guidelines determining which supervisory authorities are responsible for ongoing supervision of banks which operate in more than one national jurisdiction. However, the Concordat did not involve any agreement about responsibilities for provision of lender of last resort facilities to the international banking system.

One of the major guidelines places primary responsibility for the supervision of *liquidity* on the shoulders of the *host* authorities of foreign branches of banks. Another guideline delegates primary responsibility for the supervision of *solvency* of foreign branches on the supervisory authority of the *parent* country. A key agreement was reached that parent banks would be expected to support financially ailing foreign branches. However, these guidelines have not been fully implemented in most of the participating countries and do not characterize current practices, especially where impeded by bank secrecy provisions or by the ambiguities which arise from the institutional complexities of modern international banks using different entities within their overall structure.

Other areas of cooperative accomplishment for the committee include:

• Financial accounts must be consolidated on a worldwide business basis in order that parent-bank supervisors can meaningfully monitor an individual bank's cross-border risk exposure and its capital adequacy. This recommendation has been enacted into law by a growing number of nations.

• Fairly accurate data compilation at the BIS in the late 1970s on the maturity structure of the claims of banks in major industrialized nations.

• Several counries formulated procedures for assessing their banks' abilities to monitor and control country risk.

• Reasonably consistent data on country exposure and maturity transformation have begun to be collected, in spite of the wide diversity of national supervisory styles and techniques.

• In framing new policies, many countries seek possible models in the methods of other countries which has created a slow but perceptible trend toward convergence of supervisory techniques based on best practices.

• Extensive research on many subjects, such as the proper control of a bank's foreign exchange operations, proper endowment of capital requirements for opening up foreign branches, etc.

Exchange of information among a wider circle of bank supervisory representatives (whether or not of a confidential sort) was facilitated through periodic two-day meetings called International Conferences of Banking Supervisors. The first conference was under the auspices of the Bank of England in July 1979. One important purpose served by these conferences is to extend the dialogue to a wider circle of bank supervisors, particularly those representing major borrowing countries. Since these conferences are for exchanging ideas, not for decision-making purposes, their value is felt indirectly in better collaboration and rapport among supervisory staff.

Capital Adequacy

The question of capital adequacy has surfaced a number of times throughout this book. It also loomed important in these deliberations of supervisors. Concerns over capital adequacy stem from the continued secular decline in these ratios at the same time the risks are perceived to be increasing. U.S. Federal Reserve Governor Henry Wallich has taken a leading position in emphasizing concern with capital adequacy in an environment of increased risk. The *measuring* of capital adequacy may be entirely distinct from the normative *control* of capital adequacy by the bank supervisor. The gamut of control a bank supervisor might theoretically take runs from the flexible individual approach to a purely quantitative approach. The latter is merely rote application of decision rules based on what the quantitative ratios imply without any consideration of specific circumstances of each bank.

Most existing national systems of bank supervision combine these two opposite approaches. It is widely recognized that just because a bank meets specified quantitative requirements, there is no guarantee for a healthy financial picture and vice versa. Other factors are equally important for a bank examiner to assess such as the quality of management and the quality and diversification of loans.

U.S. bank regulators seem to think that the correct role for the banking supervisor is not to dictate which specific international (or domestic) loans should be undertaken. Rather it is to prevent solvency problems by ensuring the adequacy of bank safeguards against country risk.

Three topics now addressed by bank supervisors, according to Governor Wallich, are the questions of anticipating international lending problems, banks' rescheduling of country debt, and the degree to which banks prepare themselves to meet such risks by charging appropriate spreads and by building up adequate capital positions. Governor Wallich seems to advocate, as have other members of the Federal Reserve Board of Governors, like ex-Chairman Arthur Burns, that the growth of international lending should slow down. He and other governors see many developing countries at the saturation point in the amount of loans that they can service in a timely manner. However, not everyone including the author agrees with his approach or assessment of the ability of developing countries to service debt.

Conclusion

Bank supervisors must have a key role in how Western countries deal with expanding international lending. Judgments on borrowers are made by many people. It is to be expected that bank supervisors or regulators will be cautious. They should be, but this professional attitude does not make them good guides to bank activities. Bank supervisors must be careful that the failure of a developing country to manage its economy as the regulator prefers does not lead to a flunking grade.

17

Lessons for Lenders and Borrowers

This book, as noted in the preface, is not intended to describe current events, although it deals with current topics and concerns. Deeper understanding and broader perspectives were its aims. Certain lessons have been learned which if valid now are likely to be so for some years and are worth highlighting.

Status of Developing Countries

Developing countries are often plagued by social and political instability and frequently have chronic balance-of-payments deficits. Nevertheless, they will remain strong growth centers for international borrowing and lending. They will pay what the lenders will require. Despite their domestic adversities, they will try to meet the standards of different lenders, even when they conflict. The developing countries will try to honor their obligations and not lose access to these lenders. They will prefer less costly or concessional sources of funds to the extent available. From time to time, they will lose their creditworthiness and not be able to finance net inflow of resources. This condition will be temporary. Instead of importing from abroad, they will use available stocks of imported or substitute goods and services after taking measures to reduce external payments by monetary, fiscal, and exchange rate policies, exchange controls, or trade restrictions.

Destocking is a way to achieve an increment to the flow of goods from current production and to offset reductions in imports. In developing countries, however, such stocks of real goods like stocks of foreign exchange called monetary reserves are usually small and soon exhausted. The real economy again needs more from abroad. If external finance is not available, domestic production and consumption fall. But there is very little margin for such falls. The consequences are social disturbances, economic disruption, and often political instability. The world political system, as well as the world's economic system, is shaken by these events.

Under such conditions, expansion in international capital flows to developing countries becomes inevitable. Borrowing countries and lending countries know that such capital flows must take place. What is not inevitable are the particular investors and lenders participating in this activity at any time. The broad categories of sources of funds—equity, grants, and loans—can be divided by types of lenders: governments, multilateral institutions, export finance, commercial banks, and capital markets. Instruments like bank loans, bonds, letters of credit, etc., are also available. Sources of finance can be divided geographically among regions or nations, by maturities, by purposes, or even by character of borrowers. It is possible that official assistance will expand in the years ahead in relation to private credits, but this would reverse a trend of many years.

Many combinations of lenders can occur. However, somewhere in the maze of possible combinations is the answer to having enough external financing to keep the developing countries and the world political and economic structure functioning. The answer may be a combination of various sources, but the answer cannot be that there is no answer.

It is this conviction which forms my rule of external financing for developing countries: It will be found. A subsidiary rule is that it will *not* be found mostly in equity or grants but rather in borrowed funds. Whether official or private, external debts will rise over the decades, if not over the generations.

External Debt

The composition of external debt may alter drastically. Major changes can and do take place in the relative proportions of bilateral official aid, multilateral development banks (official capital but private borrowed funds to finance loans), commercial banks, export credit agencies, IMF, and bond markets. All create debts. The loans vary in interest rates charged, grace periods, and maturities. But until and unless forgiven, they create external debts.

The pace of increase in debts is affected by prevailing interest rates, willingness of governments to provide concessional terms, size of balance-of-payments deficits, ease of access of borrowers to credit and capital markets, rescheduling techniques or refinancing, forgiveness of debts by creditor governments, maturity practices, and regulations in borrowing and creditor countries. Such factors can significantly alter debt-servicing schedules and can accelerate or dampen the rate of growth of external debts. But they rarely cause national debt levels to decline, even though individual credits are constantly being repaid.

Rescheduling or Moratoria

External debts to private and official lenders will rise. If prompt and full servicing of debts becomes severe, the borrower will ask for relief—be it rescheduling of terms or new money. If the debts are mostly to governments, the requests will be placed before governments. The Paris Club has been the principal instrument for government rescheduling. Multilateral agencies can help with information and money. It has usually been this way in the past; it could be otherwise in the future. However, some multilateral presence is likely to be involved, and more rather than fewer institutions are likely to be involved.

If private banks are the largest creditors in any particular country case, rescheduling with them will be of major importance. In these cases, the alternatives will be narrower because commercial banks do not have as broad policy options as do governments. As international lending continues, reschedulings can be expected to become commonplace.

There will be fear of repudiations or defaults by borrowers. Although politically embarrassing and financially suicidal, repudiations or defaults should not be ruled out as impossible, however unlikely as a general practice. This is quite different from creditors declaring moratoria. One form of foreign assistance is to forgive debts owed to the creditor government or official entities or short of this to declare moratoria. The creditor government has ready access to domestic sources of finance to substitute for repayments by the debtor country in the creditors' currencies. Such actions are likely to be exceptional, unless a world economic crisis is prolonged for many years.

Moratoria or indefinite delays in debt servicing on private bank loans would be different indeed. Full moratoria are costly for commercial banks; restructuring is less costly and less damaging. Restructuring can be an acceptable substitute to the borrowing country, even if it sounds as though it is heading for a declaration of moratorium. Even moratoria would not stop external debt from rising, although it could reduce the debt-servicing obligations in the short or medium term.

Debt forgiveness can take many forms, including multilateral refinancing of bilateral debt. The critical aspect is who is the debtor. If the former debtor is replaced or the level of past debt reduced, the debts decline. The process of debt creation can be temporarily halted or reduced, and debt servicing of old debt presumably reduced. Even in such cases, the needs of developing countries will soon recreate relatively large-scale borrowing, significant debt-servicing obligations, and large external debt.

Borrowing Continues

From this perspective, the issue of borrowing from private or official sources is seen as a choice of one or another or both, with nonborrowing not a true option. Thus, we can expect that when one group of lenders believes it cannot respond to the loan requests from developing countries, it will urge the other groups to expand and vice versa. Warnings of too much lending by commercial banks will be intermingled with requests for increased lending because official sources of finance are not adequate. Similarly, private banks will urge more bilateral and multilateral financing, when they wish to hold back in their lending activities.

All lenders will urge borrowing countries to pursue policies which increase confidence in these countries. Commercial banks are pleased to have official endorsements, particularly from the IMF. Fundamentally, lenders like to lend. They want to fulfill their own lending criteria and standards. But these criteria are designed to avoid poor loans not avoid lending. Lenders will seek to reconcile the objectives of lending with the objectives of security: Guarantees, co-financing, collateral, country limits, and maturity mixes will be used. The positions of individual lenders will change, but total lending to developing countries will increase. Individual borrowing countries will find limitations on their ability to borrow, but all of them will be under pressure to create country or economic conditions demanded by lenders. To the extent that official financing is available, standards will be set by political or governmental norms; to the extent that private financing is sought, the standards will be as formulated and applied in a highly competitive market in an environment of chronic uncertainty and risk by private, commercial entities.

With experience, lenders and borrowers are learning how to reschedule and refinance more efficiently. Precedents and experience, organization, procedures, fact-finding, and financial terms help make quicker starts and shorter negotiating periods. Issues like desirable lengths of maturity stretch outs remain to be discussed. Generalized resolutions are not essential, particularly if restructuring is on a country-by-country basis.

Mechanisms have been formed within lending institutions to deal with reschedulings, which benefit from the experienced people in the major banks who have learned to collaborate with each other in these matters. Borrowing countries are also learning and using talent both within and without their countries for such purposes. Ease of action, as well as frequency, will reinforce the tendency for rescheduling or restructuring to become nearly commonplace and ordinary. The most publicized cases occur when very large borrowers are involved, like Mexico or Brazil, but the lessons learned in smaller cases are equally applicable.

Suggestions for Lenders on Renegotiations

1. Do not assume you know how much external debt is owed by entities individually or combined in any one country.

2. Do not assume that countries with relatively low debt-service ratios have less difficulties in servicing and rescheduling their external debt.

3. Try to obtain the cooperation of the central bank in the borrowing country in the rescheduling exercise.

4. Do not assume that relatively large external debt will cause other lenders to lend additional sums in case of a rescheduling when country risk conditions continue to be unfavorable, or that substantial official sources of financing will be available to facilitate debt servicing to private banks. Where official sources are available, private creditors expect to be asked at least not to reduce their exposures in the borrowing country.

5. Do not assume official assistance from national or multinational sources will be available in sufficiently large magnitudes to cope with the needs of the country being rescheduled if private bank lending stops. Be prepared for requests to increase exposure.

6. Be prepared to participate in debt renegotiations with sufficient expertise to defend your interests.

7. Avoid statements to borrowers or public which imply willingness or ability to assist borrowers in ways not compatible with needs and interests of your lending institution—a private bank is not an aid institution.

8. Do not expect to engage in debt renegotiations without agreeing to a lengthening of maturities of some or all outstanding exposure and changing the profile of interest payments. Assume important changes will emerge in your asset portfolio.

9. Distinguish clearly between renegotiation of exposure and extension of new incremental lending. New lending should meet country risk criteria of your lending institution.

10. Distinguish between countries that are eager to reestablish their country creditworthiness in ways which create confidence among private lenders and countries which cannot or will not do so, whatever the reason.

11. Indicate what conditions you regard as necessary for resumption of new incremental lending before any debt renegotiation or restructuring becomes final.

12. Commercial banks should not expect to be treated like official creditors in debt restructuring, but the differences need not be to their detriment.

13. Commercial banks should be prepared to act cooperatively and collectively with other commercial bank creditors to protect their interests as lenders.

14. Commercial banks should not expect official multilateral institutions to subordinate their preferred creditor status to the commercial banks.

15. Delays in servicing need not result in formal declarations of default. Other ways are available to protect the interests of lenders.

16. Declarations of default should be regarded as extraordinary and treated as exceptional on a one-by-one basis. Declarations of defaults and consequent defensive actions are ultimate measures not to be ruled out but not seen as likely ways to deal with external payments difficulties.

17. Debt renegotiations and restructuring entail costs to lenders and borrowers. They are not a soft option for lenders or borrowers. Their widespread use can weaken substantially the process and mechanism of international lending, even if they help cope with immediate problems. There is the danger, as experience grows in debt renegotiation and rescheduling, that the ease with which they can be used will encourage quick and unwarranted recourse. Private lenders should question in any case whether other preferable ways can deal with the existing difficulties.

Suggestions for Borrowers

1. The external debt of a country is a contractual obligation like other contractural obligations requiring payment in foreign exchange. This obligation is not unique to credit operations. Countries can lose their international creditworthiness by failure to honor their obligations for payments on goods and nonbank services, as well as bank credits and loans.

2. The servicing of external debt is, nevertheless, unique because credit provides

payments for other goods and services, as well as for the debt itself. Failure to service debt fully and promptly tends to have broader, more rapid cumulative effects than failure to meet other obligations.

3. Debtor countries which lose their country creditworthiness should seek to restore their former position as soon as possible. Short-term gains in reducing obligations to service debt by renegotiations should be weighed against longer term costs in availability and pricing of future credits and loans.

4. Frequently, debtor countries appear to be in a strategically advantageous position. The lender seemingly has more to lose than the debtor with relatively small assets to seize by creditors. Debtors may be tempted to threaten repudiation or default. This view can obscure the fundamental need of debtor countries to borrow in the future. Only the rare country which will not require future borrowing is in a strong bargaining position.

5. Debtor countries should seek the most possible improvement in their external debt profiles compatible with maintaining relations needed to service new lending and borrowing. This will probably be found more in lengthening maturities and granting grace periods than in reducing interest costs on loans being renegotiated. Interest rates are likely to be market determined, while spreads are likely to rise with restructuring.

6. Debtors need to be mindful of the conditions under which international lending is conducted and not assume that their actions will not affect future availability of funds for themselves or other borrowing countries. Debtors have an interest in strengthening confidence levels in international lending to all developing countries.

Country Risk

Country risk analysis and management systems are now a recognized need in international banking. To the lending banks, the need to know countries becomes increasingly evident, and the desired knowledge and experience are difficult to acquire. Only a few lending institutions can be satisfied with their preparation for dealing in a global world economy. Lenders would like to apply country knowledge effectively to business decisions, and are moving in many quarters to improve their country assessments. The process, however, is time-consuming. Short-cuts provided by outsiders are at best partially informative and do not provide nearly enough to guide a business decision. Banks are in danger of making major mistakes if they do not recognize this. Moreover, outside groups like the IMF simply do not have the knowledge and experience in commercial bank lending. They can, however, contribute a great deal.

There is much common ground in country evaluations. Institutions like the U.S. departments of state, treasury, and commerce; the Federal Reserve and its counterpart in other countries; and international institutions like the IMF, the World Bank, Inter-American Development Bank, Asian Development Bank, BIS, and United

Nations organizations all can provide very useful country information and are eager to do so. They all publish valuable material.

Therefore, ignorance of countries is inexcusable. More information is available than can be absorbed. The missing links are between general and specific information needed for business decisions and the experience to apply this knowledge to the business decisions of lenders. The needs are not the same, even for the same categories of lenders.

However, lending will go on. But it continues without the confidence banks need to exploit more opportunities which adequate knowledge would render acceptable. The development of highly professional country risk management systems would be a major contribution to achieving more certainty and stability in our present highly uncertain and unstable world economy.

In the meantime, I would offer the following canons to guide international lending and borrowing by commercial banks.

Canons for Borrowers

1. Borrow from private banks only for productive purposes. Create capability to judge this process.

2. Maximize the use of borrowings from private banks for export-oriented activities.

3. Assume from the outset of borrowing that future servicing schedules need to be met promptly and fully.

4. Assume that international payment requirements, including servicing of external debt, need continuous access to foreign private credit markets and therefore the criteria of creditworthiness of private banks must be met.

5. Do not borrow from private banks unless there is a reasonable degree of confidence that good economic management is likely to prevail.

6. Try to build monetary reserves. Avoid substantial use of available monetary reserves. Where necessary and available, draw on other official sources like the IMF to finance general balance-of-payments needs.

7. Avoid large-scale accumulation of private bank debt unless basic development strategy is to expand the economy efficiently through modernization and expansion of agriculture and industry led by growth and diversification of exports. Assume that the economy and exports must grow at least as rapidly as the debt-servicing obligation and, in the longer run, grow more rapidly.

8. Avoid unmanageable balance of payments, external debt, and rising levels of domestic savings with correspondingly high levels of productive investment.

9. Do not regard borrowings from private banks as a substitute for domestic savings. Instead, recognize that external borrowings for new investment frequently require increased domestic savings to offset the inflationary impact of higher levels of investment.

10. Create technical capability, policy autonomy, and management continuity in the monetary authority to manage effectively balance of payments and to help integrate fiscal, exchange rate, and other government policies with domestic monetary and balance-of-payments policies and behavior. Among other things, keep informed of changes in external debt.

11. Use balance-of-payments support from the international community as a mechanism to strengthen domestic economic management as well as a source of financing. Be prepared to meet criteria for such support.

12. Recognize that creditworthiness for borrowing from private banks will result from confidence in the country's economic management rather than availability of external assistance. This external support can be an important factor in achieving or maintaining creditworthiness, if obtained within the framework of economic programs and policies which give confidence to external lenders that adjustments to adverse developments will be done in a way which enables the country to maintain its elements of economic strength.

13. Borrowers will be more creditworthy if they are perceived as not requiring outside discipline to ensure good economic management. Reinforcement of domestic disciplinary devices are needed when doubts already exist about a country's creditworthiness.

14. Insist that lending banks know their countries and expect to supply private banks with data needed to make correct evaluations of countries.

15. Use windfalls in earnings to strengthen international monetary reserves and to repurchase loans from the IMF.

16. Do not expect to be able to eliminate current account deficits in the balance of payments in the foreseeable future and avoid commitments to do so. Consequently, ensuring access to external financing is a must for orderly development. Defaults and repudiations are not true alternatives for a country.

17. Make efforts to expand sources of private finance, including access to external capital markets.

18. Do not expect private lenders to be eager lenders during balance-of-payments difficulties or domestic distress or to continue lending after a country has lost its external country creditworthiness.

19. Seek opportunities to improve your debt profiles by new borrowings on more favorable terms to repay existing debt, when conditions permit.

20. In debt renegotiations, do not primarily aim for the longest stretch outs and grace periods with reductions in interest costs. Aim to achieve the quickest possible reestablishment of creditworthiness. This will make possible optimum refinancing of old debt as well as the largest possible net inflow of new funds.

21. Expect balance-of-payments difficulties and repeated sharp questioning of country creditworthiness. Be prepared to defend creditworthiness during such periods by strategic thinking and planning. Do not wait for the surprises to create a crisis.

Canons for Lenders

1. Do not expect developing countries to be in balance-of-payments surplus on current accounts; assume that current account deficits are normal for such countries.

2. Do not view developing countries as a homogeneous group for business decision-making purposes. Recognize their differences and judge the risks on a country-by-country basis.

3. Do not view any single developing country as a homogeneous entity within itself. Disaggregate the country into its major sectors and components to judge country risk.

4. Evaluate most carefully the creditworthiness of the individual borrower—be it a private or official entity. Apply the means and purpose tests to official entities.

5. Avoid lending to developing countries that do not meet your tests of acceptable country risk, irrespective of potential earnings. Avoid new lending to developing countries whose potential for maintaining their creditworthiness looks unfavorable.

6. Pay special attention to the actuarial principle both in subdividing global programs by countries and in lending in any one developing country for any particular purpose or to any one entity or with respect to maturities and currencies.

7. Give special attention to management of domestic economy and the balance of payments, including external debt management, in judging the country's creditworthiness. Regard domestic growth, modernization of agriculture and industry, institutional capability to encourage and allocate available savings efficiently, and export performance in diversification and expansion as primary indicators.

8. Do not be guided by only a few quantitative indicators. Rely on in-depth knowledge of the country, preferably based on firsthand experience. Be aware of the danger of applying generalizations and approaches derived from different societies and economies to judging specific countries.

9. Do not forget that past measures of ability to use capital efficiently, as well as need for capital, have become anachronistic. Do not assume that the historical experience of a country foretells its future.

10. Private banks must be regarded by borrower and lender as the most cautious sources of international credits. Continued reliance on bank sources can only be assumed if countries manage their economies so they command the confidence of private international banks.

11. Do not judge a foreign private bank by the actions of governmental institutions, whether national, regional, or multinational. The presence of official bodies can reduce country risk, but the judgments of such entities cannot substitute for a U.S. bank's own judgments on country creditworthiness.

12. Private banks should not lend based on the assumption of renegotiation and rescheduling as a way out of future difficulties. Private bank lenders should not

assume the existence of a lender of last resort. A bank's income, profitability, capital, and reserves are its financial defenses.

13. Defend against adverse developments by heeding early warnings.

14. Remember that the international environment must be continuously monitored to assess impact on borrowing countries.

15. A good credit to an individual borrower may be transformed into a bad credit by adverse economic, social, and political developments within a country subsequent to the original credit decision. Thus, countries must be continuously monitored to assess the impact of actual and potential country developments on a bank's portfolio of loans outstanding, as well as loans in prospect.

16. The size of a developing country's outstanding debt, the size of its GNP, its GNP per capita, or its natural resources do not determine its creditworthiness. Rather, dynamic criteria like rates of growth and progress in diversification and modernization of output, domestic savings, and exports are more indecisive.

17. Private bank lending should be for productive purposes directly or to governments that demonstrate management capability and pursue policies that cause domestic savings and foreign inflows of capital to go sufficiently into productive purposes.

18. Lending abroad on a nonguaranteed basis cannot be without risk. Potential country risk must be scrutinized and evaluated. Banks cannot avoid the full responsibility for their decisions on countries. Officers within a bank must take the full responsibility for their country judgments and be held strictly accountable without ambiguity.

19. Avoid simplistic modeling of countries to anticipate or judge country risks.

20. Banks should not impose policy conditions relating to government economic management as part of loan contracts. However, banks should judge economic performance and outlook carefully before making loan commitments. These judgments should be made known confidentially to the borrowing country, if requested, and should be vital in the bank's business decisions.

21. Banks should not make significant investments in countries without an adequate knowledge of the country obtained directly by its own efforts or indirectly by its business relations with other banks and entities.

22. Mechanisms used to set country ceilings (if any), implement ceilings, report exposure, evaluate countries, and assess country risk must be tailormade to suit the individual bank. The components in deciding content of particular country assessment and country risk management processes include:

- Quality of existing portfolio, including profitability, diversification, and vulnerability.
- Degree of management comfort and support for international lending.
- Strategic view of long-run activities of the bank in lending and funding.

- Size of operations abroad.
- Geographical spread.
- Business-segment spread.
- International management style: degree of decentralization and delegation of authority.
- Extent and kind of physical presence abroad—branches, subsidiaries, consortia, representative offices, visits, etc.
- Professional capability in evaluating countries and international development.
- Head office management style.
- Access to sources of information.
- Relations with other banks.
- Bank's computerization and automation.
- Relations with board of directors and regulatory authorities.
- Concerns with market standing and rating agencies.
- Significance of international earnings.
- Capital availability.

23. Be willing to renegotiate external debt in conjunction with other private lenders on longer maturities and grace periods if borrowing countries are making promising efforts to improve economic management.

24. Monitor carefully external debt and debt servicing of borrowing countries. Do not assume that all private creditors are treated alike.

25. Be neither an optimist nor a pessimist. Be informed; know your country; know what to expect. Wear neither rosy nor dark glasses. Be prepared for surprises and to react to defend against adversity. Take advantage of favorable opportunities; do not leave such deliberations to actual time of surprise.

Conclusion

In the last analysis, what is a good loan for the borrower in the developing country is also a good loan for a private lender to such countries. If this principle is not understood or applied, borrower and lender are headed for trouble. However, it would be wrong to conclude that loans to a country, which are warranted in terms of acceptable total exposure will be desirable from the viewpoint of the borrower. The borrowing country is in the best position to ensure the productive use of externally borrowed funds. The lending institution cannot be expected to exercise the same degree of care and surveillance. The lending institution focuses more on the individual credit. Whether the country would better serve its interest by other use of such increased external debt is not likely to figure strongly in the bank's judgment. The bank, however, should make every effort to ascertain whether the country is so managed as to give reasonable assurance that its total foreign borrowing is well used. The careful use of externally borrowed funds is an essential prerequisite for the longer term viability of a borrowing country.

Appendix A
Glossary*

Accrued interest receivable (balance-sheet item). Interest earned by the bank on its claims against third parties which remains uncollected due to administrative and other reasons.

Advances (a balance-sheet item). Short-term loan—maturity less than one year.

Advised line of credit (off-balance-sheet item). Credit facility confirmed in writing as to the terms and conditions under which the bank is prepared to grant credit. These facilities are normally of three types:

1. *Good until cancelled*—wherein the bank may terminate the line of credit at will, and prior to such termination the beneficiary may draw at will.
2. *Annual review*—wherein the line of credit terminates one year from date of confirmation, during which period the beneficiary may draw at will.
3. *As offered*—wherein the bank must be consulted prior to each drawing.

Annual review (off-balance-sheet item). See **advised line of credit**.

Arranged overdraft (balance-sheet item). A debit balance in the client's account arranged by the banker at the request of the client. It is a common European method of short-term lending comparable to a line of credit.

As offered (off-balance-sheet item). See **advised line of credit**.

Assets. Anything owned by a bank which has commercial or exchange value. Assets usually consist of specific property or claims against others.

Bankers' acceptance (balance-sheet item). A time bill of exchange (frequently called a time draft) drawn on and accepted by a banking institution. By accepting the draft, the bank signifies its commitment to pay the face amount at maturity to anyone who presents it for payment at that time. In this way, the bank provides its name and credit and enables its customer, who pays a commission to the accepting bank for this accommodation, to readily secure financing. When a bankers' acceptance is discounted, the discounting bank acquires a debt investment (a claim against a third party) which appears on the balance sheet. Such acceptance can subsequently be sold to another bank or investor, although the accepting bank continues to guarantee payment on maturity.

*This glossary was originally published by the Association of Reserve City Bankers (ARCB) in *Country Exposure Measurement and Reporting Practices of Member Banks*, March 1977.

Bareboat charter (transfer of country exposure). See **shipping guarantees.**

Bills discounted (balance-sheet item). Written debt instruments evidencing the obligation of one party (the drawer) to pay another a certain sum of money at a given time (transfer of country exposure). Refers to written debt instruments drawn on a payor (the borrower) by a third party (the drawer) who in turn discounts the draft with a bank. The bank may discount the draft either with or without recourse to the drawer. When there is full and unconditional recourse to a drawer who is a resident of a country other than that of the payor (the ultimate obligor), country exposure is generally transferred from the country of the payor to the country of the drawer.

Cash (balance-sheet item). This definition is restricted to "cash on hand" and noninterest-bearing deposits held by nonaffiliated banks. More frequently, cash held by nonaffiliated banks is considered to be exposure to the country where such banks are domiciled. For the most part, given the nominal amounts, cash on hand is only infrequently tabulated as country exposure.

Casual overdraft (balance-sheet item). A debit balance in a client's account. An overdraft is created when checks, drafts, money transfers, or other transactions are drawn or charged against demand deposit accounts in excess of the available balance in the account. Such an overdraft is not by prearrangement.

Charter party and charter party assignment (transfer of country exposure). See **shipping guarantees.**

Collateralized loan (transfer of country exposure). A loan granted to a customer upon the pledge of (1) liquid assets such as registered shares of stock, bonds or (2) illiquid assets (mortgage on a building, etc.). If the borrower is unable to repay the loan, the lender can then sell the security to satisfy the claim. Generally, when liquid collateral is offered a bank, country exposure is often transferred from the country of the obligor to the country where the liquid collateral is held, provided the latter is denominated in the same currency as the loan.

Comfort letter (transfer of country exposure). A written instrument issued by a third party whereby that party agrees to make every effort to assure the maker's compliance with the terms of a contract in the event the maker is unable to fulfill the obligation thereunder, but by which instrument that party is not itself obligated to perform. For the most part, ARCB banks do *not* transfer exposure from the country of the obligor to the country of the issuer of the comfort letter in part due to the uncertain legal status of such instruments.

Confiscation. Seizure of private property by a government without any compensation to the owner. Also, a seizure of assets without *fair* compensation.

Contingent liabilities (off-balance-sheet item). The term applies to the obligations of a bank when acting as a guarantor or accommodation endorser of a negotiable instrument. The guarantor or endorser has no benefit from the negotiable instrument involved but is required by law to make good the payment of the instrument if the maker defaults. The actual liability exists *with* the maker of the note (the borrower). The contingent liability exists for the duration of the instrument and is passed to the guarantor as a primary liability only if the borrower dishonors the instrument on presentation and request for payment. Once the guaranteeing bank meets the liability involved, it then has a claim (asset) against the borrower.

Because there is the potential for an actual claim to arise from a contingent liability, ARCB banks include all contingent liabilities issued on behalf of foreign customers as exposure to the domicile of the customer—unless the transaction is fully and unconditionally counter-guaranteed by an external obligor in which case exposure is allocated to the country of the counter-guarantor. In addition, "contingent liabilities" includes legal commitments to extend credit, forward exchange contracts, and guarantees whether or not reflected in the financial statements of the bank.

Contract of affreightment (transfer of country exposure). See **shipping guarantees.**

Country exposure. A term of measurement which refers to the volume of assets held and off-balance-sheet items considered to be subject to the "country risk" of a given country. In practice, one important aspect of this measurement is based on identifying the country of domicile of the entity ultimately responsible for the credit risk of a particular transaction.

Country risk. Refers to a spectrum of risks arising from the economic, social, and political environments of a given foreign country (including government policies framed in response to trends in these environments) having potential favorable or adverse consequences for foreigners' debt or equity investments in that country.

Events which may adversely affect profitability or recovery of equity investments in a given foreign country include:

- Confiscation.
- Nationalization.
- Branching limitations.
- Restrictions on earnings remittances.
- Higher local taxes levied on earnings.
- Market conditions (deflation).
- Devaluation.

Events which affect profitability of debt investments in a given foreign country include:

- Withholding and other special taxes which have an impact on existing outstandings.
- Interest rate control.
- Government-imposed delays on the liquidation of private or public sector external obligations.

Events which often affect potential recovery of debt investments include:

- Certain types of foreign exchange controls including government-imposed restrictions on the liquidation of public or private sector external obligations.
- Domestic policies often imposed in a sudden, unpredictable manner which affect client's ability to generate the necessary cash flow to repay loans. Examples are fiscal policy (increase in taxes), restrictive monetary policy, and price controls.

The above types of country risk are incurred as a result of activities undertaken in a foreign country and are distinct from considerations relating to a given borrower's creditworthiness. In varying degrees, the above examples of events can affect both local and foreign currency investments.

In this context, the term "investments" is often used synonymously with exposure.

Cross-border exposure. Exists when any subsidiary or branch of the holding company/bank, irrespective of location, lends to, invests in, places with, or otherwise extends any form of credit or credit commitment to any entity that is *located outside* the booking unit's national borders, irrespective of currency.

Deflation. Reduction in the level of economic activity in an economy. Deflation results in lower levels of national income, employment, and imports and lower rates of increase of wages and prices. It may be brought about by monetary policies, such as increases in rates of interest and contraction of the money supply or by fiscal policies, such as increases in taxation (direct and indirect) or reductions in government expenditure.

Devaluation. Reduction of the official rate at which one currency is exchanged for another.

Exchange controls (off-balance-sheet item). Any regulation or action taken by a government or authorized government agency which restricts the free flow of domestic or foreign currency into or out of its country. During recent years, such regulations have taken many forms.

Blocked exchange—exists when importers and others (borrowers) desiring to make payments abroad are prohibited from doing so by their government. That is, they are blocked from purchasing required foreign currencies. Under such conditions, deposits in local currency are sometimes made to cover the prospective remittances, but foreign creditors must wait until the block is removed or they find some way of using the local currency credited to them.

Multiple currency system—involves the establishment by law of different exchange values for the national currency, the applicable value in any exchange transaction depending on the type of commodity or service purchased abroad for which exchange is desired.

Rationing foreign exchange—a means of controlling foreign exchange by requiring that all holders of bills of exchange relinquish them to the government in return for domestic currency at a stipulated legal rate. All importers must apply for bills of exchange to the government. The government then allocates such exchange to importers or other claimants (those with external debt commitments) whose activities it wishes to encourage and denies it to others whose activities are considered less essential or perhaps harmful to the government's plan for foreign trade equilibrium.

Expropriation. Governmental seizure of assets owned by a foreign entity, with or without compensation.

Federal funds sold (balance-sheet-item). Amount due a bank for all transactions involving the disposal of immediately available funds, enabling other U.S. domestic commercial banks, *including U.S. branches of foreign banks,* to maintain their reserve requirements at the Federal Reserve.

Fiduciary accounts (off-balance-sheet item). Relationship between two or more parties whereby one party, such as a bank, gives advice, manages, controls, or holds in safekeeping assets, including foreign assets, owned by another.

Finance lease (balance-sheet item). See **lease.**

Fiscal policy. That part of government policy which is concerned with raising revenue through taxation and other means and deciding on the level and pattern of budgetary surpluses or deficits (and their means of financing) that the government can control the level of demand in the economy.

Fixed assets (balance-sheet item). Those assets of a permanent nature required for the normal conduct of a business and which will not normally be converted into cash during the ensuing fiscal period.

Foreign currency exposure. A term of measurement which refers to the volume of assets and other nonbalance-sheet items that are deemed to be subject to the country risk of a given country and denominated in a currency other than the currency of the country.

Forward exchange contracts (off-balance-sheet item). Example of a contingent liability, that is, a contract calling for delivery at a future date of a specified amount of one currency with the exchange rate fixed at the time the contract is made.

Good until cancelled (off-balance-sheet item). See **advised line of credit.**

Guarantee (transfer of country exposure). Written promise by one party, the guarantor, to be liable for the debt of another party, the principal debtor, should the latter be unable to meet the obligation. A guarantor can be resident of the same country as the debtor or can reside in a different country and is then often referred to as an external guarantor. In the latter case, the ARCB member banks almost unanimously transfer country exposure from the country of the debtor to the country of the guarantor where "hard," that is, "full and unconditional" guarantees are involved covering the bank against all risks—commercial and political.

Less frequently, the ARCB member banks also transfer country exposure from the country of the debtor to the country of the guarantor where certain types of "soft" guarantees are involved, e.g., keepwell arrangements. The term soft guarantee is generally applied to comfort letters—letters of assurance, awareness, indemnity, keepwell agreements, etc.

Guidance line of credit (off-balance-sheet item). Credit facility used to facilitate extension of credit to a given entity, the existence of which facility and its terms and conditions are not formally advised to that entity.

Indigenization. Any action by a government agency which forces the transfer of controlling interest in an entity located within that government's country from foreign to private domestic interests or individuals.

Intrabank transactions. Refers to asset acquisitions that take place within a holding company/bank, its branches, subsidiaries, and affiliates which are eliminated in consolidated financial statements.

Intracountry foreign currency exposure. Exists when any subsidiary or branch of the holding company/bank lends to, invests in, places with, or otherwise extends any form of credit or credit commitment to entities (including any holding company/other bank entity) that are located within the same country as the booking unit, but in a currency foreign to the country where the obligor and the booking unit are located.

Items in the process of collection (balance-sheet item). Payee's means of receiving payment wherein a check or clean draft is presented to a bank and settlement is completed only when payment in full is received by said bank.

Keepwell (transfer of country exposure). One of the stronger types of comfort letters whereby a provision is made by a parent of a borrowing subsidiary in which the parent specifies that its subsidiary will conform to certain requirements. Generally, these requirements are stated in financial terms. Although there are numerous potential requirements, some examples are that the subsidiary will:

- Maintain a minimum working capital or current ratio.
- Maintain a minimum net worth.
- Restrict the amount of capital expenditures.
- Not increase the current dividend rate nor increase it by some stated amount.

In addition, the parent may further provide assurance of ongoing interest in the subsidiary by incorporating the maintenance of a certain percentage of ownership of the credit taker or undertake to maintain the credit taker in a financial condition which would allow it to honor its debt.

A keepwell should be distinguished from a letter of assurance which is less specific than a keepwell and normally only acknowledges that a loan has been made to a subsidiary. The parent "assures" that its subsidiary's financial condition will meet the standards of the parent.

Letters of assurance are not legally binding on the issuer, whereby keepwell, depending on the wording, may be binding on the parent. According to many ARCB members, a strong keepwell may be justification to transfer exposure from the country of the borrower to the country of the issuer.

Lease (balance-sheet item). Contract by which one (a bank) conveys the use of property for a period of time for a specified rent. There are two types of leases:

1. *Finance lease.* A sales and financial term designating a lease which is recognized in law as providing the lessor with full ownership rights in the underlying asset but that for *tax purposes* is treated as if the lessee were "owner." In a finance lease, the lessee pays to the lessor over the term of the lease, a stream of payments that cover the full cost of the asset, the cost of administering and financing the asset, and a return on investment.
2. *Operating lease.* A lease in which the lessor provides specific services such as insurance or maintenance. The contract terms usually do not guarantee the lessor full recovery of the cost of the asset, the cost of administering and financing the asset, and a return on the investment. In such cases, the lessor assumes the economic risk of ownership.

Legal commitment to lend (off-balance-sheet item). Contractural agreement which is legally binding on both lender and borrower defining terms and conditions of a loan.

Letter of credit (off-balance-sheet item). Contingent liability, that is, a written instrument issued by a bank whereby the bank substitutes its more widely known credit for that of the lesser-known credit of a buyer, addressed to a seller (beneficiary), authorizing an individual or firm to draw drafts on the bank or one of its correspondents for its account under certain conditions stipulated in the credit.

- Sight letter of credit calls for drafts payable on presentation to the drawee at sight.
- Standby letter of credit against which the beneficiary can draw only if another business transaction is not completed. In other words, when a promissory note is given, sometimes a letter of credit is issued to back up the note; the credit will only be used if the maker of the promissory note defaults.

Line of credit (off-balance-sheet item). Arbitrary decision made by a bank regarding the maximum amount of credit which may be extended to a customer under an uncommitted facility, advised or unadvised. See **advised line of credit.**

Loan (balance-sheet item). Refer to **advances, arranged overdraft, casual overdraft, federal funds sold, loans to consortium banks, loans to multilateral agencies,** and **term loan.**

Loans to consortium banks (balance-sheet item). Consortium bank is generally established in an international money center as a financial multiproduct institution owned by two or more parents. Ownership in such banks generally is for the specific purpose of participating in cross-border Eurocurrency financings. To leverage their sales force, the parents are usually from different countries. ARCB banks assign exposure emanating from their loans to consortium banks to the domicile of the bank rather than that of its parents.

Loans to multilateral agencies (balance-sheet item). Multilateral agencies are supranational organizations such as the World Bank, International Monetary Fund, Bank for International Settlements, Comecon, Inter-American Development Bank, etc. For the most part, exposure to multilateral agencies is monitored separately by the ARCB banks and is not allocated to any specific country.

Local currency exposure. Refers to the level of assets and other nonbalance-sheet items that are deemed to be subject to the country risk of a given country and are denominated in the local currency of that country. Eurocurrency assets are often not included in the measurement of local currency exposure, even when the currency in question is the Euroversion of the local currency.

Marketable securities—trading account (balance-sheet item). Securities held by an institution as inventory for business of trading, that is, maintaining a secondary market, in such securities. These instruments may represent claims against public or private sector issuers.

Minimum risk assets (balance-sheet item). Cash or assets whose conversion to cash at a future date is virtually assured and on which the probability of loss is virtually zero.

Monetary policy. That part of economic policy which regulates the level of money or liquidity in the economy in order to achieve some desired policy objective, such as control of inflation, improvement in balance of payments, a certain level of employment, or growth in the gross national product. It contrasts with more direct measures of control.

Money market transactions (balance-sheet item). Refers to the purchase of foreign or domestic bills in a given country where the interest rate on such instruments is closely tied to prevailing, well-publicized day-to-day domestic and international market rates.

Nationalization. Ownership and operation by the central government of some enterprise previously a private or local government undertaking. Also, the act of taking over assets owned by either local or foreign entities or individuals, with compensation.

Operating lease (balance-sheet item). See **lease.**

Performance bond (off-balance-sheet item). Contingent liability—a written instrument which substitutes a strong financial risk (usually of a bank, insurance, or bonding company) for a lesser-known risk. It warranties compensation for nonperformance in accordance with certain conditions stipulated in the bond.

Placement (balance-sheet item). Interbank interest-bearing time deposit.

Price control. Fixing prices by government statute to prevent price rises in an inflationary situation.

Redeposit (balance-sheet item). See **placement.**

Risk assets (balance-sheet item). All assets of a bank except cash and minimum risk items.

Shipping guarantees (transfer of country exposure).

- *Charter party.* Agreement by which a shipowner agrees to place an entire ship, or part of it, at the disposal of a merchant or other person, for the conveyance of goods, binding them to a particular place, for a sum of money which the merchant undertakes to pay as freight for their carriage. Charters are either time, affreightment, or demise (bareboat).
- *Charter party assignment.* Contractual arrangement whereby the contract existing between the shipowner and charterer (specifically, the rents payable) is assigned to a bank as security for its loan to a shipowner. In theory, the bank actually takes possession of the rents that are due the shipowner from the charterer. These amounts are paid by the charterer directly to the bank to reduce the shipowner's loan. The ARCB member banks use three basic treatments in dealing with loans to shipowners collateralized by charter party assignments:

1. Most commonly, ARCB members consider shipping loans collateralized by bareboat or time charters to be "special situations" because political or economic developments

in the country of the owner or registration may not necessarily affect the flow of funds from the charterer to the bank. In such cases, shipping transactions are monitored separately from the other types of country exposure.

2. Alternatively, banks may assign country exposure to the country of the charterer, especially if the bareboat or time charterer is deemed to generate relatively little foreign exchange from countries other than the country of residence.
3. Finally, banks may consider that the country exposure belongs to the country of the shipowner, especially where unguaranteed loans to national flag carriers (including government maritime agencies) are involved or to the country from which the carriage of goods takes place in the case of contracts of affreightment. See below.

- *Bareboat charter*—the bare ship is chartered without crew; the charterer, for a stipulated sum, takes over the vessel with a minimum of restrictions. Also called barepole charter, bare-hull charter.
- *Contract of affreightment*—contract with shipowner to hire his ship or part of it for the carriage of goods. Such a contract generally takes the form of a charter party or bill of lading.
- *Time charter*—form of charter party issued when the vessel is chartered for an agreed period of time. It places the vessel in the possession of the charterer. It may, however, provide that the owner shall man and provision the vessel.

Sight letter of credit (off-balance-sheet item). See **letter of credit.**

Standby letter of credit (off-balance-sheet item). See **letter of credit.**

Term loan (balance-sheet item). Usually a long-term loan with a maturity from one to ten years, extended by large commercial banks to large well-established business enterprises and repayable according to a specified schedule (for the most part in periodic installments) under a legal agreement between the bank and the borrower.

Time charter (transfer of country exposure). See **shipping guarantees.**

Appendix B
Country Exposure Questionnaire and Results*

The following questionnaire highlights the general country exposure reporting practices utilized by the Association of Reserve City Banks (ARCB). The first eight questions, however, pertain to the size and general scope of the responding banks' international operations. Answers to these questions enabled the ARCB's international committee to meaningfully interpret many of the subsequent responses. In addition, information provided in the first few questions gave the committee the flexibility to tabulate separate statistical summaries (by size of bank, by size of international operations, etc.).

The Questionnaire

Numbers in parentheses indicate percent of responses for each category.

1. Size of bank—by assets at 12-31-75:
    a. Less than $1 billion (35%)
    b. $1-2.5 billion (32%)
    c. $2.5-5 billion (19%)
    d. $5-10 billion (6%)
    e. Over $10 billion (8%)
2. Significance of bank's international operations—by total balance-sheet assets under international division administration at 12-31-75:
    a. Less than 5% of total assets (37%)
    b. 5-15% of total assets (37%)
    c. 15-25% of total assets (10%)
    d. 25-35% of total assets (8%)
    e. 35-45% of total assets (4%)
    f. Over 45% of total assets (3%)
3. Number of foreign branches:
    a. Only convenience booking centers of the Nassau/Cayman type (47%)
    b. 1-5 full service branches (24%)
    c. 6-10 full service branches (4%)
    d. More than 10 full service branches (3%)
    e. None (24%)

*This material was originally published by the Association of Reserve City Bankers in *Country Exposure Measurement and Reporting Practices of Member Banks*, March 1977.

4. Foreign subsidiaries (more than 50% owned) of the bank and its holding company:
   a. None (72%)
   b. 1 (15%)
   c. 2-10 (8%)
   d. More than 10 (5%)
5. Edge Acts:
   a. None (50%)
   b. 1 (35%)
   c. 2-5 (13%)
   d. More than 5 (2%)
6. Foreign affiliates (50% or less ownership) of the bank and its holding company:
   a. None (57%)
   b. 1 (15%)
   c. 2-5 (13%)
   d. 5-10 (8%)
   e. 10-20 (2%)
   f. More than 20 (5%)
7. In approximately how many countries does your bank have assets (or off-balance-sheet items) which it believes are subject to country risk?
   a. 0 countries (6%)
   b. 1-10 countries (18%)
   c. 11-25 countries (22%)
   d. 26-50 countries (29%)
   e. More than 50 countries (23%)
8. Of those countries where the bank has assets deemed to be subject to country risk, country exposure reports are prepared on a regular basis (at least annually) on:
   a. 0 countries—not prepared (20%)
   b. 1-10 countries (10%)
   c. 11-25 countries (16%)
   d. 26-50 countries (15%)
   e. More than 50 countries (1%)
   f. All countries where bank has exposure (44%)
9. Countries for which regular country exposure reports are prepared are selected on basis of:
   a. Relative amount of exposure (19%)
   b. Opinion of risk involved—without regard to amount of exposure (10%)
   c. All countries where bank has exposure (76%)
   d. Other (7%)
10. The assets (and off-balance-sheet items) of the following booking units are included in country exposure reports (tick off all which are included):
   a. Bank head office (96%)
   b. Foreign branches (80%)
   c. Subsidiaries (27%)
   d. Edge Acts (39%)
   e. Managed affiliates (3%)
   f. Nonmanaged affiliates (4%)
   g. Other (1%)

11. How frequently are country exposure reports generally prepared?
    a. Monthly (54%)
    b. Quarterly (17%)
    c. Annually (20%)
    d. Other (19%)
12. Country exposure reports have:
    a. Standardized format (84%)
    b. Other (16%)
13. Data input for exposure reports is derived:
    a. Manually (54%)
    b. Computer (6%)
    c. Combination of a and b (43%)
14. Preparation of country exposure reports are the ultimate responsibility of:
    a. Area line officers (38%)
    b. International division staff officers (62%)
    c. Comptroller's division (9%)
    d. Other (12%)
15. It is believed that many banks' country exposure reports are disaggregated into one or more components. It is also believed that exposure report disaggregation varies greatly from bank to bank. In a general way, does your bank break out any of the following on its country exposure reports (more than one answer possible):
    a. By booking unit—does the bank report one global U.K. country exposure amount without regard to the booking unit source of the exposure or is there some breakdown of the U.K. exposure into subtotals by domestic and offshore booking units? (56%)
    b. By type of exposure—do the country exposure reports contain a subtotal(s) for loan exposure, a subtotal(s) for placement exposure, etc? (67%)
    c. By maturity—disaggregation into short-, medium-, or long-term groupings? (67%)
    d. Cross-border exposure vs. intracountry foreign currency exposure? (22%)
    e. Other/comment (21%)
16. Does the bank include as country exposure local currency assets funded by local currency liabilities?
    a. Yes (53%)
    b. No (32%)
    c. Other/comment (16%)
17. If local currency assets are not included in country exposure, does the bank have separate management controls covering these assets?
    a. Yes (55%)
    b. No (23%)
    c. Other (21%)
18. Are unpledged deposits considered as offsets to country exposure?
    a. Yes (5%)
    b. No (95%)

Defining Country Exposure

Following are more detailed responses to the ARCB survey. They identify how respondents classify items that give rise to country exposure.

APPENDIX B (continued)

			ADDED TO THE COUNTRY EXPOSURE OF:					
			UNGUARANTEED		WHEN FULLY AND UNCONDITIONALLY GUARANTEED AND/OR SECURED			OTHER
		BOOKING UNIT	DOMICILE OF BORROWER	DOMICILE OF BORROWER'S HOME OFFICE OR PARENT	DOMICILE OF GUARANTOR	COMFORT LETTER – DOMICILE OF ISSUER	LOCATION OF SECURITY	
I. BALANCE SHEET ITEMS A. MINIMUM RISK ASSETS 1. CASH								
PERCENTAGE BREAKDOWN	YES	13	27	13	10	1	4	7
	NO	57	37	46	26	30	27	52
	N/A	30	36	41	64	68	68	41
2. MARKETABLE SECURITIES A. TRADING ACCOUNT								
PERCENTAGE BREAKDOWN	YES	4	21	5	14	0	5	1
	NO	37	24	35	22	29	27	43
	N/A	59	55	60	64	71	67	55
B. OTHER SECURITIES HELD FOR BANK'S OWN ACCOUNT								
PERCENTAGE BREAKDOWN	YES	4	26	8	17	2	4	2
	NO	43	23	37	23	33	30	48
	N/A	52	51	55	60	65	65	50
C. FED FUNDS SOLD								
PERCENTAGE BREAKDOWN	YES	8	20	25	12	2	2	1
	NO	50	41	39	32	40	38	58
	N/A	42	39	36	57	58	60	41
D. SECURITIES PURCHASED UNDER AGREEMENT TO RESELL								
PERCENTAGE BREAKDOWN	YES	3	15	12	15	4	4	1
	NO	36	24	24	20	25	26	38
	N/A	61	61	64	65	71	70	61
3. BANK PLACEMENTS A. TO FOREIGN BRANCH OFFICE/SUBSIDIARY OF U.S. BANK								
PERCENTAGE	YES	13	43	51	33	8	5	4

		BOOKING UNIT	UNGUARANTEED: DOMICILE OF BORROWER	UNGUARANTEED: DOMICILE OF BORROWER'S HOME OFFICE OR PARENT	GUARANTEED AND/OR SECURED: DOMICILE OF GUARANTOR	GUARANTEED AND/OR SECURED: COMFORT LETTER – DOMICILE OF ISSUER	GUARANTEED AND/OR SECURED: LOCATION OF SECURITY	OTHER
BREAKDOWN	NO	61	45	33	23	40	39	70
	N/A	26	12	16	45	52	55	26
B. TO NON-U.S. BANK'S HEAD OFFICE								
PERCENTAGE BREAKDOWN	YES	14	62	43	27	8	4	4
	NO	54	22	25	21	36	33	71
	N/A	32	16	32	52	57	63	25
C TO NON-U.S. BANK'S FOREIGN BRANCH/SUBSIDIARY								
PERCENTAGE BREAKDOWN	YES	12	53	50	37	12	7	7
	NO	57	30	34	17	38	40	67
	N/A	32	16	16	46	50	53	26
4. ITEMS IN PROCESS OF COLLECTION								
PERCENTAGE BREAKDOWN	YES	5	26	10	12	4	3	2
	NO	62	53	67	41	47	48	70
	N/A	33	21	23	47	49	49	28
B. RISK ASSETS								
1. LOANS, EXCLUDING SHIPPING LOANS								
A. CASUAL OVERDRAFT								
PERCENTAGE BREAKDOWN	YES	12	62	37	43	12	13	5
	NO	64	32	54	26	49	39	76
	N/A	24	7	9	30	39	48	18
B. ARRANGED OVERDRAFT								
PERCENTAGE BREAKDOWN	YES	13	64	41	54	18	18	5
	NO	55	13	35	13	38	33	68
	N/A	32	23	24	33	43	49	26
C. SHORT-TERM ADVANCE								
PERCENTAGE BREAKDOWN	YES	21	83	47	85	29	30	8
	NO	60	13	46	8	49	43	76
	N/A	20	4	8	8	22	26	16
D. ACCEPTANCE FINANCING								

			UNGUARANTEED		GUARANTEED AND/OR SECURED			OTHER
		BOOKING UNIT	DOMICILE OF BORROWER	DOMICILE OF BORROWER'S HOME OFFICE OR PARENT	DOMICILE OF GUARANTOR	COMFORT LETTER – DOMICILE OF ISSUER	LOCATION OF SECURITY	
PERCENTAGE BREAKDOWN	YES	20	83	49	78	25	24	7
	NO	57	13	45	9	50	46	77
	N/A	24	4	7	13	25	30	16
E. BILLS DISCOUNTED								
PERCENTAGE BREAKDOWN	YES	17	78	45	78	25	23	4
	NO	58	13	47	11	50	48	78
	N/A	25	9	9	11	25	29	17
F. TERM LOAN								
PERCENTAGE BREAKDOWN	YES	18	84	39	82	28	28	10
	NO	57	9	51	10	51	49	72
	N/A	25	8	10	9	21	23	18
2. LOANS TO MULTILATERAL AGENCIES AND CONSORTIUM BANKS								
PERCENTAGE BREAKDOWN	YES	14	70	20	59	21	18	9
	NO	49	4	51	13	45	40	58
	N/A	37	26	29	28	35	41	34
3. SHIPPING LOANS A. CONSTRUCTION LOANS TO FINANCE NEWBUILDINGS								
PERCENTAGE BREAKDOWN	YES	3	30	13	40	7	9	11
	NO	33	9	26	4	30	27	32
	N/A	64	61	61	55	63	64	58
B. TO REFURBISH EXISTING VESSELS								
PERCENTAGE BREAKDOWN	YES	4	28	13	34	7	8	8
	NO	29	8	22	4	26	24	34
	N/A	66	64	65	62	67	68	59
C. TO FLAG OF CONVENIENCE SINGLE PURPOSE VEHICLES COLLATERALIZED BY CONTRACTS OF AFFREIGHTMENT								
PERCENTAGE BREAKDOWN	YES	5	22	15	33	8	9	10
	NO	28	14	20	5	25	23	34
	N/A	66	64	65	62	67	68	57

			UNGUARANTEED		GUARANTEED AND/OR SECURED			OTHER
		BOOKING UNIT	DOMICILE OF BORROWER	DOMICILE OF BORROWER'S HOME OFFICE OR PARENT	DOMICILE OF GUARANTOR	COMFORT LETTER - DOMICILE OF ISSUER	LOCATION OF SECURITY	
D. TO FLAG OF CONVENIENCE SINGLE PURPOSE VEHICLES COLLATERALIZED BY BARE-BOAT CHARTERS								
PERCENTAGE BREAKDOWN	YES	4	21	13	36	8	13	12
	NO	30	15	22	3	26	22	32
	N/A	65	64	65	61	66	65	57
E. TO SINGLE PURPOSE VEHICLES COLLATERALIZED BY TIME CHARTERS								
PERCENTAGE BREAKDOWN	YES	4	26	12	33	8	14	9
	NO	27	9	22	5	25	18	28
	N/A	68	65	66	62	67	67	63
F. TO NATIONAL FLAG CARRIERS INCLUDING GOVERNMENT MARITIME AGENCIES								
PERCENTAGE BREAKDOWN	YES	4	27	16	34	8	12	8
	NO	26	5	16	3	24	17	28
	N/A	70	67	67	63	68	71	64
4. LEASES								
PERCENTAGE BREAKDOWN	YES	5	24	8	22	4	10	1
	NO	26	9	24	10	23	22	32
	N/A	68	67	68	68	73	68	67
5. BANKERS ACCEPTANCES								
A. ACCEPTANCES CREATED BY ANY BANK SUBSEQUENTLY PURCHASED BY BANK								
PERCENTAGE BREAKDOWN	YES	12	45	40	46	10	11	3
	NO	50	30	34	14	43	40	63
	N/A	38	25	26	40	47	49	34
6. ACCRUED INTEREST RECEIVABLE								
PERCENTAGE BREAKDOWN	YES	11	29	16	30	12	8	3
	NO	53	48	62	42	55	58	70
	N/A	36	23	22	27	33	35	27

C. OTHER ASSETS
1. FIXED ASSETS

			UNGUARANTEED		GUARANTEED AND/OR SECURED			OTHER
		BOOKING UNIT	DOMICILE OF BORROWER	DOMICILE OF BORROWER'S HOME OFFICE OR PARENT	DOMICILE OF GUARANTOR	COMFORT LETTER – DOMICILE OF ISSUER	LOCATION OF SECURITY	
PERCENTAGE BREAKDOWN	YES	10	9	4	5	2	3	0
	NO	30	26	32	22	24	24	39
	N/A	60	65	64	73	74	73	61
2. INVESTMENTS IN AFFILIATES								
PERCENTAGE BREAKDOWN	YES	7	26	7	8	2	2	2
	NO	36	20	30	16	21	21	42
	N/A	58	54	63	76	77	77	55
3. INVESTMENTS IN SUBSIDIARIES								
PERCENTAGE BREAKDOWN	YES	4	15	3	3	1	1	2
	NO	29	18	23	15	16	16	33
	N/A	66	66	74	82	83	83	65
4. SUNDRY								
PERCENTAGE	YES	5	3	3	3	0	2	3
BREAKDOWN	NO	27	23	22	20	22	20	27
	N/A	67	74	75	77	78	78	70
II. INTRA-BANK BALANCE SHEET ITEMS								
A. DUE FROM OTHER BRANCHS								
1. PLACEMENTS								
PERCENTAGE BREAKDOWN	YES	8	18	5	3	0	1	8
	NO	41	34	39	23	25	25	40
	N/A	51	48	55	74	75	74	52
2. LOANS								
PERCENTAGE BREAKDOWN	YES	5	17	5	5	2	3	5
	NO	41	34	38	24	26	26	42
	N/A	53	49	57	71	72	71	52
B. EQUITY IN FOREIGN BRANCHES (WHERE APPLICABLE)								
PERCENTAGE BREAKDOWN	YES	9	13	3	2	1	2	0
	NO	26	20	23	17	17	17	33
	N/A	65	67	74	80	82	80	67

			UNGUARANTEED		GUARANTEED AND/OR SECURED			OTHER
		BOOKING UNIT	DOMICILE OF BORROWER	DOMICILE OF BORROWER'S HOME OFFICE OR PARENT	DOMICILE OF GUARANTOR	COMFORT LETTER - DOMICILE OF ISSUER	LOCATION OF SECURITY	
C. EQUITY IN SUBSIDIARIES								
PERCENTAGE BREAKDOWN	YES	3	12	2	1	0	1	0
	NO	27	20	22	15	16	15	28
	N/A	70	68	76	84	84	84	72
D. EQUITY IN MANAGED AFFILIATES								
PERCENTAGE BREAKDOWN	YES	4	12	4	3	1	2	0
	NO	24	16	20	13	15	14	30
	N/A	72	72	76	84	84	84	70
F. EQUITY IN NON-MANAGED AFFILIATES								
PERCENTAGE BREAKDOWN	YES	3	18	1	1	0	0	0
	NO	30	17	26	15	16	16	34
	N/A	66	64	73	84	84	84	66
F. LOSS RESERVES								
PERCENTAGE BREAKDOWN	YES	4	4	2	2	0	2	1
	NO	35	36	34	22	22	22	35
	N/A	61	60	64	76	78	76	64
G. OTHER NON-EQUITY RESERVES								
PERCENTAGE BREAKDOWN	YES	4	5	3	4	0	2	1
	NO	32	32	30	20	22	22	33
	N/A	64	63	66	76	78	76	66
III. NON-BALANCE SHEET ITEMS								
A. LETTERS OF CREDIT								
1. ISSUED								
PERCENTAGE BREAKDOWN	YES	18	62	36	57	16	17	4
	NO	55	26	51	23	52	52	74
	N/A	26	12	13	21	32	30	22
2. CONFIRMED								
PERCENTAGE BREAKDOWN	YES	21	71	50	62	21	20	5
	NO	55	23	42	21	50	51	77
	N/A	24	7	8	17	29	29	17

			UNGUARANTEED		GUARANTEED AND/OR SECURED			OTHER
		BOOKING UNIT	DOMICILE OF BORROWER	DOMICILE OF BORROWER'S HOME OFFICE OR PARENT	DOMICILE OF GUARANTOR	COMFORT LETTER – DOMICILE OF ISSUER	LOCATION OF SECURITY	
B. PREFORMANCE LETTERS OF CREDIT, LETTERS OF INDEMNITY, STANDBY LETTERS OF CREDIT, ETC. ISSUED								
PERCENTAGE BREAKDOWN	YES	18	71	41	68	23	22	5
	NO	54	20	47	16	49	49	74
	N/A	27	10	12	15	28	29	21
C. UNUSED LEGAL COMMIT-								
PERCENTAGE BREAKDOWN	YES	17	74	41	71	27	24	7
	NO	54	16	47	16	47	50	75
	N/A	28	10	12	13	26	26	18
D. UNUSED ADVISED/CONFIRMED LINES OF CREDIT								
PERCENTAGE BREAKDOWN	YES	17	61	38	53	22	18	10
	NO	55	30	53	34	53	55	75
	N/A	27	9	9	13	25	26	15
E. UNUSED GUIDANCE LINES OF CREDIT								
PERCENTAGE BREAKDOWN	YES	11	35	24	32	16	12	8
	NO	61	54	65	49	57	58	73
	N/A	28	11	11	20	27	30	20
F. FORWARD EXCHANGE CONTRACTS								
1. SPOT								
PERCENTAGE BREAKDOWN	YES	8	23	17	15	8	2	15
	NO	55	54	59	43	49	50	55
	N/A	37	23	24	41	43	48	29
2. FORWARD								
PERCENTAGE BREAKDOWN	YES	9	26	20	17	9	3	14
	NO	53	49	54	41	48	49	57
	N/A	38	25	26	41	43	48	29
3. BOUGHT/SOLD CONTRACTS (SWAP)								
PERCENTAGE BREAKDOWN	YES	9	23	17	13	7	2	14
	NO	51	47	51	41	47	48	53
	N/A	40	30	32	46	47	50	33

		BOOKING UNIT	UNGUARANTEED: DOMICILE OF BORROWER	UNGUARANTEED: DOMICILE OF BORROWER'S HOME OFFICE OR PARENT	GUARANTEED AND/OR SECURED: DOMICILE OF GUARANTOR	GUARANTEED AND/OR SECURED: COMFORT LETTER – DOMICILE OF ISSUER	GUARANTEED AND/OR SECURED: LOCATION OF SECURITY	OTHER
G. FOREIGN EXCHANGE LINES 1. SPOT/FORWARD								
PERCENTAGE BREAKDOWN	YES	10	23	17	15	12	5	12
	NO	47	46	51	41	42	47	53
	N/A	43	32	32	43	46	48	35
H. OWN ACCEPTANCES CREATED AND SOLD IN THE MARKETPLACE								
PERCENTAGE BREAKDOWN	YES	14	54	28	42	11	9	2
	NO	47	20	45	21	48	50	65
	N/A	39	26	27	37	41	41	33
I. TRAVELLERS CHECKS								
PERCENTAGE BREAKDOWN	YES	0	2	1	2	0	0	0
	NO	32	34	34	28	28	29	36
	N/A	68	64	65	70	72	71	64
J. SECURITIES AND INVESTMENTS HELD FOR FIDUCIARY ACCOUNTS								
PERCENTAGE BREAKDOWN	YES	0	2	0	1	0	0	0
	NO	35	32	30	27	27	28	36
	N/A	65	66	70	72	73	72	64

Index

5M/8-83